The Soviet Union and Postwar Japan

The Soviet Union and Postwar Japan

Escalating Challenge and Response

Rodger Swearingen

Foreword by Edwin O. Reischauer

HOOVER INSTITUTION PRESS
Stanford University   Stanford, California

The Hoover Institution on War, Revolution and Peace, founded at Stanford University in 1919 by the late President Herbert Hoover, is an interdisciplinary research center for advanced study on domestic and international affairs in the twentieth century. The views expressed in its publications are entirely those of the authors and do not necessarily reflect the views of the staff, officers, or Board of Overseers of the Hoover Institution.

Hoover Institution Publication 197

International Standard Book Number: 0-8179-6971-3
Library of Congress Catalog Card Number: 78–59866
Printed in the United States of America
TYPESET BY TED LIGDA, REDWOOD CITY, CALIFORNIA

to Olive

Contents

Illustrations

Tables

Foreword

In 1952 Rodger Swearingen, together with Paul Langer, brought out the first thorough and scholarly treatment in English of the history of the Communist movement in Japan. Entitled *Red Flag in Japan: International Communism in Action*, it was Dr. Swearingen's first major scholarly work, based in part on his doctoral dissertation. Since then he has written widely on Communism in general, on the Soviet Union, and also on contemporary China. Now, a quarter century later, he has woven together many of the various themes that have drawn his scholarly attention into this present volume on *The Soviet Union and Postwar Japan*. Having written the introduction to his maiden scholarly endeavor, I am particularly pleased to be able to do the same for this product of his mature years.

It is interesting to see how the international context has changed in the quarter century between these two books. *Red Flag in Japan* and its introduction were both written before the American Occupation of Japan had ended and before Japan had made more than the first uncertain stirrings toward economic recovery. The viability of the Japanese economy was still in doubt, and the future of democracy in Japan was even more uncertain. The Communists had only recently triumphed in China, the Korean War was in progress, and the extent to which Communism would spread throughout the world through warfare or subversion was quite unclear. The chief significance of the Communist movement in Japan seemed to be as part of a worldwide contest between democratic and Communist forms of political and social organization. In short, Japan appeared to lie on the border line between the Communist and non-Communist worlds, and the story of Japanese Communism appeared to be a significant element in the Cold War between the two.

All this is part of the postwar record of Soviet-Japanese relations and is therefore well documented in the early chapters of this book, but since then the whole world and particularly Japan have changed enormously. Cold War tensions have eased to a large extent and the "Cold War" is felt by some to have never existed. The "Communist world" is deeply divided, and the Soviet Union has itself gone through some significant changes. The non-Communist world is even less of a unit, being divided regionally by various cultural and racial groupings, and most significantly into several different levels of economic evolution, from the industrialized, trading democracies of the so-called First World, to which Japan now belongs, down to the undeveloped and resource-poor countries of the so-called Fourth World.

Japan in the intervening quarter century has experienced its "economic miracle," almost to the point of self-strangulation through pollution and crowding. It has become relatively affluent, even though precariously dependent on an ever-expanding international trade. It has developed perhaps the world's most efficient industrial economy, making it a feared competitor for all parties engaged in international trade. Despite the traumas and rapid changes of the past century, it has become perhaps the socially most stable country among the great industrialized nations. Its democratic institutions seem as solidly based and efficient as those of almost any other country in the world. It ranks near the top on most measurable scales of human well-being, such as longevity, education, relatively low crime rates, per capita productivity, or even economic standards of living.

When *Red Flag in Japan* was written, Japan had no independent relations with the Soviet Union, and the Japanese Communists were a means through which the Soviet Union contended with the American Occupation forces for influence over Japanese minds. The international triangle that involved Japan then was one in which the two superpowers met in conflict over Japan.

The international triangle that figures in the present book is the so-called "Moscow-Peking-Tokyo triangle." Economic relations with the Japanese economic giant have become important for both the Soviet Union and China. In fact, one of the five parts of this book is devoted exclusively to Soviet-Japanese economic relations. A Japan that is secure in its close defense relationship with the United States and also in its position as a major member —in fact the second largest—in the community of industrialized, trading democracies, is alternately bullied and courted by both Peking and Moscow in their desire to use Japan to better their own position in this bitter rivalry.

This change in the position of Japan in a short quarter century may not be typical of the whole world, but it helps to clarify some of the trends of our times. The changing nature of Soviet-Japanese relations in the postwar era makes obvious the great changes within Japan, gives insight into some of the changes going on in the Soviet Union, and above all, throws light on the sometimes striking, sometimes subtle, changes going on in the dynamics of East Asian strategic relations.

Red Flag in Japan was a pioneer work. Since its appearance, several large and sometimes more specialized accounts of the Communist movements in

Japan have been published. There has also been a great deal of writing on particular aspects of Soviet-Japanese relations. But ample room remains for the present book. The facts, analyses, and documentation of this important and complex phase of current world history need to be pulled together and presented in a coherent form. This Professor Swearingen has done with a masterful balance between detailed documentation and stimulating analysis. In addition, through new research into the materials in both Japan and the Soviet Union and extensive interviewing in both countries, he has delved into unexplored angles of the subject and put together already known elements into new analytic patterns. The result is the most comprehensive and authoritative account of Soviet-Japanese relations produced to date. It is factually solid and, at the same time, highly readable and intellectually stimulating. Although the area it charts is no longer completely virgin territory, it maps the terrain with greater clarity and precision than ever before, thus serving as a reliable guide for the student and a solid basis for further exploration of the field.

EDWIN O. REISCHAUER

Preface

Every book characteristically has an origin, a purpose and a plan—roots, rationale, and a road map. Each also, inevitably, has its limitations and dilemmas. Let us start with the latter. Comments from two different authors of divergent backgrounds seem curiously relevant to the present endeavor. Both authors I have met and talked with at some length. The first is Professor Arnold Toynbee who once described reactions to his celebrated multivolume study of world history. He related how "very pleased" he was to receive from scholars around the world "extraordinarily kind comments" on the comprehensiveness and quality of his magnum opus—pleased, he said, until he got around to reading the almost identical second paragraph of virtually every laudatory letter. Toynbee explained that after its typically lavish compliments on the scope, contribution, uniqueness, and quality of his broad-gauged work, each scholar (many of them of world renown) would then add, "but when you come to Germany (France, Russia, and so on), may I point out. . . ."

Let it be clear that no substantive or qualitative comparison with Professor Toynbee's celebrated scholarship is here presumed or intended. The point is quite another one: the attempt to cover in a single volume, as herein, the wide range and diversified dimensions of postwar Soviet-Japanese relations necessarily precludes attention to many relevant aspects, imposes depth and length constraints, and sadly limits inclusion of much otherwise desirable detail.

The second dilemma is implicit in the comment of a German colleague, Klaus Mehnert. Best known for his contemporary work on Moscow-Peking relations and related topics, he once confided to me: "Scholars sometimes tend to think of me as a journalist, and journalists often find my writing too scholarly." While the present volume will, it is hoped, not invite either such an accolade or such a criticism, the point does suggest the usefulness of setting forth at the outset the broad purposes of this endeavor.

This volume aims to fill some critical gaps in the literature on the subject, and to satisfy the need for a single book in the field at a time when Soviet-Japanese relations have reached a new plateau, or impasse, as the case may be. Specifically, the purposes of the volume are to incorporate between two covers analysis of the changing elements of Soviet-Japanese relations, ideological, political, cultural, diplomatic, economic, and strategic, from 1945 to 1978; to add research depth and original documentation in several important areas not substantially treated in existing books, monographs, or journal articles (at least in English); to make available in English the essence of selected, important publications (a number of them fairly obscure or quite recent) in Japanese and Russian on specialized aspects of the subject; to represent succinctly the divergent viewpoints and conclusions of other scholars (Asian, European and American), on contemporary aspects of the problem; to provide the full text or summaries in English translation of the 34 bilateral treaties signed between Japan and the Soviet Union, 1956 through 1977, most of which are not readily available even in the original Russian or Japanese.

Like most broad-gauged treatments, this one has roots in earlier research, conferences, interviews, travel, and field work. In the larger sense its origins may be traced back to World War II, where as a young language officer serving with the Supreme Commander for the Allied Powers (SCAP), my duties briefly included dabbling in precisely such matters. But that was three wars and some thirty-odd years ago. Subsequent research and publications plus a number of research/conference trips to Asia and the Soviet Union have served to sustain, indeed, to intensify my concern with the subject. Three years ago, I decided to devote full research attention to the subject, with the present volume as the objective.

There is hardly need to stress the critical and potentially decisive significance of postwar Soviet strategy toward Japan and of Japan's policies, attitudes, and relations vis-à-vis the Soviet Union. There is good reason to be surprised and concerned that so little scholarly attention has recently been devoted to the question—in this country and abroad. No comprehensive, single volume on the subject has been published to date in either Japanese or Russian although substantial articles and impressive research monographs by specialists of both countries have appeared. The same may be said in the case of Western Europe, notably Germany. Happily, when we come to the American/English language scene, the picture is somewhat brighter. The pioneering work of Professors James Morley (of Columbia University) and George Lensen (of Florida State University), on the prewar and wartime periods, is, of course, excellent and quite well known. A cursory glance at the section on "Japanese Communism" in Thomas Hammond's massive bibliography, *Soviet Foreign Relations and World Communism* (1965) confirms this curious situation to that point.

The picture during the decade since, has shown some improvement. A few pioneering works of the past decade (most of them now four or five years old) which have been invaluable in the preparation of this volume, should be noted as a kind of minibibliographic introduction to the field: Herbert Feis, *Contest Over Japan* (1968) puts the international issue in perspective, and documents the nature of the problem. Savitri Vishwanathan's *Normalization of Soviet-Japanese Relations, 1945–1970: An Indian View* (1973) is a well-documented, comprehensive historical study to the end of the last decade. Young C. Kim's short work (88 pages), *Japanese-Soviet Relations: Interaction of Politics, Economics and National Security* (1974) is the most concise and perceptive analysis of the issues as they appeared about four or five years ago. Donald C. Hellmann's *Japanese Domestic Politics and Foreign Policy: The Peace Agreement with the Soviet Union* (1969) remains extremely valuable to the understanding of such matters. John K. Emmerson's *Arms, Yen and Power: The Japanese Dilemma* (1971) while not, strictly speaking, focused on the subject at hand, demands attention for two reasons: first, because the author, a retired high-ranking American Foreign Service officer, is himself a specialist in Soviet-Japanese relations, and second, because the security issues covered in the book are critical to the topic. Similarly, Robert A. Scalapino's *The Japanese Communist Movement, 1920–1966* (1967) must also be included here, especially as it is more comprehensive than the title would suggest, providing a wealth of background information and analysis which bears directly on Soviet-Japanese relations, and for that matter, on Japanese-Chinese relations. John J. Stephan's *The Kuril Islands: Russo-Japanese Frontiers in the Pacific* (1974) is a solid, up-to-date analysis of that critical dimension. My own earlier RAND study, books and monographs, and other work in this area may be left for footnotes, citations, and bibliographical references.

A careful study of the available literature augmented by research and conferences in Washington, Tokyo, Khabarovsk, and Moscow over the past several years has led me to the following conclusions: first, it seemed clear to me that serious gaps existed in the available treatments and documentation on the subject. Among these are Soviet and Japanese Communist policy and practice in Occupied Japan; the Soviet indoctrination of Japanese prisoners of war; an overall evaluation of public opinion in Japan and the press on this particular subject; joint Soviet-Japanese economic ventures in Siberia; the fisheries question; the emergent "independent" Japan Communist Party; the impact of the Moscow-Peking split; and the security dimension in Northeast Asia.

Second, since no overall treatment of postwar Soviet-Japanese relations seems to exist, no concerted attempt at political-economic strategic synthesis, cause, and effect, could be found. For example, a study of the Soviet indoctrination of Japanese prisoners of war helps to explain the predominantly anti-Soviet public opinion in Japan today. Or, knowledge of the extensive Soviet-Japanese joint ventures and increasing Japanese trade with the Soviet Union and the People's Republic of China throws additional light on Tokyo's political policies and attitudes toward Moscow and Peking. Or, the Soviet handling of the fisheries issue, of Japanese fishermen and their response—the whole fisheries question (particularly after enactment of the new Law of the Sea)—provides a further glimpse of the very fundamental and sensitive nature of Japan's relationship with the Soviet Union. And so on. . . .

Third, several rich reservoirs of documentary material remained to be tapped: documentation from the National Archives (both Department of State and SCAP, G-2), some of it only recently declassified; Soviet and Japanese specialized journal material as well as unpublished theses and conference papers; memoirs and eye-witness accounts; key actors in the drama such as Soviet and Japanese Foreign Ministry sources, former Japanese diplomatic and trade representatives in Moscow; and United States Foreign Service specialists on the subject.

Fourth, it seemed therefore that it might be useful to bring together and augment some of my own background and experience in Japan, the Soviet Union, Santa Monica (RAND), and Washington, incorporating and augmenting interviews, translations, documentation, and ideas that I have not earlier put together in any one place. As it worked out, the augmentation took three years of sustained research, analysis, and writing.

Fifth, in academic life, during my brief association with the Department of State, for fourteen years as a consultant with the RAND Corporation as well as during the years of work on the present volume, it became painfully clear that it is impossible to lay one's hands on even the most basic primary documentation on the subject (key treaties, bilateral agreements, and so on) in any single volume. Indeed, often they are not even available separately in *full text or summary*. Thus, it seemed appropriate and useful to locate, translate, and summarize the key bilateral treaties and agreements between Japan and the Soviet Union, 1956–1977 (38 of them as it turns out) and to include *all of them* in some form as appendixes to this volume.

The study is organized into five parts and fourteen chapters. Part One deals, briefly, with the historical perspective, images, and comparative perceptions. Part Two, "The Soviet Presence in an American-Occupied Japan," looks at Soviet policy and practice, the Soviet indoctrination of Japanese prisoners, and the Moscow link of the Japan Communist Party, drawing heavily on hitherto unpublished archival material (SCAP, G-2 documentation) and interviews.

Part Three focuses on Soviet intentions and techniques in the process of normalization and the question of Japanese public opinion, and goes on to investigate the metamorphosis of the Japan Communist Party in post-treaty

Japan. Recent Soviet and Japanese sources, as well as interviews in Japan and the Soviet Union, are included as primary documentation. Part Five, on economic relations, examines in some detail the joint projects in Siberia as well as the striking intensification of Soviet-Japanese trade. Wherever possible, both Soviet and Japanese statistics and viewpoints are used and documented. Research for this dimension was updated and enhanced substantially by a month spent in Moscow at the invitation of the Soviet Academy of Sciences in the summer of 1976 and by a research/conference visit to Japan and Siberia in the spring of 1977.

Part Five, "Diplomatic and Strategic Dimensions," takes up the interrelated fisheries, territorial, and security questions within the context of the Moscow-Peking-Tokyo interrelationship. Here the cooperation of high-level Soviet and Japanese government specialists and the staffs of various Japanese government departments and agencies has been invaluable, as have the good offices of friends and colleagues in Washington and at the U.S. embassies in Tokyo and Moscow. The 38 bilateral treaties and agreements between Japan and the Soviet Union, 1956–1977, are appended either as full text or in brief summary form, depending upon their significance.

This book, then, is designed as a general overview for the serious student of international affairs, as supplementary reading for university courses on Soviet foreign policy, East Asian international relations and contemporary Japan, and as background and perspective for colleagues in the teaching, government, media, and research worlds. Secretly, if immodestly, I would hope that the volume might even find its way into the hands of a few key senators, diplomats, and foreign correspondents whose necessary preoccupation with the crisis or constituency of the moment rarely permits time or inclination to reflect upon the larger picture—even in such critical areas of evident Western concern as the escalating interaction between the Soviet Union and Japan.

Acknowledgments

Without the generous and ongoing cooperation of many individuals and institutions in several countries this study could not possibly have been completed.

I am deeply indebted to Edwin O. Reischauer of Harvard University and to Ross Berkes and Norman Tertig of the School of International Relations at the University of Southern California for their continuing support and encouragement over the years. Likewise, Andrew Kuroda and Paul Horecky of the Library of Congress have always found time to provide professional assistance whenever it may have been requested, as has Lynn Sipe, librarian of USC's von KleinSmid Library of World and Public Affairs. The vital interest and support of Richard Staar, Emiko Moffitt, and others of the Hoover Institution is also gratefully acknowledged.

My sincere appreciation for essential travel-grant and fellowship support goes to the International Research and Exchange Board (IREX) in New York (and to Daniel Matuszewski, in particular) and to the Yoshida International Educational Foundation in Tokyo (especially to its executive director, Yasusuke Katsuno, and his associate board member, Masaru Ogawa) for making possible recent research/conference trips to the Soviet Union and to Japan. The good offices of James Rosenau, director of the School of International Relations at USC, and Hammond Rolph, associate director, in arranging for additional, modest travel and research funds are also acknowledged with thanks.

I am further indebted to the government of the Federal Republic of Germany (and to its consul general at Los Angeles) for providing me with the opportunity to re-visit centers of international studies throughout Germany. In addition to the valuable perspective afforded by the visit, the consequent, continuing exchange of research materials and ideas with Joachim Glaubitz was most rewarding. Similar gratitude is expressed to the successive consuls general of Japan at Los Angeles whose good offices in connection with my several visits to Japan over the years have proved invaluable. The assistance of Ms. Peggy K. Nakaki of the Los Angeles consulate general's office is acknowledged with special appreciation.

Useful research/conference visits to the Republic of China and the Republic of Korea were arranged under the auspices of the Institute of International Relations in Taipei (Han Lih-wu, former director; Tsai Wei-ping, director) and the Institute of East Asian Studies in Seoul (Kang In-Duk, director). My thanks to the Institute directors, their staffs, and to other helpful friends in both countries.

For their assistance in providing Russian sources and Soviet perspectives, I am grateful for the time and interest of Dimitry Petrov of the Far Eastern Institute and the Institute of International Relations and World Economy, to Boris Zanegin of the Institute on the U.S.A. and Canada, to Boris Slavinsky of the Far Eastern Scientific Center in Vladivostok, and to Leonid N. Kutakov and Sergi L. Tikhvinskii, well-known Far Eastern affairs specialists and consultants to the Soviet Ministry of Foreign Affairs.

Among the many Japanese authorities on the Soviet Union (and China) whose generous help over the years has been invaluable, a few may be acknowledged with a word of special thanks: Hirokazu Arai, Shinsaku Hogen, Ki Nemoto, Kinya Niizeki, Akira Shigemitsu, Masatada Tachibana, Kazuhiko Togo of the Ministry of Foreign Affairs, and Hsiao Iwashima of the Defense Agency. The considerable contributions of members of the Japanese academic community are acknowledged in the notes to this volume. Konosuke Hayashi and Takahiko Yamato of the National Diet library provided additional, invaluable bibliographic assistance. Etsuo Kohtani, editor of *K.D.K. Information*, and his associates in the Japanese government were helpful with available public information and analyses on contemporary security issues.

To a host of graduate students who have put up with this research obsession for so many months or years, let me address a "collective word" of appreciation. A few of them whose research and administrative efforts have sometimes gone beyond the call of duty deserve special recognition and thanks: Tsuneo Akaha, Jerry Fleischhacker, William Green, John Kang, Charles Kupperman, Thomas Lenergen, John Miller, John Rose, Charles Silverstein, Tink T. Ssutu, William Stiller, and Don Wolven.

A very special, separate word of gratitude must be reserved for the excellent work of Ms. Olga Markof-Balaeff of the University of California, Berkeley, who translated and summarized the treaties and agreements (when not otherwise indicated) that appear as appendixes to this volume.

Several American scholars with substantial knowledge of the subject have assisted me greatly by reading drafts of the manuscript at various stages of its completion and making most helpful suggestions. Peter Berton, George Lensen, and Edwin O. Reischauer read early drafts of the book and made many critical and useful comments. William Caldwell's editorial assistance and suggestions are also gratefully acknowedged. John J. Stephan reviewed the chapter on the northern territories and offered helpful advice. William Van Cleave looked over the chapter on the security dimension and offered important additions and suggestions. John Emmerson read the bulk of the manuscript and provided valuable additions and corrections based in part on his extensive professional experience as a U.S. Foreign Service Officer in Moscow and Tokyo. Robert Scalapino read the entire manuscript most thoughtfully, providing many useful additions, necessary corrections, and added perspective.

My experienced and hard-working editor, Susan Welling, may be credited with ironing out numerous technical and stylistic wrinkles in the manuscript and in bringing a greater degree of unity to the book. Finally, I must thank several secretaries, typists, and administrative assistants, especially Ms. Cindy Abrams, for their long and dedicated cooperation.

Part One

Historical Perspectives

Chapter One

The Prewar Heritage: A Montage

The Russian mirror of Japan reflects as much of Shogun Hideyoshi as it does of Madame Butterfly. Similarly, Japanese perceptions of the desperate need to strengthen the nation's northern defenses against the "Red barbarians" run ominously through Japanese "defense literature" of the eighteenth and nineteenth Tokugawa era centuries.

It should be noted at the outset that the major force behind the early Russian thrust down the southward island route to Japan flowed from the activities of adventurers, merchants, and scholars, not generals and soldiers. Curiosity and trade rather than territory or conquest were the order of the day. Indeed, early Cossack and commercial encounters with Japanese or with the native *Ainu* of the northern islands seldom proved hostile. Nor were they, for the most part, sponsored by the Czarist government. Preoccupied with other, more urgent events and with a capital in St. Petersburg—a vast Euro-Asian continent away—the Russia of Catherine the Great was not particularly concerned with Japan.[1]

The Japanese of the period (including the Tokugawa authorities) were, for their part, very much concerned with Russia—no matter that such concern stemmed primarily from myth, manipulation, misinformation, and inference! Contributing to the early negative montage and resulting "official" Japanese fear of Russia were such items as the impact on Japan, in 1771, of a strange visitor, a Polish adventurer and Russian exile born in Hungary who, when stopping over in Japan (Nagasaki) for provisions "warned" the authorities of an impending Russian attack upon the Japanese empire; the emergence a few years later of a whole school of Japanese literature ominously depicting tzarist Russia as the "land of the Red barbarians"; the return to Japan of a certain castaway, Kodayu, in the 1790s after a year in

St. Petersburg, a living encyclopedia on the strange, huge and unpredictable nation to the north; the appearance of an eleven-volume major report on Russia and the Russians entitled "Summary Report of a Raft Drifting in the Northern Seas," based on Kodayu's information plus rumors and misinformation gleaned from Japanese fishermen who, shipwrecked, had washed up on "alien shores to the north"; the sudden appearance of any number of Japanese books on geography and "conditions in neighboring countries," which cautioned against the Russian threat to Japan and called for the strengthening of "northern defenses"; and attacks on settlements and shipping off Hokkaido (not apparently ordered or even authorized by the authorities) by two young Russian naval soldiers of fortune when their trade overtures were rejected by the Japanese.[2]

Sustaining and exacerbating such fears were the early and persistent appearance of Russian ships off the shores of Japan. Some of these vessels even sailed into Japanese ports before proceeding to Nagasaki as they were inevitably ordered to do. Japan of the Tokugawa era, it may be remembered, was by stern decree isolated and secluded from the alien, outside world except for one window to the West at the southern commercial port of Nagasaki. No exceptions were to be made, least of all, one suspects, in the case of the Russians. Local Russian visits to neighboring Japanese islands were likewise unwelcomed. One account notes: "Should they need food or wine, they could send Ainu from Uruppu."[3]

The Russians had, in fact, first reached Japan in 1739 as part of the Second Bering Expedition, though discrepancies in their journals and reports to their commanders caused the authorities at St. Petersburg to disbelieve that they had reached Japan. Proceeding down the Kurile stepping stones, the Russians landed on Etorofu in the 1760s and Hokkaido in 1778.[4]

That by the early nineteenth century some individual Russians were taking more than a short-range commercial or curious, cultural look at the "quaint and picturesque islands" off Siberia may be ascertained from the ship's log of a certain Captain Golovin of the Russian navy. Seeking a safe harbor, Captain Golovin and party went ashore on Etorofu where they were detained by the local authorities. During his prolonged captivity, Golovin had ample time to make observations and to ponder the future. Consider this early entry in his journal penned during the third decade of the eighteen hundreds, that is some fifty years before the Meiji Restoration and Japan's momentous decision to "Westernize":

"What must we expect of this numerous, ingenious and industrious people, who are capable of everything, and much inclined to imitate all that is foreign? . . ." Golovin asks. He answers: "If the Japanese should think fit to introduce the knowledge of Europe among them and we should then see the Chinese alleged [*sic*] to do the same; in this case these two powerful nations might soon give the situation in Europe another appearance." Captain Golovin concludes: "I do not mean to affirm that the Japanese and Chinese might form themselves on the European model, and become dangerous now, but we must take care to avoid giving cause to our posterity to despise our memory."[5]

When the race among the powers for concessions and influence in Northeast Asia (particularly vis-à-vis Japan) was accelerated following the signing between Great Britain and China of the Treaty of Nanking in 1842, the Russians seemed still very much in the maritime competition. Vice Admiral Evfimil V. Putiatin arrived in Nagasaki on August 21, 1853, six months before Commodore Mathew C. Perry's celebrated opening of Japan with the initialing of the Treaty of Kanagawa on March 31, 1854. As the Japanese apparently desired to play the Russians off against the other powers, Putiatin, while in Nagasaki, was warmly received by the shogun's representatives and given promises of favorable trade consideration. But the outbreak of the Crimean War and other factors diverted Russian efforts, and the center of Russo-Japanese interests gravitated more or less naturally back to the northern frontier.[6]

Russo-Japanese relations next entered the sticky realm of treaty diplomacy, pointedly centering on conflicting territorial and related interests along the northern frontier. After much discussion and disagreement, on February 17, 1855, the Treaty of Shimoda was signed between the two nations. It included a clause dividing the Kurile Islands between Japan and Russia. Sakhalin was left unpartitioned. This settlement was, in effect, amended by the Treaty of St. Petersburg on May 7, 1875. All of Sakhalin now became Russian territory, while the Kurile Islands were conceded to Japan.[7]

The construction of the Trans-Siberian railroad, launched in 1891, marks something of a milestone in Russo-Japanese relations, signaling as it did one more huge step in the Russian drive to the east.

Japan's latent fears and evident distrust of Russia mounted during the next years within the context of the great power rivalry in East Asia and as it became increasingly clear that Russia promised to remain a major obstacle to Japanese plans for the area. It may be remembered that it was Russia, with the help of Germany and France, that initially blocked Japanese acquisition of the Laiotung Peninsula and thus, for a time, prevented a Japanese foothold on the continent following the latter's victory in the Sino-Japanese War (1894–1895). Still elated by the victory over China and by now allied with Great Britain, Japan shocked the world with a victory over Russia—a European power—in the Russo-Japanese War (1904–1905). During the decade between the two wars, Japan moved relentlessly to intensify and consolidate its interests in Korea.

The Treaty of Portsmouth ending the Russo-Japanese War, which had been negotiated through the good offices of President Theodore Roosevelt, brought Japan rich strategic booty: Southern Sakhalin, a leaseholding of the Liaotung Peninsula, including the important areas of Port Arthur and Dalny (Dairen) and a vital section of the Chinese Eastern Railway (in Manchuria) south of Changchun. Nonetheless, from the Japanese point of view far too much Russian influence remained both in Manchuria and in Korea—a situation Japan sought further to remedy by annexing Korea in 1910.[8]

Reflecting a certain "if you can't beat 'em, join 'em" philosophy, Russia now switched to a policy of guarded cooperation with Japan for the next decade despite the continuation in being, if not in practical force, of the Anglo-Japanese Alliance. This period of Russo-Japanese calculated cordiality reached its apex in 1916 with the signing of a series of secret conventions which in the aggregate amounted to a limited mutual defense pact.[9]

The advent of the Bolshevik Revolution only two years later radically changed the leadership, significantly altered the rules of the game, and added a new ideological dimension to Russian foreign policy. From the Japanese perspective, the collapse of Russian power in Northeast Asia was looked upon as an opportunity to achieve the long-standing aim of weakening Russia as an obstacle in the path of its own pretensions to influence and empire.

The first period of Soviet-Japanese relations, 1918 to 1922, which included the celebrated Siberian intervention, centered on Japan's attempt to eliminate the "Russian menace" and to expand its own economic and political influence in order to preempt or at least forestall the spread of Bolshevism. Russia now added to its foreign policy arsenal the Comintern which, under Lenin's initial prompting, set about organizing Communist parties and conducting revolutionary propaganda—with China and Japan as major Asian targets.

The second period, 1922 to 1925, was characterized by efforts to reestablish more or less normal relations between the two nations, despite the persistent, built-in historical, cultural, and "ideological" reservations each held with respect to the other.[10]

The third period, 1925 to 1939, following the reestablishment of diplomatic relations between Russia and Japan, saw some apparent dissipation of the traditional feeling of mutual distrust and antagonism born of earlier events, perceptions, and misperceptions. This outwardly improved relationship was embodied in the Soviet policy of neutrality on the Manchurian incident, the sale of the Chinese Eastern Railway by the USSR to Manchukuo, fisheries concessions, and oil and timber concessions in North Sakhalin.

From the Soviet viewpoint, these moves must be seen as part of Moscow's worldwide United Front strategy, after 1935, designed to placate jingoist Japan and to rally unlikely capitalist friends while buying time to worry about Nazi Germany and the unthinkable consequences to the economically and militarily weak Soviet Union of a two-front war. Japan's continuing concern over Soviet policies and purposes, however, scarcely diminished; indeed, such concern became quite public in November of 1936 with the signing and announcing of the Anti-Comintern Pact with Germany. While the pact, as published, merely called for mutual help in checking Communist activities, an accompanying secret protocol was specifically directed against the "military threat" posed by the Soviet Union and called for joint defense efforts in the event of a Soviet attack upon either nation.[11]

With the consolidation of Japanese victories in Manchuria (Manchukuo) and in China during the late 1930s and as the military regime, by now in virtual control of the Japanese government, became more powerful, aggressive, and restless, tensions between Moscow and Tokyo (punctuated by Soviet-Japanese border clashes in Manchuria) reached a near breaking point.

The fourth period, 1939 to 1941, however, saw a return to the policy of rapprochement. The Nazi-Soviet Non-Aggression Pact marked a turning point, but the rationale was rooted on the Japanese side in its growing apprehension over the prospects of a hostile Soviet Union side by side with an unfriendly United States and Great Britain in Japan's plans for a "Greater East Asia co-prosperity sphere." For its part, Moscow, as suggested, was ill prepared economically or militarily for a two-front war. The result (concomitant with Japan's final decision, after much debate, to move south against the United States and its allies rather than north against the Soviet Union) was a Japanese proposal to the USSR in July of 1940 for a neutrality pact and the formal signing of such a pact in Moscow in April of 1941.[12]

The German attack on the Soviet Union with some 160 divisions in June of 1941 dramatically changed the international environment in which Japan was to operate. Should Japan now join its erstwhile ally, Germany, in the war against the Soviet Union? Or would Japan's interest better be served, prior pacts and agreements notwithstanding, by concentrating its efforts and resources on the consolidation of gains on the continent, on problems of the Pacific, and most importantly, on resolving—by force, if necessary—its deteriorating relations with the United States. Britain and France, it may be remembered, were by this time totally involved with the war in Europe and, thus, virtually out of the East Asian equation.

The complicated period from June through December 1941, as we know, resulted in the fateful Japanese decision, for economic and empire reasons, to let the Germans worry about the Russians on their own and to strike south against the United States and the other Western interests—now perceived, correctly, as the only real obstacle to the Japanese domination of

East Asia and the Pacific region. With the attack upon Pearl Harbor, the United States suddenly found itself in an incongruous situation in relation to the war. Having as a consequence declared war upon both Japan and Germany, the United States was in Europe, by definition, an ally of the Soviet Union, which in Asia had a neutrality pact with Japan, a pact that was honored by Moscow—for a combination of sophisticated, strategic reasons—*almost* to the end of the Pacific War.

Chapter Two

The Pacific War and the Emergence of a Soviet Policy for Postwar Japan

THE PEARL HARBOR DIMENSION

The prospects of a two-front war—with Nazi Germany in the West and Japan in the East—had for a turbulent decade prior to Pearl Harbor remained something of a nightmare to Stalin and his generals. It was the Japanese "sneak attack" in the Pacific and resulting major confrontation with the United States and its allies from the Aleutians to Singapore and the Burmese-Indian frontier that overnight reduced the Soviet perception of the "clear and present danger," at least temporarily. Japan's military leaders, already in control of coastal China, increasingly attracted by the critical strategic natural resources of Southeast Asia, and banking on the evident American isolationism as well as distance from the scene to obviate any formidable U.S. military response, had moved decisively and confidently. For some years before that time, we now know, the question of whether to attack "north" (against the Soviet Union) or "south" (against the United States and its allies), remained the burning issue within ruling Japanese military circles, with the army and navy very often on opposite sides and the Foreign Ministry characteristically contributing guidance such as "on the other hand. . . ."

To be sure, Moscow had only a few months earlier concluded a neutrality pact with Japan (April 1941). Furthermore, it may be recalled (not incidentally), that the Stalin-Hitler non-aggression pact signed by Molotov and Ribbentrop in August of 1939 had been rudely violated on June 22, 1941, when 160 German divisions launched a massive invasion across the western frontiers of the Soviet Union. In one of the now familiar Soviet zigzags from the role of the "bad guys" to that of the "good guys," the Soviet Union (this time through no choice of its own or of the West), had suddenly been converted from erstwhile potential enemy to friend in need, and ultimately, possible Pacific ally.[1]

The Japanese attack on Pearl Harbor and the ensuing critical military situation in the Pacific region prompted immediate and intensive consideration in Washington, as well as in the field, of the desirability and advantages of urging early Soviet entry into the war against Japan. There seems to have been little or no consideration at the time given to the possible long-range political or strategic disadvantages, not to say potential dangers, of direct Soviet involvement in the East.

The desirability of USSR participation in the war against Japan was indirectly suggested by President Roosevelt to Soviet Ambassador Litvinov the day after Pearl Harbor. On December 10, from the Philippines, Gen. Douglas MacArthur by implication seconded the motion, cabling Gen. George C. Marshall: "Information here shows that entry of Russia is enemy's greatest fear."[2]

Wheels were inevitably set in motion; discussions took place at the highest level in Washington, but on December 11, the Soviet ambassador officially informed the secretary of state that the Soviet Union "was not then in a position to cooperate with us against Japan. Russia," he said, "was fighting on a huge scale against Germany and could not risk an attack by Japan."[3]

This was the position the Soviet Union was to take for virtually "the duration." Meanwhile, U.S. military planners, in conjunction with the other Allies, continued to hold meetings, draft elaborate plans, and make serious recommendations based on the apparent assumption (or at least continuing hope) of some sort of early joint United States–Soviet military effort against Japan.

For the remaining three weeks of the year (1941) no encouragement was forthcoming from the Kremlin and no progress made, despite extensive efforts at several U.S. operational staff levels. The result was that by the end of the year the question of Soviet participation in the war against Japan had been essentially suspended; that is neither dropped nor resolved to the satisfaction of Washington. The importance of holding the Maritime Provinces of Siberia was generally recognized as an essential Allied objective; but, as we shall see, it became increasingly apparent that Moscow intended to achieve that objective short of permitting U.S. air or naval bases or units, or even isolated American personnel, on Soviet soil.

1942: STEPPED-UP JAPANESE OFFENSIVES— SOVIET NONCOOPERATION IN ASIA

During 1942 the question of Soviet participation, or at least cooperation, in the Pacific War was raised repeatedly in Washington because of both the continued possibility that Japan might attack the Soviet Union and the U.S. Army Air Force's interest in establishing air bases in Siberia. On March 4, 1942, President Roosevelt asked the Joint Chiefs of Staff to restudy the question of Soviet participation in the Pacific War.[4] In their reply to the president, the Joint Chiefs noted pointedly that such an undertaking required extensive planning, logistic and other cooperation, and that: "Up to the present, it has been impossible for our military authorities to obtain any but the scantiest information concerning Soviet forces, *and it is questionable if more information would be supplied by the Soviets*" (italics supplied).[5]

On June 15, 1942, the Joint Chiefs of Staff asked the president to obtain Stalin's approval for United States staff conversations since lower level contacts and requests had not produced any significant degree of liaison, not to say Soviet cooperation. Accordingly, President Roosevelt dispatched a message to Stalin, which noted the increasing possibility of a Japanese attack against the Soviet Maritime Provinces and offered to supply the Soviets with U.S. aircraft "providing there are available in Siberia landing fields which are adequate."[6]

When, typically, no reply had been received after almost a week, the president sent another longer and more detailed message, this time making some very specific suggestions, including a proposal that a strictly commercial U.S. aircraft from Alaska piloted by civilians be permitted to survey portions of eastern Siberia as far as Lake Baikal "to hasten air route development for ferrying aircraft and much-needed supplies."[7]

In reply, Stalin announced that work was already progressing on airfields and that he felt aircraft should be piloted by Soviet flyers who would also make the proposed survey flights across Siberia, accompanied by U.S. representatives.[8]

Some further discussions were held, vague agreements in principle reached, but little specific progress was recorded. Finally, in December of 1942, the Joint Chiefs of Staff after reviewing the problem suggested that the president be more specific and inform Stalin of U.S. readiness to commit three heavy bomber groups to Siberia. Such a proposal was, in fact, dispatched December 30, offering the immediate delivery of 100 four-engined bombers and noting U.S. intelligence indicating the increasing possibility of a Japanese attack upon Soviet territory.[9]

Marshal Stalin's replies of January 5 and 13, 1943, sum up the frustration of the year and in a succinct way reveal Soviet strategy for the Pacific War and beyond:

I have received your message concerning the Far East. Please accept my appreciation for your willingness to send 100 bombers for the Soviet Union to the Far East. However, I must say that at the present time we want aid in airplanes not in the Far East but at the front of the fiercest war against the Germans, i.e., at the Soviet-German front. The arrival of these airplanes *without fliers* (we have enough fliers of our own), at the southwestern or the central front would play an enormous role in the most important sectors of our struggle against Hitler.[10]

Finally, the president again tried to clarify the terms for U.S. assistance in the Far East, elaborating and suggesting that Stalin had perhaps not fully understood. Stalin, indeed, had understood! Accordingly, he cabled Roosevelt on January 13, 1943, restating his position in no uncertain terms:

As regards sending bombing units to the Far East, I made it clear in my previous messages that what we want is not avio-units, but airplanes without fliers, as we have more than enough fliers of our own. This is in the first place.

In the second place, we want your aid in airplanes not in the Far East, where the USSR is not in a state of war, but at the Soviet-German front, where the need for aviation aid is particularly acute.

I do not quite understand your suggestion that Gen. Bradley should inspect Russian military objects in the Far East and other parts of the USSR. It would seem that Russian military objects can be inspected only by Russian inspectors, just as American military objects can be inspected only by American inspectors. In this respect there must be no misunderstanding.[11]

1943: YEAR OF CONFERENCES AND DECISIONS— FOR FUTURE SOVIET ACTION ON JAPAN

In accordance with overall Allied policy to get the war over in Europe before concentrating on the defeat of Japan, discussions among the United States, the United Kingdom, and the Soviet Union during 1943 focused on the problem of coordinating and maximizing the war effort against Germany. Scant attention was given to Soviet participation in the Pacific War at the four interallied conferences that took place that year—the first at Casablanca in January, the second in Washington in May, the third at Quebec in August, and the fourth at Cairo-Teheran in November and December.

Casablanca was essentially a European affair, with an afterthought to the effect that the United States should be prepared to support the Soviet Union "in the case of war with Japan."[12]

At the U.S.-U.K. Washington conference in May 1943, the question of the possibility of a Soviet-Japanese war was raised once again, more as an apparent footnote. The U.S. Joint Chiefs' clear and perceptive estimate of the situation at the time concluded:

> ... both Russia and Japan desire to avoid war with each other to be free to direct their efforts against their respective enemies. Russia is likely to intervene in the war against Japan at some stage, but not before the German threat to her has been removed. After that, she will make her decision in the light of her own interests and will intervene only when she reckons that Japan can be defeated at a small cost to her.[13]

The subject of Japan occupied even less time at the Quebec conference of August (1943). The conference did not discuss steps for obtaining Soviet participation in the Pacific War, "nor did the President and the Prime Minister allude to this subject in their message to Stalin summarizing the discussions taken at Quebec."[14]

When the Moscow Foreign Ministers conference opened on October 19, 1943, again, as might be expected, primary concern was with Europe. An intriguing and sophisticated by-product relative to Japan may be noted. Major General John R. Deane who had accompanied the U.S. Ambassador W. Averill Harriman to the Soviet Union, reported on October 13 as follows:

> Stalin gave an off-the-record dinner party at the conclusion of the conference last night. The atmosphere was one of complete desire for cooperation and I feel that Mr. Hull has done a great job in this regard in the conference. It was significant that after the dinner we were shown a lengthy picture of Japanese penetration in Siberia in 1921. It was distinctly anti-Japanese propaganda and we all felt it was an indirect method of telling us their attitude with regard to Japan. In private conversation with Molotov, Vashinsky [sic] and others we have heard more direct statements indicating that they will join us in the Pacific war as soon as Germany is defeated.[15]

Secretary of State Hull also recorded that at the Moscow conference Stalin astonished and delighted him "by saying clearly and unequivocally that, when the Allies succeeded in defeating Germany, the Soviet Union would join in defeating Japan."[16]

A fourth and final series of meetings during 1943 was held by the president, the prime minister, and Marshal Stalin at Teheran preceded by meetings with Gen. Chiang Kai-shek in Cairo. The U.S. Joint Chiefs of Staff in consultation with the British at this time drew up and submitted a list of five items relative to possible joint Allied-Soviet cooperation against Japan.

This list included, for instance, a request for Soviet combat intelligence information concerning Japan, and queries on what ports, if any, the U.S. Navy would be allowed to use and what airbases, if any, the Soviets would allow the U.S. air forces to use against Japan.[17]

Late in December Molotov informed Amassador Harriman that information about the Japanese could be furnished, but that the remaining questions required further study or could not be answered "at the present time."[18]

Noting the Joint Chiefs' regular inclusion, by this time, of "if any" when they queried their Soviet counterparts on what airbases might be used by U.S. aircraft, it should have come as no surprise to the frustrated U.S. staff officers that nothing further was forthcoming from Moscow on the subject, except silence.

Still, the new plans prepared by the U.S. Joint Chiefs of Staff if and when the Soviet Union entered the war against Japan regularly included such items as "To supply and operate air forces from Siberian bases."[19] Contingency planning had, of course, to continue, however routine and unrealistic the proposals may by now have appeared to some of the experienced U.S. military working groups.

The comprehensive Department of Defense report, *The Entry of the Soviet Union into the War Against Japan: Military Plans, 1941–1945*, succinctly summarizes the situation for the year under review: "At the end of 1943 the military planners had reason to believe," the report notes, "that the Soviet Union would participate in the Pacific War after the defeat of Germany." The report continues: "Whether she would actually do so when the time came, and under what conditions, were still unknown." Then the intriguing conclusion: ". . . the political problem of what she [the Soviet Union] would want as a price remained to be settled by the heads of government."[20]

1944: FROM TEHERAN TO YALTA— PROMISES, PROMISES!

Eventually, at Teheran Soviet participation in the war against Japan was specifically promised. The United States and its allies continued on the tough Pacific "island hopping" route to victory. The planners concluded that air and sea bombardment would not be enough; that it would ultimately be necessary to invade Japan's home islands. The prospective target dates were April 1 through June 30, 1945, for the invasion of the Bonin and Ryukyu islands with the final phase scheduled to begin with an assault on the Tokyo region of Honshu at the end of December 1945. These plans were, it may be noted, drawn without reference to U.S. progress in the development of an atomic bomb and, indeed, before the U.S. refinement of the two deliverable bombs ultimately dropped on Hiroshima and Nagasaki, respectively.

Moreover, as the tide of battle in the Pacific changed during 1944 in favor of the Allies, the defeat of Japan was perceived as not contingent upon the active participation of Russia in the war. Still, Soviet cooperation could be extremely useful, and was repeatedly requested.

During the first half of 1944, it was simply impossible to arrange for any systematic Soviet–United States discussion of the war in the Pacific. Early in February Stalin slyly told Ambassador Harriman that the United States would be permitted to operate aircraft from Siberia after the Soviet Union declared war on Japan.[21] But, again, no opportunity was offered for consultation with Soviet air force officers, and nothing of consequence ever came of the matter. From time to time thereafter Stalin raised the question of the possibilities of staff conferences, yet no meetings of any kind occurred until September 23, 1944, when Ambassador Harriman and the British ambassador met with Stalin to inform him of the results of the Quebec conference. In his report to the president, Harriman related: "Stalin inquired whether we wished to bring Japan to her knees without Russian assistance or whether you still wished, as you suggested in Teheran, Russian participation. . . . He gave every indication of being ready and willing to cooperate but did not want to be an uninvited participant."[22]

The president immediately cabled Stalin: ". . . I want to reiterate to you how completely I accept the assurances which you have given us on this point [eventual Soviet participation in the war against Japan]."[23]

As the late Professor Philip Mosely, Director of the Russian Institute at Columbia University, once remarked to me, by this time the real question was "not how to get the Soviets into the War against Japan, but how to keep them out!"[24]

In response to Marshal Stalin's request for a specific role in the Pacific War, the Joint Chiefs of Staff approved on September 28, 1944, the following list of objectives submitted by General Deane:

1. The broad strategic concept of Russian participation should be aimed at the following objectives in order of priority:
   a. Securing the Trans-Siberian Railway and the Vladivostok Peninsula.
   b. Setting up American and Soviet Strategic Air Forces for operations against Japan from the Maritime Provinces and the Kamchatka Peninsula.
   c. Interdicting of lines of communication between Japan proper and the Asiatic mainland.
   d. Destroying Japanese ground and air forces in Manchuria.

     e. Securing the Pacific supply route which would include Russian
       participation.
  2. Making available for United States use:
     a. Petropavlovsk as a naval support and supply base.
     b. The areas on the Kamchatka Peninsula for air bases.[25]

Again, the military staff conversations did not materialize, nor did the
promised joint planning sessions occur. Then, on December 14, Stalin
revealed for the first time to Ambassador Harriman the price for Soviet
participation. This included the annexation of the Kuriles and southern
Sakhalin, the restoration of former Russian possessions in Manchuria, and
the recognition of the *status quo* in Outer Mongolia.[26] To add insult to injury,
General Deane was informed by General A. I. Antinov on December 16,
that the U.S. requests for air bases in the Maritime Provinces would not be
granted, "since all the available facilities would be needed by the Soviet
forces." United States protests against this reversal of Stalin's previous
assurances failed to alter the decision.[27]

1945: YALTA AND POTSDAM— THE PRICE EXTRACTED

At the Yalta conference in February of 1945, the Soviets extracted their
price for agreeing to enter the war against Japan "approximately three
months after the defeat of Germany." The terms agreed upon between
President Roosevelt and Marshal Stalin were essentially those outlined by
Stalin to Ambassador Harriman earlier: the preservation of the *status quo* in
Outer Mongolia, the restoration of the former rights of Russia in Manchuria,
the internationalization of Dairen, the return of southern Sakhalin, and the
annexation of the Kuriles. In restrospect, at least, the price seems exorbitant.
Moreover, despite additional promises at Yalta, neither a projected U.S.
survey party for Kamchatka nor an American Amur River survey team ever
entered Soviet territory.

On May 12, 1945, Secretary of War Stimson summarized the U.S. military evaluation of the Soviet role in the Pacific War as well as Moscow's
plans for the Occupation of Japan. The secretary stated in part:

  1. The War Department considers that Russian entry into the war
     against Japan will be decided on their own military and political
     basis with little regard for any political action taken by the United
     States.
  2. . . . it appears we can bring little, if any, military leverage to bear

on the Russians in so far as the Far East is concerned, unless we choose to use force.

3. With regard to Soviet participation in the military occupation of the Japanese homeland, the War Department considers this to be a matter for political decision. From one military standpoint, this participation appears desirable, since it would reduce the military requirements of the U.S. for occupation purposes. On the other hand, our experiences with the Russians in the occupation of Germany may in the future lead to considerations which would point to the wisdom of exclusive occupation by our own forces.[28]

In preparation for the Potsdam conference, Harry Hopkins and Ambassador Harriman talked with Stalin and Molotov on several occasions. At the end of May (1945), Hopkins reported to the president: "Stalin expects that Russia will share in the actual occupation of Japan and wants an agreement with us and the British as to zones of occupation."[29]

Shortly before the U.S. delegation's departure for Potsdam, the Combined Intelligence Committee completed its latest estimate of the Japanese situation. It pointed out that the Japanese navy had been virtually eliminated, the Japanese air capability reduced to suicide tactics, that the 4.5-million-man army possessed only dwindling and inadequate supplies and lacked mobility. Militarily, Japan was finished. Still, the report admonished, "Japanese military tradition" and the "question of the Emperor" make unconditional surrender unacceptable. "Japanese leaders are now playing for time," the document concluded, "in the hope that war weariness, Allied disunity, or some 'miracle' will present an opportunity to arrange a compromise peace."[30]

During these last desperate weeks, another notion—one final, if reluctant, possible way out—became increasingly attractive to Tokyo: an appeal to the "good offices" of the Soviet Union. That huge and influential nation was, at least, still formally "neutral"; and Japan's options, short of total annihilation, now appeared pitifully few, even to those stoic, unrealistic, or devoted souls still publicly determined to die for emperor and country. After a series of audiences with the emperor which may perhaps best be characterized as a curious mix of tradition, platitudes, waning hope, and stark realism, the Japanese military-political leadership accepted "the *emperor's* suggestion" that a mission be dispatched to Moscow "to discuss Japan's situation."[31]

In the Soviet capital, Japanese Ambassador Sato was instructed to inform Molotov that the emperor wished the war terminated and to that end had proposed sending Prince Konoye to Moscow as his special envoy.

Regular and "urgent" conversations had meanwhile been going on in Tokyo between Japanese representatives and Soviet Amassador Malik. On one such occasion, former Premier Hirota even offered a *quid pro quo*: "Japan," he said, "would like to trade the rubber, tin, lead, and tungsten of the southern regions in return for Soviet oil." It was, of course, no secret to anyone—least of all U.S. and Soviet intelligence—that Japan was by this time critically short of oil, but coming at this late juncture on the road to certain military defeat, such a suggestion from Tokyo must have seemed incongruous to Moscow. Then, Hirota added: "If the Soviet Union would enter into a non-aggression pact [different from a neutrality pact] with Japan, . . . [Japan] would grant Manchuria her independence, would relinquish Japanese fishing concessions in Soviet Far Eastern Waters [in return for oil], and would be willing to consider any other matters the Soviet government might wish to place on the agenda." Malik would "report the substance of these conversations to Moscow."[32]

Moscow was conspicuously in no hurry to "negotiate" with Tokyo. Soviet indifference combined with procrastination greeted virtually every Japanese initiative. Sometimes silence or even "illness" of the responsible Soviet official was the order of the day. Scarcely surprising! In light of the perhaps unnecessarily generous concessions presented the Soviet Union at Yalta, Moscow needed only to await the appropriate "agreed upon" time to enter the war against Japan, and then to claim and collect the "fair share" of the spoils due the victor. This is precisely what happened.

When the Potsdam conference convened, July 17 to August 2, 1945, the call was for the unconditional surrender of Japan. Stalin was told for the first time by the United States about the existence of a new and possibly decisive weapon on July 24.[33] He was not surprised as Soviet intelligence had kept the Soviets apprised in detail of U.S. nuclear developments and plans. On July 29, the Japanese radio broadcast the news that the Japanese government would ignore the Potsdam Declaration demanding unconditional surrender. Thus, the nuclear stage was set, and on August 3, orders to prepare to drop the atomic bomb were confirmed by the president on his way back from Potsdam. The end was near.

SOVIET ENTRY INTO THE PACIFIC WAR, THE BOMBS, AND JAPAN'S DECISION TO SURRENDER

Four days after the conclusion of the Potsdam conference, on August 6, 1945, the first atomic bomb was dropped on Hiroshima. A second (and the only remaining atomic bomb in the U.S. arsenal), was dropped on Nagasaki on August 9. Just the day before, the Japanese ambassador in Moscow had been informed by Molotov that the Soviet Union would consider itself at war with Japan as of August 9.

With the Soviet declaration of war, Russian divisions swept through Manchuria. They met only moderate to token Japanese resistance as the pride of the once vaunted Japanese Kwantung army had long since been withdrawn to protect the homeland. This fact, incidentally, does not prevent Soviet historians from regularly claiming (with scant reference, if any, to the U.S. role in the Pacific War) that victory over Japan in World War II came about as a direct consequence of the Soviet defeat of Japan's military forces in Manchuria.

Inevitably, the war came quickly to a close. After the personal intervention of the emperor, the Japanese government on August 10 conditionally accepted the Potsdam Proclamation, "provided it did not prejudice the Emperor's prerogatives." But it was not until August 14 that the Japanese government formally accepted the revised and somewhat more ambiguous terms of modified surrender designed to circumvent the question of the future status of the emperor. The same day, General MacArthur was appointed Supreme Commander for the Allied powers.

On September 2, the formal surrender ceremonies took place aboard the U.S.S. *Missouri* in Tokyo Bay. The Pacific War was over, but the contest over Japan had only begun.

Part Two

The Soviet Presence
in an American-Occupied Japan

Chapter Three

Soviet Policy and Practice in Occupied Japan

"Before the outbreak of war between the United States and Russia, the Soviet government will direct a violent anti-American campaign through the Japanese Communists with the aim of establishing a Red government in Japan." This provocative statement from a Japanese government report dated 1945 and marked "secret" was penned on the eve of Japan's defeat.[1] It coincides with the Soviet Union's belated entry into the Pacific War shortly before Japan's surrender. The comment, we are told, represents "the view of one informant," but the theme, in fact, runs through Japanese police and intelligence documents of the wartime and early Occupation period.*

SOVIET GOALS— SHORT RANGE AND LONG RANGE

For American-Occupied Japan, as for other areas of the world, Soviet grand strategy was conceived in terms of long- and short-range goals, each with its concomitant strategic and tactical aspects. Nor, as has been suggested, did any well-defined Soviet policy for postwar Japan emerge from the policy planners in Moscow any more than was the case with Washington.

---

*As a Japanese language officer serving with the Supreme Commander for the Allied Powers (SCAP) in Tokyo during the early phase of the Occupation, the author personally filled several mail bags with key Japanese government documents having international relations and policy implications. These were then shipped to Washington where they ultimately found their way to the dusty basement of the Library of Congress. It was some years later before there was occasion to review them again in preparation for a book, co-authored with Paul Langer, later to appear under the title *Red Flag in Japan* (Cambridge, Mass.: Harvard University Press, 1952).

As it turns out, once the question of Soviet troop participation (i.e., actual occupation by Russian troops) and the Soviet demand for a co-supreme commander had been settled in the negative, the policy options open to Moscow became fewer and fewer as the Occupation crystallized into a massive American venture, a personalized MacArthur enterprise.

American perception of early Soviet policy in postwar Japan is perhaps nowhere more directly and clearly stated than in a dispatch prepared for Washington by the embassy in Moscow on November 2, 1945, and significantly sent on to the U.S. political advisor in Japan by Secretary of State Byrnes. It read in part:

> It is difficult to believe that Soviet General Staff and POLITBURO are lying awake nights worrying about recrudescence of Japanese Imperialism and aggression. What may cause them uneasy moments, however, is thought that Japan like Germany might some day be utilized by Western Powers as springboard for attack on USSR. Japan as much as Eastern Europe is in Soviet zone of vital strategic interest.

The document goes on to suggest:

> Long range strategic implications of American occupation and control of Japan are therefore one reason for Soviet dissatisfaction with the situation in Japan.
>
> With USA dominant in Japan, only possible program [sic] for introducing and expanding Soviet influence, aside from establishment of Allied control mechanism with its limited utility to USSR, is exploitation through Japanese Communists and Leftists of post-war disorder and economic unrest. We appear, however, to be housecleaning and encouraging liberal tendencies in Japan. This has effect of stealing Communist thunder. And this irritates USSR because fundamentally USSR prefers crusading against reaction to competing with liberals. Our apparently intelligent internal policy in Japan is therefore a second cause for Soviet dissatisfaction with American dispensation in Japan.[2]

The dispatch proceeds to postulate what is termed a third possible cause of Soviet concern. This point turns out to be singularly relevant not only in terms of Japan but with respect to overall Soviet attitudes and behavior in the postwar era.

> Possible third cause [sic] of Soviet dissatisfaction of which no evidence has yet been seen in press but which appears inferentially in stray conversations with Russians would be feeling that USSR as one of the two

greatest powers and as Pacific power has not been accorded due "face" in disposition of Japan. Being new rich with a lingering inferiority complex and feeling of gauche uncertainty in international society USSR is inordinately sensitive regarding appearance as well as substance of prestige.

This third cause of Soviet disgruntlement could probably be eliminated to considerable degree by concessions to Soviet dignity. But it should not be assumed that such concessions would compensate in Soviet eyes for continuing American single control of Japan and a constructively liberal internal policy there. So long as these fundamental conditions exist Soviet press and government may be expected to take jaundiced view of Japanese affairs.[3]

The political, economic, and psychological arenas in which Soviet policy agencies were to operate in an American-Occupied Japan is discussed by SCAP's political advisor George Atcheson, Jr. in a telegram to the secretary of state in an early comment on the matter. After noting the probable implications of Japan's defeat, physical destruction, national disorientation, psychological and political confusion, and economic chaos, Atcheson makes a perceptive and refreshingly balanced judgment of Communist potential and Soviet involvement when he comments:

In this situation, there is obviously considerable encouragement for the Communists. Japan is groping for a new ideology to replace the shattered one which was so carefully and deliberately constructed during the years of military-feudal control. The old has been discredited and the new is attractive: liberalism is vague and difficult to define. Communism is positive and concrete. It will be favored by the present serious economic insecurity. *It will take at least moral encouragement from Soviet participation in the control of Japan.* But the popular hatred and fear of Russia and Communism will also be checks. . . [italics supplied].[4]

In this context, broadly speaking, Soviet maximum objectives in Occupied Japan in order of priority may be postulated as follows: (1) the Communization of Japan, that is the ultimate replacement of the pro–United States Japanese government by a pro-Communist regime, presumably controlled from Moscow; (2) the discrediting of U.S. policy and the American Occupation, and the eliminating of U.S. presence (military bases) and influence in Japan concomitant with the establishment of a Socialist, "neutralist" government of an essentially anti-American character; (3) the development of a coalition, nonsocialist government with strong "neutralist" tendencies reminiscent of early Third World neutralism and with only nominal ties with the United States; (4) some less desirable "friendly" combination of the above (a last, reluctant if more realistic, resort). It is doubtful, of course, that Moscow ever assumed that it would make more than modest progress on priorities 1 and 2, and as events were to show, even the third, less formidable objective, that of quasi neutralism, was an unrealistic Soviet objective for Japan.

These Soviet goals, of course, had to be modified and redefined, or at least postponed, as Moscow's policy options decreased in number and as the character of the Occupation became strictly a MacArthur show run by the general with a minimum of guidance from the Far Eastern Commission, the Allied Council for Japan—or from Washington, for that matter.

The very real limitations imposed upon Soviet policy and practice in Occupied Japan by the position, personality, policy-orientation, and predilections of the Supreme Commander of the Allied Powers, Gen. Douglas MacArthur, were balanced (as was only natural) by certain liberal (some writers have even suggested left-wing) elements on the operational level within SCAP and by disagreements within the U.S. government on the desired nature and direction of the Occupation. Indeed, in what some analysts regard as something of a contradiction in terms, the Occupation under General MacArthur (at least during its first phase) was a surprisingly liberal affair. A careful reading of the Counter-Intelligence Corps (CIC) and other intelligence field reports reveals a professional, systematic, and unexpectedly mature and moderate, though realistic, judgment of the nature of the Soviet challenge in the security issue.*

The Soviets, it should be noted, were not entirely without resources or assets in the political, ideological, and strategic competition that was to ensue—though these, of course, were not of the scope or magnitude of U.S. (SCAP) agencies, organizations, and personnel within Occupied Japan. Soviet resources included the propaganda platform provided by the Allied Council for Japan which met for a time in Tokyo (with General Kuzma Derevyanko as principal Soviet spokesman); the Soviet mission in Japan, whose personnel capabilities and organizational machinery were quite formidable and went far beyond the official, presumed, or agreed role of the Allied powers; the Moscow-oriented Japan Communist Party (JCP) essentially, if at times with difficulty or occasional apparent reluctance, serving Moscow's ends at this early juncture; Soviet radio broadcasts to Japan; and

---

*The author has examined hundreds of pages of documents for the period, many of them recently declassified and now available at the National Archives. These range from documents dealing with the Soviet mission in Japan to Soviet espionage, Soviet radio broadcasts, etc. to substantial reports on Communist activities in Japan and on the role of the problems presented by the Soviet-indoctrinated repatriates.

the Japanese repatriates, returned after a period of long indoctrination, to Japan from Soviet areas.[5]

GENERAL MACARTHUR VERSUS
GENERAL DEREVYANKO

One can scarcely imagine a greater contrast in background, philosophy, personality, and style than that which emerges from studying the military and personal history, and observing the routine, and behavior, of the two arch-protagonists and principal representatives, respectively, of the United States and the Soviet Union in Occupied Japan.

General Douglas MacArthur's long and brilliant military career, ultra self-esteem, and colorful, if controversial personality, punctuate the pages of half a century of U.S. military and political history. Statements such as "I shall return!" and "Old soldiers never die—they just fade away" are merely the more eloquent and memorable manifestations of a man preoccupied throughout his life with the "business of being great." No useful purpose would be served here by attempting to sample the volumes of published material produced over the years by the general's erstwhile admirers and critics (or the general himself), not to mention those few brave souls who would aspire to that evanescent literary quality called "objectivity." But no matter!

Suffice to recall in this comparative context and for the record that General MacArthur was: top in his class at West Point; Chief of Staff of the 42nd ("Rainbow") Division during World War I; the youngest general (at 50 years of age) to become Chief of Staff of the U.S. Army since Grant; superintendent of the U.S. Military Academy; Chief of the Far East Command (after Pearl Harbor), then Commander-in-Chief of Allied Forces in the Southwest Pacific; one of the United States' rare five-star generals; a distinguished officer in twenty campaigns and six wars (with more medals for distinguished service than any other man who ever served in the American army); and, finally, Supreme Commander of the Allied Powers in Occupied Japan.

Compared with his brilliant military record and flashy public image, MacArthur's personality and life-style, at least in Occupied Japan, appear austere, even dull. His office in the Daiichi Building across from the Imperial Palace in Tokyo was not impressive. His desk, though always neat, displayed only one distinguishing feature: a prized stand of his famous corncobs. He lived in the American embassy with an honor guard of U.S. soldiers and so many Japanese police that one American journalist was prompted to remark that "they seem to sleep in the trees." His social life was nil. He held no open houses. He rarely attended any of the numerous official functions of the Tokyo "diplomatic set." He had few hobbies, unless one considers reading a hobby (MacArthur was an avid reader). He was a devout Christian although he did not attend church except on occasion. His pet diversion appears to have been attending regular motion picture showings at the embassy. His son, Arthur, tutored at home, often went with his mother to sports functions; but MacArthur's inflexible rule prohibited undue publicity. "The boy," he insisted, "must be allowed to grow up normally."[6]

Turning to General Kuzma Derevyanko, General MacArthur's Soviet counterpart in Occupied Japan, no such record of brilliant achievement fills the annals of Soviet history. Indeed, the name of the Soviets' principal representative in Occupied Japan does not even appear in any of the standard Soviet encyclopedias or reference volumes (past, recent, or current).[7] He is, to use the celebrated Orwellian term, a "nonperson." Fortunately, for the persistent, interested researcher, the Soviet general also had a son, and that son wrote an interesting account of his father (which was published in Moscow in 1971). Moreover, several of the general's former aides, as well as his wife, reside in Moscow. It was only on my 1976 summer visit to Moscow that I came across the biography written by his son, and, by chance, encountered two of the general's former aides with whom there was occasion to chat briefly. Thus something may also be said, by way of comparison, about the background and personality of MacArthur's principal protagonist in Tokyo.[8]

General Kuzma Derevyanko was born in 1904 in the village of Kosenovka in one of the most picturesque corners of the Ukraine. It was in that then remote and backwoods region that he received education through high school.[9] His son writes that at an early age his father loved books and music and that he was very popular among his fellow students.[10] In 1922, he volunteered for service in the Red Army. By 1925, he had been accepted as a candidate for the Communist party. This was the same year that he married, and soon a son was born.[11] After commanding a rifle company and taking some further training (in 1931), he was appointed to the staff of the Ukranian military region. By 1933, he successfully passed the examinations and entered the famous Frunze military academy. Among other subjects, Kuzma studied Japanese and English and "soon he could read both languages and translate and converse on military topics."[12] Derevyanko's son also recalls that his father was very fond of children; would often stop to play soccer briefly with neighborhood children or take them from time to time swimming or on organized ski expeditions.

Most of General Derevyanko's military service appears to have been of a staff and intelligence nature. This included an assignment as aide to Marshal Voroshilov in the People's Commissariat for Defense, where among other duties he helped develop a secret advanced logistical base for supplies across the Gobi Desert (equipment and ammunition) for the Chinese (Communist) Eighth Route Army. In 1939, he was summoned to the "critical Finland border" where he served in the intelligence group which "operated behind enemy lines."[13] During the war with Nazi Germany, General Derevyanko was appointed Chief of Intelligence of the Staff of the North-West Front. He participated, we are told, in the Kursk battles, the Dnepr River crossing, and the "Liberation" of Budapest. In May of 1942, he was promoted to major general and in 1944, to lieutenant general. When General Derevyanko participated in the battle for Vienna, his son (also a military graduate) was at his side. It was Derevyanko who, after receiving a telegram from Stalin reassigning him to the Far East, signed for the Soviet Union at the celebrated surrender ceremonies on the battleship U.S.S. *Missouri.*

Bright, gregarious, and something of a ladies' man, with a formidable background in Intelligence, knowledge of the Japanese language as well as of English, and a specialization in China and Japan, General Derevyanko seems a logical choice as Stalin's man in Tokyo during the Occupation of Japan. Ironically, it was the combined force and aggregate weight of the personalities of his boss, Stalin, and principal adversary, General MacArthur, that have resulted in his modest place in history—Soviet and American.

SOVIET EXPLOITATION OF THE ALLIED COUNCIL FOR JAPAN

It may be recalled that the four-power Allied Council for Japan (ACJ), made up of the United States, USSR, China, and the British Commonwealth, was established in Tokyo to monitor the directives issued by the Far Eastern Commission (FEC) in Washington, D.C. and to "advise" SCAP. In fact, neither the FEC nor the ACJ proved effective administrative instruments, since Occupation policy and practice almost from the outset, as has been suggested, was dictated personally by General MacArthur as Supreme Commander for the Allied Powers.

Accordingly, the role of the Soviet representative on the Allied Council for Japan, as principal U.S. adversary, assumed three familiar aspects: denunciation of American policy, of the conduct of the Occupation, and of General MacArthur personally; propaganda of a blatantly pro-Soviet and pro-Communist complexion; and perhaps the most important of all—the systematic and persistent pursuit and collection of Intelligence information.

A review of the detailed *Verbatim Minutes* (VM) of the Allied Council for Japan, while hardly bedtime reading, is in its own way fascinating, and dramatically documents the Soviet exploitation of that organization for destructive propaganda and positive intelligence purposes. A full analysis of that procedure remains to be written. It would seem to serve no useful purpose here to compile even a substantial representative sampling of "quotable quotes" from General Derevyanko's sometimes almost eloquent attacks upon General MacArthur, U.S. policies, the "inadequate land reform program," SCAP controls on "democratic" organizations (i.e., the Japan Communist Party), the "catering to Japanese war criminals and former military officers," and so on. Suffice here to record some of the relevant highlights in the original, telling language.

Quite apart from the propaganda aspect, what emerges clearly from a careful reading of the Allied Council documentation is the comprehensive and persistent Soviet exploitation of the ACJ for strategic Intelligence purposes. Here the Soviets are in their element: "What was the composition of the Japanese fishing fleet at the beginning of the war, at the moment of surrender, and at present, the total tonnage of the fleet and separate tonnage according to types of vessels?" General Derevyanko asked this question— one of thousands of similar intent—early in the course of the council meetings.[14]

Similarly, here is a typical exchange between the general and the U.S. representative, George Atcheson, Jr. (who will be heard from later on this issue):

DEREVYANKO: "It would be highly desirable to obtain a list of personnel purged from Japanese public offices."
CHAIRMAN (*Atcheson*): "The 186,000 names?"
(*Then to interpreter*): "You mean the General would like to have a list of those 186,000?"

The general conceded that perhaps "for his purposes" (not specified) the central government offices' rosters would suffice. "There can't be so many people there?" he added.[15]

The same story goes on and on meeting after meeting, month by month, with respect to virtually every strategic intelligence topic imaginable until on one occasion General Derevyanko felt constrained to explain (this time relative to the repatriation issue): "We haven't requested lists of crews, but (only) lists of personnel working for the First and Second Demobilization Bureaus," and he continued, "the personnel attached to sections and divisions of these bureaus."[16]

At this point, Chairman Atcheson, obviously annoyed, interjects: "May I ask the purpose the Member has in mind in requesting such detailed information?"[17]

Again, later, probing still another key strategic intelligence area, Derevyanko persists: "It is known that during a considerable period of time the [electric] power balance has been extremely tense [critical] . . . I would like to receive information. . . ."[18] By the spring of 1947, the Soviets began requesting additional long lists, charts, and graphs on every conceivable aspect of the economic and strategic situation—with projections.[19]

Finally, apparently unable any longer to stand the Soviet representative's blatant exploitation of the council, the U.S. representative and chairman, Atcheson (on the occasion of the council's 38th meeting in August of 1947), met the issue squarely: "The purpose of the Council as originally established," he said, "was to assist the SUPREME COMMANDER with constructive advice and recommendations. It has been made abundantly clear that it has been a misuse of the Council to employ it as an information collection agency."[20]

Ultimately, at the 41st meeting of the council on September 17, replying to the Soviet representative's insistence that he had simply been doing his proper homework and that it was the United States that had been doing the "exploiting," Atcheson presented the Soviets, the council, and the world with a devastating bill of particulars.

This detailed presentation by the U.S. representative started gently enough. "I do not deny," Atcheson conceded, "that the SOVIET MEMBER has been very busy and has worked very hard since the inception of this Council . . ." and then Atcheson added, "but I do take exception to the direction which that work has taken."[21] This signaled the beginning of a systematic U.S. onslaught on Soviet obstructionism, intensive political influence, and intelligence activity.

"In a number of cases, recommendations were made by the SOVIET MEMBER which, read by themselves, leave an impression, but only an impression of sweet reasonableness and constructive effort," Atcheson noted, adding, "however, when these recommendations are read in conjunction with statements made at the meeting or at previous or subsequent meetings, they illustrate a continuous effort on the part of the SOVIET MEMBER to becloud the issue."[22]

"At the Fourth meeting the SOVIET MEMBER recommended systematic surveillance of the activities of all former Japanese officers. This," Atcheson charged, "is nothing more than an attempt to implant into Japan a system of a police state."[23]

Referring to the Soviet regular oblique support of the Japan Communist Party and its supporters, Atcheson stated: "At the same (Fourth) meeting the so-called 'Address of the People's Meeting of May 1, 1946,' is nothing more than an attempt to highlight a document written by a Japanese Communist militant minority which held itself out as a representative of labor as a whole."[24]

Next the U.S. representative took exception to the Soviets' attempt to control the proceedings. "At the Seventh Meeting an effort was made by the SOVIET MEMBER, to establish a principle of joint recommendation to the SUPREME COMMANDER by members of the Council, an effort," Atcheson asserted, "obviously designed to circumvent the Terms of Reference and to introduce the veto principle into this Council."[25]

The Soviet attempt to influence the reshaping of Japan's institutions and Japanese society along Soviet lines, in the Soviet mold, next came in for its fair share of criticism. At the ninth meeting, the U.S. representative argued, "the SOVIET MEMBER advocated workers' control of enterprises which amounts to taking over property without compensation, a doctrine entirely alien to democratic processes."[26]

At the tenth meeting, Atcheson evoked the ultimate in invidious comparisons when, on the subject of literature in Japan, he charged: "the SOVIET MEMBER, in effect, advocated a campaign of book burning which is reminiscent of what took place in Nazi Germany."[27]

Again, at the seventeenth meeting, Atcheson stated, "the SOVIET MEMBER advocated the nationalization of the *Zaibatsu* (Large Corporations/Trusts) without any compensation . . . and introduction of production quotas, an institution which would appear clearly to parallel Soviet methods."[28]

And once more at the 26th meeting, we are told, "the SOVIET MEMBER advocated the abolition of the private ownership of seashore areas used by fishermen . . . a further . . . expropriation of property."[29]

Finally exasperated (in light of the $1 million per day the United States had been pouring into the Japanese economy), at the 32nd meeting Atcheson noted: "the SOVIET MEMBER charged that, and I quote from the minutes, 'almost no serious measures have been taken to rehabilitate the economy of Japan, to improve the economic situation . . . etc.' "[30] Atcheson concluded: "the record speaks for itself."[31]

The Soviet representative replied that he had no intention of continuing the discussion on this subject, "although I could give quite a number of convincing facts to disprove what has been said."[32]

So much for a glimpse at Soviet intelligence and propaganda activity within Occupied Japan at the platform, conference level. At the rice-roots level, policies and activities were designed, organized, and implemented by and through the Soviet mission in Tokyo.

THE CHARACTER AND ROLE OF THE
SOVIET MISSION IN TOKYO

Less publicized but highly effective in implementing aspects of Soviet policy and augmenting Soviet practice in Occupied Japan was the Soviet mission. From Moscow's perspective, that mission's official role was to assist the Soviet representative on the Allied Council and to "represent legitimate 'Four Power,' especially Soviet, interests in Japan." To accomplish these tasks (and, as it turned out, a few more) required the service of more than 500 Russians. The Chinese mission, by contrast, numbered 95, and the British, 65.

When queried concerning the need for such a large staff, the Soviets characteristically explained that it was necessary since the Soviet officials preferred their own Russian chauffeurs, needed dual translation capabilities (Russian-English; Russian-Japanese), and required a special diet necessitating the importation of cooks ("We are not used to eating Japanese food"). On this point, perhaps in a moment of exasperation with some of the official Soviet nonsense, a young colleague at SCAP once quipped that it had never been clear to him why the preparation of borsch required training in electronics, or why driving a car demanded an advanced degree in physics or naval engineering.

An overall analysis of the personnel of the Soviet mission reveals a broad range of interests and capabilities. As reflected in its official duty roster, the mission comprised fourteen divisions or departments: I Executive (8); II Secretariat (10); III Foreign Assignment (19); IV General Duty Officers (35); V Record Section (31); VI Air Corps Section (14); VII Navy Department (39); VIII Department of Recreation and Education (27); IX Department of Minor Political Questions (31); X Economics Advisor Group (34); XI Housing Administration Department (41); XII Finance Department (7); XIV Garage (33); and XV Department of Domestic Offices.[33] It may be noted that there is no department number XIII, no doubt because "13" is regarded as an unlucky number quite as much in Russia as in the West.*

In terms of rank, the Soviet mission was impressive, with one lieutenant general (Derevyanko), 3 major generals, a rear admiral, 7 assorted colonels, 20 lieutenants colonels, 23 majors, 15 captains, and so on. The official roster ends with a notation, "172 men working team for a total of 530 persons." Many of their staff were listed as civilians.[34]

The majority of the Russians lived in two places: at the former Russian embassy and a large Japanese government building across from the embassy, and in a billet known as Mitsubishi 21. The Soviet officers rarely wore uniforms, and usually appeared on Tokyo streets, typically in groups of two or three, in civilian clothes.

The Soviet embassy was always a curious edifice, but during the early

---

*From time to time, a cartoon in the Soviet humor magazine makes the point. One cartoon I remember shows the inside of a Soviet movie theater. On the screen: "On Superstition, a People's Science Film." Seat number 13 from top to bottom of the theater is vacant.

phase of the Occupation, the Soviets seemed to be constantly remodeling, adding concrete garages, thick walls, and building guard houses. Journalists, both overseas and Japanese, sometimes suggested that the Soviet embassy had come to look more like a castle. The Soviets showed a great sensitivity to having their embassy photographed, probably more of a built-in Soviet "secrecy" response than for any good or apparent reason. The embassy gates were, of course, closely guarded by their own soldiers, usually selected Intelligence types.

Mitsubishi 21 was the center of Soviet mission "unofficial" activities in Occupied Japan. It was the Intelligence operations center, the social hall, the contact spot, the film library, the "cultural center," TASS headquarters, VIP room, literature distribution point, and officers' club all rolled into one.

Not surprisingly, SCAP intelligence kept close watch on the building, its occupants, visitors, and their activities. Some of this activity is summarized in an unusual SCAP document (only recently declassified from "secret"), and entitled "Watchdog of the Occupation." Here are some passages from this document, subsection, "Soviet Mitsubishi 21":

The use of Mitsubishi 21 as an Intelligence headquarters was well established. Approximately 130 persons, chiefly Soviet Army officers, including three of general officer rank and three NKVD (secret police) officers were in the building. There were two general types of personnel quartered in Mitsubishi 21: long term residents, believed to be propaganda and intelligence specialists, and short-term residents. . . .

Mitsubishi 21 was used as a Soviet contact spot for Japanese, both individually and in groups.

Within the halls of Mitsubishi 21, Soviet personnel engaged in unauthorized distribution of motion pictures. The Soviet mission announced in November 1946 the opening of a film library in the building for use of the general public. The movie "Crime and Punishment" (among others) . . . was shown at Mitsubishi 21 to an audience composed exclusively of members of Communist front organizations.

The Intelligence section of Mitsubishi 21, in close contact with TASS, was a detachment of the Soviet Mission's espionage section.

Some of the most vitriolic attacks against SCAP, the Occupation forces and American policy in general came from Soviet-sponsored publications distributed illegally in Japan. . . . American foreign policy, Occupation policies in Japan and Germany and domestic issues in the United States were held up for ridicule and derision by distorted reports of isolated occurrences and in some instances, deliberate fabrications. Much of the material of this nature was flown into Japan from Sakhalin and distributed directly from Mitsubishi 21.[35]

THE JAPAN COMMUNIST PARTY AS A
TOOL OF MOSCOW

A few critical points regarding the prewar heritage of the Japan Communist Party need first to be summarized at this point by way of introduction before examining separately that party's orientation, role, mission, capability, and actions as an agency of Soviet policy in Occupied Japan.

First, the JCP was founded in 1922 with the assistance of Soviet and Chinese and Korean Comintern agents. Second, the party functioned officially through its prewar existence as the "Japan Communist Party, Japanese Branch of the [Soviet-controlled] Comintern." Third, the JCP maintained a representative at Comintern headquarters in Moscow. (From 1931 to 1940 that representative was Sanzo Nosaka, during the postwar era to become the leading figure in the JCP.) Fourth, the "coincidence" of Soviet and JCP policy line changes are numerous enough on virtually every major issue to establish essential Soviet policy guidance, i.e., control, over the prewar JCP. Fifth, the record of extensive training in Moscow and/or secret trips for conferences to Moscow in the case of numerous JCP leaders is well documented. Sixth, a wide range of converts from Japanese Communism and defectors detail the story of Moscow training and "guidance." Seventh, the JCP's principal policies (programs) were drafted in Moscow and secretly brought back to Japan by Communist couriers.

The complicated question of the degree to which the JCP in Occupied Japan remained essentially a tool of Moscow, as well as its diverse anti-Occupation activities and SCAP's ultimate reactions, will seem significant enough to demand separate treatment.[36] Suffice to record here the initial U.S. reading of the issue.

Perhaps the earliest documented U.S. view of the question came out of Moscow in the fall of 1946. Commenting on a SCAP report on the Japanese Communist Party, Foreign Service Officer John Davies, writing from the Soviet capital, stated:

There would seem to be little doubt that the Japanese Communist Party is out to capture authority. Its relationship with Yenan and Moscow is more difficult to determine. The composition of the Japanese Communist Party Politburo, with its three leading personalities having undergone long Moscow indoctrination, suggests that the ties with the USSR are strong. If Japanese Communist publications consistently assume the same attitude in foreign affairs as Soviet mouthpieces, that fact would further suggest subservience to Soviet authority. So long as the Japanese Communist Party is able to obtain sizable sums from domestic sources, it is unlikely that evidence will be found of Moscow gold filtering into Japan.

The Embassy would suggest that it might be useful in further investigations of the Japanese Communist Party to seek to determine how many of Nosaka's Yenan "students" are now working with him in Japan. It would also be interesting to learn whether Japanese from the USSR have also been brought into positions of authority in the Japanese Communist Party.

Finally, it might be stated that the growth of a healthy economy and a strong liberal movement in Japan are, of course, developments most likely to cut the ground out from under the Japanese Communist Party. Furthermore, wide dissemination of information about the true state of affairs in the USSR would go far towards dissipating the Soviet-concocted mirage of the USSR as an oasis of democracy and well-being in a world of oppression and misery. If Soviet-controlled Communist parties in the Balkans do not hesitate to depict the United States in dark and ominous colors, there would seem to be no valid reason why our Occupation authorities in Japan should not permit independent Japanese liberals, such as Social Democrats, to publish freely the truth about the Soviet Union.[37]

By mid-1949, as we shall see, SCAP Intelligence had produced partial answers to a number of these intriguing questions. Information from documents and interviews that have appeared in the post-Occupation period provide further perspective and detail on these critical issues.

SOVIET PROPAGANDA AND RADIO WARFARE

Throughout the world during the postwar years, the Soviets have waged a massive propaganda and cultural offensive through a number of high-powered agencies of which VOKS (USSR Overseas Cultural Liaison Associations) is perhaps the most celebrated. In Occupied Japan that offensive was channeled through such blatantly pro-Communist "cultural organizations" as the Soviet Study Association (*Sovieto Kenkyn Kyokai*), the Japan-Soviet Cultural Relations Association (*Nisso Bunkakai*), and of course, the Japan Communist Party.

Much of this activity originated in and was organized and directed by the Cultural and Educational Section of the Soviet mission of Mitsubishi 21. It included, among other projects, subsidizing left-wing Japanese publishers, secretly distributing volumes of unauthorized literature in Japanese and Russian which had been printed in the Soviet Union, supporting a host of cultural fronts through liaison with JCP left-wing labor leaders, student groups, and so on.[38]

Less well publicized but thought to have had significant impact was the intensive Soviet Radio Warfare campaign against Occupied Japan. Daily propaganda broadcasts were beamed intermittently from Japan from 6:00 A.M. until 11:00 P.M., a total of some 130 minutes of news and comment. These broadcasts originated in Moscow and were relayed by powerful transmitters located at Khabarovsk, Vladivostok, Komsomolsk, and Petrapovlovsk. The signals were strong enough to be audible on the ordinary Japanese radio receiver.[39]

Program content, needless to say, bitterly opposed the U.S. methods of conducting the Occupation and attacked all aspects of U.S. foreign policy. Here are a few characteristic themes:

> The anti-people Japanese government has set up a police tyranny in Japan.
> The U.S. imperialism intends to make Japan a part of its 'empire' now abuilding.
> Semi-starving people, reactionary government, economic crisis— these are the conditions which the Occupation headquarters wants to maintain in Japan.
> The United States is re-arming Japan.
> The United States is ignoring the Potsdam Declaration.
> The United States is delaying a Peace Treaty for Japan.[40]

At the same time, the Japanese were told by a Moscow radio commentator that:

> The Soviets single-handedly fight for Democracy in Japan and on a world-wide basis.
> The Japan Communist Party is winning the support of the people in its fight against the reactionaries.[41]

Finally, the Japanese were reminded that it was the entry of the USSR into the war against Japanese militarists that saved millions of lives. Pointing to August 9, the date of the USSR's entrance into the war as an "historic date," the Soviet commentator claimed that "without the fighting friendship and partnership" of the Soviet Union, the United States and its allies "could not have defeated their insidious enemy, Japanese militarism."[42] This is, of course, a major and standard Soviet propaganda line repeated in virtually all Soviet media.

Throughout 1948, attacks upon SCAP and the U.S. government became more frequent and vitriolic. In addition to assailing the past three Japanese cabinets (Yoshida, Katayama, and Ashida), with a familiar array of uncomplimentary and slanderous adjectives, attacking all aspects of Occupation policy, the Soviet radio's biggest guns were now directed at the United States. All these things were said to be but straws showing the true direction and purposes of U.S. policy: "To restore Japanese militarism to fight the Soviet Union and the democratic movements of the nations of the Far East is the simple principle of U.S. policy in Japan."[43]

By the middle of 1949, Moscow radio propaganda beamed to Japan reached a high pitch. All stops were out, no holds were barred! "The bad odor (of U.S. policies) attacks our noses mercilessly," one colorful Soviet broadcaster deplored. Virtually every conceivable U.S. and SCAP policy and practice now came under systematic and vitriolic attack: economic policies, the foreign trade situation "which it is evident the United States controls," the "tyranny over the trade unions," taxes imposed upon the Japanese "used by U.S. monopolists to buy Japanese railroads and other industries with Japan's money," "the transformation of Japan into an arsenal for war and a U.S. base in the Far East," and so on. But Moscow radio assured its Far Eastern listeners that "the people of Japan heartily support the world movement for peace."[44] Public opinion polls, Japanese newspaper editorials, and election results suggest that by this time the overwhelming majority of nonpartisan, noncontrolled, sensible, and realistic Japanese had come to understand only too well the special Communist connotation of the term "peace."[45] At the same time there appeared to be a degree of genuine Japanese appreciation for U.S. efforts toward the political and economic reconstruction of defeated or Occupied Japan.

THE SOVIET IMAGE OF THE AMERICAN OCCUPATION

Apart from official Soviet attacks upon General MacArthur and U.S. Occupation policy and practice by the Soviet representative on the Allied Council for Japan, Soviet press and publications poured out an impressive torrent of "backup" anti-MacArthur, anti-Occupation, and anti-American propaganda designed to discredit U.S. policy in Occupied Japan in the eyes of the world. Moscow found it expedient to go to the heart of the matter by directly attacking the U.S. capitalist system, "led by Wall Street." By simple Marxist-Leninist logic (assuming there is some agreement on what that might be), what was happening in American-Occupied Japan, the Soviets insisted, could have been anticipated.

The standard Soviet treatment of U.S. policy in Occupied Japan is nowhere stated more concisely or authoritatively than by the Soviet Japan specialist, H. T. Eidus[46] in a 31-page booklet (originally a lecture presented to the Soviet Society for Documentation of Political and Scientific Knowledge [sic]) published in Moscow in 1949 and entitled *The Aggressive Policy of American Imperialism in Japan*. The main themes echoed by other Soviet specialists and propagandists are mostly contained in that volume.

Here are some characteristic passages, translated verbatim:

> The leading power in the military defeat of imperialist Japan, as well as fascist Germany, was the Soviet Union. (p. 3) [No reference to the United States and its role in the Pacific War]
>
> United States dominance of Japan has been accomplished under the leadership of the reactionary General MacArthur. (p. 5)
>
> The essence of U.S. economic policy for Japan is to make the Japanese economy dependent upon American monopolies. . . . (p. 6)
>
> Standard Oil and Westinghouse already own more than half the shares of Mitsubishi. (p. 7)
>
> General Electric has 45 percent of Mitsubishi, etc. (pp. 9–10)
>
> About 70 percent of Japanese peasants don't own their own land. That is why they must slave for the landlord. (p. 11)
>
> American and Japanese authorities are persecuting individuals of the democratic camp, representatives of progressive intelligentsia, and, above all, the Communists. (p. 17)
>
> The Soviet government stands for a prompt peace treaty with Japan and removal from Japan of the Occupation forces. (p. 21)
>
> The JCP is the only party in Japan fighting for freedom, independence and sovereignty, for real democratization and demilitarization, against Japan's enslavement by American capital, against its transformation into an American colony, for a lasting peace and against the instigators of war. (p. 25)

Time and space do not permit a review of the dozens of journal articles by Soviet Japan specialists attacking virtually all aspects of American policy and practice in Japan. A few of the predominant themes and key specialists tell the story. Here are typical characterizations by two prominent Soviet critics:

M. Markov, one of the Soviet specialists on the Occupation, in April of 1946 attacked the United States for not declaring Hirohito a "war criminal number one."[47] This theme became a prominent Soviet criticism throughout the Occupation period. In May of the same year, V. Argrin published an angry article criticizing MacArthur for not liquidating fascism.[48] Then in November of 1947, Markov "deplored" the ban on Soviet information in Japan, saying, "the Japanese are being turned into American slaves."[49]

By the summer of 1950, Markov had concluded that although "Mac-Arthur doesn't like Englishmen, he (MacArthur) considers Russians the number one enemy. Japan, for MacArthur," we are told, "is just one huge airbase from which bombers can cover the whole of Siberia."[50]

And so the stage was set for the Korean War—and for the Soviet, Chinese Communist, and JCP portrayal of Japan as an "advanced military base of United States imperialism in Asia."*

---

*See chapters 5 and 14 for details of Soviet policy and Communist activity during the Korean War and its aftermath.

Chapter Four

Soviet Indoctrination and Repatriation of Japanese Prisoners of War

THE REPATRIATION PARAMETERS

The surrender of Japan in the fall of 1945 left the Allies with the immense problem of repatriation. Japanese forces, some seven million strong, had fanned out over the Far East from Siberia to Singapore. With the war over, all interested nations, except the USSR, began the formidable task of transporting these millions of weary, disillusioned, and often wounded or ill fighting men back to their home islands.

The Soviet Union, with a huge, hungry army of Japanese prisoners of war on hand, seemed curiously reluctant to return them to their families and friends. Originally, it was the disorganized and confused situation in Manchuria, North Korea, and other areas that prevented repatriation, or at least afforded an acceptable excuse for Soviet delay. Lack of adequate transportation provided the next rationale for Soviet procrastination. Other factors were added as time passed slowly for the concerned repatriates—even more slowly, no doubt, for those waiting anxiously back home. For the most part, relatives in Japan had no idea whether their husbands, brothers, sons, or other relatives and friends in the military service were dead or alive. Repatriation of Japanese nationals from Siberia and other Russian territories did not begin officially until December 19, 1946, after SCAP and the Soviet representatives had reached an agreement of sorts on the issue. Even after this date, the Soviets continued to stall. Despite sharp notes addressed by SCAP to the Soviet member of the Allied Council for Japan,[1] repatriation proceeded at a snail's pace and was at times suspended for months on end because of "climatic and icing conditions," even though SCAP offered to dispatch icebreakers to Soviet ports.*

A Moscow broadcast of May 20, 1949, quoted in *Akahata* (Red Flag) of May 22, stated that at the time of surrender a total of 594,000 Japanese prisoners of war had been in territories under Soviet control. Of these, the same account asserted, 70,880 had been released on the spot during 1945. According to the official Moscow version, the remainder, with the exception of war criminals, were repatriated by the end of 1949. A Soviet spokesman in Tokyo, on September 5, 1951, put the total number of Japanese "war criminals" in Soviet custody at 1,479.[2] The Japanese government, on the other hand, estimated that 234,151 Japanese prisoners died in Soviet (or Chinese) camps between the end of the war and the summer of 1951 and listed 28,797 as "unaccounted for or missing." According to the same Japanese estimate, 17,637 still remained in Soviet hands.[3] The question has not been satisfactorily resolved to this day.

SOVIET POLICY AND PERSPECTIVE

The Soviets viewed the issue in twin perspective and devised policy and practice accordingly. In immediate, short-range terms, Moscow saw in this vast army of Japanese prisoners of war great potential for rebuilding the war-torn Soviet economy. Psychologically, it may be argued, this kind of "slave labor" was less open to criticism or censure—after all, "Japan lost the war!" In any case, the Soviets wasted no time in pressing their newly acquired labor force into service. But, it was the longer range, strategic, and political potential of this huge human resource that clearly captured the imagination of Soviet policy planners—after sufficient time had elapsed to collect thoughts, ponder options, and take care of more urgent matters elsewhere.

Whether preparations for a systematic, massive program of indoctrination had been made in advance of the Soviet entry into the Pacific War is a moot question. While there is little information and there are no specific documents affording perspective on this point, it is reasonable to assume that such a dramatic ideological opportunity would hardly have escaped Moscow's policy planners. At the same time, defeated Germany and the Eastern European theater were obviously being given first priority. Moreover, as the Soviet Union entered the Pacific War only weeks before its

---

*The Japanese Communist explanation for the Russian refusal to accept the SCAP offer was that the icebreakers were in bad condition and would have endangered the lives of the crew and passengers. This statement appears in an official handbook of the Communist controlled League for the Protection of Repatriates from the Soviet Union [Soren Kikansha Yogo Domei] *Telling the Truth* [*Shinjutsu wo uttaeru*] (Tokyo, 1949), p. 46.

conclusion with a sweep through Manchuria, disorganization was much the order of the day. This is to suggest that the developing, extensive Soviet program of indoctrination probably was hammered out piecemeal from a very general master plan—if that term can be used at all.

By the time of the formation of the Cominform in September of 1947, however, evidence of an extensive Soviet program of indoctrination was overwhelming.*

THE PHYSICAL AND EMOTIONAL SETTING

The logistical problem of transporting, relocating, and maintaining hundreds of thousands of stunned, disillusioned, weary, ill (and often wounded) Japanese in camps throughout Siberia and central Russia as far west as the fringes of the Ukraine and Turkey is staggering. To those familiar with the Soviet scene and system, it seems nothing short of incredible. What is surprising is not how many of the erstwhile Japanese soldiers and civilians died, but how many managed to survive.

There were, to cite but one typical sector example, about 30 camps along the Siberian Railway with approximately 1,000 to 1,500 prisoners in each camp. With some few exceptions, conditions in camps everywhere were extremely poor, sanitation deplorable, medical facilities virtually nonexistent, and starvation widespread. A statement (one of hundreds) from a CIC summary interrogation report early in 1947 reads: "The appearance of many of the repatriates on arriving in Japan with gaunt, emaciated bodies and possessing only the clothes on their backs, tells its own story of hardships and destitution."[4] Later reports indicate some slight improvement in conditions. The evidence suggests that healthier prisoners were, in fact, retained as forced labor; the sick and the old were sent home.

JAPANESE PRISONER-OF-WAR LABOR—
A SOVIET PRIZE

The Soviets clearly recognized the valuable prize they had won: a windfall labor force of hundreds of thousands of Japanese prisoners of war. A *Maizuru Shukan Asahi* newspaper report of the period (Maizuru was one of

---

*Hundreds of CIP, Civil Intelligence Section (CIS), and other SCAP field, interrogation, and intelligence reports from 1945 through 1949 (the period for which documentation is now available from the National Archives) provide data from which, put together with Japanese sources and more than 100 books plus my own interviews in Japan, this program can be reconstructed in considerable detail.

the major ports of entry for repatriates) tells the story, a story also detailed in dozens of other articles and books and in U.S. intelligence reports: "Japanese internees in Siberia, Central Asia, and European Russia are engaged in virtually all types of industrial activity under the new Five Year Plan." This activity, the report specifies, includes: "the felling of trees, mining, railway construction and other construction work."[5]

A Japanese prisoner writing of his experiences in European Russia further relates: "German prisoners were much more efficient and intelligent than the Russians, but the Russians found that we Japanese were superior even to the Germans in efficiency." Then he adds (a point made by many of the prisoners), "in spite of our good ration of food, we were hungry almost all the time."[6]

One Japanese prisoner, who had been deep in European Russia, made several observations on his trip back to the Pacific Coast, commenting on such things as, "the industrialization along the railways east of the Urals," that "many cities were being built," and noting that "construction of the Bamu [BAM] Railway [a second Siberian Railway] apparently is being hastened with the blood and sweat of Japanese labor."[7]

Throughout 1949, SCAP's Civil Censorship Division continued to intercept unmistakable evidence of the Soviet use of Japanese POWs as "slave labor." Letters charged that prisoners were being used as a source of cheap manpower and, as one prisoner put it, "driven like wild beasts for the benefit of the USSR."[8] Another repatriate noted that the situation was so bad that "suicide came to be regarded as our only recourse."[9]

THE PROGRAM OF INDOCTRINATION

The Soviets launched a systematically organized and intensively cultivated educational and propaganda program within the POW camps early in 1946. At the end of the year it was in full swing. By the spring of 1947, U.S. intelligence had put together a substantial and disturbing picture of the Soviet indoctrination program:

Considerable evidence of mass indoctrination of Japanese awaiting repatriation in Russian occupied areas has been compiled during the last few months. Practically all returnees, civilians and soldiers alike, have been exposed (often forcibly) to Communist theories and anti-American propaganda of some type. Internees showing sympathy and interest in Communist ideas were given preferential treatment and were selected for further intensive training in special schools scattered throughout Manchuria and Siberia. Interviews with recent returnees show that they were subjected to Communist propaganda through Russian-controlled newspapers, radio broadcasts, anti-American posters and banners, speeches, lectures and movies.[10]

The Japan Newspaper (*Nihon Shimbun*) and the Friendship Society (*Tomo no kai*) became the nuclei of the diverse camp organizations, training apparatus, and procedure. As the program developed, in addition to a camp newspaper and a friendship society, activities became more diversified and sophisticated with special lectures, film series, "democratic libraries," music societies, little theater groups—and all the other now familiar trappings of the worldwide Communist "cultural offensive."

The Japan Newspaper (Nihon Shimbun). From the outset, the single most important instrument used by the Soviets to indoctrinate the Japanese prisoners was the *Japan Newspaper (Nihon Shimbun)* published in Khabarovsk, Siberia. Founded by the Political Intelligence Section of the Soviet Far East Army shortly after the cessation of hostilities in the early fall of 1945, this Japanese language newspaper was originally designed as an information sheet to convey the desires and support the policies of the Soviet military and political administration. At first it consisted of a single sheet, rather crudely designed and printed. With the withdrawal of the main forces of the Red Army from Manchuria in February of 1946, the central need for administrative information largely ceased. It was about this time that the newspaper appears to have assumed its new and increasingly important role as a major propaganda organ designed to support Soviet policies, to further Soviet goals, and to create a favorable image among the repatriates of the Soviet system and of Communism as a way of life, "the wave of the future." A corollary theme was the mounting of a vitriolic attack upon the American Occupation of Japan which included a "full and frank revelation of the 'pitiful' conditions in Japan now that it is controlled by the United States."

The *Nihon Shimbun* was under the direction of a group of officers of the Soviet intelligence section, assisted by Japanese POWs who were selected because of their educational backgrounds or previous newspaper experience. The paper was issued three times weekly and had an estimated circulation of more than 100,000 copies. While this figure may not seem large by Western (not to say Japanese) newspaper standards, it must be remembered that the prisoners had little else to read. The newspaper thus had an interest, influence, and impact far larger than its statistical image might imply. It is, for example, regularly mentioned in memoirs and other accounts written by former POWs.[11]

The newspaper was an important vehicle for the ideological conversion of the huge army of Japanese prisoners captured in Manchuria, Korea,

Karafuto (Sakhalin), and the Kurile Islands and interned in centers from Vladivostok and parts of Russia proper through Central Asia, to the fringes of Turkey. By mid-1947 it was being given free distribution throughout all POW camps in eastern and central Siberia and at processing centers for repatriates. It was also distributed among Japanese nationals in Northern Manchuria and North Korea and even turned up from time to time in Mukden.

As the Soviet handling of Japanese POWs became better organized, the indoctrination program became more substantial, more diversified, and more sophisticated. The *Nihon Shimbun* was fully developed as the principal vehicle. It was in the spring or summer of 1946, that four members of the Japan Communist Party were added to the newspaper's staff and the scope and journalistic level of the propaganda began to change noticeably. The paper, thus expanded, took a new, more professional format along the following lines:

Page One: Soviet and world affairs, often translations of TASS dispatches and characteristically carrying Moscow datelines.

Page Two: "News" pertaining to conditions in Japan, dealing particularly with economic and labor problems and Japan's relations with the United States.

Page Three: Editorials on life in Russia. Topics such as collective farming, Soviet government, sketches of important Soviet leaders, and articles depicting Russia as the "workers' paradise" and "protector of world peace and democracy."

Page Four: Features deemed of special interest to POWs, short stories, cartoons, some material contributed by POWs themselves.

During 1947, emphasis of the *Nihon Shimbun* was increasingly shifted to include even more international news propaganda (notably anti-U.S. items), attacks on "capitalist democracies," frankly pro-Soviet articles and editorials dealing with the fundamentals of Communism and more particularly "dis-information" about American Occupied Japan.

The Soviet concept and utilization of "dis-information" is familiar to students of the KGB.[12] The Soviet policy toward the Japanese prisoners—a policy that channeled discrimination, bias, erroneous and distorted "news" through the several Khabarovsk-supervised newspapers for the POWs—had a discernable effect on some of the targets. The Civil Censorship Detachment in Japan, in its survey of POW mail, regularly picked up relevant items attesting to this fact. Typical is this comment from one prisoner: "In no article of the newspaper (*Nihon Shimbun*) can I find any sign of rehabilitation in Japan. I am overcome with a feeling of hopelessness when I think of the hard living of the people who are suffering from inflation, starvation and unemployment."[13] After citing many other similar instances, the same Civil Censorship report concludes: "This deluge of misinformation is dangerously effective when coupled with the idealized picture of the Communist state which is fed to the prisoners by their Soviet captors."

The Friendship Societies (Tomo no kai). A second, significant Soviet propaganda vehicle in the Soviet program to indoctrinate and influence Japanese POWs were the "Friendship Societies" (*Tomo no kai*). Directions and specific plans for the establishment of these Friendship Societies appear to have been issued from the Khabavrosk headquarters of the *Nihon Shimbun* to the headquarters at each POW camp. Programs were launched by selected Japanese internees working under the close supervision of Soviet political officers at the individual camps. Evidence indicates that a vast number—possibly the majority—of Japanese internees joined in the activities of these Friendship Societies.

A 1949 SCAP report marked "secret" and based upon numerous CIC interrogations provides a succinct description of the developing character and work of the society:

> The Friendship Society carried on its major activities in meetings held one or two evenings weekly. The principal and often only indoctrination measures during this period were lectures and discussions based upon materials in the Japan Newspaper, the publication and distribution of a wall newspaper, and showing of a few motion pictures and the staging of a few crude theatrical productions.[14]

The model of the Friendship Society was ultimately replaced by other, more elaborate organizations such as the so-called Democrat Groups, which maintained minilibraries, distributed Soviet-approved "textbooks" (printed in the Soviet Union in Japanese), held special athletic contests, "democratic" musical events, "festivals," and so on. Needless to say, the themes and propagandist tone of these and their Soviet-sponsored successor organizations were essentially the same.

Radio Broadcasts, Lectures, Movies. In conformity with general Soviet radio practice and security procedures, no American or Japanese broadcasts were permitted in Russian-Occupied areas. However, several repatriates from Sakhalin reported that carefully selected programs originating in

Tokyo and rebroadcast by the local Russian radio station occasionally were heard.[15]

Agitation against the American Occupation, designed also to popularize and "explain" Communism, was conducted continually through orientation lectures and speeches by both Russian officers and Japanese Communists at many of the larger indoctrination centers. Russian officers were said to be "blunt" and "vociferous" in venting their personal dislike and antagonism toward America and Americans. "Many openly expressed the belief that a war between Russia and America was inevitable within the next five to ten years."[16]

Motion pictures were shown to the Japanese at irregular intervals, usually two or three times per month. They depicted such themes as Soviet military might, life in Russia under a peaceful cooperative system, and Stalin as protector of the common man. One movie, stressing racial prejudice in the United States, told the story of the marriage of a white and black in America. Persecuted in America, the couple finally found happiness and peace in "democratic Russia."[17]

In addition, the so-called Democratic groups with Soviet assistance operated libraries within the internment camps. These were well supplied with appropriate books, magazines, and pamphlets on the "history" of Japan, the USSR, and the Communist movement along with pseudo-scientific "treatises" on subjects such as the Russian farming system, Soviet education, and the labor movement. Significantly, a large mass of such material printed in Japanese in the Soviet Union and Japan had by the spring of 1949 become widely available to many of the camps.[18]

Treatment of Former Japanese Officers. The indoctrination of high-ranking officers, as might have been anticipated, differed drastically from the approach to the rank-and-file Japanese POW. After their capture by the Soviets in Manchuria, North Korea, Karafuto, and elsewhere (in August and September 1945) the generals simply disappeared. Few high-ranking officers were repatriated. On this subject, as on many issues, the Soviets have chosen to remain silent. Japanese officers of company grade were interned along with their men. Former gendarmes (*Kempeitai*) and intelligence personnel were held separately and given special treatment. Two reasons may be suggested for this procedure: that they were regarded as essentially unreconstructable and had to be segregated so that they could not sabotage Soviet indoctrination efforts, and that they were considered a pool of potential Kremlin agents well worth the most intensive efforts to convert them for subsequent use in Japan. There is little, if any, evidence to substantiate the validity of either point.

Many returnees told of large groups of repatriates, consisting mostly of field-grade officers, high-ranking governmental officials, and businessmen having been taken to Russia for special indoctrination schools and camps. Rumors of their easy living filtered back. These rumors were substantiated by a Civil Censorship Detachment (CCD) study of intercepts from a special POW camp in Siberia. The education and intellectual potentialities of prisoners from this camp were, of course, greater than the general run. They were a hand-picked group.

THE JAPAN COMMUNIST PARTY CONNECTION

An obvious and very relevant question is the part that the Japan Communist Party played in this indoctrination process. In view of the prewar history of the JCP's close ties with the Comintern and its direction from Moscow, one would expect to find that party (legal for the first time) active as a vanguard of Soviet interests in Occupied Japan.[19] The repatriates obviously constituted a major ideological and political target of great potential in swelling the ranks of a resurgent Communist Party in American Occupied Japan—a point scarcely overlooked by the Soviet military/intelligence authorities or the JCP leaders.

Within the Soviet Union, indoctrination itself within the camps was handled mainly by so-called "democratic groups" organized by Communist and leftist elements among the Japanese internees, "with the Soviets remaining very much in the background."[20]

CIC and other SCAP intelligence reports abound with evidence of JCP activity among the repatriates. The following is an excerpt from one early report:

> Communist activities by repatriates from Russian occupied areas have increased with every shipment. Groups of Japanese Communists, their indoctrination completed, are beginning to return to spread Communism. Five noted Yenan-schooled Communists (probably *Minshu Remmei* members) recently were repatriated from Dairen to Sasebo with an advance element of 76 Japanese Communists. This group arrived in Sasebo with more than Y1,000,000. On docking, three of the group disappeared from the port of embarkation.[21]

The Japanese Communists launched intensive drives to gain new members among repatriates, especially after repatriation, which had been intermittently disrupted and delayed by the Soviets, was resumed in May of 1948. A special Repatriation Planning Section (*Hikiage Taisaku Bu*) was established within JCP headquarters for the purpose of formulating and directing activities among repatriates. Communist delegations frequently met trains to welcome repatriates and provide them with copies of *Akahata* (Red Flag), the party's daily newspaper published in Tokyo. On July 30, 1948, *Akahata* issued a special message to repatriates written by Sanzo Nosaka, Moscow-Yenan trained member of the central committee of the JCP.[22]

It is difficult to evaluate information on the degree to which the membership of the JCP was increased markedly by the return of the repatriates. As of August 1948, SCAP was reporting estimates of as many as 200 additional members joining the JCP ranks daily from among the repatriates. This estimate seems too high. In any case, certainly the rate of repatriate entry into the JCP did not long remain at that level—if, indeed, it ever really reached that figure.

The JCP thus established direct contact and attempted to influence the repatriates even before they finished their orientation in debarkation camps. A party directive to its *Maizuru* District Committee ordered it to report in detail the arrival and departure of repatriation ships and the number and names of returnees aboard. It was elsewhere suggested that repatriates report the substance of all interrogation (debriefings) and refuse to answer all questions about the USSR. For this purpose, party members are known to have impersonated repatriates in order to check on the content and method of Occupation debriefings.[23]

According to U.S. intelligence monitoring: "The JCP activity first actually observed in Japan in relation to repatriates took the form of train meetings. Groups of Communists began in May, 1948 to meet repatriation trains at Shinagawa, Tokyo, and Ueno stations and to go into the trains and ride to the next station." The report continues: "They wore arm bands, waved red flags, sang Communist songs, greeted repatriates by name and distributed pamphlets, Communist newspapers and magazines. JCP cooperation with the Communist-dominated Japan Railway Workers Union (*Kokutetsu*) insures knowledge of time of arrival of repatriation trains."[24]

Within Japan, The Livelihood Protection League of the Repatriates from Russia (*Soren Kikansha Seikatsu Yogo Domei*) became the nucleus of the JCP's campaign to influence and control the repatriates. The organization was established on April 20, 1948, after several preparatory meetings. It comprised essentially a core of Communist party members and a smoke screen body of repatriates, families of repatriates dead or still interned, and members of neutral and even a few anti-Communist organizations. Branches of the organization became extremely active throughout Japan. Estimated membership in September of 1948 was 10,000.[25]

Thus the JCP sought and to some degree succeeded in mobilizing a portion of the repatriates, their friends, and families for pro-Soviet Communist causes.

THE BALANCE SHEET

How successful was this elaborate Soviet program of indoctrination? Perhaps the single most authoritative official U.S. comment on this point is contained in a brief document prepared by the U.S. Political Advisor for Japan, W. J. Sebald, entitled "Communist Influence Among Japanese Repatriates from Soviet Russia," and dated August 24, 1948. Citing a Publications Analysis survey, the document states:

> The survey is somewhat inconclusive in regard to the success the Soviets are experiencing in the Communist indoctrination program. It is significant, however, that one repatriate was told by a member of the *Nihon Shimbun* staff that the Soviets would be satisfied if they converted only ten percent of the million-odd Japanese who were captured and interned at the end of the year. . . . One repatriate estimated that the number of adherents would not exceed five percent. This small ratio, however, would still provide the Japanese Communist Party with approximately fifty thousand new Soviet trained members.[26]

It was also noted, the document concludes, "that middle-aged and better-educated Japanese more frequently turned anti-Soviet after repatriation, while men in their early twenties have proved more persistent in their affiliation."[27] But perhaps the most telling—and, in retrospect, significant comment comes from a young Japanese soldier in his twenties who writes: "For the two years that I was a Russian prisoner I was taught the Communist formula. I listened to bitter criticism of Japan's national structure and social organization and became convinced of the validity of some of the Russian arguments. I learned a number of Red songs." And then his striking conclusion: "But when our repatriation ship left the port, I suddenly realized that I was a Japanese and nothing else. Back in Japan, I found myself 100 percent Japanese. All that I had been taught in Siberia faded from my mind."[28]

Estimates of the number of repatriates who joined the Japanese Communist Party vary widely. As already suggested, SCAP documentation is not very precise on the point. A strong flavor of wishful thinking, of course, pervades such JCP statements as: "From the standpoint of 30 percent of those repatriated during the war, the Party will increase by 210,000" or . . . "There are about 700,000 Japanese in the USSR. Information received from the USSR reveals that at least 20% of these will join the Party upon repatriation." Estimates by anti-Communists and neutrals are more conservative, but still grant the JCP substantial gain. From a low of 3.8 percent, neutral estimates have run as high as 100,000 gain in JCP membership during the 1948 repatriation season from this influx of new blood. The above represents the substance of what would appear to be SCAP's most definitive report on the subject. That report concludes: "Informed estimates of JCP membership gains indicate an increase of 30,000–50,000 members during a recent four-month period. A large proportion of these new comrades can reasonably be attributed to repatriates. . . . This represents about six percent of the repatriates up to 7 October 1948."[29]

It is, of course, the responsibility of Intelligence agencies and political advisors to provide the policy planners and operational staffs with both an assessment of present realities and an estimate of future trends and capabilities, including the "worst possible case." This often proves a tricky and dangerous task especially in terms of the question of retrospective accountability against what might be called the luxury of hindsight. This is not to mention the issue of possible *ex post facto* partisan criticism or deliberate distortion.

As it turned out, the Soviet program of indoctrination of Japanese prisoners of war was not a huge success by any standard. In some ways it may have backfired. The well-known care and caution with which statistics must be handled may be dramatically illustrated in this instance by a single classic case (out of hundreds):

Data from interrogation reports of the Japanese repatriates from Soviet territory returning through Maizuru and other repatriation centers indicate that up to 60 to 70 percent answered "yes" when asked whether they intended to join the Communist party in Japan. Later surveys of repatriates of former years, interviews, government and public opinion polls, establish the fact that the overwhelming majority of repatriates from Soviet territories, in fact, did *not* join the party.[30]

Reasons given by the repatriates themselves for this apparent change of heart are that they had only pledged to join the party as a way of ingratiating themselves with their captors and ensuring that they would get back to their homes; that after associating with relatives and friends, they realized the untruth of Soviet propaganda and turned against the JCP; or, simply that they were fed up with the whole business, delighted and even surprised to have made it back to Japan at all and wanted only to forget about war, Communism, and the nightmare of Soviet captivity.[31] A relatively small percentage of repatriates, for a variety of reasons (ideological and other) did, of course, join the Communist party in Japan.

That the Soviet-"indoctrinated" repatriates' lasting impact on Japanese public opinion and political trends in Japan has proved on balance anything but pro-Soviet is documented over the years by Japanese public opinion polls, which regularly register Russia as the "most hated nation"; by election results; and by the healthy skepticism with which successive Japanese governments have understandably viewed Soviet policies and overtures toward Japan.

Chapter Five

The Metamorphosis of the Moscow-Linked "Lovable"Japan Communist Party

THE INTERNATIONAL CONTEXT

To speak of the Moscow-linked Japan Communist Party during the prewar Comintern years, that is from the birth of the party in 1922 until the death of the Comintern in 1943, risks incurring the proper wrath of some latter-day Taoist, who may wish to caution us allegorically against using such redundant terms: one does not speak of "benevolent fathers"; simply "fathers!"

It is perfectly true that Communist parties of the pre–World War II era operated formally as "branches of the Comintern," which was itself an "unofficial" foreign policy, intelligence, propaganda, and influence-peddling agency of the Soviet government. The Kremlin and its Comintern subordinates went to elaborate and, at times, "indignant" lengths to deny any such relationship. But the documentation linking the pre–World War II parties to Moscow is overwhelming, and the Communist party of Japan was no exception. It bore the official title: "Japan Communist Party, Japanese Branch of the Comintern." Its unbroken record of ideological training, leadership, programmatic and operational ties with the Soviet Union can be traced in convincing detail.[1]

Yet in the postwar era, even before the emergence of China as a second Communist ideological and power center, a number of Communist leaders around the world began to express serious doubts and reservations on the question of Soviet hegemony over the "fraternal parties." Not that such questioning was a peculiarly new or postwar phenomenon, but rarely had the demonstrated disaffection with Moscow surfaced so dramatically or so publicly—and with such dramatic international ramifications—as in Tito's celebrated break with Stalin (1948) or the Cominform's curious clash with

Nosaka (1950). This is to leave aside for the moment Peking's later world-shaking, open break with the Kremlin.

Moreover, in postwar American-Occupied Japan, the Communist party found itself—for the first time in its turbulent history—a legal political party in a constitutional democracy where elections, votes, popularity, and images were not only important but decisive.

Certainly during the immediate post–World War II period Moscow's most urgent "family problems" were not with the party in Japan but with its Eastern European parties and satellites—although in the latter case the out-come seems to have been never really in doubt. The presence of formidable Soviet military forces, including tank divisions, in those hapless European nations represented a compelling argument in favor of continued and decisive control of the area by the Moscow-supported Communist party leadership. This is not to minimize the several explosive, if (alas!) forlorn challenges to the Soviet domination of Eastern Europe—but that is another story.

In Asia, if China has been, is, and perhaps forever will be, an enigma for the Soviets, from the outset Japan has been regarded in a different light, a special case—which, of course, it is. As the most westernized and industrial-ized of the Eastern nations, an advanced capitalist country, Japan according to strict Marxian logic was by definition destined to be "imperialistic." And one scarcely need be a Marxist-Leninist to discern shades of imperialism (however defined) early in Japan's emergence as a modern state. Moscow's attempts to create, maintain, and manipulate for its own purposes a Com-munist party within that unique Asian bastion of the "capitalist, enemy camp," thus comes as no great research discovery or surprise. Indeed, scarcely had the Bolsheviks seized power at home before the Kremlin and its agents, aided and abetted by Lenin's eloquent appeals to the "peoples of the East," were zeroing in on Japan. All of this is to suggest that we dare not plunge headlong into the midst of the postwar "peaceful revolution" and "lovable" Japan Communist Party scene without a brief look at that party's prewar antecedents, especially its very relevant relationship with the Comin-tern and Moscow.

COMINTERN ANTECEDENTS—MOSCOW TIE LINE

The Japan Communist Party is, in fact, a creature of Moscow. Its genesis may be traced back to the Comintern's success in selecting, radicalizing, and reorienting a portion of Japan's "social movement." The party's prewar ties with the Comintern, in terms of leadership, training, liaison, and policy formulation, were extensive and persistent. It is, thus, an unbroken (if at times fractured) tie line with Moscow that runs from the party's inception through its turbulent life and death (at the hands of the Japanese police), to its resurrection and resurgence in postwar, American-Occupied Japan.[2]

Wearing its new ideological garb, traditional Russian interest in Asia was not long in reappearing after the Bolsheviks seized power at home. In Moscow, Baku, Shanghai, Irkutsk, and elsewhere Lenin, Stalin, Zinoviev, Voitinsky, and others appealed to the peoples of the Orient to "discover the special types of contacts between the advanced proletariat throughout the world and the toiling and exploited masses of the East. . . ."[3] "Socialist" organizations were formed, liaison established, and plans for coordinated Comintern efforts to form Communist parties in the major Asian nations discussed.[4] That Japan was a tempting and timely target there could be little doubt. "The West," Lenin said, "is digging its own grave in the East."[5]

In terms of origin, leadership, and liaison, the Japanese party's Moscow connection is critical, persistent, and impressive. The JCP was formed in 1922 after veteran Comintern agents at Moscow's request had converged upon Japan from the Soviet Union, China, and the United States. Moreover, virtually all the top leaders throughout the subsequent prewar years were either trained at one of the several special schools in Moscow or made regular secret liaison visits to the Soviet capital for "suggestions," "advice," and funds.[6] No less than eighteen such key JCP leaders may be identified during the prewar period. When a top JCP leader was arrested by the Japanese police, which was increasingly the case in the late 1920s and early 1930s, he was quietly replaced by Moscow.

Table 1 represents a partial list of the JCP's ongoing Moscow-linked leadership corps, indicating time frame, role in the party, Moscow link, and date. As such a chart cannot really be summarized in a manner that will convey its overall impact as a documentary montage, it is perhaps worth pausing for a few moments to study it carefully, to absorb the important story it tells.

For the less fastidious wishing to bypass such tedium, several cardinal points may be identified by way of summary: first, only five of these eighteen prewar JCP leaders survived to serve the party in postwar Japan, but they included Kyuichi Tokuda (the postwar party's secretary general) and Sanzo Nosaka, the postwar party's principal policy planner and strategist. Both, it should be noted, had extensive Moscow and/or China backgrounds. Second, three prominent prewar leaders (on the chart), Jokichi Kazama, Manabu Sano, and Sadachika Nabeyama, all of whom defected from the party during the 1930s, also survived the war to become prolific writers and active anti-Communists in postwar Japan.[7] Thus the issue of prewar leadership-linkage to Moscow turns out to have significant, if surprising, ramifications for the Communist movement in postwar Japan. The same

TABLE 1

JCP–Moscow Linkage/Continuity

Dates (Moscow)	JCP Leader	Role in Party	Moscow Link	Fate
Jan. 1922	Kiyoshi Takase	Chairman, JCP Pub. Com.; later active First JCP.	Attended Far Eastern People's Congress, Moscow.	See below.
Nov. 1922	Kiyoshi Takase	Chairman, JCP Pub. Com.; later active First JCP.	Attended Fourth Comintern Congress.	Arrested 1923; sentenced 8 mo. jail. Joined Socialist party; active until after WW II.
1923–1924	Manabu Sano	Member, JCP Central Committee.	Comintern rep, Moscow. Visited Shanghai with Voitinsky.	Arrested 1925; 8 mo. jail.
Mar. 1928	Manabu Sano	Member, JCP Central Committee.	Fled to Moscow. Attended Sixth Comintern Congress.	Arrested; sentenced life, 1932. Defected. Anti-Communist postwar. Died 1953.
1921–1924	Sentaro Kitaura	Chief, JCP Youth Dept.	Studied Kutobe, Moscow.	Arrested 1928; suffered "breakdown." Active labor movement postwar.
1922	Kyuichi Tokuda	Member, First JCP	Attended Far Eastern People's Congress, Moscow.	See below.
Feb./Mar. 1926	Kyuichi Tokuda	Chief, organization dept. JCP.	Attended Sixth Plenum, Comintern Ex. Com., Moscow.	See below.
1927	Kyuichi Tokuda	Member, Central Committee.	Visited Moscow again; discussion of strategy and tactics.	Arrested 1928; sentenced 10 yrs.; prison Oct. 1932; released 1945. Sec. Gen. postwar party. Died 1953, Peking.
1925–1930	Jokichi Kazama	Head, JCP Control Commission; Russian interpreter.	Studied Kutobe, Moscow. Worked Far Eastern Section Comintern, Moscow and Vladivostok.	Arrested, Oct. 1932. Defected 1933. Active anti-Communist postwar. Died 1968.
1925	Shojero Kasuga	Chief, JCP organizer Osaka-Kyoto area.	Studied one year Kutobe, Moscow.	Arrested/jailed Mar. 1928; released 1937; rearrested 1938; released 1945. Active JCP 1945–1961. "Retired," poor health.

Dates	Name	Position	Moscow/Comintern Activity	Arrest/Fate
1923–1926	Eizo Kondo	Executive Committee, Organizer, First JCP.	Profintern rep. in Moscow.	Arrested 1921; pardoned. Joined Labor-Farmer party. Welfare work postwar. Died 1965.
Nov./Dec. 1926 1927	Sadachika Nabeyama	Member, First and Second JCP.	Attended Seventh Enlarged Plenum of Comintern Executive Committee. Remained in Moscow as JCP Profintern rep.	Arrested Apr. 1929; sentenced 1932 to life. Defected from party 1933. Active anti-Communist in postwar era. Died?
Nov. 1927	Masanosuke Watanabe	Member, Central Committee; chief party labor department.	Visited Moscow for discussions of strategy and tactics.	Arrested Sept. 1928; hospitalized because of illness.
1927	Fumio Sano	Chairman, Central Committee, Second JCP.	Visited Moscow for policy discussions.	Defected 1929. Died 1930.
1927	Katsuo Nakao	Candidate member, Central Committee.	Sent by party to SU for strategy discussions.	Arrested Apr. 1928; sentenced 10 yrs. prison. Defected 1933. Died in jail.
1926–1928	Sadaki Takahashi	Leader, Communist Youth League.	Studied at Lenin Institute, Moscow. Attended Sixth Comintern Congress, Moscow.	Arrested Apr. 1929; sentenced 15 yrs. prison. Died in jail 1944.
1924–1928	Ichino Soma	Party organizer; Soviet agent.	Studied at Kutobe, Moscow. Member, Soviet CP.	Arrested 1928; sentenced 10 yrs. prison.
1928	Goichiro Kokuryo	Member, Central Committee; labor expert.	Attended Profintern Congress, Moscow.	Arrested Oct. 1928; sentenced 15 yrs. prison. Died 1945.
1925–1928	Satomi Hakamada	Member, Central Committee; Presidium (postwar).	Studied in Moscow, 1925–1928.	Arrested 1928; jail until 1932; arrested again, 1935; remained in jail to 1945. Active postwar.
1930	Yojiro Konno	Member, party organization dept.; labor specialist.	Attended Fifth Profintern Congress, Moscow. Maintained liaison, Comintern agents, Shanghai.	Arrested 1932. Member postwar party politburo/presidium.
1923 1928–1942	Kenzo Yamamoto	Member, Central Committee.	Visited Russia 1923; attended Sixth Comintern Congress. Became JCP Profintern rep. in Moscow.	Victim of Stalin's purges, 1937. Died of tuberculosis, Apr. 1942.
1922 1931–1940 1940–1945	Sanzo Nosaka	Member, Central Committee. Key leader in postwar era.	Attended Profintern Congress, Moscow, 1922. Fled to Moscow 1931; remained as Comintern rep. until 1940. Went to Yenan; remained until 1945.	Arrested 1923; served 8 mo. jail; released 1933; arrested again. Fled to SU. Returned to Japan 1946. Active postwar.

may be said in the case of JCP policy and strategy.

With respect to Japanese Communist policies and programs during the prewar era, not only did the Japanese party follow the Comintern's general line, but the specific action programs (called "theses") which formed the basis for JCP theory and practice in Japan were drafted in Moscow— "jointly" by Soviet and Japanese Communist leaders. Significantly, these "theses" (notably the 1927, 1931, and 1932 theses) displayed exceptional longevity and carryover qualities as may be judged by the fact that they became focal points for major Communist party discussions—even disagreements and arguments over proper Communist strategy in post-surrender, Occupied Japan. Indeed, the 1932 thesis was to serve as the basis for JCP policy in the initial postwar period.[8]

POSTWAR RESURGENCE—
THE JCP AS A TOOL OF MOSCOW?

Having lost the policy battles for a "Control Commission" within Japan, Soviet occupation troops for Hokkaido, and a Soviet Co-Supreme Commander for the Allied Powers in Tokyo, Moscow settled for three lesser propaganda, intelligence gathering, and influence-peddling agencies within American-Occupied Japan.[9] The first was the Allied Council for Japan, which, as we have seen, was exploited by the Soviets for both propaganda and intelligence purposes.[10] The second was the Soviet mission in Tokyo, which performed a number of useful tasks for Moscow, held the distinct advantage of being under direct Soviet control, and was staffed with experienced and high-level Soviet intelligence types (numbering over 500), and boasted operational capabilities akin to those of the general staff of a field army.[11] The third, the Japan Communist Party with its long-standing Moscow connections, experienced top leadership, and new legal status ought to have represented Moscow's greatest hope and SCAP's greatest fear.

As it turns out, the JCP's role as a tool of Moscow in Occupied Japan proved almost from the outset contradictory, disappointing to the Soviets (if, indeed, Moscow ever really nurtured any high hopes), confused, and ultimately counter-productive despite some striking, temporary successes in a number of crucial areas.

On September 2, 1945, after representatives of the Japanese emperor had formally acknowledged their country's defeat and General MacArthur had been duly installed in Tokyo as Supreme Commander of the Allied Powers, Japan was to witness the beginning of a sweeping program of political, economic, and social reforms. A SCAP directive, sometimes referred to as the Japanese "bill of rights," ordered the Japanese authorities to release all political prisoners. It further directed the government to "abrogate and immediately suspend the operation of all provisions of all laws, decrees, orders, ordinances and regulations which establish or maintain restrictions on freedom of thought, of religion, of assembly, and of speech, including the unrestricted discussion of the Emperor, the Imperial Institution and the Imperial Japanese Government." Most importantly, in the present context, the directive granted legal status to the Japan Communist Party—for the first time in its tormented history.[12]

With evident reluctance and apprehension the Japanese government on October 10 finally released the political prisoners including Kyuichi Tokuda, Moscow's man-on-ice in Tokyo,[13] and Yoshio Shiga, the party's fiery theoretician (and Tokuda's long-time cell mate). It was not until January of 1946 that Sanzo Nosaka returned to Japan after sixteen years in exile (ten of them at Comintern headquarters in Moscow; six of them with Mao and Chou En-lai in Yenan).[14] Nosaka quickly assumed the role of principal strategist of "peaceful revolution" and astute advocate of "a lovable Communist party."

INTERNATIONAL ORIENTATION OF THE JCP LEADERSHIP

Long before the term "polycentrism" came into vogue as a euphemism for suggesting that not all Communist leaders and their parties in the postwar world operated under strict Moscow control, certain "national Communist tendencies" on the part of the JCP in American-Occupied Japan had been suggested in the Japanese press and by SCAP authorities. To those familiar with the Japanese party's impressive 25-year record of deep, extensive, and persistent "fraternal ties" with the Soviet Union (and to some extent with the Chinese Communists), such "rumors" undoubtedly seemed quite as outlandish as they were clearly irresponsible. They were, obviously, either "contrived" or "naïve," or perhaps merely "uninformed."

Certainly, the surface evidence suggesting a continuing powerful and close relationship between the JCP and its long-time Soviet godfather seemed overwhelming. Consider only the following characteristics of the early, postwar JCP profile:

- *Top Party Leadership:* Kyuichi Tokuda (secretary-general) and Sanzo Nosaka (policy planner and strategist), both with extensive Moscow training, liaison, and long-term Comintern ties and experience. Yoshio Shiga (party theoretician and third-ranking party leader) known to have close ties with the Soviet mission (Mitsubishi 21) in Tokyo.

- *The Party Central Committee:* Five key members of the twenty-member postwar JCP central committee with experience and training in the Soviet Union.
- *Postwar Party Policy:* In apparent line with Soviet policy on all major international issues: party press (*Akahata*, *Zenei*) regularly quoting *Pravda*, Tass, etc. Use of the prewar 1932 "thesis" drafted in Moscow as key document guiding postwar policy.
- *Party Activity:* After a very brief period of "praise" for the Occupation "liberators," anti-United States, anti-MacArthur propaganda, demonstrations, agitation, etc. (later toned down somewhat in line with Nosaka's concept of "peaceful revolution" and a "lovable JCP").
- *Party Public Image:* In the eyes of the overwhelming majority of Japanese as reflected in public opinion polls, the non-Communist Japanese press, and election results, party unpopular, regarded as pro-Soviet, essentially an agency of the Soviet government.[15]

But very often appearances are misleading. Surface manifestations may tell less than the whole story; what is hidden, left unsaid, or merely ignored may in the long run prove the most significant, even decisive element in the picture. In the case of the JCP, this is by no means to imply that the Japan Communist Party in Occupied Japan had no Soviet links at all or that it simply refused to serve as a sometimes tool of Moscow. In some areas and in a number of ways, the party served Moscow's purposes very well indeed. It is rather to suggest two relevant points with respect to Soviet-JCP relations that came to the attention of SCAP quite early in the game: first, that the Soviets apparently had serious doubts and reservations about the future of the party in Occupied Japan and second, and more specifically, that the Soviets were less than enthusiastic about the choice of veteran Kyuichi Tokuda as party secretary general. SCAP intelligence reported at the time:

Tokuda's revolutionary and independent tactics have caused some concern to the Soviets. He does not follow blindly Soviet instructions and does not want the JCP to be used only to implement a Soviet inspired program. . . . Tokuda has strong nationalist and racial beliefs. . . . Tokuda will cooperate with the Soviets and other Communist Parties, but is not willing to become an integral part of the Soviet dominated world-wide Communist machine.[16]

Another SCAP highly confidential intelligence report about one year later, makes the point in more general and even stronger terms: ". . . there is considerable suspicion of the JCP among the Soviets," the report asserts and then goes on to postulate, "a possible reflection of similar distrust in Moscow. In the eyes of the Russians," the document concludes, "the JCP is too nationalistic and not sufficiently pro-USSR."[17]

JCP RELATIONS WITH THE
SOVIET MISSION IN TOKYO

While Soviet reservations about JCP leadership must be duly recorded, along with the latent "nationalism," these apparent facts must not be allowed to obscure the very significant ties that the JCP maintained with the Soviet mission in Tokyo or that mission's persistent and, at times, effective use of the JCP and its front organizations to pursue Soviet political objectives in Occupied Japan.[18] Certainly, SCAP intelligence was also clear enough on this issue. Here is a typical passage from one SCAP, G-2 report (only one of any number that might be cited):

> Unquestionably, there exists a close link between the Soviets and the Japan Communist Party. Investigations have shown that the Soviets have close connections with pro-Soviet cultural organizations in Japan, and in many instances have given them assistance and direction. In some cases, Soviet representatives have participated directly in the organization of such groups and have attended their meetings. Japanese with long experience in Russia are believed to serve as a close link between the Soviet billet known as Mitsubishi 21 and Japanese leftist groups.

Then the report concludes:

> Japanese Communists have received propaganda material from the Soviet Culture Section in Mitsubishi 21. Yoshio Shiga, head of the Japan Communist Party Organization Magazine Department, is known to be in close touch with the Section where presumably he receives advice and material for Communist publications. Members of the Soviet Mission reportedly have supplied saleable publications to Japanese publishers.[19]

When Sanzo Nosaka returned to Japan in 1946 to take over the policy planning and strategy of the Communist party in Occupied Japan, the public image and policy orientation of the JCP began to change noticeably. Nosaka's personal relations with the Soviet mission appear to have been less direct, his strategy more sophisticated, and his reputation (as one of

Moscow's faithful supporters) increasingly suspect though his policies and practices in Occupied Japan were scarcely designed to advance long-range U.S. interests—there or anywhere else.

In many ways, Nosaka's highly sophisticated strategy of "peaceful revolution" and a "lovable" Communist party appears to have been as confusing to and misunderstood by SCAP and Washington as it was to Moscow.

PEACEFUL REVOLUTION AND A "LOVABLE" COMMUNIST PARTY

The first postwar convention of the Japan Communist Party, in December 1945, was officially designated the Fourth Party Congress, indicating that the now legal postwar party regarded itself as an extension or projection of the illegal prewar organization. As documented, the top leaders of the JCP in Occupied Japan were veterans with extensive experience in the Soviet Union. Moreover, the fact that the postwar party saw no need to replace or revise its basic policy, termed a thesis, which had been drafted in Moscow in 1932, suggests the significant continuity between the prewar and postwar JCP.

At the first postwar party congress, Secretary General Tokuda said: "Direct liaison with the Soviet Union will harm rather than assist our movement."[20] A few weeks later he stated: "At present we are aiming at the early establishment of a democracy in its real sense. In other words, democracy in the American way."[21] At the next party congress, in 1946, Tokuda made the point even more strongly: "At present," he said, "we have no ties whatsoever with the Soviet Union . . . I should like to state here that, in the future as well, our Party will never have relations with the Soviet Union."[22]

Such comments are of course difficult to assess in view of the Communists' well-known proclivity for misrepresentation and opportunism, and, more specifically, in light of the bad blood between Tokuda and Moscow.[23] What is clear is that after a brief period of consultation and confusion, by the spring of 1946 the party had settled firmly on the policy of "peaceful revolution" and the engaging campaign slogan "toward a lovable Communist party." Equally clear, and documented, is the fact that during this period the party continued to maintain contacts with the Soviet mission in Tokyo and to follow the general Soviet line on most international issues.

THE STRATEGY OF PEACEFUL REVOLUTION

Except for a brief period of uncertainty and confusion, then, immediately following Japan's surrender, Communist strategy in Occupied Japan from

1946 to the Cominform criticism of Nosaka's "moderate" policies (early in 1950) may be characterized as the era of peaceful revolution. Lest there be some misunderstanding on the fundamental nature of this strategy, it may be well to recall that Nosaka wrote in 1948: "Although at times the possibility of a peaceful revolution may exist, peaceful revolution is no more than a type of tactics. With changing conditions, the approach must also change."[24] A year later Nosaka, in clarifying his position, stated: "If pursued skillfully this policy will facilitate the development of conditions for direct revolution and make possible the seizure of power."[25]

With the onset of the Cold War and the deterioration of relations between East and West during 1947, the Kremlin launched a more militant policy. This policy, it may be recalled, crystallized as worldwide Communist strategy with the formation of the Cominform in September of 1947. Zhdanov's "Two Hostile Camps" keynote speech was accompanied by a publication of "Declaration of the Conference on the International Situation" which named Japan as an "instrument of United States imperialistic policy" and characterized Socialist parties everywhere as "tactical weapons of the imperialist camp."[26]

Japanese Communist response to the new line was the immediate abandonment of attempts to form a "top alliance" with the Socialist party, some deemphasis of the peaceful revolutionary theme, and adoption of a somewhat more anti-United States posture—one more mini-indication of JCP response to Moscow influence. From the outset Nosaka appears to have been unhappy with the position in which this placed him in an American-Occupied Japan, as was later documented in his celebrated confrontation with the Cominform.[27]

In the Communist view, Japan had become a semicolony; hence foreign imperialism (i.e., the United States) was added to the traditional enemies "monopoly capital, feudal landlords and reactionary bureaucrats." In February of 1948, the JCP officially launched its "democratic national front" offensive. Communists concentrated on establishing a united front "from below" by wooing dissident groups and individuals in the Socialist camp and by attempting to mobilize "all democratic forces" (representing the workers, peasants, "working townspeople," intelligentsia, small and medium businessmen, and even "sincere and progressive capitalists") to carry out the announced goals of the "lovable party": democratization of Japan, stabilization and improvement of living standards, complete independence, and world peace.[28] Significantly, and reflecting Nosaka's moderating influence on policies, the American presence in Japan was attacked only indirectly with a sophisticated, gentle touch reminiscent of the shrewd Chou En-lai, with whom—perhaps not incidentally—Nosaka had worked in Yenan for years.

With such a sophisticated, moderate strategy in an Occupation environment of total reform the now legal Japan Communist Party made substantial progress. By the spring of 1949, Communists dominated the strong postwar labor union and had infiltrated key government unions and departments; registered membership in the party stood at some 100,000; 35 Communists had been elected to the Diet; perhaps 40 percent of all university students in Japan supported the party's program; numerous business enterprises found the party's suggestion for trade with the continent "attractive"; and there were more than 3 million sympathizers and an indeterminate number of secret party members throughout the nation.

The critical point, however, is that while this substantial Communist support in Japan may not have been predominantly pro-Soviet in its orientation and collective attitude, it was essentially and actively Marxist-Leninist, anti-Capitalist, anti-SCAP, and anti-United States. This is to suggest that clearly the net effect of the strategy and tactics of "peaceful revolution" served Soviet and Chinese Communist purposes and advanced Moscow's, not United States, interests in Japan although the Cominform was soon to argue that Nosaka had gone soft on capitalism, would have to reform and do better.

MORE MILITANT POLICY, COMINFORM INSPIRED

Suddenly, in January 1950, Moscow "suggested" a shift to a more positive policy with an anonymous editorial in the late official Cominform journal, *For a Lasting Peace; For a Peoples' Democracy.* Nosaka's policy was branded as "anti-democratic, anti-Socialist, anti-patriotic and anti-Japanese." The Japanese party would have to improve its discipline and ideological level, become more militant and "active," stop toying with the Occupation and with "unreliable social democratic elements," and publicly declare its dedication to the Soviet cause. If because of the unique Occupation circumstances the Japanese Communists for a time had been given special dispensation, when the international Communist line became more militant in 1948, the honeymoon was over.[29] Nosaka admitted that grave mistakes had been made, concluding on the note that was to become the keynote of future strategy and tactics: "We must . . . fulfill," he said, "the important mission assigned to the Communist Party of Japan as a link in the international revolutionary movement."[30] Nosaka was significantly not removed from any of his posts in the party.

The two-year period from the Cominform criticism in January 1950 to the publication of a new party program in November 1951 was confused and transitional. In the course of adjusting a major and often violent factional dispute within the party between the left-wing, the Internationalists (*Kokusaiha*),[31] and the more moderate elements, the Main Stream Faction (*Shuryuha*),[32] and while thrashing out differences over theory and tactics, the orientation of the whole party moved steadily to the left. This shift to a more radical and internationally oriented policy can be identified by a study of the Japanese party press of the period and by the increasing number and scope of Communist-linked incidents in Japan, and of sabotage and other acts of violence.[33] Two party documents—the "1950 thesis" and the "1951 Party Rules and Regulations"—form the principal link between the old line of "peaceful revolution" and the new strategy of "national liberation" in a colonial, or dependent, area. Taken together, in terminology, emphasis, and specific content, these two documents reveal the direction of the reorientation in progress; from a moderate to a more radical approach, from peaceful to violent revolution, from an ostensible position of neutrality to outspoken alignment with the Soviet bloc.[34]

On the eve of the Korean War, most of the Communist party leaders disappeared. The Japanese government and private industry initiated a series of measures designed to control the now openly radical and frankly foreign-oriented organization.[35] Almost immediately, the party set up an interim central directorate as its overt headquarters to carry on openly for the "purged," or outlawed, central committee, and soon Japanese government reports and the Japanese press were describing a vast new Japanese Communist underground structure, including military committees, special units, labor unification committees, and an expanded clandestine press.[36] Meanwhile, the party's popularity with the general public dwindled markedly as it moved underground and to the left.

"NATIONAL-LIBERATION DEMOCRATIC REVOLUTION"

By the summer of 1951 factional strife had been virtually eliminated; the reorientation seemed complete. Shortly after the signing of the San Francisco Peace Treaty in September, the Japan Communist Party announced a new policy, the "national-liberation democratic revolution." The basis and nature of the new line are contained in three documents published by the Cominform.[37] The theoretical justification for the new approach, as given in the party documents, may be summarized as follows: owing to the exploitation by United States monopoly capital and military imperialism, Japan has been transformed—economically, politically, and militarily—into a country completely under the control of, and dependent on, the United States. And what is the fundamental standpoint from which the Marxist-Leninist approaches the problems of the revolutionary movement in the colonial and dependent countries? Here, Stalin's authority is invoked to underline the difference between an imperialist country and a revolution in a colonial or dependent area. The principal point is, of course, that only in colonial or dependent countries is it possible to utilize the national bourgeoisie "at a certain stage and for a certain period . . ." (to quote Stalin) in support of the revolutionary movement of its country "against imperialism and for emancipation."

Relating this theory directly to post-treaty Japan, the "Basis of the New Program" goes on to define the future revolution in Japan as a "national-liberation democratic revolution" and to call for a coalition government to represent the interests of all "progressive and liberation forces" in the country. This is to be based on an alliance of workers and peasants, but is not to exclude many capitalists who, we are told, will support the struggle for a free and independent Japan or at least will maintain a friendly neutrality.

The abandonment of the slogan "peaceful revolution" is evident in this passage from the "New Program": "It would be a serious mistake to think," the document warns, "that a new national-liberation democratic government will arise of its own volition, without difficulties, in a peaceful way. . . ." The earlier line on autonomy is equally cast aside in the "Basis of the New Program" which develops the theme that neutrality is impossible, that American imperialism is in the nature of a paper tiger, as is shown by its weakness in Europe and by the example of Korea, and that, therefore, any attempts to rely on American imperialism would be as disastrous for Japan as was her ill-fated alliance with the imperialists Hitler and Mussolini. "The international situation shows most clearly," the document asserts, "that the international peace-camp is a powerful ally in our national liberation democracy front. Most harmful for us at present," it concludes, "is fear of the threats of the occupation troops, the illusions about the 'free world,' and the attempt to maintain a position of neutrality."

IMPLICATIONS OF THE
POST-TREATY STRATEGY

What were the tactical implications of this new Soviet line in Japan? First, the abandonment of the tactic of "peaceful revolution," which specifically rejected the "peaceful way of liberation," seemed to suggest that the Communist line in Japan in the winter of 1951 and the spring of 1952 moved one stage closer to the final objective, the attempt to seize political power. The Korean War must be regarded as an important motivating factor. The party's ability and intention to employ violence in line with the post-treaty policy was amply demonstrated, notably in February 1952, when Communists in Tokyo and other cities throughout Japan staged the biggest series of riots and anti-American demonstrations since the outset of the Occupation, and again during the alarming 1952 May Day riots. Subsequent incidents involving the use of acid bombs, Molotov cocktails, and "action squads" armed with pistols and bamboo spears were numerous enough to suggest a definite plan. Further, discussions of the party's "military policy" and of guerrilla activity were included regularly in the Japanese Communists' principal underground publications.[38] Consequently, the initial post-treaty emphasis on violence and underground activity appears to have been party policy and not simply a series of isolated, unrelated incidents. This precise point, as we shall see, is very much at issue in the July 1955 sixth national council meeting, where the party's "military policy" comes in for rough treatment as "left wing adventurism," in a sort of Japanese Communist anticipation of the anti-Stalin line.

A second implication of the new line was the increased use of the anti-American theme as the common appeal to rally all "progressive forces" against "United States imperialism" and for "liberation." Why are the workers' conditions no better? Because of the exploitation by U.S. monopoly capital and its agent, the Yoshida—later the Hatoyama—government who are turning Japan into a colony. What accounts for the increasing plight of the Japanese farmer? The American-inspired land reform program, which was "a fraud from beginning to end," designed only to preserve the domination of the reactionary forces. Similar appeals were tailored to the needs and demands of the intellectuals, the white-collar workers, and even the businessmen, whose desire to trade with Communist China went unfulfilled because, they were told, of U.S. control over Japan. No event was too remote, absurd, or unlikely to be linked for propaganda purposes to "the American imperialists." Thus by devious logic the party even sought to show that the tragic sinking, with great loss of life, of a Japanese ferry boat really came about as a consequence of the American Occupation.

A third implication of Communist post-treaty policy is perhaps the most intriguing: Japan's official reclassification as a semicolonial, dependent area placed that country, at least for propaganda purposes, essentially in the category to which China was assigned until 1949. This suggests that a share of the theory, strategy, and tactics employed by the Communists in China had been authorized, or at least suggested for post-treaty Japan.

Part Three

The New Japan versus Soviet Intransigence: Basic Issues and Rice-Roots Responses

Chapter Six

Normalization of Relations and the Elusive Peace Treaty—An Overview

More than three decades have elapsed since the Soviet signing, along with the other wartime Allies, of the surrender document on the U.S. battleship *Missouri* in Tokyo Bay, thereby bringing hostilities, in the Pacific to an end. Still, a final peace treaty is yet to be consummated.

The United States and its friends, it may be remembered, concluded formal peace arrangements with Japan at the celebrated San Francisco conference early in September of 1951. By 1952, Japan had regained its sovereignty and had officially and formally returned to the comity of nations.

That is one version. The other is that espoused by the Soviet Union and its supporters which at that time, of course, still included the People's Republic of China. This critical, opposing, Communist view may be traced back to Soviet perceptions, policies, and dire predictions relative to Japan— notions (or at least interpretations) conspicuously different from those held by the United States. These concepts and goals Soviet spokesmen began to enunciate, then elaborate, quite early in the Occupation era. In retrospect, the contrasts are striking and provide the key to an understanding of the still "elusive peace" between the Soviet Union and Japan.

DIVERGENT AND INCOMPATIBLE CONCEPTS AND GOALS

It may be noted at the outset that divergent views, at least early in the game, were held, not only by the Soviets and the United States respectively, but also, if in a dissimilar manner and to a different degree, by the several key American authorities, individuals, departments, organizations, and agencies purporting to represent the basic and best interests of the United States on the matter of peace and the future of Japan.[1] India and other allies also voiced serious reservations. However, as the Cold War budded, blossomed, then exploded, and as Soviet doctrine and strategy became more familiar and clearer, the United States found it essential to respond more decisively to the serious Communist challenges in Europe and Asia. Japan was no exception.

The process toward peace, reconstruction, and independence for Japan was initiated and presided over by the one individual most directly associated with Japan's defeat, surrender, and Occupation, General Douglas MacArthur. As early as March 1947, the general recommended that a peace treaty be concluded with Japan as soon as possible.[2] This somewhat surprising suggestion, coming from the Supreme Commander of the Allied powers so often criticized for his "fixation" with the Communist threat syndrome, seems to have been motivated by a combination of economic considerations supported by an exaggerated confidence in the degree of progress the Occupation regime had made in launching Japan on the road to lasting peace, stability, and security—though hardly "the Switzerland of the Pacific" he once conceived. The general's position was apparently shared by the Department of State at the time, but pointedly not by the Departments of the Army and Navy. These two agencies, understandably, thought in more partisan, practical terms such as the ongoing need for military bases, area access, communications links, and other mundane, professional matters. As it turned out, these matters were to prove scarcely partisan and more than mundane.

During the ensuing year, various plans for a peace treaty were put forward including one by the United States opting for the FEC as the proper arbiter of peace and one by the Soviets insisting that the Council of Ministers, where Moscow might play a more decisive role, undertake the task. Decisive legal, procedural, and other objections were raised in each case with the result that little, if any, discernible progress was made.

THE SOVIET POSITION ELABORATED

Radio Moscow sounded the keynote of Soviet policy and propaganda with respect to Japan's future in October of 1947: "If the Japanese Peace Treaty is discussed under the leadership of one country," the Soviet commentator warned, "the growth of Japan would be directed in such a way to conform to the interest of that country. In that case," the broadcast on Japan concluded, "Japan would lose her sovereignty."[3]

As the world moved into the era of the Cold War, the Soviets' publication *New Times* took up the cause, arguing: "Even today, after the lapse of three years, there is still no peace treaty with Japan. The reason is that America is stubbornly resisting its preparation. Her occupation policy is diametrically opposed to the joint decisions taken on Japan, and" the article concludes, "in no way furthers that country's conversion into a peaceable democratic state."[4]

To those familiar with the Soviet connotation and use of the terms "peace" and "democracy," the message was clear enough.

At this juncture, SCAP's G-2 Civil Censorship organization was prompted to take a quiet reading of the situation as viewed by the Japanese themselves. In a substantial report dealing in part with the matter of the impending peace treaty, based upon samplings of letters written by friends and relations throughout Japan and entitled "Reaction to the Occupation," that agency (in December of 1948) reported: "Depressed by the international outlook and reports of growing U.S.–Soviet rivalry, writers make gloomy prophecies that 'it will be two to four years before the conference is called.' " Then citing a striking, though not isolated example, the report continues: "Perhaps the most pessimistic note is sounded by a Hokkaido man who remarks, 'the treaty will probably be postponed until after the impending American-Soviet war.' " An Osaka businessman quoted in the same document virtually hit the nail on the head when he wrote: "It would not be surprising if the United States broke off negotiations with the USSR and shelved the Japanese treaty plans until 1951 or later."[5]

In conformity with the rationale for the Marshall Plan and the Truman Doctrine in Europe and also reflecting increasing concern over Communist advances in China (not to mention rumblings and military buildups elsewhere in Asia), step-by-step, Japan came to be treated less as a defeated enemy and more as a political ally and member of the free nations of the world. This conception, we are told, was crystalized in November 1948 in a decision of the National Security Council and involved a number of measures clearly designed to strengthen Japan in terms of its economic base and potential defensive/security capability. These practical steps were essentially embodied in recommendations made by George Kennan and the Policy Planning Staff a year later.[6] They paralleled, reflected, and supported the policies of SCAP, by now vigorously pursued by General MacArthur and company as Japan was prepared for the rigors of independence and peace in a conspicuously *dependent* and *scarcely peaceful* world.

If by this time the United States was still not totally clear as to the nature of Soviet global moves and motives, America's position vis-à-vis Japan had become realistic and sensible enough to alarm the Soviets and to dampen (though not quite extinguish) whatever lingering hopes Moscow may have entertained relative to Japan as an easy "Socialist" target or even a potential "Switzerland of the Pacific." One of the Soviet's most prolific journalists on Japan, M. Markov, in June of 1949 wrote characteristically of the American-Japanese "Peace Settlement" without a treaty: "At the recent Paris Meeting of the Council of Foreign Ministers," he noted, "the Soviet Union again raised the question of expediting the peace settlement with Japan. . . ." Then, he added "[but] . . . every time the Soviet government has suggested the calling of a special meeting of the Council of Foreign Ministers to consider a peace settlement with Japan, the suggestion has been met with stubborn resistance of the American and British governments. Washington," he asserted, "is striving to prolong the occupation as long as possible, to perpetuate her status as an occupied country, arguing that if American troops were withdrawn the country would be 'defenseless.' Actually, a situation in which there is no treaty suits American business and the American Army better than any other."[7]

Finally, further deploring what he termed the "infiltration of American monopolies," the rebuilding of Japanese "war industries," the strengthening of Japan as "the chief agent of Wall Street in East Asia," and "American desire to totally control Japan's trade," as well as the U.S. fear of the "Japanese people" and of "democratic forces in China," Markov concluded: "With every month that the peace settlement with Japan is delayed, Washington policy saps the foundation of peace and security in the Far East laid down by the victory of the peoples over Japanese imperialism."[8]

Then, on August 30, only two weeks before President Truman was to announce that the State Department had been authorized to initiate discussions with the FEC regarding a Japanese peace treaty, Moscow reiterated and summarized its position in a major article in *New Times* entitled "Five Years After the Surrender of Imperialist Japan." The critical passage follows verbatim:

> It became obvious long ago that the Washington politicians were sabotaging the preparation of a peace treaty with Japan. They have rejected the proposals made on this score by the Soviet Union, for they do not want the treaty to promote democratization of Japan and eliminate the roots of Japanese militarism. Washington does not hide its desire to prepare and conclude a separate peace treaty with Japan, without China and the Soviet Union, although it is perfectly clear that no peace treaty with Japan that does not bear the signatures of the two great powers that play a leading role in Asia can have any legal validity.[9]

THE DULLES INITIATIVE
AND THE SOVIET RESPONSE

On September 14, 1950—in the midst of the Korean War, but before the one million Chinese Communist "volunteers" had intervened (in December)

—President Truman announced that the State Department had been authorized to initiate discussions with the member nations of the FEC regarding a peace treaty with Japan. Soon thereafter, a memorandum was sent to these same member countries by John Foster Dulles proposing that bilateral discussions be undertaken with any and all nations that had fought the war against Japan and now wished to ensure the peace.[10]

The Kremlin replied pointedly with seven questions:

1. The signatories of the Declaration of the United Nations on January 1, 1942, had undertaken not to conclude a separate peace. Did the United States contemplate a treaty in which only some of the powers would participate?
2. Why should the question of Formosa, the Pescadores, the Kuriles, and Sakhalin be subject to a fresh decision when it had already been decided by the Cairo Declaration, the Potsdam Declaration, and the Yalta conference?
3. Why should Japanese sovereignty be removed from the Ryukyu and Bonin islands, when the Cairo and Potsdam declarations had made no mention of trusteeship?
4. Would the treaty contain a definite program of withdrawal of American troops?
5. The Basic Surrender Policy of the FEC of June 19, 1947, prohibited the maintenance of an army, navy, or air force by Japan. What was meant by the joint responsibility of the United States and Japan for the security of the latter?
6. Was it the intention to remove all restrictions on Japan's development of a peacetime economy and grant her equal rights in world trade?
7. What was being done to ascertain the views of the Chinese People's Republic?[11]

The United States responded in turn on December 27, 1950, that the question of a separate peace treaty need pertain only to one that might be concluded before the end of the war. Territorial issues were, the United States stated, subject to confirmation by the peace treaty. The trusteeship for the Ryukyu and Bonin islands, the United States pointed out, did not violate any earlier agreements, indeed was implicitly covered by them, while the retention of American troops in Japan was within the provisions of Article 51 of the United Nations Charter. Finally, the United States noted that no restrictions on Japan's economy were contemplated, and added summarily, that as the United States did not recognize the People's Republic of China, that regime's views did not matter in terms of the treaty issue at hand and were, in fact unwelcome and irrelevant.[12] When still another proposal by the USSR, that the Council of Foreign Ministers be convened in June or July of 1951 to make preparations for a peace conference, was rejected by the United States, the stage was set for the decisive confrontation at San Francisco.[13]

SOVIET CHALLENGE AND DEFEAT
AT SAN FRANCISCO

The confrontation at San Francisco was preceded by an extensive, world-wide, whirlwind tour on the part of the principal architect of the San Francisco peace treaty, John Foster Dulles. Years before Kissinger's "shuttle diplomacy" became a fashionable conversation piece, Dulles conferred, consulted, and cajoled friends, allies, and others from Paris to Tokyo, sometimes on several occasions—logging some 100,000 miles in the process. Whatever other valid criticisms many may have had of Mr. Dulles, he appears to have understood Soviet strategy quite well, and—making him all the more reprehensible to Moscow—the Soviets understood that he under-stood![14]

This process of negotiating the treaty that was to culminate with the signing at San Francisco, Dulles spoke of as an "eleven months' peace conference." After a year of worldwide conferences, the draft treaty was ready in July of 1951, barely two months before the opening of the confer-ence in San Francisco.

The conference itself opened in the Bay City's famous Opera House on September 4, 1951, with Secretary of State Dean Acheson as chief delegate of the United States, and Mr. John Foster Dulles as second member of the delegation. Almost from the outset the confrontation was joined: the Soviets and their friends were out to block the treaty and wreck the conference; the United States sought to achieve quick approval without modification, plus endorsement, in effect, of the Security Treaty permitting U.S. troops to remain to guarantee Japan's defense.

The Soviets put forward a whole range of procedural objections, requests for reopening debate on the terms of the treaty, and then a sort of forlorn, resigned repetition of tired arguments which obviously did not impress the majority of the delegates. By the end of the first plenary session, it was clear that the Soviets had lost the battle and that it would only be a matter of time before they lost the war. This Moscow must have anticipated, for the Soviet delegate Andrei Gromyko came prepared with a detailed "documented," lengthy statement which (by Marxist-Leninist standards) eloquently sum-marized the Soviet position at San Francisco. It began reasonably enough:

". . . the Soviet Delegation," Gromyko said, "considers it necessary at the very outset to stress the importance of the question of peace with Japan." The statement then went on to chronicle "Japanese aggression" against "many of the countries represented at the present conference," a point also not open to contention, ". . . not to speak of the Chinese People's Republic, the people of which during a long period of time had to struggle single handed against the Japanese aggressor who invaded its territory." But Gromyko asserted, "While the Soviets desire to prevent the repetition of such aggression, the American-British draft of a peace treaty with Japan submitted to the conference goes to show that the authors of this draft are more anxious to clear the path for the rebirth of Japanese militarism and," he added, "to push Japan again along the path of aggression and military adventure."

Then the document gets to the Soviet heart of the matter, "To sum up," Gromyko stated, "the following conclusions regarding the American-British draft peace treaty can be drawn:

1. The draft does not contain any guarantees against the re-establishment of Japanese militarism, the transformation of Japan into an aggressive state. The draft does not contain any guarantees ensuring the security of countries which have suffered aggression on the part of militarist Japan. The draft creates conditions for the re-establishment of Japanese militarism, creates the danger of new Japanese aggression.
2. The draft treaty actually does not provide for the withdrawal of foreign occupation forces. On the contrary, it ensures the presence of foreign armed forces on the territory of Japan and the maintenance of foreign military bases in Japan after the signing of a peace treaty. Under the pretext of self-defense of Japan the draft provides for the participation of Japan in an aggressive military alliance with the United States.
3. The draft treaty not only fails to provide for obligations that Japan should not join any coalitions directed against militaristic Japan, but on the contrary is clearing the path for Japan's participation in agressive blocs in the Far East created under the aegis of the United States.
4. The draft treaty does not contain any provisions for the democratization of Japan, on the insurance of democratic rights to the Japanese people, which creates a direct threat to a rebirth of the prewar fascist order.
5. The draft treaty is flagrantly violating the legitimate rights of the Chinese people to the integral part of China—Taiwan (Formosa),

the Pescadores and Paracel Islands and other territories severed from China as a result of Japanese aggression.

6. The draft treaty is in contradiction to the obligations undertaken by the United States and Great Britain under the Yalta Agreement regarding the return of Sakhalin and the Kurile Islands to the Soviet Union.

7. The numerous economic clauses are designed to ensure for foreign, in the first place American monopolies, the privileges which they have obtained during the period of occupation—the Japanese economy is being placed in slavery-like dependence from these foreign monopolies.

8. The draft treaty ignores the legitimate claims of states that have suffered from Japanese occupation regarding the redemption by Japan for the damage that they have suffered. At the same time, providing for the redemption of losses directly by the labour of the Japanese population, it imposes on Japan a slavery-like form of reparations.

9. The American-British draft is not a Treaty of Peace but a treaty for the preparation of a new war in the Far East."[15]

Finally, Gromyko proceeded to propose certain amendments and additions to the draft. These included some clarification of territorial items, a proposal that all armed forces of the Allied and associated powers be withdrawn from Japan, a clarification on reparations, and a note on ratification.

Even more important in reflecting Soviet policy, hopes, and desires for Japan were eight proposed *new* articles. These dealt with:

(1) Removing obstacles to the survival and strengthening of democratic tendencies among the Japanese people [i.e., Communist and left-wing organizations]. (2) Vigilance against resurgence of fascist and militarist organizations in Japan. (3) Prohibition against Japan entering into any coalition or military alliances directed against any power which participated with its armed forces against Japan. (4) The strict limitation of the nature and size of Japanese defensive armed forces. (5) Restrictions on the nature of military training in Japan. (6) Prohibition against possession of/or experiments with atomic, bacteriological, and chemical weapons. (7) No restrictions on the developments of peaceful industry. (8) A guarantee of free passage of ships along the Japanese coast and its demilitarization including key straits.[16]

In effect, Mr. Dulles pointed out, the Soviet proposal would mean that only Russian naval forces could use the key straits to the north, that Japan would be cut in two, and that U.S. forces could not even operate in the straits between Korea and Japan. "That is the kind of thing," Dulles said, "the 'Jokers' that are contained in the series of proposals that are put before us that we have had to face for eleven months, and that is why it is not possible for us to come to any agreement with the Soviet Union despite our sincere desire to do so."[17]

The Soviets had overplayed their hand. The careful planning and recognized dangers to the erstwhile allies inherent in Japan's critical position between East and West resulted in a rare display of near unanimity when the time came to vote. Out of the 52 member-states attending the conference, 49 (including Japan) signed the San Francisco treaty and only three Communist states (USSR, Poland, and Czechoslovakia) refused to do so.

Meanwhile, the Korean War had erupted (in June of 1950, with massive Chinese Communist involvement in December) making the Japan–United States bilateral Security Pact signed alongside the treaty an increasingly important guarantee of Japan's security.

LIMBO OF SOVIET-JAPANESE INTERACTION

The period between the San Francisco Peace Conference (September 1951) and Soviet-Japanese bilateral talks in London and Moscow (1955–1956) may be best described as limbo, that is, little happened; nothing changed except the choice of words, and in the Soviet case precious few refreshing restatements or new formulations of old positions may be recorded.

To be sure a few not inconsequential events took place. For one thing, Stalin died, and not too long thereafter his short-lived successor, Premier Georgy Malenkov, (on August 8, 1953) stated that with the advent of the truce in Korea, the time had come for the normalization of relations between various countries of the Far East—especially, he said, between the Soviet Union and Japan.[18]

With the active appearance of Khrushchev on the scene (in 1954) and the advent of "coexistence" as the new Soviet policy catchall and watchword, a certain improvement—or at least change—in East-West relations may be identified. In this context Japan, it may be noted, is regarded as "West" and not "East." Various delegations and missions increasingly shuttled between Japan and the Soviet Union and all agreed on the desirability of normalizing relations between the two nations.

Molotov chose the occasion of receipt of a questionnaire submitted by the influential Nagoya newspaper *Chubu Nihon Shimbun* (September 13, 1954), to make a major policy statement on relations with Japan. While again it plows familiar ground, the five points stressed in the Molotov reply summarize rather neatly the limbo status and key issues vis-à-vis relations with Japan.

First, on the possibility of concluding a neutrality or non-aggression pact with Japan, Molotov replies with platitudes and generalizations about the well-known Soviet desire for world peace and then says simply that "normalizations with Japan are overdue," and concludes: "It goes without saying that settlement of this matter would enable us to examine specific questions of Soviet-Japanese relations."

In other words, Molotov proposed to achieve and advance trade, diplomatic, and other relations favorable and advantageous to the Soviet Union *prior* to or indeed *without ever* settling basic issues vital to Japan, such as the territorial and fisheries questions.

Second, on the specific matter of the desirability of normalizing relations with Japan, Molotov answered that the main obstacle is in a dependent relationship with the United States, the fact that Japan is "following the dictate of U.S. ruling circles."

In other words, the comment clearly implies the Japanese should disavow the Security Treaty with the United States, remove U.S. bases, eliminate U.S. influence, and so on. Then a "mutually beneficial" treaty would be entirely possible.

Third, on the question of the increased development of trade between Japan and the USSR, Molotov is positive, encouraging, interested: ". . . present opportunities are by no means being utilized . . . more frequent meetings of persons and delegations interested in Soviet-Japanese trade would be a concrete step towards this end."

This was to become, as noted, a favorite and attractive Soviet theme.

Fourth, on rearmament, Molotov is for "substantial reduction of arms by all countries," and, he continued, "As is known, the Soviet government proposals for a peace treaty with Japan provide for an independent peace-loving and democratic Japan to have armed forces necessary for self-defense." Again the adjective "democratic" is the quietly deceptive caveat.

Fifth, on the development of cultural relations with Japan, they should, of course, "be expanded" to develop "international cooperation and strengthen world peace."[19] On this there could be little disagreement.

The following month, a joint Sino-Soviet communiqué issued on October 12, 1954, on the occasion of Khrushchev's visit to Peking, expressed the readiness of both countries to normalize relations with Japan. Moscow and Peking now—in an important concession—no longer demanded, in order to normalize relations with the Soviet Union and China, that Japan's "friendly" relations with other countries be sacrificed.[20] This cleared the way for further Soviet-Japanese talks, as it turned out, in London and Moscow.

At the end of the year, one of Moscow's then young specialists and

spokesmen on Japan, Dmitry Petrov, was called upon to stress the importance of developing trade relations between Japan and the Soviet Union and
China—in order to avoid depending solely on America, "which at any
moment may threaten to take away the 'crutches' on which the Japanese
economy relies."[21] The Soviet emphasis on the economic trade incentive to
counter or neutralize the territorial displeasure from this point on becomes
a recurrent Moscow theme.

TALKS IN LONDON AND MOSCOW

The tough-line, Cold War Soviet policy epitomized by the Stalinist regime
began to shift midway through 1954. The spirit of the Geneva conference
of that year (reflecting shades of Asian neutralism) and the post-Stalin leadership's profound sense of insecurity and of strategic inferiority resulted in
the beginnings of calculated cordiality later exuded by the new Khrushchev
and Brezhnev regimes and combined to produce a more flexible, astute, dis-
arming, and attractive Soviet worldwide "coexistence" strategy which inevitably had its impact on and in Japan.[22] In this context, Foreign Minister
Molotov announced on September 12, 1954, that the Soviet Union was
ready to normalize relations with Japan. Foreign Minister Shigemitsu
responded on December 11, 1954, that Japan desired "without prejudice to
its cooperation with the 'Free World' to normalize relations with the Soviet
Union and China on terms mutually acceptable."[23] This was followed on
January 25, 1955, by dispatch of a Soviet note specifically requesting that
negotiations for the normalization of diplomatic relations be opened.[24]
    Moscow's timing of these moves seems anything but accidental. Nor was
Soviet policy exclusively motivated by fortuitous trends in the international
arena. In his study *Japanese Domestic Politics and Foreign Policy: The
Peace Agreement with the Soviet Union*, Donald Hellmann suggests Moscow's close attention to the Japanese political scene and explains the critical
international-domestic linkage involved. He writes:

At the time that the Soviet Union made these gestures, the Japanese
political world was undergoing far-reaching changes. Yoshida, the
prime minister for six years and the man most closely identified with
United States policy, was clearly in the twilight of his political career.
A series of domestic incidents, including a scandal which reached into
the cabinet, had brought his popularity to an all-time low and brought
his many critics within conservative ranks into unified and open opposition. The Democratic Party, which had been formed in October
1954, was truly a potpourri of political opportunists, who were united

by little more than their desire to topple his cabinet. As president they selected Hatoyama Ichiro, an old and ailing prewar party veteran, who, after his depurge in 1951, had already made several abortive attempts to unseat Yoshida. With the aid of the two Socialist parties, the Democrats brought down the government on December 7, 1954, transferring the mantle of political leadership to a motley coalition headed by Hatoyama.

Then Professor Hellman concludes pointedly:

The issue of Soviet relations was projected directly into the center of this unsettled situation. Immediately after entering office, Hatoyama proclaimed normalization of relations with both the Soviet Union and Communist China as a central policy goal, and it quickly became one of the major political slogans of the Democratic Party. Not only did it precipitate a bitter public controversy with the rival Liberal Party, since the position sharply diverged from that of Yoshida, but the fulfillment of this vague pledge came to be a trying policy responsibility for Hatoyama. Thus, from the very beginning, the issue was drawn deeply into the maelstrom of Japanese domestic politics.[25]

The London talks began on June 3, 1955, were interrupted fifteen sessions later on September 13; resumed again on January 9, 1956, and continued until March 20; reopened again on July 31, they lasted until August 13, 1956. At the end of it all, few solutions to the fundamental issues dividing the two nations had been achieved.

The London negotiations opened on the basis of a Japanese memorandum which called for repatriation of all Japanese interned in the Soviet Union; respect for Japan's rights and obligations under the San Francisco Treaty and the Security Pact; return of the Habomais, Shikotan, Kuriles, and South Sakhalin after the conclusion of a peace treaty; freedom of fishing in the northern waters and return of captured fishermen and boats; an increase in economic relations, to be discussed in separate negotiations; mutual respect for the principles set forth in the Charter of the United Nations; and Soviet support of Japan's entry into the United Nations.

Based upon Soviet performance in world affairs to that date as well as upon previous Soviet policy statements with respect to Japan, it was not difficult to anticipate the Soviet position and probable response on each of the points put forward by Japan: repatriation of Japanese prisoners had been "virtually completed," but the matter would be "looked into," and the precise nature of Japan's right under the San Francisco Treaty and Security Pact would require "serious discussion." Since, with the exceptions of Austria and Iran, the Soviets have not retreated from control of territories they had occupied (the situation in Eastern Europe is a case in point), the return of the Northern Territories seemed most unlikely. The fisheries issue would be discussed separately. The Soviets, of course, welcomed increased economic relations "to the mutual benefit of both nations." And, finally, the Soviets expressed nothing but respect for the Charter of the United Nations, and as part of a peace treaty would support Japan's entry into the United Nations.

Thus, the real issues would come down essentially to three: Japan's relations with the United States, especially matters of the Security Treaty and continued presence of United States troops in Japan; the question of the disputed Northern Territories, claimed by Japan but controlled and occupied by the Soviet Union; and, an acceptable fisheries agreement.

After long negotiations in London, it became clear that these issues would not be easily resolved and that (most distressing), the Soviets were not willing to concede to Japan cession of other than possibly two small islands to the north, the Habomais and Shikotan; that, in short, these and other matters must await resolution and conclusion of a formal peace treaty.[26]

At the end of July 1956, formal talks looking toward the restoration of diplomatic relations opened in Moscow. These talks constituted the third major negotiating attempt to resolve the issues that had divided Japan and the Soviet Union since San Francisco. When it became clear that the Soviets would remain adamant on the territorial issue, intended to hold on to *their* Kuriles, and were prepared to discuss only the return of the Habomais and Shikotan, the negotiations were broken off by Tokyo.

On August 19, 1956, Hatoyama, after consulting with key members of his then ruling party, announced that he was prepared to go to Moscow. This, it may be noted, would be the first visit of a Japanese prime minister to the Soviet capital. A young Japanese foreign ministry officer (who shall remain nameless) said to me at the time, in a singularly Japanese formulation: "Hatoyama is a man perfectly unsuited for negotiating with the Soviets."

Though opposition from both the Yoshida and the Shigemitsu factions continued to be strong, the talks in Moscow were reasonably friendly, if not cordial. To the ailing Hatoyama, nothing of less significance than a sacred campaign promise was at issue, perhaps even a cherished place in diplomatic history. After only four days of negotiations, on October 19, a joint declaration was signed. This document was ratified by the Japanese Diet on November 15, and the requisite ratified documents formally exchanged on December 11, 1956. Thus, after a decade in limbo and two previous false starts, formal diplomatic relations between Japan and the Soviet Union had been restored, but the fundamental issues between the two nations—including peace itself—remained to be settled.

THE JOINT DECLARATION OF 1956 AND
THE RESUMPTION OF DIPLOMATIC RELATIONS

While, as suggested, the Joint Declaration did not settle fundamental, outstanding issues, it does represent a milestone of sorts along the complicated and (from the Japanese standpoint) frustrating road to "peace" with the Soviet Union. Accordingly, the principal items covered by the declaration need only be recorded briefly here as we shall encounter them again in more detail, in their proper setting, in due course.

The short declaration of ten articles was signed on October 19, 1956, by Bulganin and Shepilov for the Soviet Union and Hatoyama and Matsumoto for Japan.

Articles 1 and 2 end the state of war, reestablish diplomatic relations, and initiate the process of establishing appropriate embassies and consulates.

Article 3 affirms mutual adherence to the principles of the United Nations, particularly the Charter's prohibitions against the threat or use of force, or intervention in one another's internal affairs.

Article 4 certifies Soviet support for Japan's application for United Nations membership.

Article 5 promises the release of Japanese prisoners in the USSR and continuing efforts to determine what happened to those still listed as missing.

Article 6 renounces all Soviet reparation claims against Japan.

Article 7 proposes increased trade.

Article 8 brings into force the deep-sea fishing convention of the northwestern section of the Pacific and the agreement on rescue of persons in distress at sea, both signed on May 14, 1956.

Article 9 pledges both nations to continue negotiations on a final peace treaty.

Article 10 deals with ratification.[27]

The Joint Declaration, while falling short of the "peace" desired by Japan and clearly failing to come to grips with the central, burning issue from the Japanese viewpoint—the Northern Territories question which remained deadlocked—did achieve some notable, if limited, results:

First, there can be no question that the psychological impact of the agreement on Japan in apparently—finally—getting Soviet-Japanese relations off dead center, was substantial.

Second, the activation of the fisheries accord, while limited and temporary, either placated or pleased a great many Japanese fishermen whose displeasure with Soviet policy and practice was becoming increasingly vocal.

Third, Soviet support for Japan's desire for United Nations membership produced an understandable degree of appreciation as that nation moved actively into its new sovereign status.

Fourth, the prospect for increased economic relations with the Soviet Union implied by the agreement—especially when accompanied by a whole range of attractive Soviet trade and joint venture initiatives, struck a responsive chord with the Japanese business community.

Fifth, the Soviet cancellation of all reparation claims and promises to look into the question of unaccounted-for Japanese prisoners added a further note of reasonableness—precisely the tone the document seemed designed to convey.

THE DEADLOCKED 1960s: FOCUS— "FRIENDSHIP," "CULTURE," AND TRADE

Recalling Khrushchev's candid remark to the effect that Moscow values trade as much for political as for economic reasons and aware of the Soviets' unique employment of "culture" as a strategic weapon, it should come as no surprise that the deadlocked Soviet-Japanese peace treaty negotiations of the 1960s witnessed a marked Soviet policy shift to the "cultural" and economic spheres. In effect, having evidently failed to advance their interests by political means, the Soviets shifted to the realm of economics hoping that massive economic involvement would ultimately result in more cordial, or at least useful, political relationships.

The keynote of the new policy was sounded by the venerable old Bolshevik Anastas Mikoyan when he visited Japan on the occasion of a Soviet Trade Fair in August of 1961. In a significant article by the authoritative "Observer" published in *New Times* that same month entitled "Japanese Neighbor," we are told pointedly that "A. I. Mikoyan's speeches have met with a lively response and will doubtless do much to achieve better understanding. The national interests of both countries," the article concludes, "require peaceful coexistence and promotion of economic intercourse."[28]

By the spring of 1963, the seeds of this idea had sprouted and grown into a full-blown "cultural," trade, and economic co-offensive with expanded Soviet-Japanese economic relations—an alternative to a formal peace treaty. Michael Nesterov, Chairman of the USSR's Chamber of Commerce, visited Japan at this time as head of a USSR-Japan Society delegation for the Seventh National Congress of that society. In an interview in Tokyo, he said:

Nor should it be forgotten that so far our countries have not signed a peace treaty or concluded a cultural agreement.

Still Japanese people become increasingly aware of the importance of good, friendly relations for the two nations. . . .

In the course of my stay in Japan I have met many businessmen and saw that they were keen to trade with our country. . . .

The position of the businessman who really seeks broader trade with the Soviet Union is well illustrated by the activity of the prominent industrialist, Yoshinari Kawai. In August last, Mr. Kawai led a group of prominent businessmen on a tour of the Soviet Union. On his return home, Mr. Kawai, despite his 76 years, made over 50 radio, TV and other public appearances describing his impressions and explaining what wide opportunities trade with the Soviet Union offered Japanese business.[29]

Again in May of 1964, on the occasion of his second trip to Japan, Mikoyan—after suggesting that it was the United States that was impeding progress on the peace treaty—stressed the alternative importance of economic relations between Japan and the Soviet Union, identifying specifically Soviet resources which he said were of greatest importance to Japan, namely timber, oil, and coal.[30]

When a new Japanese ambassador, Toru Nakagawa, arrived in Moscow in the winter of 1965, he echoed Mikoyan's comment: there are issues, he said, but he then went on to suggest that there are also some immediate practical avenues that can be pursued. In an interview in the Soviet capital the Japanese ambassador put it this way: "Take trade, for instance," he emphasized, "It is important for the Soviet Union. For my country, it is vital. There are ample opportunities for expanding it still more . . . it is time we turned from general problems to increasing trade."[31]

The late 1960s saw a burgeoning of Soviet speeches and articles stressing the significance of Soviet-Japanese economic cooperation and stressing the proximity of the two nations. Delegations, conferences, and joint working committees multiplied as the Soviet economic offensive gained momentum. The theme was always the same. Here is the standard formulation from a typical article in *New Times* entitled neatly, "Our Trading Partner."

Economic cooperation between Japan and the USSR is very important to both. Two of Japan's acutest problems today are sources of raw materials and stable markets for her industrial goods. For nearly all key raw materials have to be imported. Oil, coal, ores, timber and many other essential materials are brought over great distances. Yet close at hand, just across the Sea of Japan, lies that rich treasure-house of nature, Siberia and the Soviet Far East.

The Soviet Union is fast developing these areas. The day is not far off when Siberia will become, as one Japanese paper aptly put it, "the industrial heart of Russia."[32]

During the late 1960s, this rhetoric was translated into action with the signing of eleven bilateral treaties between Japan and the Soviet Union. Soviet strategy was designed to circumvent a formal peace treaty by substantially increasing "mutually beneficial" economic arrangements.

An examination of these eleven treaties (February, 1965, through March, 1969) leaves little doubt as to their essentially economic character, though political overtones are also evident. The essence of the treaties is as follows: Consular Fees (February 1965); Seizure of Fishing Boats (April 1965); Trade and Payments (January 1966); Aviation Communication (January 1966); Consular Convention (July 1966); Rescue Sea Disaster (July 1967); Cooperation in Commercial Fishing (July 1967); Joint Development of Forestry Resources Soviet Far East (August 1968); Japanese Airline Flights over Siberia (March 1969); Trade and Commodity Exchange (March 1969); Aviation Communication (December 1969);[33]

NEGOTIATIONS SHORT OF "PEACE"—THE 1970s

While the economic and trade treaties of the otherwise deadlocked 1960s may be viewed as progress of sorts along the road to strengthening and regularizing Soviet-Japanese relations, from Tokyo's vantage point the two most significant areas of disagreement over two decades remained unresolved well into the 1970s: they are, of course, the question of the Northern Territories and the fisheries issue.

To be sure several attempts at resolving these key issues were made by the Japanese, but with frustrating and highly unsatisfactory results until the half a loaf progress represented by the Soviet-Japanese Fisheries Agreement of May 1977. (Discussed in detail in Chapter 12; full text of Agreement as Appendix E-5.)

As if to end the matter, it may be recalled in this context, that Khrushchev had earlier responded to a personal letter from Prime Minister Ikeda in September of 1961 on the need for normalization by stating that the territorial problem had been settled by a series of agreements and that the Japanese government was trying to create artificial barriers to the normalization of relations by raising the issue. Then, after stimulating Japanese hopes by suggesting a possible linkage of the return of Okinawa by the United States and the question of Soviet return of the disputed islands, by 1966 the Soviets again restated the position that the problem of the Northern Territories had already been settled. By 1969, Soviet policy called simply for maintaining the *status quo* determined at the end of the Second World War, that is to say: the issues had been settled once and for all at Yalta. While the Japanese (including the JCP, government, and people) remained adamant on Japan's right to regain at least some of the disputed northern islands, it was not until Prime Minister Tanaka visited the Soviet Union October 7 through 10, 1973, that one of the central issues of normalization, the Northern Territories question, could be officially raised for "summit" discussion.

The front page headlines of the *Japan Times* for three successive days reflect the familiar results: Tuesday, October 9: Tanaka, Brezhnev Hold First Round of Summit Talks"; Wednesday, October 10: "Tanaka-Brezhnev Talks Deadlocked Over Islands Issue"; Thursday, October 11: "Talks to Resume Next Year for Japan-Soviet Pact."

The talks, in fact, did not resume "next year" (1974) or even in 1975 but rather in January of 1976 when Foreign Minister Gromyko paid an official visit to Japan at the latter's invitation for meetings with Foreign Minister Miyazawa and a visit with Prime Minister Miki. The Soviet foreign minister was even given an audience with Emperor Hirohito.

Once more we are indebted to the *Japan Times* headlines for so succinctly simplifying the negotiating process and progress of the 1976 talks: Friday, January 9: "Gromyko Leaves for Tokyo"; Saturday, January 10: "Gromyko Arrives Here for Talks"; Sunday, January 11: "Territorial Isles Dispute Locks Japan-Soviet Talks"; Tuesday, January 13: "Japan, Russia Fail to Make Progress on Northern Islands Issue."[34]

Gromyko would go no further than to say that the Soviet Union welcomes further discussions on the territorial issue. Miyazawa said that Gromyko's visit this time had two objectives for the Soviet Union: the first was that a proposed Japan-Soviet Friendship Treaty could serve as an intermediate step to the conclusion of a full treaty. The second was for Moscow to learn more about Japan's view and stance toward China, the Soviet Union's arch rival.[35]

Despite the continuing failure during the 1970s to reach comprehensive agreement on the elusive peace treaty (notably the familiar Northern Territories issue), in addition to the important Fisheries Agreement of 1977, sixteen other bilateral treaties and agreements were initiated between Japan and the Soviet Union during the preceding period September 1971 through July 1975. Once again the economic and trade aspects predominate, as may be seen from the essences of these treaties: Aviation Communication Appendix (April 1971); Trade and Payments (September 1971); Foreign Trade (February 1972); Aviation Communication (June 1973); Scientific and Technological Cooperation (October 1973); Exchange of Scientific and Research Workers (October 1973); Exchange of Official Publications (October 1973); Distribution of Informational Materials (October 1973); Cultural Exchange (January 1974); Credit/Banking (July 1974); Credit/Foreign Trade (April 1975); Crab Fishing (May 1975); Fishing for Tsubu (May 1975); Whaling [Pacific] (May 1975); Fishing Operations (June 1975); Tax Exemption—

International Sea and Air Transport (July 1975).[36]

The process of normalization during the 1970s then, while far from complete, made discernible progress. The situation may be summarized as follows: first, extensive economic treaties and agreements, many of them with important political overtones, were concluded. Second, a major breakthrough was achieved with the signing in May of 1977 of the fairly comprehensive and important Fisheries Accord. But (and of course, from the Japanese point of view, the crux of "peace"), no progress may be recorded on the matter of resolving the deadlocked Northern Territories question.

The persistent Soviet position on the Northern Territories issue as the key to a peace treaty is summed up in a recent work by V. N. Berezin entitled *Courses on Good Neighborliness and Cooperation—and Its Enemies: From the History of Normalization of Relations Between the USSR and Postwar Japan*, published in Moscow in 1977. The pertinent passage reads: "The Soviet Union looks toward the ultimate conclusion of a broad-gauged peace treaty encompassing all of the many-sided issues and dimensions involved. But Japan insists upon seizing and blowing out of all proportions one aspect, namely: the territorial issue."[37]

The record of Soviet diplomacy in Europe, overall Soviet strategy, considerations of the precedence involved in reopening for discussion "issues already settled at Yalta," possible future Soviet bargaining cards, and other military and technical aspects related to Northeast Asia suggest that the Northern Territories issue is not likely to be resolved to Japan's satisfaction in our lifetime. Thus, to the question, When are Soviet-Japanese relations likely to get back to normal? one must answer, regrettably, this *is* normal—for now and the foreseeable future!

Chapter Seven

Japanese Public Opinion and the Press

Public opinion polls are almost an obsession in Japan. In the sense that they are the daily fare of Americans and Japanese, they are, of course, non-existent in the Soviet Union. This is to suggest that while it may be possible to examine in some detail Japanese public attitudes toward a variety of critical political, economic, and security problems surrounding relations with the Soviet Union, we must be satisfied with (or at least settle for) the official Soviet press pronouncements and commentary on policies, issues, and events vis-à-vis Japan and related matters.

The Japanese, traditionally introspective and, at least culturally, curiously balanced between East and West, are in the throes of a collective inclination toward self-analysis.[1] Moreover, Japanese attitudes and opinions on a wealth of sensitive international questions are of quite as much concern to Japan's friends and/or potential adversaries as they are to the Japanese themselves. It comes as no surprise, then, that the Japanese government and the Japanese people as well as their neighbors, friends, and critics around the world take more than casual notice of Japan's international posture and changing post-war opinions toward the Soviet Union, China, the United States, and attendant areas and issues.

EVOLUTION OF PUBLIC-OPINION RESEARCH IN JAPAN

For a combination of reasons, public opinion polls in postwar Japan have flourished and multiplied as in perhaps no other modern industrial nation. What started as a modest Occupation exercise in opinion sampling, has developed over the years into a major professional preoccupation enlisting the intense interest, substantial time, and determined effort of professional polling groups, radio and TV enterprises, newspapers, political parties, foreign governments, individuals, as well as the prime minister's office.

The business began rather modestly during the Occupation era. One of SCAP's first steps in this direction was to order creation of a Public Opinion Survey Section in the Japanese government's Board of Information. Initially, efforts were somewhat unprofessional, crude, and unreliable although methodology and even results improved noticeably as several Japanese groups and individuals became fascinated with the subject and began to learn and to profit from the experience of a small team of sociological research specialists assembled by SCAP's Civil Information and Education Section (CIE). A number of American experts in the opinion survey area visited Japan as advisors, and in 1948 the first genuine professional organization in the field was established. This was the Japan Public Opinion Research Society, which incorporated elements from governmental agencies, private independent research groups, and a number of newspapers in addition to enlisting the services of interested individuals.

By the summer of 1949, a substantial organization, the National Public Opinion Research Institute, had been created. It was to serve as the focus and became the major center for public opinion analysis throughout the remainder of the Occupation; indeed, it remained so until July of 1954 when it was abolished.[2] The intense and increasing interest in public opinion research during the Occupation and immediate post-Occupation years may be judged from the total figures for polls conducted in Japan between 1949 and 1954: 217 in 1949, 138 in 1950, 374 in 1951, 603 in 1952, 787 in 1953, and 852 in 1954. During these Occupation years and beyond, the new institute perfected methodology, trained interviewers, encouraged innovations, sent members abroad for consultation with counterpart organizations, and collected a substantial reference library on the subject.[3]

During the 1960s and the 1970s, while an increasing number of organizations and individuals have been active in the area of public opinion research, the most substantial and sustained effort in the field has been that of the Public Opinion Division of the prime minister's office; it has been paralleled by a similar group in Japan's leading newspaper, the *Asahi Shimbun* (circulation 7,000,000). Surveys, reports, and conclusions from these two basic sources augmented by interviews in Japan and recent research monographs provide cryptic information on and mini-insights into this fascinating and important world of ideas and attitudes.

JAPANESE ATTITUDES DURING THE OCCUPATION

It is only natural and inevitable that public opinion polls conducted in an American-Occupied Japan, either by the American authorities themselves or by Japanese groups (presumably with full SCAP sanction) may be regarded with a degree of skepticism. Nor is the suggestion, though true, that the political atmosphere in American-Occupied Japan was intrinsically different from the situation that prevailed in Soviet-Occupied Eastern Europe likely to satisfy the dogged critics of the MacArthur era. The fact seems to be, however, that the results of Japanese opinion polls conducted in Occupied Japan in the late 1940s and early 1950s display an amazing degree of continuity and similarity to those more sophisticated samplings undertaken strictly by the Japanese in a post-treaty, independent, sovereign Japan. Unless one were to argue (as the Soviets and the Chinese Communists, of course, often have done) that Japan remains essentially an American satellite or dependency, the question as to continuity of change in Japanese opinion in Occupied versus post-treaty Japan is intriguing and highly significant.

As noted, the Occupation authorities attempted to keep a finger on the opinion pulse of the nation. In this respect, SCAP's Civil Censorship Division engaged, among other activities, in the now (and perhaps always) dubious business of reading other people's mail—in this case that of the then recently defeated enemy. A typical report concluded that: "More than three-fourths of 2,135 current comments on the Occupation deal with SCAP programs and implementation and approximately 80 percent of the reaction was favorable."[4] The same very detailed summary-report, based on documentation supplied from CIC detachments operating at the city and town level throughout Japan, contains an intriguing section dealing with "letters to friends and relatives abroad." Here are two striking excerpts from that SCAP intelligence opinion survey: "Approximately 90 percent of the Japanese letters to friends and relatives abroad point up beneficial aspects of the Occupation and comment on the remarkable political, economic and cultural progress made during the past three years (1946–1948)." At the same time, the letters inevitably reflect the "Cold War" apprehensions of the time. The SCAP document continues: "The fear of progressive Communist expansion in Asia has prompted some writers to express hope for a continuation of the Occupation in their letters abroad. . . . Although these intercepts point out that Red influence to date has been kept subdued, it is predicted that a Communist-agitated civil war would break out if American forces were evacuated. . . ." "We heartily hope," one such letter cited in the same document states, "that U.S. Occupation forces will not evacuate Japan until she is completely revived as a democratic nation!"[5]

A national random sampling public opinion poll (sample, some 6,000 responses out of 8,000) conducted by the *Jiji* News Agency in May of 1949 produced dramatic results on the questions, Which foreign country do you like most? Dislike most? On the most liked country, 62 percent responded,

"America." On the country most disliked there was only slightly less agreement: 53 percent replied, "Russia."[6]

FROM OCCUPATION TO INDEPENDENCE—
SOME TRANSITIONAL ISSUES

The complicated questions of a peace treaty, U.S. troop withdrawal, the military issue, the need for Japanese rearmament, and a host of other concerns were inevitably linked in the Japanese public mind to the matter of Soviet and Chinese Communist intentions. With the outbreak of war in Korea (June 1950), these questions became even more complicated, controversial, and urgent. It is at this point that the Japanese population's curiously favorable overall reaction to occupation by their American conquerors and the Japanese traditional fear and "hate" of Russia converge to produce the strange and unusual context in which polls on the peace treaty, rearmament, the Korean War, and the future of Japan's international relations must be read.

Coming as it did on the eve of Japan's anticipated transition from Occupation to independence, the outbreak of the Korean War inevitably had a dramatic and highly significant impact upon the majority of Japanese. Rarely in history had a nation displayed a more active, total, and genuine reborn dedication to peace. Barely in the process of recovering from the physical and psychological effects of total defeat, unconditional surrender, and national humiliation, most Japanese looked with apprehension and shock at the new Communist inspired war in Korea—on the very doorstep of what remained of the once proud and again peaceful Japan.

Asked in August of 1950, "Do you think the Korean War will bring insecurity to Japan?", 38 percent of those Japanese polled answered, "yes," 40 percent answered, "a little," and only 13 percent replied, "no"; as to whether the Korean War would extend into a world war, however, 37 percent answered, "yes," 30 percent said, "no."[7]

Japanese transitional attitudes in the peace and security area may perhaps best be represented and summarized by the results of a *Yomiuri Shimbun* poll conducted in March 1951, about six months before the peace treaty was signed in San Francisco. That poll asked the question: "Do you want U.S. troops to remain in Japan after the peace treaty?" Out of a total of some 3,000 respondents, 18.5 percent said they thought U.S. troops should stay in Japan; another 45 percent also said, "yes," but added, "only for a while"; 16.7 percent said, "no." Some 20 percent were undecided.[8] By this time, it may be noted, the one million Chinese Communist "volunteers" had entered the war in Korea.

Japanese public opinion and the political parties generally reacted favorably, if in a qualified manner, to the San Francisco peace treaty which officially ended the state of hostilities with the United States and a number of other nations—except the Soviet Union, which it may be remembered, dissociated itself from the results of the conference.

When on May 23, 1951, *Pravda* attacked the American draft of a peace treaty for Japan, representatives from all major political parties in Japan (not, of course, including the Communists) quickly came to the American/Japanese government's defense.[9] The Japanese public at large, asked in a poll after its signing, "Are you satisfied with the Peace Treaty?" answered, "yes, very much," 12.6 percent; "yes, fairly," 59.6 percent; "no, partially," 12 percent; "no, extremely," 2 percent; and "don't know," 13.8 percent.[10]

On the related issue of the attendant Japan–United States Security Pact, the need for a continued U.S. military presence to guarantee Japan's defense against possible aggression from abroad, Japanese public opinion was united as on almost no other major issue. An amazing consensus of some 80 percent of more than 1,000 Japanese interviewed in Japan's two major cities, Tokyo and Osaka, for example, supported the Japan–United States Security Pact. But, significantly, asked in the same poll how long such a defensive alliance with the United States should last, there was conspicuously more diversity: "Less than 2 years," 13.5 percent; "less than 3 years," 12.7 percent; "less than 5 years," 23.1 percent; "more than 5 years," 19.1 percent; "others," 8.6 percent; "don't know," 21.1 percent; "no answer," 1.9 percent.[11]

That it would be necessary and desirable for Japan to rearm after the peace treaty was an opinion regularly reflected in poll after poll at this transitional juncture. The Japanese reacted strongly in favor of rearmament "in order to protect the security of this country (Japan) after the peace treaty." For example, a national poll of some 3,000 Japanese taken in June 1951 showed apart from those registering "no opinion," 63 percent in favor of rearmament and only about 20 percent against; the remainder were undecided.[12] When, on the eve of Japan's resumption of sovereignty, the question was posed in a more sophisticated way (that is offering diversified options) the results remained clearly on the rearmament side: better rearm quickly, 25 percent; rearm after economic stability, 51 percent; should not rearm, only 12 percent.[13] Thus, Japan moved through the transition from Occupation to sovereignty with a reasonably well-defined and clear-cut public conception of the need for self-defense if Japan were to achieve and maintain independence in a still hostile world. Indeed, in September of 1951, the very month the San Francisco peace treaty was signed, when asked: "Should an independent Japan have a defensive army?" 71 percent of some 2,500 Japanese polled nationally answered, "yes," only 16 percent replied, "no."[14] The mandate seemed clear; but the constitutional, political, economic, and psychological battles were far from over.

CONTRADICTORY AND CHANGING
JAPANESE VIEWS OF CHINA

The period of the early 1950s was, of course, one of exceptional turbulence, conflict, concern, and adjustment in East Asia. Central to most of the critical issues of the era was the emergence of the People's Republic of China as a second Communist military and ideological power center in Asia —concomitant with Japan's resumption of sovereignty and punctuated by war in Korea. Japanese attitudes toward the significance of the events of the time and their implications for Japan were, as might be expected, diversified, contradictory, sometimes confused, and ever changing.

Utilizing twelve Japanese public opinion polls covering the period September 1951 to February 1955, Professor C. Martin Wilbur reflects on some interesting attitudes and trends and makes some perceptive observations on Japanese attitudes toward China.[15]

A poll taken in Tokyo in September of 1951 (344 respondents) at the time of the San Francisco Peace Conference indicates attitudes highly unfavorable to Communist China. Among fifteen countries rated in terms of those most admired or "liked," China did not fare well; while America was again ranked first, China was tenth—outdone in the "not liked" category, as consistently, by Russia (fourteenth) and Korea (fifteenth).

By April of 1953, China's image was improving, if only slightly: in a poll conducted in Tokyo, of some 800 Japanese, about 20 percent saw points to admire or respect; some 34 percent did not, and 37 percent said they simply didn't know or had no opinion; the remainder failed to reply.

Professor Wilbur summarizes the reason for these conflicting images of Communist China as follows:

> The points of respect, in descending order of frequency: kind dealing with repatriates; power and good administration; thoroughgoing social policies, constructive spirit and productivity; communism; strong unity; good points as a race. . . .
>
> Despised points were: against humanism; dictatorial; scorn communism; out-and-out Sovietism; absence of freedom."[16]

China's image-ranking in Japan is again pinpointed by a nationwide poll conducted in November 1954 to determine what countries the Japanese "liked" or "disliked." Here is the list of "liked" countries in descending order of percentage of votes received:

United States	33.3%
United Kingdom	26.3
Switzerland	22.5
France	22.3
India	21.2
Communist China	11.9
West Germany	11.2
Canada	10.0
Australia	5.4
Soviet Union	5.1
East Germany	5.0
Nationalist China	4.0
Republic of Korea	3.1

In the same November 1954 poll, the countries *disliked* by the Japanese respondents were:[17]

Soviet Union	37.3%
Republic of Korea	30.3
Communist China	21.3
Nationalist China	13.1
United States	10.6
East Germany	5.7
Australia	4.5
United Kingdom	3.9
West Germany	2.8
France	2.4
Canada	1.7
India	1.1
Switzerland	0.5

When we come to the increasingly active issue of international trade, however, a very different pattern begins to emerge. Money apparently talks —whether yen, ruble, or dollar! Asked whether they favored promoting trade with China and Soviet Russia, out of some 800 Japanese polled in Tokyo in July of 1955, 76.7 percent said, "yes"; only 5 percent said, "no"; 18 percent replied, "don't know."[18]

During the 1960s the China issue was in part obscured by the variety of foreign policy issues that confronted and confused the Japanese government and competed for public attention. Central foreign policy issues, it may be recalled, included negotiating with the Soviets, revision of the Japan–United States Security Treaty, and the Okinawan problem. This leaves aside domestic issues such as economic problems, which it can be demonstrated were of more immediate concern to the Japanese voter in any case. One overall analysis of Japanese public opinion polls on China, 1965 through 1969, focuses on the issue with striking results: ". . . while China seemed to be the most prominent foreign policy issue in early 1965, it had dropped to third place by the end of the year, fourth place by mid-1966, fifth place by mid-1968, and sixth place by late 1969."[19]

Once again, however, when we come to the foreign trade area, as in the case with the Soviet Union, unfavorable Japanese images of China are put aside and there is widespread public agreement that trade with Communist China should be increased. This point is underlined by a mid-1970 *Yomiuri* poll: while only one-fifth of the respondents favored normalization of relations with China, more than one-half wanted either to expand economic interchange or improve friendly relations.[20]

JAPANESE PRESS AND EDITORIAL COMMENT ON THE SOVIET UNION AND THE PEOPLE'S REPUBLIC OF CHINA—SOME SAMPLES

Short of a detailed and lengthy content analysis, it is, of course, not easy to generalize confidently on the recent diversity and changing Japanese editorial and press commentary on the Soviet Union, the People's Republic of China, and related issues. On the question of Soviet policy and practice, the Japanese press, on the whole, may be characterized as curious, skeptical, sometimes confused, critical, outspoken, and often apprehensive.

Time and purpose permit only a minisampling, a fleeting glance at recent (1975–1977) Japanese press comment and editorial opinion on the subject— from several of the most widely read and respected journals (*Chuo Koron*, *Sekai*, and others) and from two of Japan's most influential newspapers, the substantial *Asahi Shimbun* and the almost equally well-known *Yomiuri Shimbun*. Such random, though representative sampling, necessarily adds more flavor than conclusive substance, but the brief press selections that follow are nonetheless interesting and I think also, each in its own way, highly significant.

Perhaps there is no more appropriate place to start than with an editorial in the *Asahi Shimbun* in January 1975 entitled "How Should Japan-Soviet Friendship be Pushed?" Here *Asahi* is both realistic and mildly hopeful. Alluding to Japanese foreign minister Miyazawa's then recent return from conferences in Moscow, the editorial concludes: "It will probably be impossible to expect concessions of the Soviet side through one or two rounds of talks. We hope again that the Government will hold persistent talks without changing its principles, in the future, too."[21]

During the ensuing months and years, *Asahi*'s advice has been largely followed and *Asahi*'s apprehension that "it will probably be impossible to expect concessions . . ." has so far been essentially confirmed. On the question of the Soviet position toward developing relations between Japan and China, *Asahi*, by mid-1975, had become outspokenly critical of Moscow's policy. In a major article, entitled "Sino-Soviet and Hegemony Problems," *Asahi* takes the Soviets to task in very specific terms: "Frankly speaking, we should say that the Soviet statement [*sic*] has excessively intervened in Japan's independent position. . . . The Soviet Union has displayed various moves, for some time now, designed to impede the conclusion of that treaty [between Japan and the People's Republic of China] prior to conclusion of a Japan-Soviet treaty [regarding the former] as the establishment of a barrier to the Soviet Union's policy toward Asia."[22]

To the extent that the Japanese Diet is a measure of Japanese attitudes and opinion, its action in July of 1975 shelving the Japanese Soviet Fishing Operations Agreement must be regarded as something of a milestone. The Japanese Foreign Ministry was shocked. A ministry spokesman noted: "Of all agreements concluded between Japan and the USSR since the two countries' diplomatic relations were restored, the above agreement was the first case failing to obtain approval from the Diet. The Ministry, therefore, is at a loss to explain it to the USSR."[23]

Some of the kinds of doubts and concerns about the Socialist system and Soviet policies, as reflected daily in the Japanese press—and specific reasons for them—are neatly summarized in the February 1976 issue of *Sekai*. Professor Mitsuru Yamamoto of Senshu University criticizes the "neutral" position of the Japan Socialist Party, writing:

> The "superiority" of the socialist system has been doubted and questioned with anguish, not only by socialists but by all others interested in socialist thought and movements, wherever such incidents as the Hungarian and Czech incidents, the Sino-Soviet border clashes, the independent policy lines of Yugoslavia, Romania and West European communist parties and the voices of liberals in the Soviet Union occurred after Stalin was criticized. But this problem and the like are all pushed aside or sidestepped in the Action Policy (of the JSP) as if the "superiority of the socialist system" were a holy oracle not permitting anyone to doubt it or to seek verification.[24]

A further perspective on Soviet-Japanese relations as viewed by the Japanese press is afforded by Akio Kimura, Chief Researcher of the *Asahi* Survey and Research section. Writing in the influential journal *Chuo Koron*, he comments on the "Meaning of Dispatch of a Big-Shot Soviet Ambassador" to Tokyo (in mid-1976). He makes two interesting conclusions:

"It may be possible to assume," he writes, "that the appointment of the new ambassador is to elevate Japan-Soviet relations from the administrative level to the political level." Then he adds: "It seems unmistakable that the Kremlin attaches importance to Japan's moves." Finally, possibly by way of alerting the Japanese readers to be prepared for the worst, the *Asahi* research chief concludes: "Former Ambassador Troyanovsky moved energetically to keep the Sino-Japanese treaty negotiations from making quick progress. The Soviet Union wants to press Japan to conclude a treaty of good neighborliness and cooperation at this juncture to make it an important cornerstone for its grand design, called an Asian collective security treaty. Is it not that Ambassador Polyansky, well aware of the Kremlin's intentions, will show bold political moves?"

Perhaps the most straightforward and direct statement on the nature of the potential Soviet threat to Japan comes (not surprisingly) from the Superintendent of Japan's Defense Academy, Masamichi Inoki, in a substantial article in *Chuo Koron* of November 1976 entitled, "How to Cope with the Soviet Threat." After detailing the process of the Soviet military buildup, Inoki argues: "It is quite natural for other countries to fear that the Soviet Union may have an intention of expanding its sphere of rule or influence by its expanded military power. Even if the Soviet side does not think that it is 'threatening,' a 'threat' exists at least potentially, when seen from an objective point of view."

Then Inoki's pointed conclusion: "Therefore to counter such a 'threat,' we must prevent this potential 'threat' from becoming an actual threat first of all. From Japan's position, the prerequisites are: (a) to improve its defense and rear support capabilities as a deterrent, and (b) to increase the dependability of the U.S.–Japan Security Treaty, so that the Soviet Union will not feel tempted to threaten Japan."[25]

In the same issue of *Chuo Koron* (November 1976), that journal's man in Paris, in an interview with Andrei Amalric, Soviet historian in exile, quotes him as warning Japan to have armaments, including thermonuclear arms, and not to be misled by the false optimism that the Soviet Union will not attack Japan.[26]

The importance of strengthening Japan's defenses represents the persistent opinion of a large segment of the Japanese population as sustained by a public opinion poll conducted about a year earlier by the Public Relations Office of the Cabinet Secretariat. That survey showed that 79 percent of the Japanese polled saw the need for Japan to develop its own self-defense forces. The report included a chart, Figure 1, reflecting Japanese opinion on the issue for the ten-year period 1965 through 1975.[27]

In the face of a torrent of Japanese press and editorial comment along

FIGURE 1

Perceived Need for the Self Defense Forces Over Time

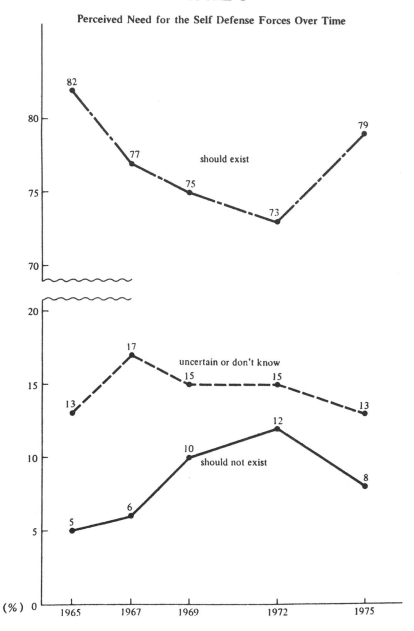

SOURCE: *Japan Report* (Issued by Japan Information Service, Consulate General of Japan, New York), May 1, 1976.

the above lines appearing in that nation's most widely read and influential newspapers and journals, in view of Japan's historical, traditional fear of "the neighbor to the North," we may not be surprised at the results—only the intensity—of very recent public opinion polls in Japan on the subject of the most "liked" and most "hated" nation and related international issues.

NATION BRANDING—THE JAPANESE
INTERNATIONAL ATTITUDE SPECTRUM

It is not usual to find in most major nations of the world the regular polling of the population on the question of "most liked" and "most hated" nation. But then, Japan is unusual in a number of ways. Several 1977 *Asahi* polls asking the questions "liked/disliked," and offering a spectrum of nation-choices, sum up present Japanese attitudes on the Soviet Union, the United States, and related political and security issues.

Some 1,500 Japanese were asked by *Asahi*, nationwide, early in 1977 their choice of the "most liked" country (*suki na kuni*). Here are the results:

Switzerland	30.2%
United States	30.0
Italy	22.0
Great Britain	19.0
China	6.8
Soviet Union	1.9
North Korea	0.6
South Korea	0.5

Apart from the traditional and consistent dichotomy between the "liked" United States (30 percent) and the very much "less liked" Soviet Union (1.9 percent) several other points may be noted. First, the attractiveness of the "policy of neutralism" and other national traits symbolized by Switzerland (30.2 percent) which emerges as the people's choice—however irrelevant or unrealistic in terms of Japan's present situation. Second, the Soviet Union (1.9 percent) appears, if possible, to be even losing ground in this curious popularity contest. Third, China remains low on the popularity scale (6.8 percent) for a variety of reasons already discussed. And fourth, North and South Korea compete (with 0.6 percent and 0.5 percent respectively) for the bottom of the chart.[28]

When the question is turned around and becomes, "most *hated*" country, Japanese anti-Soviet feeling (as of 1977) is unmistakable. In order of disdain (*Kirai*):[29]

Soviet Union	33.7%
South Korea	22.0
North Korea	21.1
China	12.0
United States	4.7
India	3.8
West Germany	3.1
Great Britain	1.5
Switzerland	0.1

Interviews by this author in Japan during 1975, 1976, and again in 1977 with leading Japanese government officials, Japanese businessmen, journalists, university professors, and others, suggest the following reasons (not necessarily in the order of importance) for the present state of Japanese public opinion on the Soviet Union, China, the United States, and related international and security issues.

- Traditional, historical Japanese distrust of Russia dating from early Tokugawa fear of attack on the northern frontiers, and sustained through the Russo-Japanese War, the Bolshevik Revolution, the several Soviet-Japanese border incidents in Manchuria, and so on.
- Japanese prewar fear and postwar memories of the Soviet-controlled Comintern and of "the dangerous thoughts" represented and fostered by International Communism and its agents in Asia.
- Soviet behavior toward Japan immediately before and during the Pacific War, especially the Soviet violation of the 1941 Neutrality Pact, the treatment of Japanese prisoners of war in Russia, and the later perceived seizure of "Japan's Northern Territories."
- The persistent Soviet capture of Japanese fishing boats and the internment of their crews accompanied by what is viewed in Japan as an excessively tough Moscow stand on the fisheries question.
- The perceptible Japanese feeling of isolation and insecurity in an increasingly Communist postwar Asia, especially after the Communist victory (read: U.S. defeat) in Vietnam and the possible implications for the "reliability" of other U.S. security and defense commitments in Asia, notably those with Japan, Taiwan, and the Republic of Korea.
- Japanese uncertainty over the direction of politics and opinion in the United States especially in the light of the change in administration in Washington in the direction of what many Japanese apparently regard as a confusing, passive, or at least something of an unknown quantity in foreign affairs, especially vis-à-vis Asia.

Chapter Eight

The Evolution of an "Independent" Japan Communist Party in a New Japan

Although perhaps out of tune with the Soviet policy of detente and at apparent odds with the message of the new Eurocommunism, it may still be correct to suggest that a Communist party—including the "independent" JCP—is not a political party in the usually accepted sense of the term. In the first place, over the years and throughout the world, Communist parties have not been primarily interested in votes at election time. Second, a full-blown formal ideology (Marxism-Leninism/Maoism in the case of Communist parties) is not normally espoused by or associated with most of the traditional Western-style political parties. Third, Communist parties are organized according to their members' place of work rather than their place of residence. Fourth, membership in a Communist party demands strict adherence to party discipline, mandatory dues, and regular (weekly) meetings. Fifth, the international orientation of a Communist party—at least until very recently—has always been its most distinguishing feature.

Another universal, though by no means unique, feature of Communist parties, is their inevitable totalitarian characteristic once in power (total planning implies total police power). At the same time, the manner in which this power is organized and employed has depended very much on the cultural and environmental variable as well as the nature of the particular leadership: Stalin was for all intents and purposes a later-day tsar; Tito a Balkan partisan; Ceausescu an Illyrian nationalist; Castro a Latin guerrilla; Hoxha a descendant of warring clansmen of the Gegh and Tosk tribes of Albania; Mao, the peasant emperor deified.[1] To the extent that such a perception suggests shades of nationalism and even the great-man theory of history (if turned on its head), it is, of course, a very un-Marxian view, but then so are innumerable other historical realities.

The JCP, then, in the New Japan, reflects in its policies and changing image an admix of external influence, the domestic environment, and the leadership variable.

POST-OCCUPATION READJUSTMENT
AND RETROSPECTION

The depths of readjustment and retrospection into which the JCP plunged in the post-Occupation period can only be fathomed within the context of the world-shaking events that occurred throughout the Communist realm during these critical years. One way or another individually or in the aggregate these events inevitably affected virtually all parties and peoples almost everywhere on the globe.

Whether one pursues the point down the twisted ideological path or along the rough power-politics road by computer or common sense it is difficult to escape the conclusion that immense changes were occurring in the wake of World War II, changes that would fundamentally alter attitudes, relative power positions, political alignments, even options of parties and nations for years to come.

Leaving aside for the moment the broader questions of changing strategic/ nuclear balance and comparative national economic prowess, certain decisive international political events of the postwar decade inevitably had powerful reverberations within the JCP ranks. By way of instant recall, we may remember in order of occurrence: the Soviet domination of Eastern Europe (1945–1947); Tito's celebrated break with Moscow (1948); the emergence of a Communist China as a second Marxist-Leninist-Maoist ideological power center in Asia (1949); the Cominform's criticism of Nosaka (1950); the Communist-initiated Korean War (1950–1953); the deaths of Stalin and Tokuda (1953); Khrushchev's "secret" anti-Stalin speech (1956); and the Polish and Hungarian revolutions (1956).

No wonder that the period following the deaths of Stalin and Tokuda (both in 1953) resulted in uncertainty and confusion within the JCP ranks, even as the radicalism and violence sanctioned by the party during the Korean War period (which witnessed intensification of the MacArthur crackdown on Communism) had produced disastrous, counter-productive results. During this same time span, it should be noted, a number of JCP cadre members fled to Peking where they were trained in special Chinese Communist schools before being returned to Japan some years later to join their Yenan-trained comrades and to enhance the degree of latent Peking orientation of the JCP.[2]

Some drastic post-Occupation policy changes were clearly in order if the

JCP was to meet the challenges at hand and seize the opportunities afforded in the new, democratic Japan within a "revolutionary" Asia. Attesting to the nature and degree of the JCP's immediate post-Occupation adjustment are the following trends and events within the party for the critical year 1953: continued self-criticism and "study" of the reasons for the resounding defeat of the party in the October 1952 and April 1953 elections in Japan—a defeat generally interpreted as public disapproval of the party's 1951–1952 violent tactics; the conspicuous absence (apart from minor and isolated incidents) of violence such as characterized the February and May riots of the previous year; the development by the party of an extensive "peace movement" coincident with the end of the Korean War; increased activity in the legal-political realm; concentration with renewed vigor on the labor movement, especially the 3 million member *Sohyo* trade union confederation; an increase in the number and circulation of legal JCP publications and the emergence of several organs from covert to overt status; a deemphasis of military activities (i.e., military action squads, "shock troops").[3]

A new "interim party program," adopted in November 1953, frankly admitted that the balance of power between the East and the West was unfavorable to the Communists and called upon the party to "increase Communist strength by strengthening the Communist Party, the National Liberation Front, and the Democratic United Front." It also characterized as "nonsense" any attempt to schedule a revolution at what it called "the present stage." Instead, it placed emphasis on strengthening a united front for bringing about an anti-American, anti-Yoshida, and antirearmament movement, in essence, it may be noted, precisely the policy of the "independent" JCP. The party then listed nine items as tactical objectives for attaining the larger goal: opposition to the San Francisco Peace Treaty, the Japan–United States Security Treaty, and U.S. interference in Japan's domestic affairs; opposition to foreign military bases; demand for the withdrawal of foreign troops; restoration of just and fair relations with all countries including the Soviet Union and Communist China, revival of free trade on the basis of equality and reciprocity, opposition to international trade under U.S. unilateral control; freedom to travel to foreign countries; opposition to the militarization of industry, guarantee of peaceful development of industry; freedom of assembly, speech, and association, complete guarantee of people's democratic rights; opposition to the revival of militarism and to the mercenary armed force of the United States; opposition to the Pacific military alliances and all other aggressive military alliance under any name; overthrow of the Yoshida government.[4]

Seven of these nine planks, it may be noted, were directly related to the party's formal reentry into the arena of international relations concomitant with Japan's reassertion of sovereignty.

THE CHANGING INTERNATIONAL SCENE
AND PREVAILING PARTY UNCERTAINTY

Given the traumatic events that followed in the wake of Stalin's and Tokuda's deaths and in view of the confused situation within the JCP during the immediate post-Occupation era, the months between November 1953 and the Sixth Party Conference of mid-1955 may perhaps best be described as a time of prevailing uncertainty. The struggle for the helm in Moscow among Beria, Molotov, Malenkov, Kaganovich, Bulganin, and Khrushchev, in effect, left the international Communist ship adrift. The death of JCP leader Kyuichi Tokuda in November 1953 in Peking (where along with numerous other Japanese party members he had been in self-imposed exile) further complicated the confused leadership issue in Japan. The result was a hiatus in JCP–CPSU (Communist Party of the Soviet Union) relations during which interval the People's Republic of China came to acquire a measure of the proletarian international symbolism traditionally reserved by the JCP for the Soviet Union.[5]

Moreover, it may be recalled in this context that while the JCP under remote control by Tokuda had engaged in the military activities already described, a rising star, Kenji Miyamoto (ultimately to become secretary general of the party), and his group opposed this policy as, in effect, being of misguided Peking inspiration. Yet in August of 1951 when Satomi Hakamada, Miyamoto's right-hand man, had accompanied Tokuda to the Soviet capital to meet the boss, Stalin is thought to have supported Tokuda's policy and virtually ordered Hakamada to dissolve a "unity committee" which he and Miyamoto had organized to attempt to heal the wounds within the troubled and uncertain party.

In any case, by the time of the historic JCP Sixth National Council Meeting in July of 1955, the former so-called "mainstream" leadership faction (whose leader, Tokuda, had meanwhile died) and the group that had come to be known as the "international faction" (under Miyamoto and Hakamada) had affected a reconciliation. A new consolidated alignment emerged, which significantly included in its ranks the venerable Nosaka, whose fine hand over the years was never to be found far from the scene of decisive party action.[6]

The extent of Chinese Communist interest and influence in JCP affairs by this time may be judged from the report of a participant in a discussion of high-ranking Japanese Communist leaders in 1955. According to veteran JCP leader Kasuga Shojiro, when the issue of self-criticism of "ultra-left adventurism" was being debated, Nosaka cautioned that extensive self-criticism regarding militant tactics might "disturb" the Chinese comrades. "Nosaka then proceeded to mention the names of several Chinese leaders, asserting that they had promised to provide any form of aid that the Japanese Communist Party would need, including military equipment when and if it were required."[7]

It should be added for the record that the Moscow-Peking Treaty of Friendship and Alliance concluded in 1950 was at this time presumably still firmly in place, so it was not a matter of the JCP—as yet—being obliged to choose sides.[8]

RETURN TO LEGALISM—
ON THE MOSCOW-PEKING TIGHTROPE

The Sixth National Party Congress of the JCP, held in 1955, formally signaled the party's return to legalism. It also, in effect, placed the party on the tricky Moscow-Peking tightrope. It was at this juncture that a number of the JCP leaders, including Nosaka, emerged from hiding for the first time since 1950.[9] Moreover, in the period from 1953 through 1957 some 1,500 Japanese Communists are reported to have been "in training" in Communist China. Many of them returned home in 1958 to bolster Peking's influence within the once Moscow-oriented JCP.[10] A transitional period thus began with the Sixth National Council meeting in the summer of 1955; it encompassed the important Moscow Declaration of November 1957,[11] and struck a new strategic note with the Seventh JCP Congress in July of 1958.

The party now attempted to walk a tenuous tightrope with a policy that presumed somehow to be both pro-Soviet and pro-Chinese at the same time. Since the JCP had not yet even hinted that trouble was brewing between Moscow and Peking, this policy presented fewer obstacles than would otherwise have been the case. On one hand, in its response to the new program of the 20th Party Congress of the CPSU (1956), the JCP had nothing but praise for the Soviet efforts—if with no reference to Stalin. On the other hand, the JCP's 1957 program (officially presented to the Seventh Party Congress which after a delay actually convened July 21 to August 1, 1958) displayed a strong Chinese flavor.

The parameters of this JCP ambivalent policy were defined in two major articles that appeared in *Akahata* about this time. Not far below the verbal surface, one senses the depths and dimensions of the party dilemma, indeed, the spark of "autonomy." The party was "to keep on friendly terms with all countries." The party strongly backed the peaceful unification of Vietnam and Korea. It was also necessary to reopen "equal diplomatic relations" with East Germany. The party called further for the immediate conclusion of a peace treaty with the Soviet Union, restoration of diplomatic relations with Communist China, increased trade with the continent, and the return of

Okinawa to Japan. The delicate question of the "Northern Territories" was handled gingerly by pointing out that the Socialist party, victim of Liberal-Democratic party propaganda, was demanding return of southern Sakhalin and the entire Kuriles, which, the party insisted "will rather confuse the people." Finally, the JCP asked for the revision of the "unequal peace treaty," and abrogation of the Japan–United States Security Treaty and the Administrative and MSA agreements.[12]

THE INTERVAL OF CAUTIOUS NEUTRALITY

A brief interval during which the JCP leaders displayed a conspicuous tendency toward cautious neutrality in the Sino-Soviet dispute may be dated from the Moscow conference of 81 Communist parties in November 1960.[13] It was Khrushchev himself who set the tone when he said that Communist parties in the future would be able to "synchronize their watches" without direct guidance from Moscow, but merely by the light of their common interests.[14] This moderate tack seemed clearly designed to placate Peking and counsel unity, and was no doubt so regarded by the JCP leadership which, once more, chose to remain silent on the matter.

On the occasion of the 22nd Congress of the CPSU in Moscow in the fall of 1961, Khrushchev's public attack upon Albania (read: China) and Chou En-lai's hostile response signaled a discernible public escalation in the Moscow-Peking dispute. Communist parties throughout the world and delegates at the conference in particular were now under obvious pressure to declare their alliance to Moscow as that was what the conference was all about in the first place.[15] In his speech before the Soviet Congress on October 23, 1961, Sanzo Nosaka pointedly refrained from criticizing the ever irascible Enver Hoxha and other pro-Peking Albanian leaders, preferring instead to urge world Communist unity on the basis of the 1957 and 1960 Moscow agreements.[16]

Then, on November 18, 1961, in a Tokyo speech paying tribute to the Russian revolution, Nosaka placed the CPSU ahead of all other parties in the "task of constructing Communism" and alluded to the Sino-Soviet dispute only obliquely by stressing the necessity for continued unity on the part of Communist parties, which he said (without specifying) "no imperialist machinations could destroy."[17]

By the end of the year, however, JCP neutralism, or at least caution, was waning, for on December 29, 1961, an *Akahata* editorial for the first time clearly implied disapproval of Khrushchev's open criticism of Albania.[18] It seemed now only a matter of time before the JCP would be forced to take a public stand rejecting any suggestion of continued Moscow control.

THE SWING TO PEKING

During the years 1963 through 1965, JCP policy began to swing noticeably in the direction of Peking. This development should have come as no
complete surprise to observers of Soviet foreign policy, the world Communist movement, or the Asian scene. Only a few of the salient reasons for such
a move need be recorded here, not necessarily in order of importance.

The JCP's retrospective perception of prewar Moscow as a ruthless,
dictatorial overlord could hardly have been favorably changed by Soviet
postwar policy and practice in Eastern Europe. Until the advent of the
Moscow-Peking split, however, and the emergence of a second Communist
power center in Asia, no viable world Communist leadership alternative was
available to the Japanese—even assuming that such an alternative might
have been welcomed. Moreover, the experience of the Chinese comrades
with perceived Soviet dictatorial high-handedness during the height of the
Moscow-Peking treaty years (1950–1958)—as no doubt related by the Chinese in excruciating detail to the Japanese comrades—must have reinforced
doubts as to the virtue of close future JCP relations with the CPSU.

On the more positive side (if that's the word for it) the proximity, the
historical and cultural affinity of Japan and China, as well as the increasing
number and influence of JCP cadres with varying degrees of training and
experience in the People's Republic of China must also weigh in the equation. The advent of the Soviet policy of coexistence and detente, then, merely
added opportunity to rationale. Looked at in another way, the JCP swing to
Peking may be viewed as a kind of balance-of-power maneuver, with
greater JCP autonomy within the world of Communism as the unstated,
ultimate goal.

Evidence that the JCP had at this juncture decided to cast its lot on major
policy questions with Peking is overwhelming. A reading of *Akahata* of the
period (beginning with the autumn of 1963) supplies abundant detail.
Concise and convincing documentation is provided by the following four
issues: on the Sino-Indian border dispute, the JCP supported its Chinese
comrades, reproducing the complete text of China's denunciation of Nehru
in *Akahata*; during the Cuban crisis, the JCP reproduced the Chinese not
the Soviet arguments against American imperialism; on the Albanian-
Yugoslavia issue where the JCP was considerably more friendly toward the
Albanian (pro-Chinese) than the Yugoslavian comrades; with respect to
the partial Nuclear Test Ban Treaty, *Akahata* published an article in
October 1963 strongly opposing the treaty—Soviet participation in the
agreement was barely mentioned.[19]

This swing to Peking may also be traced through the turbulent meetings
of the *Gensuikyo* (Japan Council against Atomic and Hydrogen Bombs).

The ninth conference of that organization took place in August of 1963 with both Soviet and Chinese delegates present and only ten days after the United States, the Soviet Union, and Great Britain had signed the Limited Test Ban Treaty. That treaty, it may be remembered, was bitterly opposed by Peking as strongly suggesting a Soviet-American rapprochement, if not nascent conspiracy against Communist China. The sessions in Tokyo during August produced new heights of bitterness: Zhukov branded the Chinese "madmen" for opposing the Test Ban Treaty, and then reminded the Chinese comrades of the Soviet assistance in Mao's revolution. Had they forgotten? Chou, incensed and pointedly sarcastic, insisted that China had achieved the revolutionary victory quite on its own.[20]

With the convening of the JCP's Seventh Central Committee Plenum in October of 1963, there could be no doubt as to where the party stood on the delicate matter of relations with Moscow and Peking, despite the still slightly veiled language: ". . . in the open criticism against the Chinese and Albanian Parties at a number of fraternal party congresses from the end of 1962 to the beginning of 1963" the Central Committee resolution states, "our Party has made active efforts dedicated to the solidarity of the international Communist movement and the Socialist camp." But, the resolution concludes: ". . . as evidence of solidarity within the international Communist movement has grown stronger, and disputes among [between] Parties have become more severe, particularly in the case of the Chinese Communist Party . . . the argument is spreading to the effect that the CPSU has the right to be trusted unconditionally by each fraternal party . . . as if it were wrong to criticize [Moscow]."[21]

In this atmosphere the JCP could hardly remain neutral—and did not. The leadership (mainstream) now not only systematically removed all pro-Soviet elements from key party posts, but began curtailing the activities of such key front organizations in Japan as the Japan–Soviet Union Society. Japan Communist Party headquarters even began restricting or prohibiting the dissemination of what was for the first time tabbed "Russian propaganda in Japan."[22]

When in May 1964 the partial Nuclear Test Ban Treaty came up for the long-awaited vote in the Japanese House of Representatives, Anastas Mikoyan, Soviet First Deputy Premier, was sitting in the visitors' gallery. Only one JCP delegate out of four, Yoshio Shiga, voted for the treaty. For this action, which he later defended, he was suspended as a JCP Diet member and ultimately expelled from the party, along with several other "errant" JCP members. On June 30, 1964, Shiga announced the formation of the "Voice of Japan Comrades Society," a move suggesting that a rival Communist party in Japan might be on the horizon. As the mainstream of the party continued to lean toward Peking, Shiga was to become the alternate "darling" of the Soviets—Moscow's man in Japan.

This all took place even as a bitter exchange of letters between the CPSU and the JCP continued. Moscow charged: under Chinese influence the JCP had begun to "cater to nationalist and chauvinist sentiments"; at meetings between the JCP and CPSU delegations held in Moscow in March, JCP leaders had "ignored fundamental issues" and directed all their efforts toward "accusing the Soviets of interference in the affairs of their party."

The JCP rejoinder insisted that the first issue that was to be settled was the "unpardonable interference of the Soviet Union in the internal affairs of the Japanese Communist Party." The Soviet party was guilty of "big nation chauvinism." Moreover, the Russians had not hesitated to "use spies in an effort to disrupt the JCP." The Japanese party better understood the meaning of true Marxism-Leninism. And on and on. . . .[23]

The 1972 official Japanese party history, published by the Central Committee and entitled *Fifty Years of the JCP*, directly attacks Soviet interference in the internal affairs of Japan, or more particularly of the Japan Communist Party, during the mid-1960s and leaves no doubt as to the seriousness of the matter. The pertinent passage reads:

> Khrushchev and others had been engaged in the interference of the internal affairs of the JCP in an attempt to demand uncritical and blind obedience to the CPSU, but in August of 1963 when the JCP made public its independent and critical view with respect to the conclusion of the Limited Nuclear Test Ban Treaty, Khrushchev and others published Zhukov's essay, "The Voice of Hiroshima," in *Pravda* and openly began attacking the Party and stepped up their pressure and interference.
>
> The Party had from the beginning consistently made its position clear: it would fight against invasion and war by American imperialism; maintain its independent position of not following any foreign party nor allowing interference by any party. . . .[24]

THE BREAK WITH PEKING AND
BRIEF JCP-CPSU SECOND HONEYMOON

Charges of "Big Powerism" were not long confined exclusively to attacks on Moscow. Peking soon came in for its share of criticism as the Japanese party struggled through the turbulent sixties on the "inevitable" road to "independence." After an unsigned article in *Akahata* had urged an international Moscow-Peking front against U.S. imperialism, a JCP mission headed by Miyamoto toured Communist China, North Vietnam, and North

Korea. While details are fragmentary, it seems clear from subsequent developments that the trip proved a disappointment, if not a rebuff. One account speculates: "Miyamoto had gone to Communist China to persuade the Peking leaders to agree to his line. When he met Mao Tse-tung at the latter's villa in Hangchow, however, he found Mao in no mood to be persuaded." Then this account adds: "Mao dealt with Miyamoto as a representative of an insignificant Communist Party in a capitalist society which had not yet achieved the revolution."[25]

Miyamoto, for his public part, makes no reference to disagreement or disappointments during his trip to China. Indeed, while stressing the "independence" of the JCP, throughout his writings and speeches, he carefully avoids leaving the impression of hostility toward the People's Republic of China. "Simply because we do not take time to praise every event that takes place in China does not mean," he cautioned (shortly after his trip), "that we are unfriendly toward China."[26]

In any case, the JCP's anti-Peking policy now became increasingly evident and active; attacks in *Akahata* against the Chinese multiplied as the elimination of pro-Peking members of JCP organizations—paralleling the earlier pro-Soviet ousters—was stepped up. At the same time attacks on the Soviet Union were continued. On August 8, 1966, in an unusually direct article in *Akhata* entitled, "On the Strengthening of International United Action and the United Front Against American Imperialism," the Japanese party went so far as to accuse Khrushchev of having been responsible for disunity within the International Communist movement and to request a new assessment of Soviet leadership.[27]

By the summer of 1967, worsening relations between the JCP and Peking had reached the point where the JCP began naming Chinese names. The Japanese party's open criticism of the Chinese party now included among other items the following serious allegation against the CCP:

(1) Treading on the principles of autonomy, equality, and non-interference in internal affairs, which have been the basis of friendship and solidarity between the Japanese and Chinese people since last year [1966]; (2) Unilateral imposition upon Japan-China friendship and trade organizations of praise for "Mao Tse-tung's thoughts" and Chinese "Great Cultural Revolution" and support for the attack on the JCP; (3) Destruction of the solidarity of these organizations; (4) Declaring the intention to deal, on "Japan-China friendship" matters, with only those elements that destroy the solidarity of the above organizations and blindly follow the ultra-leftist opportunist and big-powerist elements of the Chinese Communist Party.[28]

How concerned Moscow by this time had become over the disintegrating revolutionary situation in Japan may be judged by the fact that in January of 1968, a top-ranking delegation led by none other than Presidium member and top ideologue, Mikhail Suslov, visited Japan to attempt to repair the ruptured interparty relations. A high-level JCP-CPSU conference was held from January 31 to February 5, 1968, with a resulting joint communiqué published in *Akahata*, which said in part:

> ... the delegates of both parties agree to re-examine the virtual sever-
> ance of all ties between the JCP and the CPSU since 1964 and further
> pledge to solve the major problems impeding normalization of the
> relationship between the parties. In addition, the delegates of both
> parties acknowledge the prime importance of the principles of inde-
> pendence, equality, and non-intervention in the internal problems of
> the fraternal parties as specified in the Statement of the Moscow Con-
> ference of the Communist and Workers Parties in 1960.[29]

Contacts and follow-up discussions continued and in August of 1968 a JCP mission headed by Hakamada visited Moscow for formal discussions between the Communist parties of the two countries.[30]

But talk is cheap, and the second honeymoon was short-lived. Concilia-tion was abruptly reversed by the Soviet invasion of Czechoslovakia barely six months after the perennial pledge of non-interference in internal affairs. On August 25, 1968, *Akahata* categorically denounced the Soviet Union for its violation of the sovereign independence of another fraternal nation and demanded an immediate end to the intervention and prompt troop with-drawal.[31] Why in the light of the Soviet historical record in Eastern Europe and elsewhere, yet another such Soviet act of aggression should have come as a surprise or shock to anyone, especially a seasoned Communist party, must remain a mystery.

THE CONSOLIDATION OF INDEPENDENCE

That the errant comrades in Japan were, from the Moscow or Peking perspectives, increasingly up to no revolutionary good could be discerned by even a casual reading of the Japanese Communist press and the Soviet and Chinese responses during the years of JCP consolidation of "independ-ence," 1970–1978. The two issues on which the JCP and the CCP have had the most fundamental disagreement are the CCP's placing "Soviet revision-ism" and "American imperialism" on the same level, as "enemies," and the JCP's stated policy of seeking power through parliamentary means.

As if to remove any lingering doubts regarding its dedication to "independence," JCP Presidium member Koreto Kurahara, at a rally on May 26, 1970, criticized both the Russian and Chinese Communist parties for what he termed "big-powerism" and "chauvinism." He then went on to stress the party's autonomous line, indicating that the meaning of "dictatorship of the proletariat" must be redefined and insisting that violence need play no part in future revolutionary activities.[32] The JCP now proceeded down a relatively consistent and determined path designed to consolidate, clarify, and even elaborate its concepts, policy, and practice of "independence."

A few of the highlights of the many milestones of the 1970s along that strategic road served to illuminate the scene brightly enough for the question to become of obvious and vocal concern to the erstwhile fraternal and sometime controlling parties in Moscow and Peking.

Toward the end of 1971, Party Secretary General Kenji Miyamoto initiated the JCP's own version of people's shuttle diplomacy with the first of a series of visits to Romania, Italy, North Vietnam, and elsewhere. Then on the occasion of the Japanese party's 50th Anniversary, on July 15, 1972, the JCP held an "international" conference to which it invited like-minded representatives from Australia, West Germany, Britain, France, Italy, Spain, and the United States. The conference, which lasted four days, could only have been calculated to cause further consternation within the twin capitals of world Communism. This process of "people's diplomacy" continued and expanded over the next months.

The 50th anniversary of a history studded with lavish thanks for the assistance of "fraternal Soviet and Chinese Parties" was a year, by contrast, which saw only JCP criticism of Moscow and Peking plus a persistent party hammering on the "independence" theme. Generally conceded to be related to its new, self-projected image, the elections in December of that same year brought the party's strength in the House of Representatives to an unprecedented 40—the third-ranking party after the Liberal Democrats (LDP) and the Japanese Socialist parties (JSP).

While the JCP continued to attack Peking, the Chinese Communists for their part lost no opportunity to express their contempt for the "independent" JCP. On one occasion, Chou En-lai said, "The revisionism of the JCP is unthinkable." On another, Chou castigated the JCP, lumping it together with the conservative wing of the LDP and the Chiang Kai-shek government on Taiwan as an "ultra-rightist" force opposing the normalization of Japan-China relations.[33]

At the same time, the "independent" party continued to blast away at Moscow and at virtually all that "international communism" of the past presumably stood for. The JCP's fourth Central Committee plenary session held August 2 to 4, 1974, was unusual, among unusual happenings in some very usual years. Its decisions on a study of education included shockingly unorthodox comments and actions such as "the writings of Marx and Lenin may not always elucidate all revolutionary movements in the future world," and removing from the authorized book list 22 classic texts including *The Manifesto of the Communist Party* and *State and Revolution* as well as both the Moscow Declaration of 1957 and the Moscow Statement of 1960 in order "to prevent Japanese Communists from displaying dogmatic obedience to them."

By the spring of 1975, the consolidation of "independence" on the part of the JCP seemed virtually complete. The party had sorted out its "anti" priorities. Accordingly, *Akahata* reported in an unsigned (and therefore very authoritative article): "The biggest hegemonist in the World is U.S. imperialism, but both the Soviet Union and China are abusing their big power-ist hegemony."[34] The year 1975 also saw JCP "independent" international relations in the form of personal mission and delegate diplomacy blossom profusely. In that single year alone the following activity may be recorded: JCP mission to Yugoslavia and Vietnam (January/February); two separate JCP delegations to Romania (March/August); visit by Romanian President Nicolae Ceausescu to Tokyo for talks with Miyamoto (April 4–9); JCP delegation to Cuba (May 10–19); JCP delegation named to 21st Congress of the CPUSA (visa refused, June); JCP delegation to Laos, Vietnam, and Lebanon (August); Nosaka to Hanoi (August/September); Communist parties of France, Vietnam, and Romania send representatives to JCP "Akahata Festival" in Tokyo (October 10–11); French Communist party delegation, led by Paul Laurant (member of Politburo) to Tokyo for talks with Miyamoto (October 12–19).[35]

Perhaps to add thrust and international recognition to the new independent party, the JCP official publications gave unusually prominent and pointed coverage to the joint declaration issued in mid-November 1975 by the heads of the Communist parties of Italy and France expressing commitment to independence, democracy, and human rights—principles which, it was suggested, paralleled those of the JCP.[36] The Japanese party seemed to be insinuating itself into the ranks of Eurocommunism, and this was only the beginning.

During the ensuing years (1976–1978), the substantial "practical contacts" developed and expanded earlier were sustained and augmented. Continued visits to and from Spanish and French Communist parties appear to have especially troubled Moscow. Visits by the JCP also included important conferences in Romania, Yugoslavia, and Algeria while representatives of the Communist party of Cuba visited Japan upon JCP invitation. The JCP also sent an observer to the conference of nonaligned nations in Colombo, Sri Lanka (in August of 1976). Top JCP officials attended the Vietnam party congress in Hanoi at the end of the year.[37]

Thus, the JCP's "independent" international relations now moved from the realm of rhetoric and policy to what can only be regarded in Moscow and Peking as an even more dangerous plane—the field of action with like-minded "independent" parties jointly "plotting" autonomous moves everywhere.

The top leadership of the "independent" JCP consists of the "Godfather" Sanzo Nosaka (in semi-retirement); the "father," powerful Party Presidium Chairman Kenji Miyamoto; and a newcomer, Secretary Tetsu Fuwa. Each in his own way has displayed conspicuous inclinations toward "independence" for varying periods of time.[38]

There is considerable evidence to suggest that since 1976 Moscow had become sufficiently concerned over the rapid deterioration of its relations with the Japanese party and by the advent of Eurocommunism in East Asia (added to the burden of Chinese chauvinism) for some Soviet conciliation to be in order. It was in this context that the JCP was invited by the Soviet party to attend its 25th Congress in the spring of 1976. Moscow even sent two Soviet Central Committee members to Tokyo to "persuade" the Japanese colleagues of the value of repentance or at least cooperation. But the Japanese politely turned down the invitation on the grounds that *Pravda*'s earlier support of the pro-Soviet splinter group, "Shiga's Voice of Japan," had not yet been disavowed. Moreover, the CPSU was not invited to be represented at the JCP's Thirteenth Extraordinary Congress in July of 1976. The meeting nonetheless was given extensive coverage in the Soviet press and Moscow cabled congratulations expressing "solidarity with the struggle of the JCP members . . . who are striving to create a Japan founded on peace, democracy and social progress."[39] Then, putting the cap on official Soviet overtures, at a plenary session of the Central Committee of the CPSU on October 25, 1976, Brezhnev—in an obvious "if you can't fight 'em, join 'em" public mood, expressed his hopes for success in the activities of "popular Communist parties" in Japan, France, and Italy, three of the six advanced capitalist countries.

A year later (November 1977), in his report on the "Great October and the Progress of Mankind," Brezhnev again struck a somewhat cautious and ambivalent note when referring to the troublesome parties: "Their theoretical principles . . . ," he said, "contain some interesting propositions although probably not everything can be regarded as finally decided upon and incontrovertible. This is understandable," Brezhnev added, concluding: "A search is a search. What is important is that it proceed in the right direction."[40]

The fortunes of the JCP during 1977 and 1978 have wavered and waned. Its claims that party membership grew from 7,500 in 1946 to "nearly 400,000 in 1977" must be viewed against other known facts. The jubilation engendered by the 1972 victory where the party won the largest number of seats in its history (39) and polled 10.49 percent of the popular vote, was not to last. Having lost more than one-half its seats (dropping from 39 to 19) in the December 1976 lower house elections, a further Communist defeat was registered in the July 1977 upper house election when the JCP seats were reduced from 20 to 16. Moreover, a serious crisis in the top leadership culminated in January of 1978 with the expulsion from the party of veteran leader Satomi Hakamada.

Hakamada will be remembered as a Moscow-trained party member since 1928, Chairman of the JCP Central Committee during the turbulent 1930s, and one of the triumvirate (with Nozaka and Miyamoto), which led the mainstream and guided the party during the late 1950s and 1960s. Perhaps even more significantly, he had been Vice-President of the Standing Committee of the Presidium, the all-powerful politburo. "His unforgivable sin," John Emmerson writes, "was to break into non-Communist print," with a series of articles in which, among other things, he accused Miyamoto of murder during an incident in 1933, which has for years been a matter of embarrassment within JCP ranks. The reaction in Japanese political circles has been the most "interested" since the celebrated ouster of Yoshio Shiga for, in his case, pro-Soviet sentiments.

What does the future hold for Communism in Japan? First, the party is not likely to revert soon either to a pro-Moscow or pro-Peking stance, but is likely to continue to pursue the more appealing, "peaceful, independent" line. Second, the party can scarcely hope to return, in the near future, to the day when it controlled 70 seats in the Diet. Third, confidence in the party leadership is bound to have been shaken by the Hakamada expulsion, but the JCP, as we have seen, has been accustomed in the past to unexpected leadership challenges. (The full impact of the Hakamada affair upon the rank and file has yet to be recorded.) Fourth, the JCP despite its "independent" stand, will most certainly continue to focus on "the evils of American imperialism" and the dangers of the "military alliance between Japan, South Korea, and the United States." Finally, it would be difficult to improve on John Emmerson's perceptive prognosis, to wit: "Anything but dead, the Communist party of Japan will undoubtedly continue to play an active if modest role in Japanese politics though both trends in Japanese public opinion and the increasing sophistication of the other Japanese political parties may be expected to reduce the JCP's political leverage and curtail its propaganda potential for the immediate future."[41]

Part Four

Economic Relations:
Joint Ventures and Trade in Siberia and Elsewhere

Chapter Nine

Joint Economic Ventures in Siberia

Sailing into the crowded commercial port of Nakhodka on a Soviet ship, traveling on the Trans-Siberian Railway, viewing the new Soviet cities of Siberia (even via television from Moscow), or in Khabarovsk, listening firsthand to plans for Siberian development from specialists at the New Scientific Center in Vladivostok, leaves one with the inescapable conclusion that the Soviets have recently rediscovered Siberia.[1]

SIBERIA—RUSSIA'S TREASURE HOUSE

In a very real sense, Siberia and the Soviet Far East may be called the Russian treasure house. A major portion of the nation's natural resources may be found in these, until very recently, remote regions. With respect to certain strategic raw materials, the area holds perhaps the leading position in the world. Half the country's coal reserves, 37 percent of its lumber reserves, some 32 percent of the utilizable water energy resources, huge deposits of iron ore, nonferrous metals as well as rare and precious metals, chemical raw material, and a host of other valuable resources abound in the region.[2]

The conclusions accompanying an analysis of "Soviet Dependence on Siberian Resource Development" prepared in 1976 at the Library of Congress by Alan B. Smith place the Soviet treasure house in economic perspective and underline its vital and growing importance to the Soviet Union and Japan:

The U.S.S.R. is accelerating development of Siberian resources out of economic necessity. Continued growth of the Soviet and East European economies will depend to an increasing degree on Siberian resources.

About 80 percent of the energy used in the Soviet Union is consumed in the European part of the country, but 80 percent of the reserves of primary energy lie east of the Urals.

. . . Exports of Siberian oil and gas, timber, gold, diamonds, platinum group metals, and perhaps eventually other minerals and metals can finance needed imports from the West. Development of chemical complexes and other types of industry based on Siberian electric power and raw materials can reduce dependence on certain types of imports. Development of Siberian resources will be greatly facilitated if the U.S.S.R. has access to Western technology and equipment either through joint ventures, commodity pay-back arrangements, or conventional commercial deals. This is especially true in the case of exploration and development of offshore oil and gas reserves, and in certain branches of the chemical industry. Development of Siberian resources is inevitable, however, and can and will be carried out entirely with the Soviet's own resources if need be. In this case, development will be somewhat slower and more expensive. . . . Production east of Lake Baykal will support development of the Soviet Far East and exports, primarily to Japan and other Asiatic countries, but perhaps also in some small part to the U.S. west coast.[3]

THE SOVIET REDISCOVERY OF SIBERIA

Over the past decade, with the rediscovery of Siberia, the Soviet leadership has assigned increasingly high priority to the economic development of that great Russian treasure house—and in this effort Japan has been encouraged to play a significant role. That this Soviet policy and process, so evident in the bilateral treaties and joint ventures of the 1960s, is likely to continue—even accelerate—may be judged from the prominence given the matter by Premier Kosygin and company on the occasion of the 25th Soviet Party Congress early in 1976. Soviet interest and rationale may be judged from the following passage taken from the latest plan:

The "Directives for Development of the U.S.S.R. National Economy in 1976–1980" adopted in March at the 25th Congress of the Communist Party of the Soviet Union call for: Further build-up of economic potential of the eastern regions and the raising of their role in all-union industrial output; accelerated development of the fuel industry and of energy-intensive production facilities for ferrous and nonferrous metallurgy and for the chemical and petrochemical industries;

comprehensive development of the economy, increase in the extraction of rare and precious metals, and of diamonds, and in the output of products of the timber, pulp and paper and furniture industries.[4]

These recent major Soviet policy enunciations merely formalized and elevated to the highest governmental level the essence of a great many earlier statements and actions: the economy-linked bilateral treaties of the 1960s; the initiation of a series of joint conferences on "Business Cooperation" in 1966; the first timber agreement of 1968; increasing attention in *Pravda* and other Soviet publications to the economic importance of Japan in Soviet development plans.

Moscow moved aggressively into the 1970s—still bypassing agreement on the fisheries and territorial issues—by continuing, even upgrading, the series of joint conferences on mutual economic cooperation and joint Siberian development. The fifth such joint conference of the "Soviet-Japanese and Japanese-Soviet Commissions for Business Cooperation," which met in Tokyo in February of 1972 at the headquarters of the Japanese Federation of Economic Organizations (*Keidanren*), provided *Pravda* with the occasion to review the situation and to stress the progress to date of the several Siberian joint development projects.

"The results of previous conferences have taken concrete form in three general agreements already in effect. The agreement (in 1968) on cooperation in developing the lumber resources of the Soviet Far East is being successfully implemented," the report notes. "In December 1970," the report continued, "an agreement was concluded on cooperation between Soviet and Japanese organizations and firms in building a new port in Wrangel Bay, near the port of Nakhodka." Then the review adds: ". . . a short time ago, in December 1971, an agreement was signed on cooperation between the appropriate organizations of the two countries in setting up facilities in the Soviet Union for production of industrial chips and deciduous pulpwood."

Finally, we are told in the same *Pravda* report, "K. Uemura, President of the Japanese Federation of Economic Organizations and head of the Japanese delegation, opened the session." Pointing to the future, Uemura announced that "the chief items on the agenda would be discussion of these questions: Construction of an oil pipeline to the port of Nakhodka—through which pipeline Tyumen oil could reach Japan; development of Southern Yakutia coal deposits; and prospecting for oil and gas on the shelf of Sakhalin Island."[5]

Several significant advances in communications and trade further serve to underline the Soviet rediscovery of Siberia and to make clear Soviet intentions of maximizing efforts toward: the exploitation of the Siberian strategic resources; the development, settlement, and integration of the area more closely into the USSR—that is, the more effective linkage of European and Asiatic Russia; the encouragement of Japanese scientific, technical, and economic participation in the joint Siberian development projects; and a substantial increase in trade between the two nations with special interest in trade between Japan and the Soviet Far East.[6]

These communications advances and developments involve several substantial endeavors: first, a crash program designed to complete work on the celebrated and important Baikal-Amur second Siberian railway (BAM); second, the construction of a second major port, Wrangel, to augment the crowded, inadequate facilities of Nakhodka and designed specifically to meet the requirements of trade with Japan; third, the conclusion with Japan of a whole series of treaties and agreements covering scientific and technical exchange, Siberian airspace and related regulations, as well as a wide range of other "communications" linked matters.

Treaties and agreements in the communications area concluded during the decade 1966–1975, having direct or indirect bearing on Siberian development, tell the story in impressive, formal terms. The communications aspects covered by the documentation include Aviation Communication (January 1966); Japanese Flights over Siberian Air Space (April 1969); Letters and Appendix, Aviation Communication (December 1969); Aviation Communication (April 1971); Modification, Appendix Aviation Communication (June 1973); Scientific and Technological Cooperation (October 1973); Exchange of Scientists and Research Workers (October 1973); and International Sea and Air Transport (July 1975).[7]

So much for important bilateral treaties and agreements of the past decade, in one way or another related to the communications aspect of joint Soviet-Japanese Siberian development activities. Construction of the Wrangel Port will be treated separately as one of the joint development projects. This leaves only the new BAM railway, which because of its extraordinary potential in the future development of Siberia, and ultimately its importance to the success of expanded large-scale economic exchange between Japan and the USSR, we dare not pass by without appropriate consideration.

THE BAIKAL-AMUR MAINLINE RAILWAY (BAM)

Clearly one of the major projects destined to play a critical role in both Siberian development and the enhancement of Soviet-Japanese economic relations is BAM, a second trans-Siberian railway now under active construction. Stalin had, in fact, begun construction of BAM in the 1930s, but work was interrupted during World War II, again resumed after the war with Japanese POW labor, then halted after Stalin's death. As early as 1969 *Izvestiia* once more could report that construction of the BAM railroad would start from the western end in 1970. Brezhnev later announced that the Soviet Union would embark on construction of BAM in March 1974. As to Japan's role in the project, the Soviet leadership had told Prime Minister Tanaka when the latter was visiting Moscow in October 1973: "The Soviet Union will construct on her own a trans-Siberian railroad . . ." and "although the construction of the railroad will be accomplished solely by the Soviet Union, the Soviet Union would like to cooperate with Japan if that nation is interested in the development of the resources, because there are rich natural resources along the course of the railroad."[8]

When completed BAM will stretch some 3,145 kilometers (2,000 miles) from Ust-Kut on the Lena River, northwest of Lake Baikal, to Komsomolsk, on the Amur, where it will connect with a line to Vladivostok, via Khabarovsk. From Komsomolsk on the Amur, BAM will terminate its last 200-mile segment at the new Soviet port, Sovetskaya Gavan, on the Sea of Japan. Overall, the new railway will be roughly two-and-one-half times the length of the Alaska pipeline and will challenge difficult terrain and impossible climatic conditions not unlike those encountered in the formidable, now operational, Alaskan pipeline venture. "BAM," we are told, "will cross seven mountain ranges, sixteen large rivers and transverse 500 kilometers (more than 300 miles) of permafrost."[9] Completion of BAM was originally scheduled for 1982, but for the reasons suggested, plus the usual bureaucratic conditions characteristic of the Soviet system, the Plan appears to be about three years behind schedule.

The cost of constructing the BAM railroad has not been made public by the Soviet authorities. However, a French journalist who recently returned from on-the-spot reporting in Siberia was quoted in a French magazine to the effect that "the average cost of the BAM mainline railroad is nearly 2 million rubles per kilometer. Including the cost of constructing station buildings, adjacent communities, and other facilities, the total cost of BAM construction will run some 6,000 million to 8,000 million rubles. This constitutes one-fifth of the 1975 national budget of France."[10] Other Western experts estimate that BAM may cost as much as $15 billion, that is, about twice the cost of the Alaska pipeline.

The strategic implications of the new railway have inevitably concerned a number of Japanese and American political observers. Speaking to this point at the Second Joint Soviet-Japanese Conference on Peace in Asia held in Moscow in the spring of 1974, Kiichi Saeki, president of the Nomura Research Institute of Tokyo, had this to say:

I do not believe that [the] railroad from Ust-Kut to Komsomolsk was

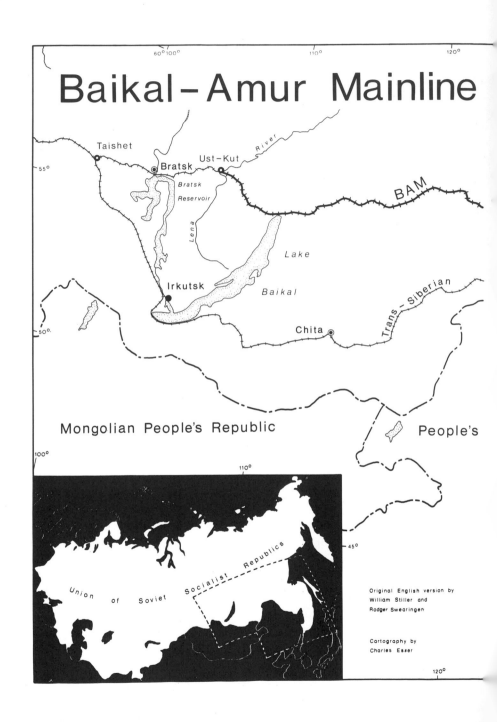

Baikal – Amur Mainline

Taishet

Ust–Kut

Bratsk

River

BAM

Bratsk
Reservoir

Lena

Lake

Irkutsk

Baikal

Trans-Siberian

Chita

Mongolian People's Republic

People's

Union of Soviet Socialist Republics

Original English version by
William Stiller and
Rodger Swearingen

Cartography by
Charles Esser

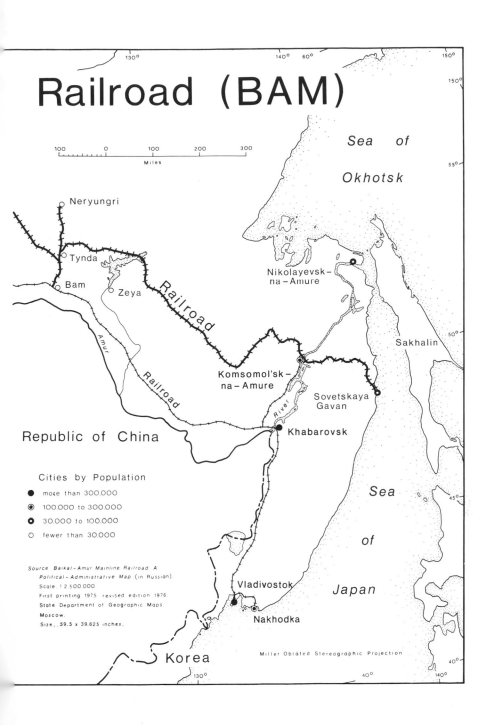

Railroad (BAM)

100 0 100 200 300
Miles

Sea of Okhotsk

Neryungri

Tynda

Bam   Zeya

Railroad

Nikolayevsk-
na–Amure

Amur

Railroad

Sakhalin

Komsomol'sk-
na–Amure

River

Sovetskaya
Gavan

Republic of China

Khabarovsk

Cities by Population

● more than 300,000

◉ 100,000 to 300,000

◑ 30,000 to 100,000

○ fewer than 30,000

Sea

of

Japan

Source: Baikal–Amur Mainline Railroad. A
Political–Administrative Map (in Russian).
Scale: 1:2,500,000.
First printing 1975 revised edition 1976.
State Department of Geographic Maps.
Moscow.
Size: 59.5 x 39.625 inches.

Vladivostok

Nakhodka

Korea   Miller Oblated Stereographic Projection

planned primarily for the strategic and security considerations of the Soviet Union. Such objectives may very well be secondary, however, and the end result would be an upgrading of Soviet military and strategic status. . . .

If the second Trans-Siberian Railway (BAM) helps Soviet Far Eastern development, aids to populate the area more and strengthens Soviet military potential, then the Sino-Soviet balance of power in the area will shift further in favor of the Soviet Union. . . .[11]

Focusing, rather, on the economic potential of BAM, Brezhnev stated (the same year): "The construction of the railway which will cut through the Siberian massif with its inexhaustible natural riches, opens the way to creating a new, large industrial region. Alongside the railway settlements and towns, industrial enterprises and mines will spring up, and naturally, new lands will be ploughed and put into industrial turnover."[12]

A volume entitled *BAM: Problems and Perspectives* published late in 1976 (in Russian) in Moscow combines the personalized experience and eye-witness accounts of a number of participants and observers of the great Siberian railway project to add perspective and to bring the story more or less up to date. The short volume (173 pages) is divided into three parts plus a postscript-conclusion. As the colorful table of contents may suggest, this little book, in its own way, captures the essence of BAM. Its contents:

Part I - BAM—Its Roots
1. Along Lost Trails
2. On the History of the Idea and the Roots of its Development
3. In the Region of Sleepy "Taiman" (an Amur fish)
4. The Main Base Operations

Part II - BAM—Under Construction
1. The King's Highway of the Young Communist League
2. A Nationwide Effort
3. A Second Gateway to the Ocean
4. Burning the Midnight Oil in Komsomolsk

Part III - The Development of the BAM Railway Zone
1. Yakutsk's Potential
2. The Role of the Siberian Branch of the Soviet Academy of Sciences
3. New Concerns for Ancient Lands
4. The Local Geography of the BAM Zone
5. Additions to the Geographical Map
6. The Social Development of the People of the North

It is in the postscript-conclusion of this colorful little volume, however, that the reader senses the significance of the new railway as the Soviets see it—or wish it to be viewed. Here is summary-translation of those two concluding pages:

> BAM is called the way into the future. Such construction has no parallel. In so short a span of time, 3,200 kilometers of railway will be complete. This not only staggers our imagination, but also dramatizes the tasks before us in the future. More than 3,000 complexes of various types must be constructed. The scope of the task far exceeds that required in constructing the original Siberian railway. Moreover, the route transverses permafrost and earthquake prone regions. Without exaggeration we may say that BAM is the construction project of the century. All the changes that will take place in Siberia and the Soviet Far East are connected with this important new transportation system. It will awaken the area from its century old sleep. . . . The whole world watches with mixed feelings of puzzlement and admiration.[13]

The problem faced by the outside observer in looking at BAM is, of course, similar to that encountered by all Western analysts when evaluating Soviet plans, establishments, and endeavors: to avoid the twin dangers of either overestimating Soviet capabilities or underestimating Soviet potential.

JAPANESE MOTIVATIONS FOR PARTICIPATION

Japan's rationale or multimotivation for participation in the Siberian development need only be noted briefly. The fact that the third-ranking economic power in the world must import the overwhelming bulk of its raw material and virtually all its oil is alone a near decisive argument for doing urgent business with the Soviets assuming suitable arrangements can be worked out. With respect to oil, this argument became increasingly compelling when the price of distant Middle-Eastern oil skyrocketed after 1970 even as the oil-gulping Japanese economy was growing at the astronomical rate of a 10 percent GNP increase per year.

Linking the oil and coal issues with Japan's geographical location off the coast of Siberia, Young C. Kim, in his pioneering, brief study of Soviet-Japanese relations, quoting Japanese sources, summarizes the key twin economic aspects that underlie Japan's Siberian involvement:

> Geographic proximity is an important factor affecting cost. Japan pays about $18.00 per ton for transporting coal from the United States, compared with about $3.00 a ton for transporting coal from the Soviet Far East. The Tyumen project would constitute an enormous saving in

transportation. It takes Japan 29 days via 100,000-ton tanker and costs 1000 yen to transfer a ton of crude oil from the Middle East. The cost from Nakhodka to Japan would be about one-fifth of this amount, and would take two days via tanker in the 25,000 to 50,000 class (*Asahi Shimbun*, 1973). The Tyumen project would guarantee delivery of crude oil for 20 years. . . . Moreover, the oil would be of low sulphur content (*Nihon Keizai Shimbun*, 1972).[14]

During his visit to the Soviet Union in October 1973, the then prime minister of Japan, Kakuei Tanaka, is reported to have told the Soviet leadership: "On the resource development project, the *Keidanren* (Japanese Federation of Economic Organizations) will serve as the private window for Japan," and "if concrete content of development conditions is determined between this window and the Soviet authorities, the Japanese Government will provide financial backup."[15] This statement indicates the position of the Japanese government on the long-term Soviet desire to bring up to the governmental level economic issues between the two countries, such as the present joint economic venture projects.

The commitment of the Japanese government to the joint ventures is appreciated by the Soviet side. In the matter of Siberian development cooperation, the so-called "supplier's credit" was approved by the Japanese government, as compared with tne credit export to the Soviet Union, on earlier ventures including the new Wrangel Port construction, the First Far East Timber Resource Development Project, and the industrial chip and pulp development.

Since the approval of supplier's credit, the scale of development cooperation items expanded and the Japanese government embarked on the sanctioning of bank loans, e.g., the South Yakut coal development, the second Siberian timber development, and Yakutia natural gas development, all initiated in April 1974. These developments have been positively recognized by the Soviet Union as signifying efforts to bring economic cooperation up to the governmental level.[16]

More recently, several bank loans have been approved, including the export to the Soviet Union of 500,000 tons of steel pipes (approved in February 1976) and the export of ammonia, nitrogen, and other production equipment and petroleum gas processing installations (approved in July 1976).

As of October 1976, the total bank loan contracts amounted to as much as $2,000 million, of which $900 million was for the so-called national projects which involved the development and export of natural resources.[17]

On the political side of the coin, the Japanese have been understandably aware and concerned over the impact their Siberian involvement might have upon China. The closer political relations with Moscow inevitably implied by Japan's participation in joint Siberian economic development (when accompanied by the growth of Soviet-Japanese trade relations) could hardly have been designed to please Peking. However, from Tokyo's perspective, this negative political consequence had to be weighed against the positive balance-of-power factor as well as economic considerations. The "equidistance policy," which Japan has insisted must govern its relations with the two continental neighbors, has been one result.[18]

DOING BUSINESS WITH THE SOVIETS IN SIBERIA

The joint projects in Siberia have met with varying degrees of success, or in Moscow's parlance, "Plan Fulfillment." Problems, when discernible, may be traced at least in part to the intrinsic difficulties encountered by private enterprise attempting to do business with a totally controlled, sometimes suspicious, but not always perfectly planned socialist state.

An early case study of Soviet-Japanese economic relations written by U.S. Foreign Service Officer Jack F. Matlock, and based primarily on interviews with Japanese officials and businessmen, anticipates some of these problems and difficulties. The spectre of state control and monopoly, Matlock's report notes, "on one hand precludes competition among Soviet organizations for contracts, while Soviet trade officials are able to play off one foreign firm against another. On the other hand, it entails rigidity, red tape and slow decisions, which hamper the negotiating process and may often lead to missed opportunities."[19]

Specifically, with respect to Soviet-Japanese joint development projects, the paper continues: "Negotiations on major Siberian development projects are conducted by the Japan Chamber of Commerce and the Federation of Economic Organizations (*Keidanren*), which select the Japanese participants for the U.S.S.R.–Japan Joint Committee for Economic Development."[20]

The report elaborates: "When large projects are considered, the pattern has been for one major Japanese firm with a primary interest in the project to take the lead in the negotiations either within the Joint committee framework or outside it. If a basic agreement is reached, the 'lead' firm organizes other companies interested in participation into a loose consortium and a new specialized firm is established to coordinate transactions related to the project." The conclusion: "The Japanese system is designed to create to the extent possible a united front in dealing with the Soviet trade monopolies. It does not, however, prevent all competition among the Japanese.... Nevertheless, results indicate that the system of guidance, coordination and consensus has served the Japanese well in dealing with the Soviets."[21]

An interview in Tokyo in May of 1977 by the author with Keisuke Suzuki, *Keidanren*'s man in Moscow for more than ten years (1967–1977), provided a unique opportunity to hear from a seasoned participant something of the practical side and to make an overall evaluation of the character and conduct of the joint economic arrangement. Here are a few of the questions asked, accompanied by the essence of Suzuki's responses:

Q: Have you noticed any trends or changes in the Soviet approach to economic and joint development relations with Japan or procedures over your ten years in Moscow?

A: Yes, three: (1) Compared with ten years ago the Soviets now know very well the equipment and products that the Japanese have which they need. (2) The Soviet consumers seem to have somewhat more to say about products. On a decision over the kind of plant to be purchased (for Siberia, for example), the "consumer" may say to the authorities, "We don't want that kind of plant." (3) Today, the Soviets may say to us, "If you don't lower your prices we will buy in Europe or America."

Q: What are some priority items that Japan has provided for Siberian development?

A: In the machinery area, lumber mills. Actually, again the Soviets wanted to buy from the United States; but the United States would not do business because the Soviets had no money.

Q: What about the Soviet negotiators? Did you find your Russian counterparts bright, able?

A: I found them first rate; perhaps they are the most able and intellectual of negotiators all over the world. Most of them have had some experience in the United States. The top-level negotiators were in their sixties. There were few in the 50-year age bracket, as most had been killed in the war. Under 30, the younger group, all know two foreign languages besides Russian.

Q: The Soviet practice of utilizing economic and other missions for political and intelligence purposes is well known. What was your experience or information on this subject?

A: In the large [Japanese] enterprises, probably not. With some of the small and medium, so-called pro-Russian companies, there have been such allegations. [Note: Suzuki was understandably vague and obviously reluctant to get into this touchy subject; and, accordingly, the point was not pursued.]

Q: The Soviets often hold trade fairs in Japan and elsewhere. Would you regard these as of economic value or merely as propaganda devices?

A: They do have important economic value to the Soviets. Not all Japanese businessmen visit the Soviet Union so trade fairs are useful in introducing new products. But, above all, they are a way for Moscow to "secure scarce foreign currency."

Q: As of 1977, what would you regard, respectively, as Moscow's and Japan's number one joint Siberia priorities?

A: The Soviets regard *all* Siberian development projects as important. It would be difficult to establish a priority. In the case of Japan, coking coal must be rated number one on our priority list.

Q: How do you project the future of Soviet-Japan joint development in Siberia?

A: As continuing at about the present level—not as good as might be hoped, but not bad either.[22]

THE JOINT DEVELOPMENT PROJECTS—AN OVERVIEW

Assuming the Soviets are moderately sensible about their own long-term economic interests and that the Japanese are reasonably perceptive and cautious with respect to their interrelated economic and strategic future, the joint development projects undertaken over the past decade make a certain degree of mutual sense. The complicated issue of the feasibility or desirability of U.S. involvement in one or more of the projects adds a further controversial dimension. From the Soviet perspective, the lure of advanced technology, equipment, economic and financial assistance, and possible Japanese political goodwill is clearly attractive. From Japan's point of view, the need for the Siberian resources and the yen for dollars must be balanced against the political, strategic, and security risks and considerations. The question of U.S. participation has been cast largely in terms of the pocketbook—both by Congress and by potential participating U.S. corporations.

Timber, Timber, Timber. Timber is one of the principal natural resources of the Soviet Far East. Total timber resources are estimated at 23.4 billion cubic meters; this is thought to represent about 30 percent of the national timber reserves. Over 30 percent of the total Soviet resources of fir and spruce, the best material for producing high-grade cellulose, and about 70 percent of the industrial reserves of valuable leaf-bearing trees, e.g., ash, oak, elm, maple, and nut trees, are concentrated in this area.[23]

Arrangements for joint Soviet-Japanese exploitation of this tremendous timber resource are covered by the first agreement on the joint Soviet-Japanese development of Siberia. Known as the K-S Plan from the initials of the two chief negotiators, Kawai and Sedov, it was initiated in July of

1968. It provided for the export of $163 million worth of Japanese goods to the USSR ($133 million of earth-moving and lumbering equipment, and $30 million of consumer goods) in return for which the Soviets agreed to export to Japan $183 million worth of timber over a five-year period.[24] The key to this arrangement was credit. The terms of Japanese credit for the equipment: 20 percent deposit, with the balance to be paid over a five-year period at 5.8 percent.

The joint development of Siberian timber resources was given a major shot in the arm in April of 1974 with the signing of a protocol, according to which the Export-Import Bank of Japan granted the Soviets $1,050 million in long-term credit for the exploitation of coking coal, natural gas, and timber resources of the Far East. Commenting on the agreement, the head of the Soviet delegation, V. S. Alkhimov, stated: "The agreement reached is beneficial to both sides. . . . The long-term nature of the agreement will further the stabilization of Soviet-Japanese economic relations."[25]

Japanese business circles, we are told, also expressed great satisfaction with the agreement. In a speech during the signing of the protocol, S. Sumita, president of the Export-Import Bank, declared: "This document lays firm foundations for Soviet-Japanese economic cooperation" and "marks a new stage in the economic relations between the two countries."[26]

Linking this timber agreement to the construction of BAM, F. Dyakonov, section head of the USSR State Planning Committee's Council for the Study of Productive Forces, wrote early in 1975: "BAM is surrounded by vast tracts of forest. There are plans to set up ten lumber-industry enterprises in these areas; their total output will be 5,000,000 to 6,000,000 cubic meters of wood per year."[27]

Japan imports timber from the Soviet Union through general trade, coastal trade, cooperative trade, and national projects such as "The Far East Timber Resource Development Project." Within the framework of this last project, Japan has supplied to the Soviet Union a bank loan amounting to $550 million and necessary equipment, machinery, materials, and ships to carry timber. In return Japan will receive from the Soviet Union 18,400,000 cubic meters of raw and processed timber over the 1975–1979 period.[28]

The New Wrangel Port, Vostochny. Soviet-Japanese discussions involving joint enterprise toward enhancement of port facilities in the Soviet Far East initially centered around improvement and expansion of Nakhodka. Aboard a Soviet vessel traversing the crowded, narrow twists and turns of that outmoded facility, one is immediately struck by the desirability—indeed, necessity—for a larger, more modern port. From the vantage point of the hills above the city of Nakhodka, it becomes equally evident that the setting, terrain, access from the sea, and other geographical and geological considerations have left the planners no place to go—but elsewhere. Accordingly, the final decision was made probably early in 1970 to construct a new port facility at the nearby location on the eastern side of Wrangel Bay and after "preliminary" discussions and negotiations, a design agreement was signed in April of the same year. Japanese engineers visited the proposed site and at the end of the year a general agreement was signed on the supply of equipment for the new port.[29]

According to this basic contract, initialed in December 1970, the first period includes the construction of timber berths capable of handling 40,000 cubic meters of timber annually, chip berths to handle 800,000 cubic meters of wood chips a year, and coal berths to handle five million tons of coal each year. Of the estimated cost of $330 million, Japan is to supply to the Soviet Union $80 million worth of port construction machinery and materials.[30]

A Trade and Payments Agreement between Japan and the USSR for 1971 to 1975 signed in Tokyo on September 22, 1971, included a letter from N. Patolichev, foreign trade minister of the USSR, expressing satisfaction with the agreement reached concerning the supply to the USSR of equipment, machinery, and materials necessary "in the construction of a sea port in Wrangel Bay."[31]

The Fifth Session of the Japan-Soviet Joint Economic Committee, postponed from February of 1970, opened on February 12, 1972, at Keidanren Hall, Otemachi, Tokyo. While questions of oil, coal, and natural gas vied for top billing, the Wrangel Port also found an important place on the agenda.

Subsequent to the Third Session of the Japan-Soviet Joint Economic Committee, there had been three rounds of negotiations, including a field survey. Japan's cooperation was now seen as involving equipment for and construction of a pier with an annual loading capacity of ten million tons of coal together with necessary facilities, and an overall loading plant for wood chips, as well as an all-purpose plant for loading 120,000 to 140,000 containers annually. Japan's cooperation in the supply of materials and equipment as well as construction machinery totals about $80 million. The redemption was to be made over a period of seven years.[32]

In 1975, the first of three cargo piers was completed. This alone represents an increase of 100 percent in total lumber, coal, and general cargo processing at Soviet Far Eastern seaports.[33] With respect to Japan, especially, when BAM is completed, transit transportation of containers via the USSR should prove of increasing importance in economic relations between the two nations.

Soviet Pulpwood and Chips for Japanese Industrial Equipment. Beginning in 1967, the Oji Paper Company of Japan and associated enterprises started negotiating an agreement to supplement the timber arrangement.

This envisaged the Soviets paying for Japanese forestry, pulpwood, and wood-chip processing equipment by the delivery to Japan of a share of the product. Deliveries to Japan were to extend over the period 1972–1981 with initial Japanese credits of some $45 million to be repaid over six years at a 6 percent interest rate.

An exchange of notes between the Government of Japan and the Government of the Soviet Union on February 23, 1972, sanctioned the General Agreement behind the Japan Chips Trading Corporation and the Soviet "Exportles." The deal: Japanese machinery for Soviet chips.[34]

By the summer of 1972, *Pravda* could thus report with enthusiasm and in more detail (under Tokyo dateline):

> A new commodity—commercial wood chips, which are used in the pulp-and-paper and chemical industries—has appeared in Soviet trade with Japan. A contract has just been signed here for the delivery to Japan of 3,650,000 cubic meters of commercial chips between 1972 and 1977. The chips will be delivered in payment for equipment, machinery, materials, and means of transport that Japan is to supply the Soviet Union in order to ensure the production of this raw material. The contract's total value exceeds $100 million.[35]

In Moscow, in March of 1974, in his meeting with a high-level delegation from *Keidanren*, Deputy Premier Nikolai Bailov expressed hope that Japan would speed up efforts on various projects related to the development of Siberia. Once more, along with the question of Tyumen oil, the question of pulp supply—which we are told was discussed when Prime Minister Kakuei Tanaka visited Moscow in October of 1973—was also taken up at the meeting.[36]

The next month an exchange of notes was initiated concerning a new General Agreement between K-S Sangyo Kabushi Kaisha and "Exportles" and involving a further credit agreement between the Export-Import Bank of Japan and other Japanese banks and the Foreign Trade Bank of the USSR. As before, Japanese equipment, this time including ships, was to be exchanged for Soviet wood products.[37]

Abundant, Much-Needed Natural Gas. Proposals involving the Japanese financing of a pipeline to supply Soviet natural gas to Japan have remained under discussion for the best part of the past decade. Japanese caution related both to Tokyo's sensitivity to Peking's strong objections to the plan and to concern that Moscow might under some future circumstance simply cut off the supply to Japan. While the Japanese have displayed changing and mixed feelings about the matter, the Soviets have pressed the issue almost from the outset.

At a meeting with members of a Japanese delegation to the annual Japan-Soviet Joint Economic Committee meeting in Moscow in February of 1970, Premier Kosygin "advised" Japan to import natural gas produced in the Yakutsk region, whose reserves, he said, were estimated at between 700,000 million and 1,000,000 million cubic meters.[38]

The conclusions contained in a recent study entitled *Soviet Economy in a New Perspective* prepared for the Joint Economic Committee of the United States Congress would seem to substantiate Kosygin's lavish claims:

> The Soviets have enjoyed considerable success in expanding Siberia's known reserves. The region's "unexplored" reserves of natural gas are more than 36 times the level of 1965, and constitute approximately two-thirds of all explored reserves of gas in the U.S.S.R. . . . Most of these reserves are located in the Northern Tyumen Oblast, near the Ob Gulf. . . . The Urengoy field, the largest known in the world, has reserves estimated at 4–6 trillion cubic meters, about one-fifth to one-fourth of total Soviet explored reserves of gas. Development drilling of this field began in 1975, and commercial production is expected by 1978. The U.S.S.R. has sought foreign financing to develop facilities. . . .[39]

Early in February of 1974 in Moscow, Japan and the Soviet Union agreed to begin joint prospecting for natural gas in Yakutsk. It may be noted that at a meeting between Japanese and American experts held in Hawaii a month earlier, the United States had expressed willingness to join the multimillion dollar project. Hiroshi Anzai, chairman of the natural gas subcommittee of the Japan-Soviet Economic Cooperation Committee and also chairman of the Tokyo Gas Company, was quoted as saying that terms for the $150 million loan to be made by Japan and the United States to the Soviet Union would be discussed in March in Tokyo. Anzai immediately left Moscow for Paris for a meeting with Howard Boyd, president of the El Paso Natural Gas Company, in an effort to overcome the problems involved in U.S. participation, which included congressional opposition to granting the Soviet Union long-term credit loans.[40]

Natural gas exploitation was included in the protocol signed between Japan and the USSR extending about $1,050,000 in bank loans to the USSR to help finance several Siberian development projects. Commenting on the significance of this agreement (at the signing ceremonies that took place in Tokyo, April 22, 1974) the head of the Soviet delegation, V. S. Alkhimov, said: ". . . Soviet trade organizations up to now received credits in Japan only from private companies. Bank credit gives our trade organizations themselves opportunities to select partners in Japan for concluding these and other commercial contracts."[41]

In an unusually candid review article on Siberian development, *Litera-turnaya Gazeta* in April of 1975 pointed up the progress, problems, and pitfalls with respect to U.S. business involvement in the Yakutia project:

"The only project that is now at a standstill," the article states flatly, "is the agreement on geological prospecting for Yakut gas deposits." The article explains in detail:

> The project is to be carried out on a tripartite basis, with the participation of American firms. The principle is the same. We get equipment and know-how on credit, and Japan and the U.S.A. each get 10,000,000 cubic meters of gas per year over a 20 to 30 year period.
>
> The three parties, we are informed, signed the general agreement in Paris in December 1974. Our Ministry of Foreign Trade, Japan's Tokyo Gas Co., and two American companies, the El Paso Natural Gas Company and the Occidental Petroleum Corporation, participated in the agreement. In April 1974, the Japanese side had already committed $100,000,000 in credits. It was then up to the Americans to equal that amount.

Then the conclusion which Special Correspondent, V. Syrokomsky, the author of the review article, had perhaps been leading up to all along:

> As a result of the discriminatory trade law passed by the U.S. Congress, the Export-Import Bank of the United States was only allowed to grant the Soviet Union $40,000,000 in credits, and they could only be used for prospecting not for production.
>
> H. Anzai, President of Tokyo Gas, told me on this occasion, "I have devoted almost three years' time and effort to the Yakut project. I was shaken by what happened. It is clear the Americans not the Soviets are at fault. The law passed by the [U.S.] Congress is, in essence, interference in the international affairs of the U.S.S.R."[42]

Coal and Iron—Close, Essential.   Exploratory talks regarding the development of coal deposits and iron in the rich region of southern Yakutia began as early as 1968. More than 60 percent of the Soviet Union's explored resources of coal are found in Siberia and the Far East. In August of 1970, Japanese specialists were allowed to visit the site of the coal deposits and 10,000 tons of coal from the area were shipped to Japan for testing. The tests showed the coal to be of usable quality for the production of steel, though somewhat inferior to U.S. and Australian coal.[43]

After further talks, tests, and tribulations, an agreement was initiated in the spring of 1974 under which Japan would provide a $450 million bank-to-bank loan to the Soviet Union and receive about 104 million tons of coking coal from 1979 to 1998. To transport the coal the Russians plan to build a 400-kilometer railway linking the coal mines in southern Yakutsk with the Siberian Railway.

A succinct summary of the coal project is contained in the article on economic cooperation in *Literaturnaya Gazeta* previously cited. In detail and conciseness, it would be hard to improve upon. Here are the relevant passages:

The Yakut project was under study for seven years, and intensive, difficult negotiations were conducted. S. Tanabe, General Manager of the Nippon Steel Corporation, made more than 10 trips to the Soviet Union in connection with the project. In June, 1974, a general agreement was signed on the delivery from the U.S.S.R. to Japan of Yakut coking coal and on the delivery from Japan to the U.S.S.R. of equipment, machinery, materials and other goods for the development of Southern Yakutia's coal deposits, including the construction of approximately 400 km. of railroad.

The terms of the agreement are as follows: The Japanese Export-Import Bank has granted us $450,000,000 in credits, $60,000,000 of which are earmarked for the purchase of consumer goods. Over a 20-year period we are to deliver 104,000,000 tons of coking coal at a cost of $4,000,000,000 based on the current price (the price, however, will be determined annually on the basis of the world market price). In this way, the credit will be repaid quite rapidly, and we will then begin to receive solid profits.

Deliveries of Southern Yakut coal will begin at a level of 3,200,000 tons per year and rise to 5,500,000 tons per year. The Neryungra Opencut, which has a capacity of 12,000,000 tons of coking coal per year, has already been prepared for industrial exploitation without Japanese credits or equipment. The proven reserves of this deposit are in the hundreds of millions of tons, and the projected reserves of various grades of coal in Southern Yakutia are calculated in the tens of billions of tons.

Deliveries of equipment to the U.S.S.R. for the coal and lumber projects will be handled for the most part by the Kato machine-building firm. Ours is the largest order in the history of the company. We will be receiving 1,000 units of equipment at a cost of $110,000,000.[44]

Vital Petroleum—Near and Cheap. The advent of the Soviet global navy coupled with Japan's emergence as the world's third-ranking industrial power—which occurred in parallel during the past decade—dramatize the vital importance of oil to both nations. Japan imports 99 percent of its crude oil; the Soviet Union is a potentially substantial petroleum exporting nation —if the Soviets' extensive resources (largely in Siberia and Sakhalin) can, with Japanese and perhaps U.S. assistance, be tapped.

During the 1960s, the largest gas-and-oil bearing area in the USSR was discovered in West Siberia. Academician Trojimuk, President of the Siberian Branch of the Soviet Academy of Sciences, writes concerning the region that "its exploration would allow the Soviet Union to increase our output by 1980 over 600 million tons, and by the end of the 20th Century attain a level of oil production of over a billion tons." This would make the USSR, he concludes, "the world's leading nation in oil production."[45]

Plans for 1980 adopted at the 25th Party Congress in March of 1976 call for West Siberian production of oil to reach 300 to 310 million tons, nearly half of the planned national output of 620 to 640 million tons.[46] Moreover, huge potential reserves offshore from Sakhalin await the advanced deep drilling and specialized technology and equipment available in Japan and the United States, but not yet in the Soviet Union.

It is not surprising then that one of the first and most important of the joint ventures was the Tyumen oil field development plan initially advanced by the first Japan-Soviet Joint Economic Committee in 1967. A Petroleum Committee was set up and studies undertaken, but it was not until May of 1971 that the matter received top priority when Soviet Premier Kosygin revealed to Japanese Ambassador Kinya Niizeki in Moscow his interest in the joint Japan-Soviet development venture.[47]

Accordingly, at the meeting of the Japan-Soviet Joint Economic Committee in February 1972, the following plan for development of the Tyumen field was presented: Japan would secure from the Soviet Union a guarantee to supply petroleum from that field; Japan would obtain from the Soviets concrete data on oil deposits, and so on, and would dispatch a survey team to the Soviet Union during the summer of the year; direct participation of the United States in the project would be avoided, but American capital would be introduced, at the responsibility of Japan, for the work east of Nakhodka.

Under the development plan of the 6,700 kilometers from Tyumen to Nakhodka, the existing pipeline of some 2,400 kilometers between Tyumen and Irkutsk would be reinforced and a new pipeline of about 4,300 kilometers between Irkutsk and Nakhodka would be built. Steel pipe and other materials would be supplied by Japan together with credits amounting to about $1 billion. After completion of the project, Japan would receive an annual oil supply amounting to 30 to 50 million tons of crude oil for 20 years.[48]

When Kogoro Yemura, president of *Keidanren*, and Shigeo Nagano, president of the Japan Chamber of Commerce and Industry, met with Soviet officials in Moscow in March of 1974 to discuss the joint development projects, the Soviets intimated that 25 million tons of Tyumen oil "which Russia has promised to supply Japan annually was the amount which could be guaranteed at present."[49]

This apparently came as something of a shock in Tokyo, and the shock waves were not long in reaching Moscow. On June 1 of the same year, *Pravda*, under the title "Idle Fabrications," felt impelled to respond. The full text of that brief article reflects Soviet sensitivities and concern over economic relations with Japan:

> After meeting with V. D. Shashin, U.S.S.R. Minister of the Petroleum Industry, certain journalists from bourgeois news agencies suddenly began to spread ridiculous rumors to the effect that the Soviet Union has allegedly lost interest in selling oil to Japan.
>
> These reports are tendentious and distort what the Soviet Minister said. In reality the Soviet Union has consistently supported the development of commercial and economic ties with all countries including Japan. It is no secret that the Soviet Union is now delivering oil to Japan and specialists believe there are great, as yet unrealized, possibilities for further development in this area. Experts in both countries are working and there are good grounds for this; to expand commercial and economic cooperation on a mutual and advantageous basis, which would be in the interests of both countries.[50]

Assume the successful completion of BAM and add to the already impressive list of achievements further extensive mineral exploitation, thermal and hydroelectric power, related ocean resources development, a hundred other plans and projects underway or envisaged for future joint eastern economic development, and it must still be said that the Soviets have only scratched the surface of Siberia. The implications for Japan—economic, strategic, and political—are immense. A number of Japanese in positions of governmental authority seem to be quite as aware of the potential pitfalls as some colleagues in the Japanese business world are excited over the economic prospects. Moreover, as obstacles mount—but not incentives—in efforts to project plans for Soviet-Japan cooperation in Siberia, it is probably fair to say that both Japanese politicians and business leaders are far less optimistic today than they were in the late 1960s and early 1970s. The United States, for its part, has adopted a wait-and-see attitude.

If Japanese enthusiasm over involvement in Siberia was, at one point, fairly substantial, it has waned noticeably in recent years. The "joint projects" on which activity continues to interest Japan are timber and coal—

those with rapid payoff and little strategic risk or political implication. Discussions on joint offshore Sakhalin oil development are proceeding with the support of U.S. industry. The Japanese may yet reconsider the Yakutsk project as the energy crisis deepens, but the Tyumen plan seems dead, except in the unlikely event that U.S. corporate cooperation should be forthcoming.

Chapter Ten

Trade Between Japan and the Soviet Union

As suggested by the Soviet concentration on joint Siberian economic ventures with Japan, Moscow over the past decade has launched and sustained a major strategic resource and economic offensive in the East designed to enlist Japanese technology and financial backing in the development of Soviet industrial complexes, particularly in Siberia; improve Soviet capacity for economic exchange and trade with Japan through a major overhaul of port facilities, the construction of the new Wrangel Port, and a crash program for the completion of a second Siberian railway (BAM); obtain much-needed foreign currency, preferably in dollars; and utilize this economic offensive and economic inducements as political weapons pointedly in an effort to keep the Japanese leaning too far in the direction of Peking. In this scheme, trade has come to play a striking and increasingly prominent role.

THE PREWAR AND OCCUPATION PICTURE

Prior to World War II, trade between Japan and the Soviet Union had never been particularly significant, accounting for less than 2 percent of Japan's exports and about 2.5 percent of its imports. When the Pacific War destroyed the "yen bloc" as well as some 80 percent of Japanese industrial capacity, Japan (under Occupation controls) was forced to look for new, if limited, markets and suppliers. By 1947, arrangements had been made for a control clearing mechanism, a somewhat unsatisfactory system which remained in force until 1957.[1] The extremely small role played by Soviet-Japanese trade both in Japan's prewar and Occupation economy may be seen from the data in Table 2.

TABLE 2

JAPAN'S SHARE OF USSR FOREIGN TRADE
(selected years)

| | USSR Exports | | USSR Imports | |
	Total (million rubles)	Percentage to Japan	Total (million rubles)	Percentage from Japan
1918	6.4	—	82.5	—
1925/26	551.1	1.8	567.3	0.4
1930	812.7	1.6	830.3	1.6
1935	288.1	1.5	189.3	4.5
1938	229.8	0.5	245.3	1.1
1940	239.7	0.1	245.5	0.3
1948	1,177.3	0.4	1,101.6	0.2
1950	1,615.2	0.2	1,310.3	0.0

SOURCE: *Vneshiaia torgovlia USSR 1918–1966* [International trade of USSR] (Moscow 1967). Quoted in Jan Slankovsky, "Japan's Economic Relations with the USSR and Eastern Europe," *Japan in der Weltwirtschaft*, ed. A. Lamper, *Probleme du Weltwirtschaft*, No. 17 (Munich, Veltforum Verlag, 1974).

The Soviets, for their part, reacted understandably to SCAP's Occupation controls, objecting, for example, to the "fruits of MacArthur's policy" which were "turning Japan into an appendage of the American economic system"[2] and charging that the control of Japanese trade by the United States had merely resulted in "huge profits for American corporations at the expense of the average Japanese."[3] The fact is that the United States, over the strenuous objection of members of the Far Eastern Commission, began feeding Japan as early as the spring of 1946. This food input, in the form of grain and other staples, amounted to up to one fourth of the monthly ration requirements needed to sustain the hungry Japanese population.[4]

In 1950, the Soviet Union expressed the specific desire to place orders for Japanese textile machinery, tankers, freighters, small and large cranes, and electric motors. SCAP refused on the grounds that the USSR must first pay some $4 million already owed. The Soviet Union wanted to pay in kind, but of the products offered, Japan needed only the coal from Sakhalin. A $1 million agreement was signed for the supply of 100,000 tons of coal, but only 74,000 tons were delivered.[5]

The escalation of the Cold War with the advent of hostilities in Korea in June of 1950 projected a new urgent dimension into Japan's trade picture with a resulting expanded strategic embargo. The initial unilateral action taken by the United States to inhibit the military buildup of the Moscow-Peking bloc now was considered insufficient, and a series of conferences and consultations with allies in Asia and Europe resulted in new and increasingly strong control measures, now encompassing Communist China, North Korea, and North Vietnam. Three types of controls were instituted and each specified by a separate list: List I (embargo), List II (quantitative control), and List III (surveillance).[6]

Still, during 1951 direct Japanese-Soviet negotiations for trade on a barter basis continued although the intensification of the Soviet- and Chinese-Communist-supported war in Korea inevitably resulted in decreased trade between Japan, the Soviet Union, and Communist China.

In his chapter on Soviet-Japanese trade, Indian scholar Savitu Vishwanathan summarized the situation to the time:

Although the Soviet government issued invitations to Japanese businessmen for the World Economic Conference held in Moscow in 1952, and though the Soviet Mission in Tokyo sought to persuade Japanese businessmen and Diet members of the desirability of expanded economic relations with the Soviet Union, a glance at the following figures [see Table 3] reveals that the total trade did not substantially increase until 1955.

TABLE 3

JAPANESE TRADE BALANCE WITH THE USSR, 1950–1957
(in thousand dollars)

Year	Export	Import	Balance
1950	723	738	(15)
1951	0	28	(28)
1952	150	459	(309)
1953	7	2,101	(2,094)
1954	39	2,249	(2,210)
1955	2,067	3,073	(1,006)
1956	760	2,869	(2,109)
1957	9,295	12,326	(3,031)

SOURCE: Savitri Vishwanathan, *Normalization of Soviet-Japanese Relations, 1945–1970* (Tallahassee, Fla., 1973), p. 48.

The above figures [Table 3] do not include ship repairs, which brought the barter trade into balance.[7]

JAPANESE TRADE POLICY, INSTITUTIONS, AND PRACTICE VIS-A-VIS THE USSR

Governmental Measures.   A series of intergovernmental trade and commercial treaties provides the formal structure, the framework, for ongoing economic relations between Japan and the Soviet Union.

The Soviet-Japanese commercial treaty of 1957 marked the beginning of a new era in Soviet-Japanese trade relations. This Treaty of Commerce went into effect on May 9, 1958. The following month, on June 3, an agreement was signed establishing a sea route between the ports of Yokohama and Nakhodka and between Japan and the Black Sea.[8]

In March of 1960, this agreement was followed by a longer term 1960–1962 Japanese-Soviet trade agreement which was later extended for the period 1963–1965, and revised and augmented by subsequent agreements.[9]

A new five-year trade treaty was initialed January 21, 1966, covering the period 1966–1970. In addition to listing Soviet exports (mostly raw materials and mineral ores) and Japanese imports (fishing and cargo ships, factory and laboratory equipment, machinery and parts), a central feature of the treaty was Japan's agreement in principle to participate in the development of Siberia.[10] A 1971–1975 trade and payment agreement signed in September 1971 broadened the scope of trade relations and contained lists of some 300 export/import items, including two separate lists of items to be traded between Japan and the Far Eastern regions of the USSR. An attached letter from the Soviet side proposed that the total volume of exports in 1971 should not exceed £4,630,000 for either side and might reach £6,940,000 in 1975.[11]

In April of 1975, in an Exchange of Notes Concerning the General Agreement between "K-S Sangyo Kabushiki Kaisha" and "Exportles" and the Credit Agreement between the Export-Import Bank of Japan and other Japanese banks and the Foreign Trade Bank of the USSR, the Soviet government "welcomed the agreement to exchange Japanese machinery, equipment, ships and other material for Soviet wood products." It further pledged full support toward the future broadening of trade between the two countries.[12]

The controversial Soviet-Japanese Fisheries Agreement of May 1977, while not essentially a trade treaty, inevitably has important trade-related implications for both nations as fish, quite as much as wood products, are, of course, basic to the economies of both nations—and therefore part of the politics of each.[13]

Corporate Institutions.   Japanese companies and firms, large and small, involved in trade with the Soviet Union in the mid–1960s formed themselves into an "Association for the Promotion of Trade with the U.S.S.R. and the European Socialist Countries." This organization has over the years been instrumental in concluding various agreements in the areas of trade and scientific cooperation, both with the Soviet Union and with other COMECON members. Moreover, to plan, supervise, and operate aspects of economic cooperation, a Japan-Soviet Joint Cooperation committee was established in 1965. Its first meeting was held in 1966. The Japanese half of the committee is headquartered and staffed at *Keidanren*, the composition of which is, in turn, made up of executives from member firms with business interests in the Soviet Union. Since the Japanese firms must deal with a centralized, planned, economic structure, the value of coordination and collective Japanese strength is evident. Also, as the Japanese government will initially be involved in the final transactions, an official from the Economic Affairs Bureau of the Japanese Foreign Ministry usually represents the Japanese government in negotiations with the Soviet government and serves as a liaison link with the Japanese committee. In this way, the Japanese firms can bring the greater strength of numbers as well as a degree of government support and pressure to bear in a given negotiation with the Soviets.[14]

Company Roles and Representation. Ideally, each Japanese firm, especially the larger ones, should have its own representation in the Soviet Union as well as in key Eastern European capitals. In practice this turns out to be both difficult and expensive. Some fifteen Japanese companies do maintain representation in Moscow. All Japanese firms are housed in a single, closed block in the center of the city. About a dozen large concerns handle up to 60 percent of total Japanese exports and more than 70 percent of Japan's imports. Japanese firms were among the first to open branches in Moscow.[15] Anyone with experience in corresponding with organizations or individuals in the Soviet Union or Eastern Europe will appreciate the importance of maintaining a field representative in Moscow. Those Japanese assigned to such roles soon came to appreciate the differences, difficulties, and special problems inherent in doing business with the Russians especially on their home ground. Still, as we shall see, a considerable amount of business does get done.

Coastal Trade. Soviet officials, diplomats, scholars, and journalists have long underlined or played up the importance of Japan's proximity to the Soviet Union. Recent Soviet preoccupation with Siberia, especially its communications and port development, have further focused attention on the economic hands-across-the-Japan Sea theme. It is within this context that Soviet-Japanese coastal trade has increased and taken on new importance. Coastal trade is handled on the Soviet side by the Dalnitorg Trade Organization. By 1971 coastal trade had reached a level of $20 million. The new air route from Khabarovsk to Niigata, operated with Japanese aircraft and crew, is one more aspect of this picture.[16]

Items involved in this coastal trade for the first quarter of 1977 may be seen from Table 4 showing imports and exports.

TABLE 4

JAPANESE EXPORTS AND IMPORTS, 1977

| | Exports | |
Items	Quantity/Price	Status
Canning machine parts	?/$400,000	Contracted
Wire rope	700 tons/?	Contracted
Textile products	?/$300,000	Contracted
Scarves and garments	?/$200,000	Contracted
	Imports	
Items	Quantity/Price	Status
Timber	30,000 cubic meters/?	Contracted
Fern	550 tons/?	Contracted
Honey	?/$900	Contracted
Jam	?/$500	Contracted
Sperm whale meat	?/$370 per ton	Contracted

According to a report by Dalnitorg, the coastal trade volume in 1976 between the two countries was as follows:[17]

Japan's exports:	$30,670,000
Japan's imports:	$27,470,000

AN UNPARALLELED DECADE OF SOVIET-JAPANESE TRADE—THE 1960s

Before examining the pattern of expansion and describing the character of the export/import structure during the 1960s, it may be useful to isolate a few trends and traits peculiar, or at least singularly pertinent, to trade between Japan and the Soviet Union.

First, the spectre of the world's third-ranking economic power, a "capitalist state," doing business with the world's second-ranking and "socialist" state evidenced all sorts of political and strategic issues which go far beyond the purely economic realm. The most important of those, of course, are the fisheries and territorial questions.

Second, appreciative of the U.S. role in rebuilding Japan's war-ravaged economy, the Japanese government and people had generally gone along with U.S. efforts to limit trade with Communist countries during the Cold War years. However, with the advent of "coexistence," and as Japan's economy expanded, plans for joint economic development and increased trade with the Soviet Union replaced deference and restraint.

Third, the general relaxation of tensions between East and West after 1956 and the advent of successive Soviet policies of "coexistence" and "detente" saw Moscow, in its policy toward Japan, soft-pedaling the deadlock over the fisheries and territorial problems and stressing the themes of "proximity," "friendly neighbor," and "natural trading partner."

Fourth, the polarization and intensification of the Moscow-Peking dispute during the 1960s produced conditions favorable to the normalization of Japanese-Chinese Communist relations. (Actual Japanese recognition of Peking did not take place until 1972.) The subsequent Tokyo policy of "equidistance" toward its two continental neighbors, however, did not preclude major joint economic development activity and intensified Japanese trade with the Soviet Union. Precisely within this complex framework, Japan's trade with the Soviet Union began to show marked growth and development.

Fifth, the USSR's per capita foreign trade is substantially behind that of the United States and Japan, which suggests that even the relatively striking development of Soviet-Japanese trade relations during the decade of the 1960s may represent only the tip of the iceberg.

THE NATURE, SCOPE, AND DEVELOPMENT OF SOVIET-JAPANESE TRADE, 1958–1970

As a backdrop for describing the character of Japan's trade with the Soviet Union, the export/import commodity picture, it may be useful to establish and document the rapid development of trade between the two nations during the decade of the 1960s. Tables 5 and 6 show Japan's share of Western trade with the East, including Eastern Europe, and the proportion of Eastern trade in Japan's foreign trade. The main point demonstrated is the striking increase in both the import and export areas in the case of Japan's trade relations with the Soviet Union.

With respect to the composition of Japanese-Soviet trade, it may come as no surprise that oil figured prominently in the needs of the island nation's trade with the Soviet Union even before the Middle East oil embargo. As noted, Japan must import 99 percent of its crude oil. Japan's economy, expanding at the rate of 10 percent GNP annually during the 1960s, simply gulped oil. But there were problems. Not only did U.S. corporations and the U.S. government object to trade with Communist countries, but Japanese imports of oil were, for a time, limited by the higher freight charges in force during the period that the Suez Canal remained closed. Imports of Soviet crude oil began in 1958 and by 1960 were augmented by petroleum products. Gradually during the decade of the sixties as problems were overcome

TABLE 5

JAPAN'S SHARE OF WESTERN TRADE WITH THE EAST, 1955–1971
(percentages)

	Exports			Imports		
Year	Eastern bloc total	USSR	Eastern Europe	Eastern bloc total	USSR	Eastern Europe
1955	1.2	0.8	1.4	0.7	0.7	0.7
1956	0.5	0.3	0.7	0.8	0.6	0.9
1957	1.1	2.1	0.7	1.2	1.9	0.6
1958	1.7	4.2	0.5	1.6	3.6	0.3
1959	1.9	4.6	0.6	2.4	5.0	0.4
1960	3.2	7.8	0.3	4.4	9.0	0.6
1961	3.5	7.7	0.9	7.2	13.2	2.0
1962	6.8	14.9	1.2	6.4	13.1	1.1
1963	6.8	14.9	1.3	6.3	13.0	1.1
1964	6.8	13.5	1.4	8.4	17.7	1.7
1965	6.6	15.0	2.1	7.7	15.5	1.8
1966	7.1	17.0	2.3	8.6	17.2	2.1
1967	5.5	11.7	2.5	12.4	22.6	4.3
1968	5.1	10.8	1.9	12.0	21.7	4.1
1969	6.8	13.4	2.4	10.9	20.3	3.8
1970	7.5	14.8	3.0	10.1	19.4	3.3
1971	8.2	16.2	3.8	9.0	18.6	2.2

SOURCE: Jan Stankovsky, "Japan's Economic Relations with the USSR and Eastern Europe," *Soviet and Eastern European Foreign Trade* (Spring 1976, p. 71).

and Moscow came to view oil as a significant political weapon, Japan became one of the most important consumers of Soviet crude oil in the non-Communist world.[18]

Raw materials, which had occupied second place in Japanese imports from the Soviet Union and Eastern Europe up to 1965, by 1970 had become most important with a value of some $280 million, 47 percent of imports. Two-thirds of these imports consisted of timber from the Soviet Union, a substantial import commodity which had reached the $200 million figure by 1970. Textiles, particularly cotton, which ranked second among Japanese imports from the Soviet Union reached a high point of $50 million in 1968

TABLE 6

PROPORTION OF EASTERN TRADE IN JAPAN'S FOREIGN TRADE, 1955–1972
(percentages)

	Exports			*Imports*		
Year	Eastern bloc total	USSR	Eastern Europe	Eastern bloc total	USSR	Eastern Europe
1955	0.1	0.0	0.1	0.3	0.1	0.2
1956	0.2	0.0	0.2	0.3	0.1	0.2
1957	0.5	0.3	0.2	0.4	0.3	0.1
1958	0.8	0.6	0.2	0.8	0.7	0.1
1959	0.8	0.7	0.2	1.2	1.1	0.1
1960	1.6	1.5	0.1	2.1	1.9	0.2
1961	1.8	1.5	0.3	2.9	2.5	0.4
1962	3.4	3.0	0.4	2.9	2.6	0.3
1963	3.3	2.9	0.4	2.7	2.4	0.3
1964	3.3	2.8	0.5	3.2	2.9	0.4
1965	2.5	2.0	0.5	3.4	3.0	0.4
1966	2.8	2.2	0.6	3.7	3.2	0.5
1967	2.2	1.5	0.7	4.8	3.9	0.9
1968	1.8	1.4	0.4	4.4	3.6	0.8
1969	2.1	1.7	0.5	3.8	3.1	0.8
1970	2.3	1.8	0.6	3.1	2.5	0.6
1971	2.2	1.6	0.6	2.9	2.5	0.4
1972	2.6	1.8	0.8	2.9	2.5	0.4

SOURCE: Jan Stankovsky, "Japan's Economic Relations with the USSR and Eastern Europe," *Soviet and Eastern European Foreign Trade* (Spring 1976, p. 73).

before decreasing to about one-half that figure by 1970. About 5 percent of Japan's import needs in cotton were supplied by the Soviet Union in 1970.

Among other important imports accounting for the impressive Soviet-Japanese trade expansion during the 1960s were foodstuffs and luxury goods (such as fresh fish and meat), chemical products (including fertilizer), semifinished and finished goods, and nonferous metals (almost half of Japan's needs in platinum, for example, are met by the Soviet Union).[19]

When we come to the matter of Japan's exports to the Soviet Union during the 1960s, heavy industrial items and strategic resources increasingly came to dominate the list. For example, from 1963 to 1965 ships and steel represented the major part of Japan's exports to the Soviet Union, though emphasis shifted to machinery, textiles, and clothing toward the end of the period. Moreover, Soviet orders for ships during the first half of the 1960s played a significant role in the rapid development of Japan's shipyards and tonnage capacity. But after 1967 or 1968, when urgent requirements had been satisfied and as the Soviets became relatively more self-sufficient in these areas, ship deliveries to the Soviet Union declined markedly. Steel continued, however, to constitute some 20 percent of Japanese exports to the East.

One sentence tells the story: Japan witnessed a twentyfold increase in total volume of trade with the Soviet Union between 1957 and 1970.

CHARTING THE 1970s—TREATIES, TALK, AND TRENDS

Two events set the tone for Soviet-Japanese trade activity during the 1970s. The first was a Soviet-Japanese economic conference held in Moscow during February of 1971 where Japanese delegates were surprised and "honored" to be greeted personally by Premier Kosygin. The second was the important five-year trade and payments agreement (1971–1975) signed in 1971 which specified 64 items for Japan to export and 87 items for import from the USSR and called for the exchange of goods valued at $5.2 billion.[20]

Early in 1973, Y. Nakasone, the Japanese Minister of International Trade and Industry, could report that exports to the USSR rose 41 percent in 1972 to $560.97 million. By the spring of the same year he was predicting that exchanges with the USSR could rise to between $3 and $4 billion annually.[21]

The relationship between the trade area and the joint projects in Siberia emerged clearly in April of 1974 when the $1 billion Japanese agreement with the USSR to finance projects involving the development of coal and other resources in Siberia became heavily entwined in the question of trade practices and pricing, since Soviet prices are determined by the state and

Japanese prices largely by market forces.

While the Soviet trade deficit with the United States, Great Britain, France, Japan, and West Germany was put at $1.4 billion for the first six months of 1975, Japan increased its exports to the USSR by 143 percent during the same six-month period to a total of $583 million.

In a succinct article in the fall of 1976 noting that "Japanese-Soviet Trade Will Be the Largest in History," the influential Japanese newspaper *Sankei* stated that with respect to Japanese-Soviet trade between January and June (1976) Japanese exports amounted to $1,020 million, up 16.9 percent over the same period in 1975, while Japanese imports amounted to $540 million, down 6.3 percent over the same period. "It is now certain," the article concluded, "that the volume of Japan's trade with the Soviet Union will exceed the $3 billion mark both ways for the first time in history."[22]

Japan's 1977 White Paper on International Trade. Tokyo publishes annual White Papers in several important areas with an international dimension, trade and defense being the most notable.

The White Paper on trade published by the Japan External Trade Organization (JETRO) at the end provides an overall, up-to-date picture of Soviet-Japanese trade relations as viewed from Tokyo.

The following brief analysis is taken almost verbatim from the 1977 White Paper on International Trade, as it would seem difficult to improve for our purposes on this succinct summary:

In Japan's trade with the Soviet Union in 1976, exports increased substantially, up 38.5% over the preceding year to $2,251.9 million, favorable while exports to other Communist countries in 1976 were inactive. The rate of increase was also higher than that of Japan's total exports. As a result, the share of the Soviet Union in Japan's total exports rose from 2.9% in 1975 to 3.3%. On the other hand, imports from the Soviet Union were stagnate, down 0.2% to $1,167.4 million and as a result, the Soviet Union's share in Japan's total imports declined, from 2.0% in 1975 to 1.8%.

1. Exports

Japan's exports to the Soviet Union in 1976 recorded marked increases for iron and steel goods—the principal merchandise item—and some growth for machinery and mechanical apparatus, but fell for fiber goods and chemical goods.

Iron and steel exports increased markedly, up 93.3% over the preceding year. In quantity, the growth was 2.8-fold or much higher than the growth in value; this was because of a decline in the export price of iron and steel. Among iron and steel items, exports of pipes and joints associated with petroleum and natural gas development witnessed a big increase of 2.3-fold because of the marked growth for welded steel pipes (of ordinary steel).

Exports of machinery and mechanical apparatus increased 21.5% over the preceding year. Among machinery and mechanical apparatus items, exports increased substantially for general machinery, up 46.8% on the same basis, because the delivery of plant equipment was continuing and due to the marked increases for mechanical apparatus for heating and cooling, and for cocks and valves. Exports also increased for agricultural machinery because of the Soviet Union's policy to promote agriculture, but were inactive for other types of general machinery. Exports of electrical machinery were off 11.4% because of marked decreases in exports of manufactured goods of carbon and graphite for electrical usage, although high-voltage electrical apparatus, telecommunications apparatus, and insulated electric wires and cables witnessed a substantial increase due to increased buying by the Soviet Union from Japan. Chemical goods were off 14.9% from the preceding year, the inactivity in reaction to the big increase in 1975. The decrease was particularly substantial for inorganic chemical compounds, but organic chemical compounds and artificial resins and plastics also saw some decreases. Exports of fiber goods were off 15.7% from the preceding year.

2. Imports

Japan's imports from the Soviet Union in 1976 were virtually flat, down 0.2% from the preceding year. Japan's imports from the Soviet Union were on a down-trend along with the recession in Japan. Imports in 1976 were also flat because, as a result of the slow recovery of business activity, imports were off for all items, including lumber, the principal item, as well as cotton, coal, nonferrous metals, etc.

Imports of raw materials were off 6.5% from the preceding year because of the weakening demand in Japan. Among these items, cotton saw a decrease of 25.3% on the same basis due to the decrease in the import price of the item and the poor business in the Japanese fiber industry. Lumber imports, though flat (down 0.5% on the same basis), increased 3.7% in quantity on the same basis.

Imports of mineral fuels were up 15.4% over the preceding year with coal witnessing a 6.9% rise on the same basis due to a rise—though small—in prices. Petroleum refinery products achieved a large increase of 37.5% over the preceding year. Imports of processed and manufactured goods were flat, down 2.8% from the preceding year. Imports of organic chemical compounds increased substantially, but imports were flat for inorganic chemical compounds and were off substantially for chemical fertilizers; as a result, chemical goods as a whole showed a 26.0% decrease from the preceding year.[23]

TRENDS, CONCLUSIONS, PROJECTIONS

- Japan is the Soviet Union's second most important trading partner in the Free World, but the Soviet Union accounts for a relatively small portion (3 to 4 percent) of Japan's growing foreign trade volume.

- The asymmetry between the Soviet Marxist-Leninist-Socialist totally planned economy and Japan's capitalist, modified free-enterprise system results in a wide range of frustrations, difficulties, and roadblocks for Japanese government officials and representatives of business industry in the attempt to achieve satisfactory trade relations with the Soviet Union.

- Technological exchange and the import of heavy industrial commodities (such as ships, machine tools) and strategic items (computers, electronic innovations) constitute a vital asset in the development of the Soviet economy and military establishment.

- Moscow continues to use the lure of trade as a political weapon in an attempt to offset the adverse effects of its adamant, and from the Japanese point of view, unyielding and unsatisfactory position on the question of the Northern Territories and to compensate for Japan's increasingly close political and economic ties with Peking.

- Early Japanese enthusiasm over prospects of massive trade resulting in part from joint economic development plans in Siberia (such as the Tyuman Oil Project), has waned as Japanese government officials and economic leaders have apparently concluded that the advantages to Moscow would far outweigh those accruing to Japan and that Soviet plans are as much strategic as they are economic in character and intent.

- As the new Soviet Wrangel Port facilities are completed, concomitant with Siberian resource development, some additional modest increase in Soviet-Japanese trade may be anticipated.

- The overall trend in Soviet-Japanese trade relations in the past several years has been toward a substantial increase in exports, particularly iron, steel, and heavy industrial components, but imports from the Soviet Union (as in the celebrated case of the Japan–United States trade) have not kept pace—a trend that may be expected to continue.

Part Five

Diplomatic and Strategic Dimensions

Chapter Eleven

Peking versus Moscow vis-à-vis Japan

In comparing and contrasting Peking's with Moscow's postwar policies toward Japan, we must inevitably consider the two Communist giants' changing relationship with one another and, in turn, with the United States. Beyond this, Japan's curious and sometimes contradictory responses to her huge continental neighbors demand equal time. Here, clearly, is the subject for another book—indeed several books. Fortunately, a number of serious scholars—Asian, European, and American—have over the past several years looked carefully at these interrelationships. The essence of their findings provides divergent approaches, multinational dimensions, and complementary judgments on this critical aspect of the subject. Accordingly, along with examining and documenting certain Soviet and Chinese Communist positions and policies, the following montage will be devoted to a comparative consideration of the perspectives, perceptions, and conclusions of some of these knowledgeable colleagues.[1]

The Moscow-Peking alliance of the 1950s, directed against Japan and the United States, disintegrated rapidly after 1960 into an increasingly hostile confrontation which, in turn, spawned more or less independent Soviet and Chinese Communist approaches and policies toward Japan. After the death of Stalin, Japan's positive attitudes were encouraged and conditioned by the more flexible Soviet policies of "coexistence" and "detente"[2] and in the early 1970s, by overtures to Peking. At the same time, Japan's political ties with the Soviet Union and Communist China continued to be inhibited by Tokyo's ongoing security involvement with the United States and by the sense of successive Japanese governments that Japan's best interests lay in maintaining a healthy economic and security relationship with the West.

The 1971 Nixon-Kissinger shock, after Kissinger's secret trip to Peking, and the Nixon visit to Peking early in 1972 in effect paved the way for Tokyo's recognition of the People's Republic of China (in September of 1972) and for the consequent emergence of a curious Sino-Soviet-American triangle.[3] The new political climate in Northeast Asia, thus engendered, was further modified by three other dramatic developments of the first half of the 1970s. The first was, of course, the debacle in Vietnam and the questions it inevitably raised everywhere, especially in Asia, about the credibility of the United States as a defense partner.[4] The second was the Soviet economic offensive resulting in development of substantial joint Soviet-Japanese economic ventures, and the parallel if less spectacular growth of Soviet-Japanese trade.[5] This development was accompanied, to a smaller extent, by increased Japanese trade with the People's Republic of China and, notably, with Taiwan. The third was the surprising dialogue between North and South Korea which was arranged by the Koreans in the summer of 1971.

No wonder, then, that Tokyo, while speaking of the importance of separating politics from economics, has opted for the best of three worlds: increased economic ties with, but "equidistance" from, the two huge continental neighbors (plus ongoing trade and cultural ties with Taiwan), side by side with continued close and substantial economic and security relationships with the United States.

SOVIET WORLD PERSPECTIVES AND GLOBAL GOALS—EASTERN TARGET: JAPAN

Amid the shattered dreams and persistent hopes for a more reasonable, peaceful world, and in the confusion over detente, it is well to remind ourselves—with Japan as the point of reference—of the fundamental differences between Western and Soviet (and Chinese Communist) perceptions of peace and normalcy. To many Americans at least, peace traditionally has been understood as a state of nonwar, noncrisis quietude (perhaps reminiscent of the nostalgic 1920s) where "mutual misunderstandings" may either be ignored until they go away or simply regarded as healthy differences of opinion ultimately to be resolved by honest discussion and give and take— as in the case of an essentially well-meaning but occasionally difficult neighbor next door. But we are not dealing with the neighbor next door, least of all, one concerned with our well-being. On the contrary, to the Soviets (and the Chinese Communists) *struggle* is regarded as normal, desirable, inevitable—and the "capitalist" United States as the arch, ultimate enemy. Thus, "wars of national liberation" along with continued, selective attacks on "capitalism," "imperialism," and western society, including Japan, are seen as perfectly consistent with detente. We have Brezhnev's recent testimony on that point.[6]

Within this Soviet world perspective and as part of the rationale for Soviet global strategy, Japan (always seen as part of the West) has been cast successively as an "imperialist nation" (which in the prewar era, of course, it was); then as a "dependency" of the United States (against which the 1950 Soviet-Chinese Alliance was directed); and, since Japan's recovery of sovereignty (at least until very recently), as a co-conspirator, security-treaty ally of the United States and as a nation harboring a succession of governments bent on supporting "U.S. aggression and imperialism in Asia."

SINO-SOVIET RELATIONS—FROM ALLIANCE TO CONFRONTATION—THE CHANGING POSITION OF JAPAN

The 1950 Treaty of Friendship and Alliance signed between the Soviet Union and the People's Republic of China keyed on cooperation against future aggression by Japan or "any other state that may collaborate with Japan directly or indirectly in acts of aggression."[7] That the United States was that "any other state" an editorial in *Jen Min Jih Pao* took immediate pains to make clear. "This alliance," the official Peking *People's Daily* stated, "will effectively prevent Japan and other countries allied directly or indirectly with Japan from renewing aggression and breaking world peace. For this reason," the editorial concluded, "it is a heavy blow against American imperialism which is now fostering the re-emergence of Japanese aggression."[8]

Malcolm Mackintosh sums up the Soviet rationale of the first postwar decade, including the Sino-Soviet alliance period, when he writes:

At the end of the Second World War . . . [the Soviets'] main preoccupation appears . . . to have been the defense of the Far East and the weakening—if possible, the elimination—of American power in mainland China, South Korea and ultimately Japan, using newly acquired political, territorial and military strengths in the area. The first task was in fact performed by the Chinese Communists in 1948-1949; the second, tried by the North Koreans assisted by the Chinese in 1950-51, failed; the third was briefly attempted, as evidenced by the waves of violence in Japan in the late 1940s [and early 1950s]. However, from the Soviet point of view at the time, much more important than those last two setbacks were the conquest of mainland China by the Communists, the Sino-Soviet alliance (particularly its military potentialities for the USSR) and the readiness of Mao Tse-tung to defer in public, as late as 1957, to the "leading role" of the Soviet Union in the "World Communist Movement."[9]

A significant article in *Izvestiia*, reviewing the ensuing decade of what were termed Soviet attempts to patch up relations with Peking, stated that Moscow's efforts included several offers to hold summit meetings with the Chinese leaders (1964, 1965, 1970, 1973) and to conclude interim accords on the resumption of border trade, long-term agreements, renewed cultural cooperation, and so on, which the Chinese purportedly totally rejected or simply ignored.[10]

The initial postwar period of the Sino-Soviet alliance was followed by four fairly distinct phases in the Sino-Soviet relationship, each with clear implications for Peking's policy toward Japan and the world: the first, 1957–1960, produced increasingly acrimonious debate behind the scenes; the second, dating from the end of 1960 to the summer of 1963, centered on the struggle for adherents within the Communist movement; the third began with Peking's open break with Moscow in the summer of 1963 and lasted to the opening of border talks in October of 1969.[11] With little evident amelioration of Moscow-Peking tensions, a fourth period, since 1970, has witnessed the establishment of diplomatic relations between Japan and the People's Republic of China and the emergence of a new, more positive relationship between Peking and Washington dictated in large measure, it would appear, by the former's problems with Moscow.

JAPAN'S PLACE IN PEKING'S WORLD VIEW AND GLOBAL GOALS

Students of Chinese history argue, sometimes rather persuasively, that the Chinese world view is rooted in the term *Chung-Kuo* with its implications of that nation's perceived place as "the center of the universe."[12] That China, like India, has been over the centuries a cultural hub of Asia, from which many of the predominant ideas and forms of the civilization on its periphery have radiated, there can be no question.

It is within this context that Chou En-lai's characterization of the world in his report to the National People's Congress in January 1975 is most interesting, and it does serve to focus the issue sharply in contemporary Marxist-Leninist-Maoist terms. Emphasizing the contradictions between the United States and the Soviet Union and the contradictions between the two superpowers and the Third World (the developing countries) and what is termed the Second World (Europe and Japan), Chou on that occasion went on to stress: ". . . the contention for world hegemony between the two superpowers, the United States and the Soviet Union, is becoming more and more intense." Then he added a point no longer a public part of Soviet doctrine—indeed, since 1953, specifically rejected by Moscow: ". . . their [US/USSR] fierce contention," Chou states, "is bound to lead to world war one of these days."

Finally, Chou defines China's central place, and Japan's role, in the scheme of things: "The Third World is the main force in combating colonialism, imperialism and hegemonism. China is a developing socialist country belonging to the Third World," Chou contends. "We should enhance our unity with the countries and peoples of Asia, Africa and Latin America. . . . We support the countries and peoples of the Second World [Japan]," he concludes, "in their struggle against superpower control, threats, and bullying."[13]

In a confidential document of the Chinese People's Liberation Army issued early in 1973 (obtained and made public by the Chinese Nationalist Government on Taiwan), the Soviet Union was described as China's "most dangerous enemy" and the Nixon visit to China in 1972 was seen as "the great victory of Chairman Mao's revolutionary diplomatic line," designed to frustrate the Soviet attempt to encircle China and to "aggravate the contradictions between the United States and the Soviet Union."[14]

From Peking's perspective, the following steps taken by the Soviet Union are viewed as dramatic proof of Moscow's design to "encircle" China militarily and to isolate her diplomatically. First, there is the massive Soviet military buildup of strategic nuclear weapons to the north and west. Second, the Soviet Union has been negotiating with Japan for economic cooperation in the development of Siberian resources, which Peking sees as aimed both at undermining Sino-Japanese rapprochement and strengthening the Soviet strategic position in the Far East vis-à-vis China. Third, Soviet ties with India and the Soviet naval presence in the Indian Ocean (as part of the advent of the Soviet global navy) pose problems for China's southern flank. Peking is, of course, also concerned with India's "go nuclear" decision, and, to a lesser degree, with the annexation of Sikkim. Fourth, in Southern Asia, Moscow has been making steady if unspectacular efforts to woo China's non-Communist neighbors.[15]

THE EVOLUTION OF JAPANESE-CHINESE RELATIONS

With the Sino-Soviet alliance as the centerpiece, several fairly distinct periods in relations between Japan and China (before, during, and following the alliance), may be identified. The first period runs from the end of the Pacific war (in 1945) to the establishment of the People's Republic of China (in October of 1949). For Japan it was, of course, a period of American Occupation; for China, an era of revolution and economic chaos which saw the emergence of Chinese Communist control over the mainland and the retreat of the Chinese Nationalist government to Taiwan. Both Soviet and U.S. policies toward China at this juncture, it may be recorded, were indecisive and sometimes uncertain and the "New China's" policy toward Japan as yet undetermined.

The second period runs from the founding of the People's Republic of China to the outbreak of the Korean War (in June of 1950). Japan was now seen by Peking as an "advanced base for American imperialism in Asia" and the prospects of Japanese rearmament as a "major threat to the peace of Asia."

The third period begins with the North Korean attack on June 25, 1950 (or perhaps more precisely with the massive injection of Chinese "volunteers" into the Korean War in December), and ends three years later, with the ceasefire in June of 1953. Communists in Japan were encouraged, especially by Peking, to conduct militant, revolutionary activities in support of the war. As part of a general toughening of U.S. Asian policy, Japan, after regaining its sovereignty, was incorporated into the U.S. strategic security system against the strong opposition of both the Soviet Union and Communist China.

The fourth period extended from 1953 to 1957. Peking's support for a revolution in Japan was now replaced by emphasis on culture and trade looking toward the importance of normalizing relations with Japan.

The fifth period, from the end of 1957 to early in 1959, coincided with China's "Great Leap Forward" and saw both Chinese domestic and foreign policy become more radical and extreme. The Sino-Soviet alliance began to show serious signs of strain. Relations between Peking and Tokyo deteriorated. Trade with Japan, which had been growing, was all but discontinued.

The sixth period from 1959 until the summer of 1966, when the cultural revolution began, has been characterized as that of "adjustment period diplomacy." The Liao-Takasaki (L-T) trade agreement of January 1962 made Japan the only country in the world to trade freely with both Taiwan and the Chinese mainland. As might have been anticipated, this raised a number of delicate political questions. For example, Peking according to Chou En-lai's Four Principles, distinguished between "friendly" and "unfriendly" firms in deciding which Japanese firm was "acceptable" for trade with the People's Republic of China. By this time, of course, the Sino-Soviet alliance had disintegrated.

The seventh period, 1966 to spring 1969, witnessed the cultural revolution within China which preempted Peking's attention to matters of foreign policy. The consequence for Peking was, in effect, no foreign policy at all.

The eighth period, during the early 1970s, following the Ninth CCP Party Conference, saw this situation remedied and a steady return to near normality, the restoration of diplomatic machinery and initiative, and substantial attempts to enhance China's image throughout the world—notably in Japan. In this process, people-to-people diplomacy and trade as a political weapon came to play increasingly significant roles.[16]

PEOPLE-TO-PEOPLE DIPLOMACY— PEKING STYLE, FOCUS: JAPAN

Peking's people-to-people diplomacy vis-à-vis Japan must be credited in some large measure for the recruiting of selective Japanese public opinion, the influencing of key Japanese political and economic organizations, and ultimately, moving the Japanese government "positively" in the direction of recognition of the People's Republic of China.

What is people-to-people diplomacy? It is the intense, centrally controlled, highly coordinated assault on and wooing of an adversary nation's political, economic, and social institutions, opinion-molding and policy-making groups, and key organizations and individuals so as to engender ideas, attitudes, sympathies, and, ultimately, political leadership and policies in line with one's own perception of the "correct path" for that nation—in this case Japan's official recognition of the People's Republic of China. For this task, Peking has shown itself singularly adroit.

Peking's people-to-people diplomacy has taken the form of invitations by Chou En-lai to various Japanese Diet groups, labor leaders, student organitions, farm representatives, and others, to "visit China to see for themselves." Sometimes, in earlier years, a brief audience with Chairman Mao was even arranged. While this activity on Peking's part was somewhat muted during the Sino-Soviet alliance and necessarily curtailed during the period of China's cultural revolution, after 1970 it became highly visible and very effective. Simultaneously, numerous Chinese trade and "cultural" exhibitions have been held in Japan over the years. Characteristically on such occasions, the head of the Chinese delegation will speak of "friendship, peace, and trade"— in that order.[17]

In the months and years immediately preceding Tokyo's recognition of the People's Republic of China, both the Chinese and Japanese press were replete with elaborate stories of the visits of an endless number of Japanese individuals and groups of all political complexions to China.

A significant article entitled "Fruits of Joint Protracted Struggle of Chinese and Japanese Peoples," in *Peking Review* in October of 1972 acknowledged the role of people-to-people diplomacy in specific and detailed terms. "The Normalization of China-Japan relations," the article begins, 'is the result of the joint protracted struggle of the Chinese and the Japanese people."

Stressing the importance of the Japan-China Friendship organizations in "promoting non-governmental contacts and the restoration of diplomatic relations between the two countries," the article goes on to say: "exhibitions, lectures, and discussions to publicize China's socialist revolution and socialist construction were held in different parts of Japan under the auspices of friendship organizations including the Japan-China Friendship Association (Orthodox), the Japan-China Cultural Exchange Association and the Japan Association for the Promotion of International Trade, thus greatly promoting mutual understanding between the Chinese and Japanese peoples."[18]

Due credit is also given to the "tremendous efforts by Japanese opposition parties." The Japan Socialist Party, the Komei Party, and the Democratic Socialist Party are singled out for the "tremendous efforts to promote the normalization of relations between Japan and China." Finally, the contributions by well-known Japanese personages going back over the years are recalled.[19] This, then, is people-to-people diplomacy—Peking style.

THE NORMALIZATION OF JAPAN'S RELATIONS WITH THE PEOPLE'S REPUBLIC OF CHINA

Several interrelated issues and factors account for the delay and ambivalence in Japan's decision to recognize the People's Republic of China. Certainly, Tokyo"s close relations with Washington, including the Japan–United States Security Treaty, must be ranked high on the list of inhibiting factors. Moreover, within the ranks of Japan's ruling Liberal-Democratic Party there was no clear consensus on this issue. In what he describes as the "Alice in Wonderland qualities" of the internal debate, Donald Hellmann quite correctly suggests that on this issue as on others, "Foreign policy discussions among the conservatives have transpired mainly in private and in response to external (international) pressures and have been colored by intraparty factional considerations." He adds: ". . . the opposition left and the media have either rigidly clung to abstract moral positions (e.g., anti-Americanism and an undifferentiated moral commitment to peace) or used specific issues to further their own political purposes."[20]

The Japanese business community, on the other hand—for its part having no apparent trouble in separating economics from politics—had been carrying on an increasingly lucrative trade with mainland China even as influential business and trade organizations within Japan applied their own brand of pressure on the Japanese government in the direction of "normalization." All the while, of course, the key question persisted as to what to do about Taiwan (Nationalist China) as Japan not only maintained official diplomatic ties with the Chinese Nationalist government there, but concurrently carried on a highly valued and extremely lucrative trade relationship with that large and prosperous island in limbo.

A look at the *Peking Review* for the years 1971 and 1972 reveals the striking *volte face* made by the government of the People's Republic in its treatment of Japan, "Japanese militarism," and "U.S. aggressive plans in Asia" before and after (or for that matter, on the eve of) the restoration of diplomatic relations between the two nations.

The pages of the official Peking mouthpiece during 1971 are crammed with long articles bearing such ominous titles as: "Indisputable Evidence of Revival of Japanese Militarism" ("Collusion with U.S. imperialism in hope of dominating Asia") January 22, 1971; "True Colors of Japanese Militarism Exposed" ("To meet the needs of U.S. imperialism in carrying out its policies of aggression and war in Asia . . .") May 21, 1971; "Oppose Revival of Japanese Militarism by U.S.-Japanese Reactionaries," June 25, 1971; "U.S. and Japan Tighten Military Collusion," August 13, 1971; "The Danger of Japanese Imperialism's Policies of Aggression and Expansionism" ("The Japan-U.S. 'Security Treaty' has put Japan under the U.S. 'nuclear umbrella' 'and bound it tightly to the U.S. chariot of aggression") September 10, 1971.

During the first half of 1972 (as Peking pointed toward the reestablish-- ment of formal diplomatic relations with Tokyo), the *Peking Review* became a different journal.

The Nixon-Sato talks of January, for example, merely displayed "stepped up collaboration and inseparable contradictions" while continued use of Okinawa as a U.S. base was moderately deplored on several occasions. Otherwise the stormy weather had changed. By the fall of the year, with the Tanaka-Nixon Joint Statement, Peking could report *without comment* that the Joint Statement "reaffirmed the intention of the two governments to maintain the treaty of mutual cooperation and security" (September 8, 1972).

What replaced China's voluminous coverage of "Japanese militarism in collusion with U.S. imperialism" and "design to dominate Asia"? Here are a few typical "cultural" events and now nonbelligerent assertions from the *Peking Review* for the year 1972: "Chou En-lai and others see Japanese Theatrical Performance," February 28, 1972; "Chinese Carrier-Pigeon" ("The Activist Delegation of the Japan-China Friendship Association [Orthodox] brought a carrier pigeon with them . . .") March 24, 1972; "Second Japanese Komeito Delegation Visits China," June 2, 1972; Shanghai Dance Drama Troupe in Japan," July 21, 1972; "China-Japan Friendship Association Reception," October 27, 1972; "Bridge of Green," ("1,000 cherry saplings were shipped from Tokyo to Peking [by Japanese Foreign Ministry]"), November 10, 1972 (full page); and "Giant Pandas—Token of Friendship" ("The two giant pandas 'Lan Lan' and 'Kang Kang', gifts from the Chinese people to the Japanese people, made their first appearance before the Japanese public on November 5 at Tokyo Ueno Zoo"), November 17, 1972.

Peking Review concluded the year with a generous full-page review of cultural and economic ties entitled "Time-Honored Sino-Japanese Friendship," December 22, 1972. In addition, of course, the stream of VIPs—capped by the visit of Premier Tanaka in October—between Japan and the People's Republic of China during 1972 was reported in sympathetic detail.

THE SIGNIFICANCE OF TRADE BETWEEN THE PEOPLE'S REPUBLIC AND JAPAN

Sino-Japanese trade accounted for some 15 percent of Japan's prewar trade (1934–1936 average) and about 20 percent of China's trade just prior to World War II. With the Communist takeover of China in 1949 and with Japan under Allied (U.S.) occupation, mutual trade fell to less than 1 percent for each partner. After the Korean War, the embargo policy against China initiated by the United States was lifted and Sino-Japanese trade began to expand. This period and immediately thereafter also coincided with the deterioration of Moscow-Peking relations.[21]

One of the important, inevitable consequences of the Sino-Soviet split was the Chinese decision to shift the bulk of its trade away from the Soviet bloc to non-Communist countries. As the Cold War atmosphere abated somewhat and the United States became increasingly tolerant of Japanese trade with the continent, Sino-Japanese trade grew rapidly. By 1965, Japan had become China's leading trade partner and by the end of the decade, she accounted for 16 percent of China's foreign trade.[22]

Within two years after the normalization of Japanese-Chinese relations (in September 1972) Japan's total trade with the People's Republic of China had increased nearly threefold. Significantly, Japan's trade with Taiwan also doubled between 1972 and 1974. Japan's principal exports to China have consisted of iron and steel, trucks and ships. Japan's main imports have included coal, cotton, and food products. But it is Chinese oil and its potential that excites Tokyo as Japan must import the vast majority of the increasingly large bulk of oil consumed. In 1975, China was committed to export 7.8 million tons of crude oil to Japan. Japan's projection (hope) is that new explorations in China will place it as the fifth largest oil producer in the world by 1980 and that it would then be able to spare 50 million tons for export.[23]

On February 16, 1978, Japan and China concluded a $20 billion eight-year private trade agreement. Under the terms of the pact, Japan will import Chinese crude oil and coal while China will purchase Japanese industrial plants, construction materials and equipment.[24]

It is idle to speculate whether or not the Communist world still values trade (as Khrushchev once remarked) "as much for political as for economic reasons." That China's (and the Soviet Union's) close economic ties with Japan have strategic-political implications for all three nations—and for the United States—seems clear. Certainly as a rationale for Japan's recognition of the Peking government economic factors must be rated as very significant.

THE SINO-SOVIET-AMERICAN TRIANGLE

Strange alliances born of strategic/political necessity have not been uncommon in our lifetime. Compared with the Soviet-Nazi marriage of convenience (1939–1941) or the United States–Soviet wartime relationship (1941–1945) or even the Sino-Soviet alliance (the 1950s), the Sino-Soviet-American triangle may not be any more "unholy" than the rest. It does seem fair to suggest, however, that Far Eastern international relations of the 1970s—and Japan's place at the center of that arena—must be approached within a distinctly different context from the Cold War assumptions of the 1950s or Peking's twin-enemy (U.S./USSR) perceptions of the 1960s—and for some intriguing reasons.

Doak Barnett puts the contemporary issue neatly when he writes: "Peking now appears to base its policies on two different conceptualizations: on the one hand, its publicly articulated three-world schema, in which both superpowers are labeled adversaries; and, on the other, its unstated view of five major power centers, in which the United States is regarded as a limited 'ally' against the Soviet Union. Although overlapping to some extent," he concludes, "these two world views are very different in their implications and involve inevitable 'contradictions'."[25]

But it would be wrong to infer (and certainly Doak Barnett does not) that Peking has gone soft on capitalism. On that, most specialists on China and the Soviet Union agree. Perhaps the most colorful and authoritative warning against the dangers inherent in such a notion, indeed in the Sino-Soviet-American triangle itself, is the celebrated analogy put forward by then Vice-Premier Teng Hsiao-ping: "In the current struggle against colonialism, imperialism, and hegemony," he told delegates to a special session of the United Nations in the spring of 1974, "we [sic] developing countries must especially guard against the danger of 'letting the tiger [the USSR] in through the back door' while 'repulsing the wolf' [the United States] through the front gate."[26] The United States is thus seen as a lesser immediate threat, a more reasonable enemy to be dealt with later.

The same point emerges clearly from a "captured" Chinese Communist military document obviously intended to assure the faithful that China's tilt toward the United States was purely tactical and temporary. The document, which found its way out of China early in 1974, explains: "In the present situation: U.S. imperialism's counterrevolutionary global strategy has met with setbacks; its aggressive power has been weakened; and hence, it has had to make some reaction and adjustment of its strategy." Then the document goes on to say: "Soviet revisionism on the other hand, is stretching its arms in all directions and is expanding desperately. It is more crazy, adventurist, and deceptive. That is why," the document concludes, "Soviet revisionism has become our country's most dangerous and important enemy."[27]

When Secretary of State Henry Kissinger visited Peking the following year, in October of 1975, Foreign Minister Ch'iao Kuan-hua "urged that the U.S. wage a 'tit for tat' struggle against [Soviet] hegemonism." The Secretary replied that "the United States would resist hegemony . . . but that the United States will also make every effort to avoid needless confrontation when it can do so without threatening the security of third countries."[28] In spelling out a new Pacific Doctrine, at Honolulu in December of the same year, President Ford noted that the United States, the Soviet Union, China, and Japan were all Pacific powers with intersecting security concerns in Asia. The United States, he said, stands for "peace with all—and hostility toward none."

Even when elaborated, the new doctrine left unanswered a number of key questions, among them relations with the two Koreas and the issue of Taiwan, not to mention security problems related to Japan. These will be dealt with briefly in the final chapter, "The Security Dimension."

Professor Robert Scalapino sums up the rationale and significance of the Sino-Soviet-American triangle when he writes: "The limited detente China achieved with the United States, despite the homage that should be paid to the Nixon administration's receptivity and initiatives, was basically the product of Chinese decisions. These decisions," he concludes, "were in no sense a result of ideological or political convergence; they were grounded in the Chinese need to counter the Soviet threat. Militarily weak or politically isolated, Peking could neither fight nor negotiate from an advantageous position."[29]

CONTROLLING CONCEPTS:
"ANTIHEGEMONY" AND "EQUIDISTANCE"

With the emergence of Tokyo's flexible foreign policy during 1972, the concepts of "antihegemony" and "equidistance" became dominant, if controversial, factors in the conduct of Japan's foreign relations with the People's Republic of China and the Soviet Union. The Joint Statement issued upon the resumption of diplomatic relations between Tokyo and

Peking, in September of that year, includes, verbatim, the hegemony clause of the Shanghai Communiqué signed by President Nixon and Premier Chou En-lai six months earlier. With respect to Asia, the doctrine stipulates: "Neither [country] should seek hegemony in the Asian-Pacific region and each is opposed to efforts by any other country or group of countries to establish such hegemony."[30]

The Soviet reaction was slow, but predictable. If for a time, Moscow (surprisingly) showed few outward signs of active concern over the issue, by the spring of 1975 Soviet public indifference had ended. When China and Japan began to discuss the hegemony clause during negotiations looking toward the conclusion of a final peace treaty, TASS warned the Japanese government that a Sino-Soviet treaty including the hegemony clause would complicate relations between Japan and the Soviet Union. TASS further appealed to Japan, in a thinly veiled reference to the People's Republic of China, to reject "all activities of *Third World* countries [italics supplied], which are aimed at blocking the improvement of Soviet-Japanese relations."[31]

Perhaps the clearest explanation of the rationale of Japan's defense and foreign policy officials in dealing with the hegemony issue is that put forward by a Pakistani scholar and diplomat, Golam W. Choudhury, after high-level discussions with Japanese authorities in Tokyo in July of 1976. Choudhury reports that they cited three specific reasons for reverberations over hegemony:

(1) The word "hegemony" has acquired a definite meaning and significance in the context of Sino-Soviet feud, and Japan would like to remain neutral in that conflict; (2) China's 1975 Constitution speaks against "hegemony of the two superpowers." Japan is not willing to oppose the U.S. presence in Asia, which is vital to Japanese security, and the "anti-hegemony" clause could be construed as a commitment to do just that; (3) If Japan signed the treaty with the "anti-hegemony" clause in it, Moscow would be so offended that Japan would have no hope of getting back the four islands that the USSR seized after Japan's defeat in World War II and that Japan still claims.[32]

Nonetheless, for economic, political, and strategic reasons, Tokyo has, so far, found a flexible policy involving "equidistance" from its two more militarily powerful and contending continental neighbors, the only sensible policy among very few realistic options.

Chapter Twelve

Fisheries, Whaling, and the Law of the Sea

PERSPECTIVES ON THE ISSUES— HISTORICAL AND INTERNATIONAL

One does not ordinarily think of a fish as a strategic or tactical weapon, except perhaps in the metaphorical sense of a submarine or in the case of a dolphin retrieving an underwater missile. But to the first and second largest consumers of seafood in the world, Japan and the Soviet Union, fish is a fighting word: verbal attacks punctuate regular conferences on fisheries and the Law of the Sea; "fishing boats" turn out to be spy vessels or electronic eavesdroppers, while Russian and Japanese fishing fleets "sweep and deplete" each others' precious, endangered fishing grounds—even as scores of Japanese fishing craft are seized and their crews detained by Soviet authorities. Only on the issue of whaling is there a curious meeting of Russian and Japanese minds.

Before oil came to dominate the world economic scene, it was properly said of Japan that "she (like England) is built on coal and surrounded by fish." The Japanese eat more fish than any other large nation in the world. For the Japanese, fish have often spelled the margin between starvation and survival. Tiny villages of half fishermen–half farmer peasants have from ancient times dotted the picturesque Japanese coastline. During the Meiji era (1868–1912), fishing was concentrated in the coastal waters. As part of Japan's emergence as a major industrial power in the early twentieth century, large fisheries enterprises were established to exploit more distant seas. "Floating factory" vessels began to appear in Soviet waters along with other ominous indicators of growing Japanese power and questionable economic-military intentions. Total fisheries catches more than tripled between 1910–1914 and 1930–1934.[1]

It seemed only a matter of time before Japanese and Soviet economic and strategic interests would inevitably clash in the North Pacific region.

Soviet diplomatic historian and recognized specialist on the Far East, Leonid N. Kutakov (one-time Soviet number three man at the United Nations), specifically links the fisheries problems of prewar years to Japanese aggressive intelligence and military activities. He writes: "The Japanese took advantage of the fishing and crabbing lots and the right of Japanese fishermen to pull up at the Soviet shores during the fishing season in order to process the catch at the canning factories, to engage in sabotage and espionage against the U.S.S.R. . . . ." Then he makes his central point: "In 1937–1938, 12 groups were found spying. The solid structures erected by the Japanese at their fishing bases and canning factories were suitable for military purposes."[2]

SCAP'S CONCERN WITH THE FISHERIES QUESTION

With Japan's surrender ending the Pacific War and the reduction of the once far-flung and powerful empire to essentially the four main islands, Japanese fishing in the open sea was correspondingly curtailed. A very limited area where fishing could be conducted was initially delineated by SCAP on August 20, 1945. Military security considerations were given as the determinant factor.[3] The northern fishing regions near the Kurile Islands and opposite China and Soviet Siberia were designated as strictly off limits.

Even with these restrictions (since some 85 percent of Japanese fishing operations had always been conducted in the waters adjacent to Japan proper), by 1947, with SCAP-authorized construction of new fishing boats, production had been essentially restored to prewar levels, except for sardines and herring.[4]

Recognizing the critical importance of fish to Japan's economic future, indeed to the very livelihood of her people, SCAP authorized a successive series of limited extensions of the September 1945 "MacArthur line"— notably in November 1945, June 1946, and September 1949. In May 1950, SCAP directed that a special area in the region of the Trust Territories be made available for mothership-type tuna expeditions only.[5]

The Northern Pacific, Kurile, Soviet, and Chinese coastal waters continued to remain off limits during the remainder of the Occupation period to the growing and increasingly restless Japanese fishing fleet.

HEIGHTENED ACTIVITY AND CONFLICT IN POST-TREATY JAPAN, 1952–1956

The period from the signing of the San Francisco Peace Treaty in 1951 to the initialing of the Soviet-Japanese Fisheries Convention in 1956, as part of the process of Soviet-Japanese normalization of relations, saw heightened activity and growing conflict, as well as an occasional agreement, over fisheries issues.

The San Francisco Peace Treaty provided for the reopening of the Northern Pacific region to Japanese fishing, but the Soviet Union had, of course, not signed the treaty. Representatives of several Japanese fisheries companies sought to remedy this situation by meeting with Soviet representatives in Tokyo in 1952 "to attempt to secure Soviet permission."[6]

When that didn't work, in August of 1953, Kensaku Onishi, President of the Hokuyo Suisan Company, visited the Soviet Union, among other countries; and there, in addition to discussing general matters of trade, he is thought to have conferred confidentially with Soviet authorities on the fisheries problem.[7]

Moreover, Tsunejiro Hiratsuka of the Greater Japan Fisheries Association (*Dai Nihon Suisan Kai*) aired Japanese grievances about fishing in northern waters at the World Peace conferences at Berlin and Stockholm during May and June 1954 and called for the convening of a World Fisheries conference. He even distributed a pamphlet at the same conference advocating "mutual understanding with the Soviet Union and a more positive approach toward normalization."[8]

These and other overtures (plus persistent pressure from fisheries circles within Japan) were not lost on the Haoyama cabinet which, as noted, upon taking office in December of 1954, was favorably inclined toward normalization of relations with the USSR. Some progress appears to have been made and permission for an increased number of Japanese fleets to operate in Soviet waters was granted; but an agreement between fisheries representatives and Soviet officials for the exchange of teams of specialists to study each others' fishing failed to materialize when the Japanese government refused to issue the required visas.[9]

One of the principal Soviet worries over Japanese fishing operations near its borders in these years involved the decline in salmon stock in the North Pacific. At the United Nations Conference for Conservation of the Living Resources of the Sea, held in Rome between April 18 and May 16, 1955, the Soviet delegates linked the decrease of pink salmon in the Far East to the resumption of fishing in the northern seas.[10]

After a series of Soviet accusations and Japanese denials over this and other fisheries problems, the Soviet government was unwilling to postpone resolution of the matter any longer, and in a radio broadcast of March 21, 1956, unilaterally limited Japanese fishing beyond what was to become commonly known as the Bulganin line.[11] The issue now became critical, and the need for talks became increasingly urgent.

THE 1956 SOVIET-JAPANESE FISHERIES CONVENTION

As an adjunct to the talks on normalization, the northern fisheries talks were held in Moscow April 28 to May 14, 1956. The advantage of separating the possibly more manageable fisheries issue from the very difficult territorial problem seemed the key to the matter. The Japanese delegation was headed by Ichiro Kono, the Soviet delegation by Fisheries Minister A. A. Ashkov.

By 1956 "coexistence" had become the centerpiece of Soviet foreign policy, Moscow was on the brink of a major dispute with China, and the Japanese were becoming increasingly restless following their return to sovereign status. On the territorial issue, as we shall see in greater detail, the Soviets were willing to make no concessions. But the fisheries question provided Moscow with both political leverage and bait. Moreover, there were areas of conflicting fisheries concern, such as overfishing, where it was in the Soviet interest to arrive at some formal agreement. All this was, of course, over and above the public relations value for Moscow of placating the Japanese fishermen and assuring them, and the world, of the usual Soviet policy of "non-interference in the internal affairs of other nations."

A number of important consequences of the Soviet-Japanese fisheries dispute, some of them perhaps unexpected, flowed from the Soviet policies associated with the "conservation decree," the Bulganin line. Not only were the London talks broken off, but Soviet warnings now failed to deter the Japanese from their avowed intention of defying Moscow. On April 1, "over 100 trawlers exited Hokkaido for the fishing grounds off the central and southern Kurile Islands. On April 3, 13 Japanese crabbing fleets left for western Kamchatka waters. Two crabbing fleets left the port of Hakodate on April 10 and 20 boats sailed for Bristol Bay and the Bering Sea. It was clear that Moscow's threat of force was not sufficient to stay the Japanese fleets. . . ."[12]

It is within this context that fresh exploratory conversations started in Moscow on April 20, with full-blown fisheries talks underway a week later. After disagreements, maneuvering, and some minor concessions, the fisheries agreement was signed on May 14, 1956. It came into force December 12, 1956.

The agreement, in fact, made little substantial change in the situation that had prevailed earlier. Except for granting the validity of locally applicable Japanese regulations, Japan's situation, if anything, even deteriorated slightly. For example, the so-called "conventional zone" was enlarged to embrace the open waters of the Bering Sea and the seas of Japan and Okhotsk. Also, the sector within which salmon fishing would be jointly regulated was enlarged, again clearly to the advantage of the Soviets. The key questions as to the width of the respective territorial waters remained unanswered. Enforcement details of the agreement were conveniently left to be worked out later by a Soviet-Japanese commission.[13]

POINT AND COUNTERPOINT, 1956–1975

The frustrating long two decades between the Soviet-Japanese Fisheries Convention of 1956 and the limited Fisheries Accord of 1975 witnessed impressive economic growth on the part of both nations. In the process, fisheries issues inevitably multiplied and tended to become more specific, complex, and urgent from Japan's point of view. This situation, in turn, set up a pattern of point and counterpoint involving a variety of vital questions— none of them particularly new—such as size of the salmon and crab catches, the limits of respective fishing areas, the length of the fishing season, types of nets allowed, accusations of reckless Japanese fishing practices, and the Soviet seizure of "errant" Japanese fishing boats.[14]

Moreover, the fisheries issue continued to be employed by Moscow as a useful political lever in dealing with larger strategic issues involving Japan and the Soviet Union.

A few cardinal facts reflect the nature and dimension of the interfisheries agreements of the point-counterpoint period. The issue of the size of the salmon catch revolved around persistent Soviet attempts to maintain the Japanese catch at a low figure, finally established at 65,000 tons. The duration of the fishing season was also a matter of heated controversy, with the Russians insisting the Japanese cease fishing after July 15 or 25 in order not to disturb or prematurely take the large number of baby salmon in the waters by August. Then, the whole matter of length of drift nets and the width of the mesh came up for annual agreement.[15]

Using conservation as the catchword, both sides wrestled over the precise zones where fishing would be permitted and under what conditions.[16]

During the first half of the 1970s informal talks on the fisheries question at the joint committee level continued, with the Soviets once more, quite obviously, using fisheries as a political weapon. When Gromyko visited Tokyo in January of 1972, after a lapse of six years, "safe fishing" was one of the items on his tentative agenda. But no satisfactory agreement could be reached "pending the signing of a formal treaty." As the annual Japan-Soviet fisheries talks got underway in March of 1973, the *Japan Times* editorialized: "During the past few years, the negotiations were, more or less, carried out in a businesslike atmosphere. We hope this year's talks will be carried out in the same manner." Then the editorial added: "However, there are complicating factors which may induce the Soviet Union to take a tougher position towards the Japanese. For instance, this is the first Japan–Soviet fishery discussion to be held after normalization of our relations with the People's Republic of China."[17]

Again, when Premier Tanaka visited Moscow in October of the same year, the problem of "safe fishing" which was to be discussed between Foreign Ministers Ohira and Gromyko, was apparently preempted by agreements on "cultural exchange" and "migrating birds."[18] The joint communiqué issued at the end of the talks avoided any reference to "safe fishing" and merely promised continued negotiations on the fisheries issue.[19]

The *Japan Times* sums up the frustration of the first half of the 1970s: "For Japan and its fishing industry and fishermen, the yearly talks have always marked a period of great anxiety, for they have seldom proceeded smoothly. Hard bargaining, to be sure, is a part of any negotiation. But the results of the Japanese-Soviet fisheries talks have invariably presented disappointments to the Japanese side."[20]

THE 1975 LIMITED FISHERIES ACCORD

A limited fisheries accord was signed in Moscow by Japan and the Soviet Union early in June of 1975. This three-year, renewable agreement was aimed primarily at preventing or substantially reducing trouble arising from the operations of Soviet fishing vessels off the coast of Japan. "According to officials concerned, damage inflicted on Japanese fishermen's fishing equipment such as fishing nets and buoys totaled an estimated Y340 million, including some 1,000 cases, between October 1974 and March this year, 1975."[21] The treaty also restricted the volume of fish to be caught by both sides and established a first Northwest Pacific Japanese–Soviet Fishing Committee.

Concomitant with the signing, Japan and the Soviet Union issued a joint communiqué calling for closer fishery cooperation between the two nations. The communiqué, among other things, pledged to "take into consideration" Japanese fishing control rules, agreed to conduct joint salmon breeding in the Sakhalin area, and recognized the need for close bilateral cooperation at the United Nations Law of the Sea Conference.[22]

Japanese press reaction to the new Fisheries Accord was cautious and mixed.

The *Yomiuri Japan News* editorialized: "In the short-term sense, to be sure, Mr. Kono achieved the primary purpose of his trip. But in any broader sense, it is impossible not to feel that the Russians, by dangling salmon as bait, have succeeded in forcing Japan to accede to their political demands. . . ."[23]

The *Asahi Shimbun* noted that: ". . . provisions are generally proper as far as international agreements of this kind are concerned," and then went on to say, in effect, "we shall wait and see" what happens.[24]

The *Yomiuri Shimbun* added a note of caution, asserting: "Evaluations differ as to whether the Japanese-Soviet Fisheries agreement was a success or failure, but it is an undeniable fact that North Pacific fishing hereafter will suffer considerable restrictions. We do not oppose restrictions on catches in the least if they are for the purpose of protecting fish resources. But that obligation," the editorial concludes, "should be borne by the countries concerned on a free and equal basis as proclaimed in the treaty itself. We would like to know exactly what measures the Soviet Union is planning. . . ."[25]

It remained for the *Mainichi* to put the issue squarely on the line: ". . . the fisheries agreement itself is disadvantageous to Japan," the editorial begins, "because it includes in principle all of the Soviet demands. The Japanese fishing industry, which pioneered fishing in the North Pacific, has been forced to make a big withdrawal and it will have to curtail and reorganize operations. . . . Even if we grant that fishing allowed this year is all to the good," the article concludes, "the problem is the [nature of] the fisheries agreement which will go into effect after restoration of diplomatic relations."[26]

PERSISTENT, THORNY QUESTIONS: "SAFE FISHING" AND INTERNATIONAL POLITICAL RAMIFICATIONS

Two persistent and thorny questions that are an integral part of the larger fisheries issue relate to the matters of "safe fishing" and the international ramifications of agreements between Japan and the Soviet Union, particularly as the latter are perceived in Peking.

Concern with "safe fishing" is anything but new. Over the years, for a variety of reasons, and sometimes for apparently none at all, the Soviets have seized Japanese fishing boats and detained their crews, occasionally for long periods of time.

Despite the limited fisheries accord of 1975, throughout the remainder of that year and during 1976, the Soviets continued to seize Japanese fishing boats and to detain their crews. Available Japanese Fisheries Agency figures for these two years are as follows: 1975—27 vessels seized, 157 crew members detained, 23 of these vessels returned along with 148 crew members; 1976 (through August 30)—1,526 vessels seized, 12,701 crew members detained, 935 of these vessels returned along with 12,624 crew members.[27]

Equally, international political factors bear directly on questions of Soviet-Japanese fisheries. Notably, the ongoing Soviet ideological/political confrontation with the People's Republic of China cannot be separated or isolated from any of Japan's problems with Moscow, least of all the fisheries question. Accordingly, as might be expected, Peking has in recent years supported Japanese protests against large-scale Soviet operations near Japan's coastline as well as its claims to the northern fisheries.[28]

Though written before the May 1977 Fisheries Accord and before the 12-mile limit and 200-mile zones changed the rules of the game, the brief analysis by Pamela Houghtaling of the Library of Congress staff summarizes the twin issues to that time about as neatly as might be done:

> On balance, the Soviet Union appears to have an advantage over Japan in the fisheries issue in that it can limit access to traditional Japanese fishing grounds. Secondly, a large-scale fishing operation just beyond the three-mile Japanese territorial seas has been at the expense of the Japanese fishermen.... Also, Peking's support of Japan may strengthen the latter's position vis-à-vis the Soviet Union by adjusting the power alignment. Nonetheless, as past experience has shown, the Soviet Union will continue to exert a dominant influence in bilateral fishing relations at least in the immediate future.[29]

WHALING—THE FADING ISSUE

Turning to a related problem, it is perhaps not quite accurate to label whaling a fading issue. It has never really been an issue between Japan and the Soviet Union in the same sense that the fisheries problem along with territorial disagreements have dominated discord between the two nations. Indeed, more often than not, at international conferences and elsewhere, Japan and the Soviet Union have found themselves on the same side of the argument against the other nations of the world which are determined to end whaling altogether.

At a time when most of the traditional whaling nations of the world have reduced or even dropped out of the whaling business, the Japanese and the Russians continue to pursue the prey with persistent and, in the Soviet case, some critics insist, even enhanced vigor. The largest factory ships in the world, for example, were built by the Soviets in the early 1960s, exclusively for the purpose of whaling, even though it was clear that whales were being badly overhunted and were rapidly entering the tragic domain of other endangered species. These Soviet ships are more than 700 feet long (two football fields, making them among the largest commercial oceangoing vessels in the world—larger than all but a very few of the World War II aircraft carriers.

The same Soviet and Japanese dominance over the whaling scene is dramatically reflected in the statistics of the "number of whales caught by flag." For the period from the early 1950s well into the 1970s, both the Soviet Union and Japan continued to harvest some 20,000 whales each per year. These figures may be compared with Norway's catch which dropped from more than 15,600 whales to something over 1,000 during the same period, or the United Kingdom which recorded a hunt of some 7,620 pelagic whales in 1953–1954 but none since 1963–1964. The United States take remains at a consistent level of about 200 whales per year.[30]

During this author's visit to Japan's Fisheries Agency in the fall of 1976 for conferences and discussions of this issue, one of the young Japanese specialists on whaling and related problems answered a question on the nature of the whaling issue between Japan and the Soviet Union: "There is no serious issue with respect to whaling," he said, adding that the fisheries problem "is quite another matter."[31]

A paper entitled "Whaling Controversies—Japan's Position" published by the Japan Whaling Association in the spring of 1977 takes exception to the increasing antiwhaling sentiment, again linking Japan's interests with those of the Soviet Union: "The antiwhaling campaigns headed by private groups of the United States and Canada have been increasingly accelerated. . . . Many antiwhaling groups in the United States have repeatedly urged boycott of goods from Japan and the Soviet Union, the two major whaling nations . . ." the report asserts. The report ends with a sort of comparative economic plea: "We are not being facetious when we say that killing whales is no more cruel than killing steers or deer. While beef steak or venison may appear to westerners to be more appetizing than whale meat, nonetheless beef cattle, deer and whales are all sources of animal protein, a vital part of the human diet."[32]

THE 1976 JAPANESE GOVERNMENT WHITE PAPER ON FISHERIES

Because the fisheries issue is so central to Soviet-Japanese relations, it seems useful to review the key points emphasized in the 1976 White Paper on Fisheries, particularly those bearing on the international dimensions.

The White paper is divided into two parts: Part I, "Characteristics of Fisheries in 1975 [a review]," and Part II, "The Advent of the New Ocean Order and Japan's Fisheries Response."

The relevant point made concerning overall characteristics notes that fish caught in the foreign (including would-be) 200-mile fisheries zones represent about 40 percent of the total catch, while those caught in Japan's 200-mile zone constitute about 60 percent. Two other significant points are also included: that the average per capita income of a fishing family was

Y440,000 a year, which is 81 percent of that of the average farm family and 86 percent of that of the average worker family. Also noted is the fact that the number of Japanese engaged in fishing shows a gradual decline.

With respect to the importance of the 200-mile zone, the document is very direct, noting that 40 percent of the total fisheries production in 1975 came from *the 200-mile zones of foreign countries*; stating that the Bering Sea and the Sea of Okhotsk and other North Pacific waters are the most important fishing areas for Japan; and, concluding that much of the success in the future depends on successful negotiations "with the neighboring states."

Japan must adjust to the changing international fisheries environment mainly in the following areas, the document concludes:

1. 12-Mile Territorial Waters and 20-Mile Fisheries Zone: Due to the recent increase in large-scale fishing operations by foreign vessels in Japan's nearby waters, coastal fishery is suffering from limitations on its operations and from damage to its vessels and equipment. In response to the pressure from the industry, the government decided in January 1977 to take necessary legislative measures to realize the establishment of 12-mile territorial waters as soon as possible.

   It is necessary for Japan to respond to the advent of the 200-mile age by establishing her own 200-mile fisheries zone. But, in order to maintain the present fishery order vis-à-vis her neighboring states, Japan must choose the best timing for the establishment. In the meantime Japan must continue effective dialogues with her neighboring states.

2. Pelagic Fishery: Japan must undertake active fisheries diplomacy to secure as much as possible the present level of pelagic fishery. For this, it is imperative that a stronger government-industry system be developed. Furthermore, fishery cooperation with developing nations must be promoted through technical and financial assistance. It is also desirable to develop new marine resources such as *okiami* [krill] of the Antarctic region as well as new fishing grounds such as the deep seas.

3. Promotion of Coastal and Offshore Fishery: When there is mounting pressure on Japan's pelagic fishery, it becomes increasingly important to promote coastal and offshore fishing. In addition, development of technologies to cultivate fish must be promoted nationwide. The combination of "*hatazukuri* [field development]" and "*tanezukuri* [planned development]" will lead to the so-called "*tsukuru gyogyo* [fishery based on creation, rather than sheer exploitation]."

4. Improvement of Harbor Facilities: In order to promote coastal and offshore fishing and improve the welfare of fishing families, fishing harbor facilities must be upgraded.
5. Effective Utilization of Marine Products: Japan has utilized marine products on a selective basis as the demand for them increased and pluralized. But, with the coming of the age of the 200-mile fishery zone, pressure on fisheries increases. In order to achieve a meaningful response, effective utilization of resources limited both in quality and in quantity must be promoted.[33]

THE 1977 SOVIET-JAPANESE FISHERIES AGREEMENT AND THE NEW LAW OF THE SEA

The fisheries negotiations between Japan and the Soviet Union, which had been going on at various levels for years but took on a new urgency with the Soviet, then Japanese, establishment of the 12-mile limit and 200-mile zones, reached a climax on May 27, 1977, with the signing of the Soviet-Japanese Fisheries Agreement by Ministers Suzuki and Ishkov. It may be noted, not incidentally, that the Japanese government had rushed a new Sea Law through the Diet on May 2, establishing Japan's legal claim to these now almost universal expanded claims so that Tokyo might go into the final negotiating stage with at least "legal" equality.

Accordingly, the fishing quota for the remainder of 1977 was set at 425,000 tons excluding salmon, trout, and herring. With the addition of the March catch of 245,000 tons, the total was 700,000 tons, a drastic decline as compared with the actual catch of 1,396,000 tons in the same area in 1975. It was not an ideal session at the negotiating table for the Japanese, but apparently the best that could be done in a difficult, and (from the Japanese point of view), urgent situation. The agreement was ratified by the Japanese Diet on June 9, and became effective upon verbal note exchange between the two countries in Moscow on June 10, 1977.

Since the full text of that agreement is appended (Appendix E-5) and because much of the document is fairly technical, only the salient relevant points need be included here, plus the important "data sheet" on "Regulations Governing Japanese Fishing in the Soviet 200-Mile Zone" (Table 7). A summary of the document follows:

Article 1 establishes procedures and conditions for "the people and vessels of Japan" with respect to fishing in waters adjacent to the coast of the Soviet Union on the basis of the December 10, 1976, edict of the Presidium of the Supreme Soviet of the USSR.

TABLE 7

REGULATIONS ON JAPANESE FISHING IN THE 200 MILE ZONES

Type of Fishing	Fishing Area	Species	Number of Vessels	Catch Quota (tons)
Northwest Pacific crab fishery	Okhotsk, East Karafuto, Nijoiwa, Chishima (Pacific side)	—	67	5,300
Northwest Pacific	North Okhotsk, East Karafuto		30	3,500
Hokutensen	Chishima (Okhotsk side)	Cod	15	7,300
Offshore dragnet	East Karafuto, Nijoiwa, Chishima (Pacific side), Sea of Japan, etc.	Cod	188	212,300
Squid fishery	East Karafuto, Chishima (Okhotsk side), Sea of Japan	Squid	Small— 212 Medium—2,470 Large—1,324 4,006	132,000
Mackerel pike fishery	East Karafuto, Chishima (Okhotsk side, Pacific side)	—	880	63,400
Shrimp fishery	Sea of Japan	Shrimp	23	1,200
Octopus fishery	Chishima (Okhotsk side, Pacific side), Sea of Japan	Octopus	375	1,900
	Sea of Japan		39	2,300
	Chishima (Okhotsk side, Pacific side), Sea of Japan	Sole	712	9,400
Other	—		—	16,400
TOTAL			6,335	455,000

Article 2 talks about the broad mutual interests of the people of the two nations.

Article 3 defines "living resources [of the sea]," "fishes," "fishing," and "vessels."

Article 4 specifies boundaries and catch quotas, appending an important fishing data chart on quotas by type of fish, number of vessels, and so on (Table 7).

Article 5 requires licensing of Japanese vessels operating in certain waters under Soviet jurisdiction.

Article 6 in effect warns that vessels of Japan not observing the agreement of the fisheries regulations of the USSR referred to in Article 1 may be seized.

Article 7 authorizes Soviet inspection of licensed Japanese vessels "without hindrance" and indicates that the Japanese government will be duly apprised of any vessel boarded and found in violations and that the vessels and crews of such seized vessels will be returned as soon as the issue can be resolved satisfactorily.

Article 8 accepts the ocean law under discussion at the Third United Nations Law of the Seas Conference as binding on both countries.[34]

The fisheries problem centers on the fact that Japan takes considerably more fish from Soviet waters than vice versa. Thus the Soviets have been harder hit than Japan by the imposition of the 200-mile zones. Since some 60 percent of the Soviet catch came from non-Soviet waters, they must make up for their own shortfall by limiting foreign fishing—with obvious negative implications for Soviet-Japanese relations. The 1977 fisheries accord, it should be noted, is an interim agreement and is to be replaced eventually. Given Moscow's evident desire to preserve leverage over Japan, particularly in connection with the upcoming Sino-Japanese Peace Treaty, we may expect Moscow to continue to procrastinate on a long-term accord. Fisheries is about the only area where the Soviets can hurt Japan without hurting the USSR even more.

Chapter Thirteen

Northern Territories: The Lingering Issue

In the sometimes turbulent course of postwar Japanese-Soviet relations no issue has been more central, none more difficult, and few more persistent than that of the disputed Northern Territories. Moreover, it is an issue that clearly transcends the narrower confines of Moscow-Tokyo negotiations and rhetoric. Indeed, the military, political, psychological and economic ramifications of the territorial question go to the heart of vital Soviet, Chinese, United States, Japanese, and Korean strategic concerns in that important and often troubled region of the world.

Over the past several decades both Japan and the Soviet Union have laid conflicting claims to various of the 36 islands, spanning some 1,200 kilometers, which lie in a northeast arch between Japan's big island of Hokkaido and the Soviet Kamchatka peninsula. Each nation has put forward arguments resting on mutually disputed grounds of discovery or occupation, or claims based on law and earlier treaties. Moreover, Moscow for its part, has intermittently suggested the possible return to Japan of certain islands close to Hokkaido "after the reversion of Okinawa to Japan," "on the condition that Japan abrogate its security treaty with the United States," or (slyly) "after the successful signing of a peace treaty between the Soviet Union and Japan." Since 1960, the Soviet leadership has essentially restated and attempted to reinforce the position that the territorial question was settled once and for all at Yalta; that, in effect, there is nothing to negotiate. Moscow's presentation of this tough line has sometimes been accompanied by contradictory shades of calculated reasonableness—the continued stated Soviet "readiness to discuss outstanding issues" (in recent years, however, pointedly omitting specific reference to the territorial issue).

Thus, the Japanese government as well as political and business leaders of all ideological or sentimental persuasions are encouraged to sustain that degree of optimism appropriate to their individual perception of Soviet intentions, policy, and practice. Not surprisingly, those most familiar with the Soviet scene—including Chinese and Japanese Communist party leaders as well as academic and governmental students of Communist affairs—tend to be the most realistic and, therefore, the least hopeful on the matter of Japan's prospects for a satisfactory contemporary solution to the age-old problem.

That certain recognized Japanese specialists on Soviet-Japanese relations view the territorial issue with a healthy, though hardly reassuring, degree of professionalism may be judged by a few of the comments made by Professor Fuji Kamiya in an unusually candid paper presented before Soviet as well as Japanese colleagues at the third "Peace in Asia" Japan–USSR Symposium held in Tokyo in April of 1976.[1] "The Soviet viewpoint will most likely continue dictating a hard line on the Northern Territories," Kamiya states, "so long as Japan-China relations continue to pose major imponderables." To this point Kamiya adds ". . . the fact that West Germany, also a defeated nation in World War II, has recently given up a region larger than that demanded by Japan is certainly a minus when it comes to negotiations. . . ." Kamiya concludes ". . . Japan is unfortunately not presently endowed with the means to gain acceptance of that [her] claim."[2]

THE REGION IN DISPUTE—DIMENSIONS

Before examining the several dimensions of the problem, it is necessary to define more precisely the area or islands in dispute. The Japanese, it turns out, use the term Northern Territories (*Hoppo Ryodo*) in two different ways —in broad terms, all the territories north and northeast of Japan proper under Japanese sovereignty prior to the Pacific War, encompassing southern Sakhalin (Karafuto) south of 50° N. latitude, the entire Kurile Island chain, Shikotan Island, and the Habomai group just off Hokkaido (see Map, Figure 3); in the narrower sense, the southern Kuriles (encompassing Etorofu and Kunashiri), Shikotan, and the Habomais. The official claim of the Japanese government has been confined to the Northern Territories in the second sense. Thus, the lingering territorial dispute involves essentially only these latter four locations.[3]

At the same time there remains the larger question of what is and is not part of the Kurile Islands, or more precisely, how Japan and the Soviet Union, respectively, answer that question. The Japanese government distinguishes Kunashiri and Etorofu from "the Kuriles," to which Japan renounced all claim in the San Francisco Peace Treaty. The Soviet Union,

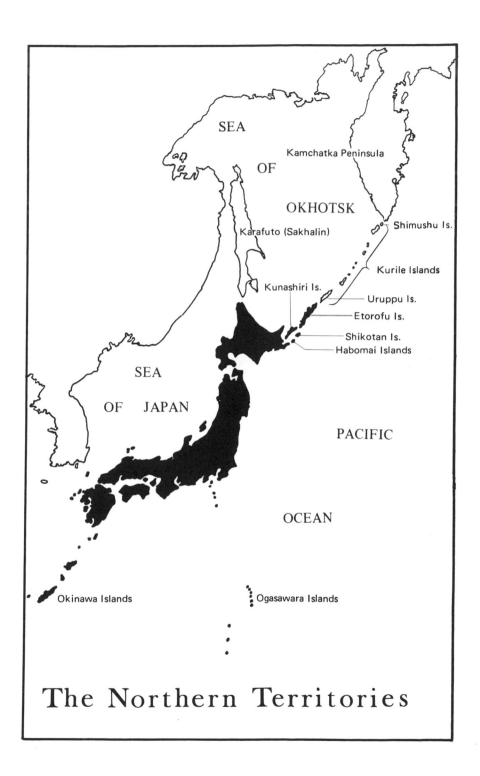

SEA

OF

OKHOTSK

Kamchatka Peninsula

Karafuto (Sakhalin)

Shimushu Is.

Kurile Islands

Kunashiri Is.

Uruppu Is.

Etorofu Is.

Shikotan Is.

Habomai Islands

SEA

OF   JAPAN

PACIFIC

OCEAN

Okinawa Islands

Ogasawara Islands

The Northern Territories

on the other hand, chooses to regard not only Kunashiri and Etorofu as Kuriles, but also some of Hokkaido's offshore islands—Shikotan Island and the Habomai group—significantly referring to the latter as the "little Kuriles."[4]

It is essential to keep in mind when considering the territorial issue that much more is involved than real estate. To put it another way, the acquisition of a few more square kilometers of land to add to the Soviet Euro-Asian empire, in and of itself, would seem hardly worth Moscow's negotiating candle or justify the prolific propaganda mill. Thus, from the Soviet, and, to a lesser degree the Japanese, point of view, the dimensions of the issue are several and overlapping: strategic, economic, psychological, and diplomatic.

A glance at a map of Northeast Asia will suffice to underline the strategic significance of the Kuriles as part of the Soviet North Pacific defense perimeter and gateway to the Sea of Okhotsk. Similarly, the Japanese have from earliest times regarded, sometimes fearfully, these islands stretching beyond Hokkaido as their own northern frontier and vital defense barrier.[5]

With the advent of the Soviet global navy during the decade of the 1970s and the Soviet, Japanese, and U.S. adoption of the 200-miles sea zone (in the spring of 1977), these critically located islands off the Soviet Far Eastern shores, some of them visible from Hokkaido, take on an even more important if still quite limited strategic character. Roles and missions assigned by Moscow to the islands after their occupation following World War II include those of advanced Soviet mini naval bases, small radar sites, and weather stations. Kunashiri and Etorofu are, in fact, replete with air bases and radar installations with long-range surveillance and antisubmarine capabilities. Buroton Bay on Shimushiru affords wide sea-lane interdiction while numerous weather and radar stations dot the smaller islands.[6]

Economically, the region is valuable both as a source of food and as a ministorehouse of important raw materials. Paramushiro, for example, houses extensive processing facilities for herring, cod, crab, and other marine products. The Soviet whaling fleet is based at Shikotan and maintains two factories on Etorofu, which island also boasts the largest salmon hatchery in the world.[7] The Soviets are developing the mineral and chemical industries throughout the islands even as joint Soviet-Japanese offshore oil exploration (particularly in the vicinity of Sakhalin) continues to be regarded as "encouraging" by both nations. Moreover, the Soviets appear to be integrating the islands economically into the Siberian and Soviet Far Eastern development plans.[8]

No less significant than strategic and economic considerations is the diplomatic dimension of the Northern Territories question. This aspect the dean of Moscow's Japan specialists, former U.N. representative, diplomatic historian, and senior Soviet foreign ministry consultant, Leonid Kutakov, took pains to make clear to me over luncheon in the Soviet capital during the summer of 1976. When I asked why Gromyko had earlier taken such a tough, even belligerent line in his then recent negotiations with the Japanese in Tokyo over the territorial issue, Kutakov replied, "That was primarily for *Chinese*, not Japanese ears." The point was not a new one. The Soviets have in recent years studiously avoided any signs of vacillation on the territorial question lest they rekindle Eastern European, or worse, Chinese hopes, that wartime territorial and other "settlements" at Yalta may be regarded as subject to renegotiation. Moscow obviously has no intention of opening that Pandora's box.

RIVAL CLAIMS: THE CONFLICTING HISTORICAL AND DOCUMENTARY RECORD

To the extent that history is the record of what people say, the documents they write, and the conflicting interpretation placed on those documents, the Northern Territories have at least two histories. As Professor John Stephan points out, "Japanese works generally give credence to early (not proven) links between Matsumae and the southern Kuriles. They portray Cossacks as intruders but applaud Tokugawa explorers as pioneers. Soviet authors," by contrast, Stephan notes, "claim that Russians discovered the Kuriles, elevate a raid on Etorofu (1807) into a patriotic rebuff of Tokugawa imperialism, and depict Kurile Ainu welcoming Russians as liberators."[9]

To substantiate and further document its historical claims that the disputed northern islands are legally Japanese, Japan usually cites two treaties with tzarist Russia: the Shimoda Treaty (1855) and the Treaty of St. Petersburg (1875).[10] Article 2 of the first treaty (the Russo-Japanese Treaty of Commerce, Navigation, and Delimitation) specifies that the boundary between Russia and Japan in the Kuriles stretches between the islands of Etorofu and Uruppu. Thus, the Kuriles from Uruppu north are, in effect, conceded to Russia, while Etorofu and Kunashiri are recognized as Japanese territory. The island of Sakhalin was to remain as a joint possession of Russia and Japan. Under Article 1 of the Treaty of St. Petersburg (the Kuriles, Sakhalin Exchange Treaty), Japan ceded to Russia part of Sakhalin, and Russia, in exchange, ceded to Japan the Kurile Islands. The names of the islands ceded were listed in the treaty, with Shumushu and Uruppu included, all lying north of Etorofu and Kunashiri.[11]

While insisting, contrarywise, that history is on their side, the Soviet claim to the Northern Territories is based, however, primarily on wartime agreements among the Allies and on the San Francisco Treaty of 1951. Japan's claim on the basis of the treaties of Shimoda and St. Petersburg is rejected out of hand; and, in any case, Moscow argues, is invalidated by Japan's "war of aggression" against Russia in 1904. Moscow also puts forward a series of lesser legal and technical arguments rejecting Japanese rights and assertions and claiming the territory by virtue of exploration, prior settlement, occupation—and Yalta.[12]

THE CURIOUS AMERICAN RECORD

It is probably fair to say that prior to World War II few Americans had ever heard of the Kuriles. Fewer still had set foot on the islands. During the Pacific War both the Japanese and the Soviets sought to keep it that way.[13]

American involvement with the Kuriles and in turn with the Northern Territories issue dates from the controversial Yalta conference when President Roosevelt, ill, uninformed as to the State Department's position on the issue, and apparently under the impression that Japan had seized the Kuriles from Russia in 1905, somewhat casually, in a brief meeting with Stalin, sanctioned their transfer ("return") to Russia.[14]

The subsequent curious postwar American policy toward the Kuriles has been aptly described as oscillating between pragmatism and negligence.[15] With the revelation of the secret Yalta clauses (in January of 1946) and the onslaught of the Cold War, and as criticism and concern mounted within the United States, a reevaluation of wartime words and deeds at Yalta seemed to many Americans, in and out of government, clearly in order. A document prepared by George F. Kennan, Director of the Department of State's Policy Planning Staff (dated October 14, 1947), represents the first clear evidence of an impending shift in U.S. policy in the territorial issue. Designed for use as a basis for discussing the upcoming Japanese Peace Treaty with SCAP, one of its provisions stipulated: "The Southern-most islands of the Kurile archipelago would be returned to Japan."[16] Amid the "give and take," deliberate vagueness, and curious confusion at San Francisco in 1951, this provision did not find its way into the San Francisco Peace Treaty. It turned out to be, however, precisely the position the United States was to take after 1956 in the wake of the Korean War, the Soviet consolidation of Eastern Europe, and other ominous signs of Soviet and Chinese Communist hostility and intransigence.

Apparently anxious to keep all options open, to be flexible, to offend no one, to wait and see, John Foster Dulles at the San Francisco Peace Conference had equivocated on the territorial issue. Having earlier dismissed the Yalta Agreement as merely a "statement of common purposes," Dulles said that the Allies were obliged to observe only the Potsdam surrender terms and then went on to assert that the Habomai Islands were not included in the geographic term "Kurile Islands." The matter, he said, should be settled by future international agreement.

During the next years, the Department of State sought belatedly to "adjust" and salvage the situation. Responding to an inquiry from the Japanese government, which had become understandably concerned and probably confused by this time, the United States expressed the following— now firm—views in July of 1955:

1. The Habomais and Shikotan are an integral part of Hokkaido, geographically, historically, and legally, and not part of the Kuriles.
2. The Yalta Agreement is a statement of common purpose by leaders of the participating powers and is not in itself a legally effective instrument. Since the Potsdam Proclamation does not mention the Yalta Agreement, the provisions of the Agreement are not binding on Japan. The conclusion of the Yalta Agreement predates the Potsdam Proclamation and hence cannot determine or interpret Paragraph 8 of that Proclamation [in response to the question whether Paragraph 8 of the Potsdam Proclamation refers to the Yalta Agreement].
3. The Potsdam Proclamation stipulates that the final determination of Japanese territory will be made later by the participating countries. The Soviet Union cannot solely and unilaterally declare southern Sakhalin or the Kuriles to be its own territory under Paragraph 8 of the Potsdam Proclamation.
4. None of the following three has determined the final status of the territories: General Order No. 1 of the SCAP, the Decree No. 677 of the Headquarters of Allied Forces, or Article 2 of the San Francisco Treaty.
5. The final disposition of southern Sakhalin and the Kuriles has not been made and is a matter to be determined by international agreement.[17]

A cap seemed to have been put on this emerging forthright American position when, at the request of Japanese Foreign Minister Shigemitsu, the U.S. government issued a memorandum on September 7, 1956, which read in part:

After careful examination of the historical facts, the United States has reached the conclusion that the islands of Etorofu and Kunashiri (along with the Habomais and Shikotan) have always been a part of Japan proper and should, in justice, be acknowledged as under Japanese sovereignty.[18]

To the extent that this memorandum was intended in some small way to nudge Soviet policy in the proper direction from Washington's viewpoint, injection of the phrase "in justice," may seem as curious to serious students of Soviet affairs as it must have been amusing to Moscow.

JAPANESE PERSPECTIVES

The Northern Territories issue has never captured the imagination of the Japanese population as a whole in the manner that "the return of Okinawa" became a burning issue throughout Japan. There are understandable reasons for this: about a million Japanese reside on Okinawa; none currently reside in the Kuriles, some 16,500 having been repatriated when the Soviets occupied the islands. Moreover, while there is general agreement within Japan that some of the northern islands rightfully belong to Japan, Japanese political parties, organizations, and activist groups differ as to precisely which of the northern islands should be "returned" to Japan, and when and under what conditions. It is a strange, perhaps typically Japanese, quasi consensus—*kitto dessho*!

The Japanese government's position is based upon a sometimes tenuous working consensus of numerous groups and organizations with overlapping memberships: the Hokkaido chapter and northern Honshu representatives of the Liberal-Democratic party, the civil bureaucracy, the Hokkaido Prefectural Office, Hokkaido municipal councils, and several irredentist organizations.[19] This position has remained fairly consistent. It is ". . . Etorofu, Kunashiri, Shikotan and the Habomais, called the Northern Territories, which are still occupied by the Soviet Union, some twenty-five years after the war . . . are part of Japan's inherent territory, historically and juridically, and should naturally be under this country's sovereignty."[20]

The principal positions taken by Japanese political parties on the question may be summarized as follows:

- *Liberal Democratic Party*: The Habomai, Shikotan, Kunashiri, and Etorofu islands are the inherent territories of Japan which are not included in the Kurile Islands that Japan gave up under the San Francisco Peace Treaty. These islands must be demanded by Japan; the status of the other islands to the north must be determined by a conference of the countries concerned.

- *Japan Socialist Party*: Not only Etorofu and Kunashiri, but all of the Kurile Islands, including Uruppu Island and northward are the inherent territories of Japan. The return of the Habomais and Shikotan must be made a condition for a successful Soviet-Japanese peace treaty. While continuing efforts for the dissolution of the Japan–United States Security Treaty, negotiations must be carried on with the Soviet Union for the (peaceful) reversion of the whole Kuriles as inherent territories of Japan.

- *Komei Party*: The Habomai, Shikotan, Kunashiri, and Etorofu islands must be returned. The Kurile Islands, that is Uruppu Island and northward, should be proposed as belonging to Japan or be designated as a U.N. control area under Japanese administration. Tripartite negotiations among Japan, the United States and the USSR should be held to clear the way for the return of the Northern Territories.

- *Democratic Socialist Party*: The Habomai, Shikotan, Kunashiri, and Etorofu islands as well as the Kurile Islands, that is, Uruppu Island and northward, should naturally be included under Japanese sovereignty. Early and full return of the Northern Territories (that is, the above islands), must be demanded from the Soviet Union.

- *Communist Party*: The Kurile Islands were handed over to the Soviet Union as a condition for Japanese surrender based on the Potsdam Declaration. But the Kurile Islands are not among the areas that Japan had taken from other countries by war or aggression. The solution of the question lies in developing friendly relations between the Soviet and the Japanese people. A peace treaty with the Soviet Union should be concluded immediately and reversion of the Habomai Islands and the Island of Shikotan must be realized. The Japan–United States Security Treaty should be terminated, and, after disassociating militarily from the United States, Japan should endeavor, in its negotiations with the Soviet Union, to accomplish reversion of the entire Kuriles. [In the past several years, the JCP's association with Eurocommunism has become even closer in a rare show of unity. The JCP's position in favor of return of the northern islands to Japan has remained even more adamant than that of the Japanese government. As JCP leader, Kenji Miyamoto must, no doubt, remind Soviet ideologue Mikhail Suslov, "Don't forget, comrade, our Japanese Party in a multiparty system depends for its influence on votes at election time!"][21]

THE SOVIET POSITION ELABORATED— ESCALATION OF THE DISPUTE AFTER 1960

The territorial war of words between Moscow and Tokyo clearly escalated with the conclusion of the Revised Security Treaty between the United States and Japan early in 1960. Augmenting earlier arguments, Moscow now took the position that since the new treaty was obviously directed against the Soviet Union and the People's Republic of China, extending the territory available for foreign troops by turning the Habomais and Shikotan over to Japan would be considered only after all foreign troops had been withdrawn from Japan and a peace treaty signed between the USSR and Japan.[22]

Somewhat amusingly, the commander of the Soviet Far Eastern Military District had warned earlier, in an article in *Pravda* on January 20, 1960, that if Japan became involved in military plans against the USSR, the *Soviet people* (italics supplied) would find it difficult to understand why the Habomais and Shikotan should be handed over to her, as they could be immediately used by foreign armed forces.[23]

The new Soviet position, linking resolution of the territorial issue with the abrogation of the revised (1960) Japan–United States Security Treaty and the removal of U.S. military bases and troops from Japan, was restated in a letter from Khrushchev to Prime Minister Hatoya Ikeda on August 12, 1961. It read:

> The Soviet Union desires to completely normalize relations with Japan, resolving through discussion all outstanding issues. Regrettably, however, the full opportunity for cooperation and improvement of relations is not yet adequately being utilized. Your excellency Mr. Prime Minister, I would be less than sincere in this connection if I failed to point out . . . [the reasons] . . . Japan's military alliance with the United States of America and continued maintenance of foreign military bases on Japanese soil.[24]

Two additional Khrushchev letters in the same vein followed on September 29 and December 8. After further almost identical letters were exchanged between Khrushchev and Prime Minister Ikeda insisting the territorial question had been solved and, putting forth Japanese claims to the islands, in October 1964, Khrushchev elaborated the same position to a group of visiting Japanese Diet members.

Despite occasional Soviet "straws in the wind" eagerly grasped at by the frustrated Japanese press and public, no basic change in the Soviet position on the territorial question was forthcoming during the remainder of the 1960s.

PEKING'S CHANGING ATTITUDES AND RESPONSES

As might be expected, Peking's position on the Northern Territories issue reflects the changing character of its political relationship with the Soviet Union, Japan, and the United States. China has no claims of its own to the

Kuriles, but clearly vital Peking interests are at stake in the issue.

During the Moscow-Peking alliance of the 1950s and early 1960s, the People's Republic of China supported the Soviet position. As Chinese Communist volunteers prepared to enter the Korean War en masse, on December 4, 1950 Chou En-lai spoke out in favor of Russian possession.[25] By 1964, with the deterioration of Soviet relations with China, Mao Tse-tung announced to a visiting Socialist delegation from Japan: "I approve of the Kuriles being returned to Japan. Russia already has taken too much land."[26]

In the long decade since, Peking's position on the Northern Territories has been stated forcefully and repeatedly. For example, to the question "What is behind Gromyko's Tokyo visit?" Peking answered early in 1972:

> Nominally, Gromyko's visit was to resume Soviet-Japanese regular consultations at ministerial level, but actually it was an important step taken by Soviet revisionist social-imperialism to step up collusion with Japanese reactionaries in opposing the people of China and other Asian countries and to contend with U.S. imperialism for spheres of influence in Asia.[27]

Over the ensuing months and years, the same theme was played by Peking in a variety of ways: "We Japanese people," *Peking Review* echoes, "should not sit with folded arms and let the Soviet Union lord it over us. We will surely recover the Northern Territories! These were the rightful demands," we are told, "of the visitors to the Northern Territories Exhibition held during September 7–9 [1973] in Akita City in Northeast Japan."[28]

The Japanese "Fishermen's Nostalgia for the Northern Territories" is detailed in another article in the *Peking Review* which describes a pavilion on the easternmost tip of Hokkaido "furnished with telescopes, radar, maps, charts, models and other materials on the Northern Territories and meticulously run by the League of Residents of Chishima and Habomai Islands. . . ." The article concludes: "All this demonstrates the Japanese people's resolve to recover the Northern Territories."[29]

An editorial entitled "Return of Four Northern Islands Demanded," in the *Peking Review* in June of 1974, makes the point in strong, unequivocal terms: "The Japanese people's demand that Soviet social imperialism return to them the four Northern Islands en bloc and unconditionally," the article states, "is the legitimate right of the Japanese nation to the restoration of the independence and sovereignty of Japan and the guarantee of territorial integrity."[30]

This was the position Peking was to elaborate and reinforce throughout the next years as Soviet "negotiations" on this and other outstanding issues resumed in 1973 to usher in the "negotiating" era of the frozen 1970s.

THE FROZEN 1970s—NEGATIVE SOVIET INDICATORS

Soviet policy and practice vis-à-vis Japan during the 1970s suggest that Moscow intended the territorial issue to be frozen for the foreseeable future. No progress for that matter may be recorded on the Soviet-Japanese territorial issue in the seventeen-year interval between the 1956 Joint Declaration and Prime Minister Tanaka's visit to the Soviet Union during October of 1973. Meetings between Tanaka and Brezhnev on that occasion, it may be recalled, merely resulted in a decision to resume negotiations "next year." After Foreign Minister Gromyko's meetings with Japanese Foreign Minister Miyazawa, it seemed clear that the Soviet-Japanese territorial question had been frozen by Moscow. Indeed, the joint Japanese-Soviet statement issued on October 10 at the conclusion of the talks made no direct reference to the territorial problem, only a reference to "outstanding questions" to be settled. When subsequently asked at a press conference whether the clause on "outstanding questions" included the territorial issue, Tanaka responded, "there are no such things as outstanding problems which do not include the territorial problem."[31]

The joint communiqué following the Tanaka-Brezhnev talks in Moscow seemed hardly designed to create a jubilant atmosphere in Tokyo, nor did it reflect any new departures:

> Both sides confirmed that the settlement of problems outstanding since World War II and conclusion of a peace treaty would contribute to the establishment of good neighborly relations, and negotiations were held concerning the contents of a peace treaty. The parties agreed to continue negotiations for the conclusion of a peace treaty at an appropriate date in 1974.[32]

The period since has witnessed Foreign Minister Iichi Miyazawa's visit to Moscow in 1975 and Soviet Foreign Minister Gromyko's visit to Tokyo in 1976 with both sides reasserting familiar positions. If possible, the Soviet stand has become more resolute, partly in response to the "hegemony" question which arose (during 1975 and 1976) as noted, in connection with the projected Japan-China Treaty of Peace and Amity.

Thus, during the frozen 1970s, the Soviets have repeatedly rejected a solution of the Soviet-Japanese territorial question and a genuine peace treaty based on mutual concessions and judicious compromise, preferring instead to talk somewhat vaguely about a Japan-Soviet Treaty of Peace and Amity, to stress the further development of "mutually advantageous" economic endeavors (in Siberia and elsewhere), and to put forward the vague notion of a Collective Security Treaty for Asia—with what degree of seriousness and for what attainable purposes remains somewhat unclear.

Chapter Fourteen

The Security Dimension

JAPAN'S INESCAPABLE PLACE IN THE SECURITY SCHEME OF THINGS

In an oft-quoted remark uttered during the Occupation period, General MacArthur characterized Japan as a potential "Switzerland of the Pacific." That curious comment has come back over the years, amplified, to haunt both U.S. officials and Japanese government policy planners. The point is, of course, that the relevant strategic similarities between Japan and Switzerland are few and not terribly important while the key differences are many and critical.

The population of Japan tops 100 million. Switzerland's population numbers only one-fifteenth of that total or about seven million. Japan ranks third among industrial nations of the world. Switzerland, while long a center of banking and commerce and boasting one of the highest standards of living in Europe, may not in the same sense be called a major industrial power. Moreover, Japan's strategic location at the northeast approaches to the Soviet Union and China and flanking the Korean peninsula entitles Japan to a place in the global security scheme of things neither assumed by nor assigned to Switzerland in Europe. Finally, Japan still remains the cornerstone of the U.S. defense system in the Western Pacific and one of America's staunchest and most important allies.[1]

CHANGING JAPANESE PERCEPTIONS OF THE SOVIET AND/OR CHINESE "THREATS"

Conclusions as to the extent of any possible Soviet and/or Chinese military threat to Japan must necessarily flow in some measure from assumptions about the purposes or rationale of Moscow's and Peking's foreign policies. Indeed, the East-West defense dilemma, in the case of Japan as elsewhere, is ultimately rooted in conflicting perceptions of the expansion-oriented Soviet/Communist system itself. Moreover, the strategic alignments of both Communist parties and nations and the policies of the Soviet Union and the Chinese Communists in their responses to the new situations, as noted, have changed dramatically over the years. What may have been properly perceived in Tokyo in 1950 to 1951 at the height of the Cold War (and in the midst of a hot war in Korea) as a "clear military threat" to Japan may in the era of Moscow-Peking disaffection with each other and detente with the West, be regarded rightfully as less immediately threatening.

A leading Japanese specialist on Communist and security affairs, Professor Fuji Kamiya of Keio University, has noted the influence of this changing climate:

> With regard to security in Northeast Asia, it was sufficient for Japan, up to the late 1960s, to cling to the Japan-U.S. Security Pact. However, although the significance and necessity of the Pact have been reaffirmed in the communiqués issued after the Japan-U.S. summit meetings in 1972 and 1973, it is obvious that the Japanese people's understanding of the necessity of the Pact is growing more vague and their evaluation of the Pact will be ever lower hereafter. . . . I believe that detente in Northeast Asia will also start on the basis of the Japan-U.S. Security Pact and will have fruitful progress. However, considering the characteristically fast-changing moods of the Japanese people, I am not very sure whether they will continue to grant a sufficient consensus to this well balanced idea.[2]

To be sure, for a reinforcing combination of reasons, by the 1970s the danger of a direct Soviet or Chinese military attack upon Japan (if ever immediate) had become remote. The reasons include: the continuation in force of the Japan–United States Security Treaty; the pointed nonresolution of the Moscow-Peking dispute coupled with some apparent improvement in Washington-Peking relations; the sophisticated Brezhnev policy of calculated cordiality (detente) toward the West, including Japan; Japan's evident economic power, enhanced foreign policy influence, and increasing, though still limited, local defense capability; and the disintegration of Communist ideology as a unifying international political force—or as an effective tool in the service of Soviet or Chinese Communist political objectives.

That the security issue has not disappeared, but merely changed in form and context is the persistent message of those most familiar with U.S. and Soviet policies and with Northeast Asia. Speaking at the third "Peace in Asia" Japan–USSR symposium in Tokyo in April of 1976,[3] Professor Shunkichi Eto of Tokyo University addressed the security issue squarely.

"... the rapid expansion of Soviet naval power in Asia," he said, "gives us pause. As long as the naval forces of capitalist America were predominant in Asia, we felt secure.... Should the Soviet Union ..." he added, "gain overwhelming suzerainty over Asian waters, however, how can we be sure that eventually the critical mass may not be reached and that naval presence act in such a way as to suddenly restrict Japan's economic activities? In that sense," Professor Eto concluded, "we cannot escape a gnawing sense of uncertainty regarding the future of Asia."[4]

Almost identical high-level Japanese government concern with a potential or growing Soviet "threat" was recorded in November of 1976 by Masamichi Inoki, Superintendent of Japan's Defense Academy: "... it is inadequate to judge the presence or non-presence of a Soviet 'threat' and its size," Inoki wrote, "premising only the Soviet military power deployment in the Far East at present."[5] During 1977 and 1978 a number of high-ranking U.S. admirals, generals, and diplomats, as well as important Japanese authorities, have warned of the increasing Soviet military and naval threats in the Western Pacific and their implications for Japan and for the United States.

MOSCOW'S CONCERN OVER JAPAN'S "REARMAMENT"; PEKING'S AMBIVALENT VIEW

As has been suggested, Soviet perceptions of Japan's "international role" have also undergone significant changes over the past two decades. While in the early postwar years Japan was viewed from Moscow as a strategic pawn of the United States in the Far Eastern international chess game, more recently the Soviets have come to recognize Japan's autonomous power, especially in economic affairs, but also pointedly (if to a lesser degree) in the defense area. Accordingly, the Soviet press after 1970 for a time stepped up its campaign deploring the prospects of Japanese rearmament and warning against "aggressive tendencies" on the part of the new "military-industrial establishment." Such warnings characteristically focused on Japan's increasing military capabilities, the "offensive" character of the F-4s, the "aggressive potential" of Japan's newest missiles, and the "provocative nature" of recent Self-Defense Force air and naval exercises. Such attacks were subsequently soft-pedaled in favor of a more positive economic and cultural offensive.

Evidence of intensified Soviet concern over Japan's growing military posture began to surface dramatically as early as 1971 when one of Moscow's senior Japan specialists (a former *Pravda* correspondent in Tokyo), I. A. Latishev, wrote: "... closely connected with the extension of the American-Japanese Security Treaty [1970] is the concept of Japan's 'self-defense.' This concept," Latishev asserted, "is turning Japan into an 'inde-

pendent military power.' " Latishev elaborated: "At first sight this concept
does not contain anything new. It is not a secret to anyone," Latishev argues,
"that despite the fact that article 9 of Japan's Constitution prohibits the
country from having any armed forces, Japan since 1954 has got an army
of her own. The strength of the army called 'The Forces of Self-Defense'
reached the figure of 285 thousand by the end of 1969. It is also common
knowledge," he continues, "that nowadays Japan pursues the policy of systematic increase in budget allocations for the maintenance and modernization
of her armed forces, equipped with tanks, aircraft carriers, missile launchers
and other kinds of modern weapons. But the point is," Latishev concludes
ominously, "that the advocates of the 'self-defense' idea are not satisfied
with the present state of Japan's armed forces and with the rate of their
build-up."[6]

This theme, the resurgence of Japanese militarism, has since intermittently occupied the pages of *Pravda* and *Izvestiia* and until 1972 constituted
a parallel Peking theme. With the establishment of diplomatic relations
between the People's Republic of China and Japan and as Washington-
Peking relations warmed somewhat, Peking dropped, or at least shelved,
direct attacks on the "Japanese military establishment."[7]

It was for a variety of reasons that Moscow moved into the mid-1970s
playing a different public tune toward Japan. Detente, technological exchange,
joint economic ventures, and good neighbors—in short, a colossal courtship—
largely replaced Soviet anti-rearmament rhetoric. Apart from the evident
economic rationale, this more moderate policy is, no doubt, in part designed
to minimize the effect in Japan of the Soviet continued refusal to make even
a token concession on the lingering Northern Territories issue and is most
certainly related to Soviet concern over improved Tokyo-Peking relations.

The changing pattern is evident from the pages of *Pravda*. The "influential circles in Japan" that during 1970 were repeatedly pictured as "striving
to play an increasingly active military role in the Far East and Southeast
Asia,"[8] seem to fade away. Those people who "in the 1930s plunged Japan
into a catastrophe"[9]—such culprits—became fewer and weaker during 1971
though they were by implication still around, to wit: "Japan's revanchist
claims to Soviet soil [the Northern Islands] breathes a spirit of the most
blatant kind of militarism."[10] At mid-year (1971), the Moscow line continued
to refer to the "Japanese ruling circles" growing strength and persistent
attempts to establish "hegemony in southeast Asia—first economic, then
political, and possibly, militarily."[11] Within a year the military theme had
been largely replaced by hopes for improved trade relations and friendlier
ties: ". . . it is necessary [for Japan] to improve good-neighbor relations with
the Soviet State."[12] This was also the year that Japan recognized the People's
Republic of China.

During the last half of 1972 and all of 1973, Moscow switched to praise and high hopes for its relations with Japan. The military theme was now almost totally absent from the Soviet press. The need was to "create a new climate in Soviet-Japanese relations . . . an intensification of contacts in all spheres, including the political sphere."[13] As economic and cultural cooperation became the hallmarks, the years 1974 and 1975 saw expansion of Soviet-Japanese trade and produced added attention to the development of joint projects in Siberia, Sakhalin, and elsewhere. In a major article entitled "Bridge Across the Sea," the Soviets highlighted trade and economic ventures between the two countries for the decade past. The article concluded by deploring "right-wing circles," "anti-Communists," and the role of Peking.[14] Conspicuous by its absence was any specific reference to "Japanese militarism."

The year 1976, which was to start with new Japanese hopes for a peace treaty and a series of substantial economic and trade agreements, also witnessed the Soviet MIG-23 incident, when a Soviet pilot defected, landed in Northern Japan, and thereby delivered one of Moscow's most advanced fighter aircraft into Western hands. After detailed examination by Japanese and U.S. experts (over angry Soviet protests), the aircraft was returned to the Soviet Union, but the pilot, at his request, was ultimately turned over to U.S. authorities and flown to the United States for valuable debriefing.[15] This incident threatened to wreck Soviet-Japanese relations—or, at least, Moscow attempted to use the occasion to pressure and intimidate Japan. However, the signing of the Soviet-Japanese Fisheries Treaty the following year, renewed calls for economic cooperation, as well as Moscow's continued adherence to a policy of calculated cordiality in its dealings with Tokyo suggest that the massive economic and cultural momentum generated by the Soviet Union in its policies toward Japan after 1969 is not likely to be so easily checked, inhibited, or diverted by such incidents—whatever the immediate Japanese government response and however strong the Soviet protest. For the immediate future then, Soviet attacks on aspects of Japanese militarism are likely to appear in various subtle and low-key forms, but will most probably continue to be subordinated to the more positive and productive themes of "cultural and economic hands across the sea," which may be more precisely defined as pro-Soviet and sophisticated anti-U.S. propaganda, on one hand, and trade and technological exchange on the other.

JAPAN'S DEFENSE CORNERSTONE: THE SECURITY TREATY WITH THE UNITED STATES

Long before Japan had recovered from the ravages of war and the agony of defeat and with the Cold War not fully joined, experienced Japanese statesmen in then still American-Occupied Japan perceived a U.S.–Soviet conflict as "inevitable," neutrality as an "illusion," and Japan's destiny for the foreseeable future inextricably bound to that of the United States. Such pessimistic, or as it turns out, realistic conceptions of Soviet policies and purposes and their implications for Japan were for a prolonged postwar period apparently not fully appreciated, not taken seriously in Washington, or simply ignored by U.S. officials.

A kind of international political indifference verging on naïveté similarly dominated the U.S. domestic scene, reflecting no doubt, the understandable desire of most Americans of the immediate post-World War II era to get back to "business as usual." With the Soviet Occupation of Eastern Europe and the series of Communist-inspired militant moves in Greece and Turkey, coupled with a generally more aggressive Soviet public posture after 1947, the prospects for the cooperative, peaceful world of the kind envisaged by the United Nations Charter began to fade—to the disappointment and despair of millions and the enhanced apprehension of the already concerned few.

In Japan, as early as the summer of 1947, Mr. Hitoshi Ashida, then foreign minister in the Katayama cabinet, had attempted unsuccessfully to explain his views by memorandum on the urgent need for a mutual security arrangement with the United States which would include an explicit U.S. guarantee against external attack, a base-leasing agreement, and provisions for consultation and joint action to defend Japan.[16]

It was not until 1951 in the midst of the Soviet and Chinese Communist-backed Korean War that Japan's urgent security needs were partially realized with the signing of the Japan–United States Security Treaty. By this time Tokyo was apprehensive, but Washington still seemed somewhat reluctant to become overly committed. John Foster Dulles wrote in *Foreign Affairs* at the time the peace treaty with Japan went into effect: ". . . the United States assumes no treaty obligation to maintain land, air or sea forces in and about Japan, or to guarantee the security and independence of Japan although this will be the practical result of the exercise by the United States of its right to station its forces in Japan."[17]

The continuity of Japanese security policy since the celebrated Ashida memorandum is striking: Prime Ministers Yoshida, Hatoyama, Kichi, Ikeda, Sato, and Miki have all formulated defense policy on the assumption that the Soviet Union posed the principal potential threat, both external and domestic, to the security of Japan and that a continuing defense relationship with the United States was, therefore, essential. This has remained the position of the Japanese government.

In specific, practical terms, these defense policies have been reflected in the Japan–United States Security Treaty of 1951–1952, the revised Japan–United States Security Treaty of 1960, and its reaffirmation in 1970 and thereafter.[18] The unique feature of these mutual security treaties with Japan as distinguished from other pacts, such as U.S. treaties with Korea, the Republic of China, the Philippines, Australia, New Zealand, and so on, is that the United States has the obligation to defend Japan while Japan has no similar obligation in regard to the security of the United States.

THE QUASI REARMAMENT OF JAPAN—
POINT AND COUNTERPOINT

Article 9 of Japan's controversial "MacArthur" Constitution—a document still in force—states that Japan shall not in the future have an army, navy, or air force. In the legal spirit of that instrument, Japan's graduated response to its perceived security needs since recovery of sovereignty in 1952 may perhaps best be labeled "quasi rearmament." However defined, there can be no question but that by 1978 Japan had embarked upon a substantial course of limited rearmament, dictated, it would seem, in no small measure by the alarming Soviet naval build-up in the Pacific area and the increasing military stature of the People's Republic of China and of North Korea concomitant with decreasing U.S. commitments in Asia.

The central point made by the advocates of Japanese rearmament is that a nation's sovereignty and its right to defend itself are indivisible.[19] Critics of this position argue, contrarywise, that Japan's is a special case: born of historical circumstances, sanctified by law, and sustained by elements of public opinion. In point of fact, the policies of all the parties in power as well as public opinion in Japan during the past two and one-half decades have strongly supported the need for some degree of rearmament. (See chapter 7, "Japanese Public Opinion and the Press.")

The process of quasi rearmament began modestly enough. It was in the summer of 1950, a little over two weeks after the outbreak of the Korean War, that Japan, upon instructions from General MacArthur, embarked upon its course of quasi rearmament with the formation of a 75,000-man Police Reserve Force to deal with "internal disorders." By the fall of 1951, the Liberal Party (*Jiyuto*) in a document labeled "Basic Policy Outline in the Post-Treaty Era" called for the establishment of defense guidelines and for a gradual build-up of defense capability. After lively debate among Japanese political parties and U.S. and Japanese government officials, on October 15, 1952, the Security Agency (*Hoancho*) was established with jurisdiction over ground and maritime forces and capabilities sufficient "to maintain internal order." With the passage of defense bills in both houses of the Diet (in May and June of 1954), a new security agency, now called the Defense Agency (*Boeicho*), and the ground, maritime, and air Self-

Defense Forces were formally set up on July 1, 1954.[20]

The essence of Japan's post-Occupation defense principles first appeared in the form of a document labeled *Basic Policies For National Defense* issued by a newly formed Japanese Government Defense Council in May of 1957. These principles were, in turn, elaborated over the subsequent years in Japan's Defense Agency's four five-year defense plans and most recently detailed in the 1977 Defense Budget.[21]

Four basic principles of defense enunciated by the Defense Council two decades ago continue to guide Japanese defense planning. They are:

(1) To support the activities of the United Nations and promote international cooperation, thereby contributing to the realization of world peace, (2) to stabilize the public welfare and enhance the people's attachment to their country, thereby establishing a sound basis essential to our national security, (3) to build up effective defense capabilities progressively within the limits necessary for our self-defense, with due regard to national resources and the prevailing domestic situation, and, (4) to cope with external aggression on the basis of the Japan-U.S. security arrangement pending more effective functioning of the United Nations in the future in deterring and repelling such aggression.[22]

To implement these principles, Japan has completed four five-year defense plans, the fourth covering the years 1972–1976, and is currently embarked on a new, more vigorous course of rearmament and systems upgrading. A triservice complex comprised of a ground self-defense force, a maritime self-defense force, and an air self-defense force constitute the heart of these plans, the body of the new Japanese defense establishment. The evolution of Japan's military forces under these several five-year plans has been gradual and conspicuously limited when compared with that of its neighbors in East Asia. The total authorized strength of this triservice increased only about 3 percent from 1957 through 1977—from 255,000 to about 265,000—while the defense expenditures (some 20 percent annually) have been made possible by the high rate of increase in Japan's GNP. Figure 4, *Trends in Defense Expenditures, 1955–1976*, and Table 8, *Self-Defense Forces—Authorized Strength*, reflect the limited character of Japan's rearmament. Moreover, Japan's 1977 Defense Budget suggests little substantial change in this pattern.[23]

The major characteristics of Japan's rearmament, as reflected in the development of the Self-Defense Forces (SDF) over a two-decade life span (1957–1977) may be summarized as follows: The SDF represents a civilian-controlled triservice force clearly defensive in character; the authorized personnel strength has increased less than 5 percent over those twenty years

FIGURE 4

TRENDS IN DEFENSE EXPENDITURES, 1955–1976

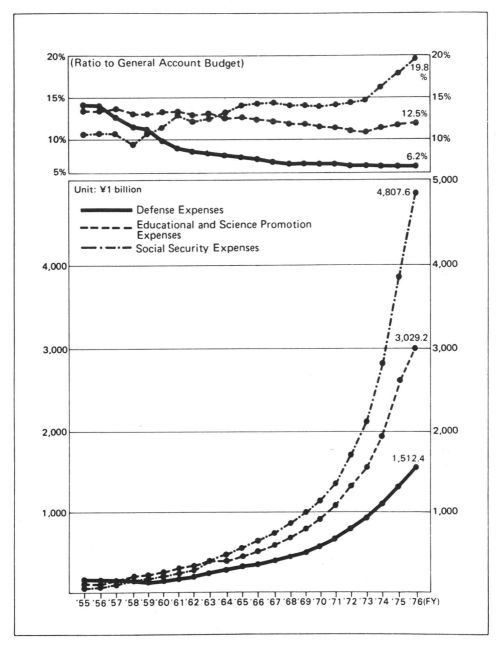

SOURCE: Japan, National Defense College, *Defense of Japan in Brief*, 1977, p. 23.

while defense expenditures have increased 500 percent; emphasis has been on the quality of new military systems and equipment, particularly more sophisticated radar and sonar equipment (to upgrade older naval vessels), antiaircraft missiles, and modern patrol and fighter aircraft; the regional capabilities of the combined Japanese SDF, as documented, are not sufficient to threaten or alarm any other nation; and, finally, the need for some sort of defense establishment on the part of the third-ranking economic power in the world is acknowledged by all Japanese political parties (except those of the extreme left) and regularly supported by Japanese public opinion polls.

Purporting to find even in such a modest defense effort an "ominous trend," the Soviets returned early in 1978 to a cautious attack upon what are termed "Japanese military preparations." Vsevolod Kalinin, one of Moscow's Japan specialists, writes: ". . . it is not just Washington that is giving impetus to Japan's military preparations." Then he asks, with shades of *Alice in Wonderland*, "For what purposes is Japan stepping up its arms race?" His answer is not likely to strike serious students of Soviet or Japanese affairs as very accurate or original: "Evidently, the primary purpose," Kalinin concludes, "is to strengthen the military and political role of Japan as a counterweight to the national liberation movement of Asiatic peoples and to their efforts to follow the path of independence and social progress."[24]

THE NUCLEAR OPTION

The debate within Japan as to whether the world's third-ranking economic power should opt to become a nuclear power goes on. The Liberal Democrat Party has, over the years, stood on four nuclear principles: not to possess or manufacture nuclear weapons and not to admit them into the country; efforts on behalf of nuclear disarmament; dependence on the American nuclear deterrent; and promotion of the peaceful uses of atomic energy.

The Japanese government signed the Nuclear Non-Proliferation Treaty (NPT) in February 1970, and that document was ratified by the Japanese Diet on January 8, 1976, after a long and heated debate. Moreover, Japanese public opinion is divided on the issue, but with a substantial minority of Japanese (some 20 percent) answering nationwide public opinion polls to the effect that Japan *should* have nuclear weapons "in the future," "ten years from now," and another important 25 percent "undecided."[25]

It seems clear that Japan possesses the technology to develop the Bomb, should it choose to do so, in a reasonably short period of time.[26] The questions are: At what economic and political price? Under what conditions? and, What may be the larger strategic implications?

One high-ranking Japanese official, writing under a pseudonym, puts the

TABLE 8

Self-Defense Forces— Authorized Strength

	Authorized Strength	Uniformed Members	180,000
Ground Self-Defense Force	Basic Units	Units Regionally Deployed in Peacetime	12 Divisions 2 Combined Brigades
		Units for Mobile Operation	1 Armored Division 1 Artillery Brigade 1 Airborne Brigade 1 Training Brigade 1 Helicopter Brigade
		Low Altitude Air Defense Surface-to-Air Guided Missile Units	8 Antiaircraft Artillery Groups
Maritime Self-Defense Force	Basic Units	Antisubmarine Surface Vessel Force (for Mobile Operation)	4 Escort Flotillas
		Antisubmarine Surface Vessel Force (Districts)	10 Divisions
		Submarine Force	6 Divisions
		Minesweeper Force	2 Flotillas
		Land-Based Antisubmarine Aircraft Unit	16 Squadrons
	Main Equipment	Antisubmarine Surface Vessels	Approx. 60
		Submarines	16
		Operational Aircraft	Approx. 220
Air Self-Defense Force	Basic Units	Aircraft Control and Warning Wings	28 Aircraft Control and Warning Groups
		Fighter Interceptor Squadrons	10 Squadrons
		Fighter Support Squadrons	3 Squadrons
		Air Reconnaissance Squadron	1 Squadron
		Air Transport Squadrons	3 Squadrons
		Airborne Early Warning Squadron	1 Squadron
		High Altitude Air Defense Surface-to-Air Guided Missile Groups	6 Air Defense Missile Groups
	Main Equipment	Operational Aircraft	Approx. 430

Source: Japan, National Defense College, *Defense of Japan in Brief*, 1977, p. 32.

Note: This table presupposes an equipment system possessed at the time of decision on the present Outline or scheduled to be acquired in the future.

issue starkly: "If . . ." he argues, "the United States should persist in pressing for Japanese ratification of the NPT, then the emergent Japanese nationalism and imperative created by Tokyo's view of deterrence may well coincide. That would result, I am deeply afraid," he concludes, "in driving the Japanese to embrace both out-and-out anti-Americanism and unilateral nuclear armament."[27]

If such a projection must be regarded as a worst-case scenario from the present American perspective, neither is it a view likely to engender any unmitigated degree of enthusiasm in Moscow (or, for that matter, in Peking) for while the Soviet Union looks with evident hope and favor upon hints of any weakening of Tokyo's ties with Washington, the concomitant resurgence of ultranationalism or the mere thought of a Japan armed with nuclear weapons greatly disturbs Moscow and clearly worries otherwise ambivalent Peking. Kaihara Osamu, chief of the Secretariat of Japan's National Defense Council, however, has suggested that whatever Japan may do in the nuclear weapons field is not likely to alter the nuclear balance for some years to come or to render Japan self-sufficient in the security domain. Responding to the argument that (Japanese) submarines carrying MIRVs (Multiple Independently Targetable Reentry Vehicles) would be effective for Japan's security, Kaihara countered that such is a "beautiful dream," but concluded that "since we start from nothing in nuclear armament, whatever we build would be merely tiny fireworks compared with the Soviet nuclear arsenal."[28]

On the key question, Will Japan exercise a nuclear option? there would seem to be little reason to modify John E. Endicott's balanced conclusions of a few years ago (1975), a view with which I essentially agree. In his thoughtful book entitled *Japan's Nuclear Option: Political, Technical and Strategic Factors*, he writes:

> . . . a Japanese decision to embark on a nuclear weapons program will be postponed until a serious international threat is perceived that cannot be countered by existing bilateral or multilateral mechanisms. Such a threat, in all likelihood, would involve a grave danger to the physical security of Japan, and the very existence of what is considered the Japanese way of life. However, one would be naive not to include in these conditions of grave peril the possibility of irresponsible economic warfare that could threaten calamitous ruin to the Japanese economy. Japan as an independent sovereign state will ultimately act in a manner to preserve its inherent sovereignty but will attempt to delay a decision to possess nuclear weapons until it is the last policy alternative. Of especial importance will be the continued perception of viability on the part of the Japanese leadership of the U.S. nuclear guarantee.[29]

The "tiny fireworks" analogy is, one suspects, neither likely to reassure those Japanese opposed to Japan's perceived nuclear syndrome nor may it be expected to extinguish the "beautiful dreams" of the more avid nuclear option proponents.

PERIPHERAL SECURITY CONCERNS— OKINAWA, TAIWAN, AND KOREA

Okinawa, Taiwan (the Republic of China), and Korea may be characterized as peripheral security concerns only in the geographic sense. Certainly, each in its own way is central to the broader consideration of security issues in Northeast Asia. Significant differences in context, time frame, and relative importance to the matter of Soviet-Japanese relations seem readily apparent. Okinawa as a burning international security issue has for all practical purposes been extinguished.[30] In 1972, after prolonged and heated debates in Tokyo, Washington, and on the island itself, Okinawa reverted to Japanese sovereignty though the United States retains certain military base rights there. The Taiwan issue is primarily political, if with important strategic implications for Japan; but the question is related to Soviet-Japanese relations mostly by remote control via the Moscow-Peking dispute.

In point of fact, the question of how America will maintain its evaporating credibility toward its long-time ally, the Republic of China (now on Taiwan), while concocting a formula for regularizing relations with the People's Republic of China (which regards Taiwan, unequivocably, as a part of China) is a *political* dilemma and has largely replaced military and strategic considerations as the rationale for resolution of that difficult and delicate problem.[31] To be sure, a Taiwan in hostile hands could represent a serious strategic liability both in terms of Japan's ocean shipping lifelines and with respect to already diminished U.S. naval defenses in the Western Pacific. Taiwan's viable economy, substantial, independent military establishment, large trade volume with Japan and with other non-Communist nations, as well as active mutual defense treaty with the United States are not matters easily negotiated away, except to the potential disadvanage of Taiwan, Japan, and the United States. Fortunately, to the topic and task at hand, neither Okinawa nor Taiwan are critically central to the present consideration of Soviet-Japanese relations. Divided Korea is a different matter.

On Korea the key questions are: How essential is the Republic of Korea to Japan's and the United States's security interests in Northeast Asia? and What are Soviet objectives, policy, and strategy for the divided peninsula?

Clearly, concern over the security of Japan figured prominently, along with questions of principle and the defense of the Republic of Korea itself, in the U.S. decision to resist the Soviet-supported North Korean invasion of June 1950. The subsequent United States–Republic of Korea Security Treaty as well as more than two decades of U.S. military and economic assistance to South Korea have been essentially designed to promote economic viability, military security, and political stability in the South—with unmistakable economic and security implications for Japan. The Sato-Nixon Communiqué of March 1969 included a clause which stated that the security of the Republic of Korea was "essential" to the security of Japan.

Following the Miyazawa-Kissinger and Miyazawa-Ford talks in Washington in April 1975, Foreign Minister Miyazawa sought to clear up a variety of doubts concerning the question raised in the Japanese Diet, by party leaders, and among journalists. Miyazawa reaffirmed the Sato pledge of 1969 that the security of the Republic of Korea was, indeed, essential to Japan. Then on June 10, 1975, before the Budget Committee of the House of Representatives, Premier Miki explained (as Sato had, essentially, earlier) that the U.S. bases were still available for the Republic of Korea's (ROK) defense should the Japanese government judge that the situation warranted it.

For Japan, the issue is inevitably linked with a variety of domestic and international considerations: article 9 of the Peace Constitution, the extremely low Japanese public opinion ratings for both North and South Korea, Tokyo's policy of equidistance from the Soviet Union and from the People's Republic of China, the Japanese attempt to separate economics from politics, and Tokyo's diffident attitude toward U.S. policy and preferences on the question. Professor Morley's balanced comment on the issue neatly sums up the matter:

> . . . it is important to understand that no postwar Japanese government has considered the ROK's security so "essential" as to obligate itself to help strengthen the ROK's armed forces. None has sent military advisory missions. None has pledged itself to send troops to the ROK in time of trouble. Premier Miki does not propose to do so now. Of course it is also true that no postwar Japanese Government has wanted to see changes take place in Korea by other than peaceful means.[32]

It may be added that few Japanese government officials, business executives, or responsible political party leaders in Japan (left-wing socialists and Communists excepted) have expressed other than varying degrees of concern over the prospects of early U.S. withdrawal of its forces from South Korea, which policy is ominously seen as reflecting a diminishing U.S. willingness or capacity to deal successfully with security issues in Asia—or anywhere else for that matter.

For the Soviet Union, too, the Korean issue is inevitably linked to broader interrelated international problems, policies, and actors: the North Korean leadership, Moscow's relations with Peking, the pros and cons of unification, reactions in Japan, relationship to the Soviet policy of detente.

The Soviets trained and brought Kim Il Sung back and installed him as Communist boss in North Korea in September 1945 but it was not until the fall of 1948 that he had eliminated rival factions within the party and installed himself as premier.[33] His quite successful, opportunist policies early vacilated from pro-Moscow (1945–1950) to pro-Peking (1950–1953), no doubt in some measure responding to the replacement of Soviet Occupation forces by one million Chinese Communist "volunteers." Kim has successfully transcended, even capitalized upon, the Moscow-Peking dispute, managing substantial economic support from both Moscow and Peking— 1957: $325 million from Moscow and $336 million from China; 1959: $125 million from the Soviet Union; 1960: $105 million from China; 1961: Treaty of Friendship, Cooperation and Mutual Assistance with both Moscow and Peking, and so on. In September 1962, North Korea supported China in its attacks on Yugoslavia and India, and relations with Moscow increasingly worsened to the extent that by 1964 North Korea had stopped retransmission of Radio Moscow; shut down the Soviet-Korea friendship societies; recalled Korean students from Moscow; and forbidden the showing of Soviet "documentary films" in North Korea.

It appears that neither Kim Il Sung nor the Soviets were happy with the trend toward total alienation, and the change in leadership in the Soviet Union coupled with the Moscow-Peking split provided an opportunity for a drastic shift in policy. About a month after Khrushchev's political demise, a North Korean politburo member attended the November 1964 anniversary in Moscow. The following year, in February, Premier Kosygin returned the favor with a four-day visit to Pyongyang. The result: two new defense agreements with North Korea, trade expansion, and an increase in arms supplies. By mid-1970, the Soviet Union had become North Korea's largest trading partner and most important arms supplier.

The increasingly "independent" Pyongyang position since that time is is reflected in the fact that whereas in 1972 some 80 percent of North Korean military assistance came from the Soviet Union and the rest from China, since early 1975, 50 percent of North Korea's military equipment has come from Russia and 50 percent from China.[34]

Since 1975, there have been persistent signs of new strains in Soviet– North Korean relations. These include the failure of Kim to visit Moscow after a summer tour which took him to China, Eastern Europe, and Africa, his first trip outside Korea in ten years; a conspicuous playing down of anniversary occasions which in the past have been utilized to dramatize friendly relations between the two states; efforts by North Korea to join the so-called non-aligned bloc; Pyongyang's increasingly political identification with Peking, including a visit to Peking by Kim in April of 1975 where he was received personally by Mao Tse-tung, on which occasion the joint communiqué referred to a complete identity of views; and finally and perhaps the most critical of all, Moscow's reluctance to give wholehearted support to Pyongyang's strategy for reunification.[35]

Donald Zagoria, in his perceptive recent analysis "Moscow and Pyongyang: The Strained Alliance" (from which some of the above has been drawn), concludes:

> In sum, Moscow has refused to endorse Pyongyang's recent efforts to delegitimize South Korea; it has refused to echo somber North Korean assessment of the North-South dialog; and it has refused to go along with Pyongyang's cavalier responses to American proposals for firming up the armistice. In private, Soviet specialists say that a "two Koreas" solution is the only solution to the Korean problem. And on a number of recent occasions, despite obvious disapproval from Pyongyang, the Russians have admitted South Korean sportsmen and other groups to Moscow in order to participate in international conferences. Indeed, one of the principal sources of strain between Moscow and Pyongyang seems to be North Korea's fear that Moscow may yet recognize the South Korean government, a fear strengthened by the American proposal for cross recognition of the two Koreas by the great powers. In January, 1975, shortly after the cross-recognition proposal was advanced by Assistant Secretary of State for East Asian Affairs Philip Habib, a North Korean party newspaper warned that socialist states "cannot deal with puppets . . . still less recognize them." It was later that year that Pyongyang enunciated its position that it was the "sole sovereign state" on the Korean peninsula—a position yet to be embraced by the Russians.

This suggests that the Soviet Union may be more concerned with Tokyo's and Washington's (and, perhaps, Peking's) immediate responses to its own strategy for Korea and to North Korea's attitudes and policies than with the feelings of Pyongyang. This, in turn, would seem to square with Moscow's present policy of detente with the West, including Japan.

THE BREZHNEV COLLECTIVE SECURITY SCHEME FOR ASIA

Side by side with the celebrated expansion of its navy in the Pacific and Indian oceans and concomitant with its massive technological exchange and increased trade with Japan and with the West, the Soviet Union has since 1969—as a kind of Eastern aspect of detente—pursued the theme of collective security in Asia. This plan is essentially conceived as a nonmilitary association of states and, therefore, envisages no military alliances. The three most conspicuous characteristics of the scheme are that it has remained vague and amorphous for almost a decade despite occasional feeble Soviet attempts to inject elements of substance into the plan; it has appeared to most Asian and Western observers to have been designed not only to isolate the People's Republic of China and to rally support for the Soviet position in the ongoing Moscow-Peking "ideological" dispute but also to facilitate the ouster of "Western [read: U.S.] imperialism from Asia"; and its broader, "second-stage" goal for Asia seems conspicuously similar to detente toward the West; it is calculated to project an image of a vital, peace-seeking, cooperative Soviet Union interested only in the security and well-being of its neighbors—the corollary of which suggests that political or ideological apprehension regarding Moscow's motives is unjustified and defense preparations against any perceived Soviet military threat are unwarranted, if not downright unfriendly.

On June 7, 1969, Brezhnev appeared before the International Conference of Communist and Workers' Parties in Moscow with a suggestion: "We think the course of events . . ." he said, "places on the agenda the task of creating a system of collective security in Asia."[36] This was the time, it may be remembered, of new problems in Czechoslovakia and elsewhere in Eastern Europe, renewed military conflict with China along the disputed and tense border, intensification of the war in Vietnam, increased Soviet economic overtures toward Japan, to mention but a few of the relevant contextual factors.

In apparent response to Asian and Western reactions that the concept as put forward by Moscow seemed vague beyond meaningful understanding, the Soviets by the fall of 1971 sought to elaborate, but only slightly.

> The Soviet Union's policy in Asia is aimed at building a solid foundation for peaceable, good neighborly relations between all of its sovereign, independent states, for the solution of all outstanding issues, territorial included, without the use of force, through equal consultation and negotiation. The Soviet Union wants to see every country order its internal affairs without any outside interference, it wants to see full equality of all countries, big and small, in accordance with the principles of peaceful co-existence.[37]

After Brezhnev, in March of 1972, "clarified" the confusion by essentially restating the familiar "Five Principles of Co-existence," Soviet spokesmen on the subject during 1973 elaborated further, explaining that the collective security notion contained such important principles as "the right of each people to be master of its own destiny, the inadmissibility of the annexation of territory by means of aggression, and the settlement of international dispute by peaceful means."[38]

The Soviets updated their position on the collective security plan in a major signed article in *Izvestiia* in August of 1975. Written in the wake of the U.S. debacle in Vietnam by one of Moscow's Asian specialists, V. Kudyavsev, the article begins: "There is no doubt that Asia is a continent that, for objective reasons, has an especially acute need for the creation of a system of security and cooperation." Alluding to the "imperialist bitter defeats in Vietnam and Cambodia . . . the bellicose statements by certain Pentagon spokesmen threatening the use of nuclear weapons if the situation on the Korean Peninsula worsens . . . as well as the attempts to tie Japan to military commitments with respect to this area. . . ," the article goes on to quote Brezhnev from a speech made in Alma Ata on August 15, 1973, which turns out to be about as precise a statement as has been forthcoming on the dimensions of collective security in Asia, as the Soviets view the issue: "We seek to rule out war, armed conflicts and imperialist aggression on the Asian continent; we want every country and people to be guaranteed conditions for free development and national rebirth, so that a spirit of trust and mutual understanding will reign in relations among Asian countries."

How have the Asian states reacted to the Brezhnev scheme? As might be expected, Peking continues to denounce the collective security idea as a form of encirclement. Other Asian governments, which must take the Chinese Communist position into account, have expressed independent doubts based upon Soviet behavior in Eastern Europe, Africa, and elswhere. For obvious reasons, neither China (in light of the territorial/border dispute) nor Japan (because of the Northern Territories issue) has been prepared to recognize existing frontiers as "inviolable." The Indonesian government has long been strongly opposed to any form of regional cooperation that would involve the creation of some sort of supernational organization dominated by a non-Asian power. Indeed, it has been suggested that Indonesia's strong opposition to collective security agreements in Southeast Asia "may well have been decisive in frustrating the Brezhnev proposal."[39]

While growing tensions between India and Pakistan may have induced the Indians for a time to pay lip service to the Soviet proposal, neither sophisticated party leaders nor the Indian military leadership have found the Brezhnev scheme basically compatible with India's national interest especially as New Delhi has watched Russian naval forces fill the vacuum created by the withdrawal of the British navy from the Indian Ocean.[40]

The Brezhnev collective security scheme for Asia, then, remains vague and generally unattractive to most Asian nations. None of the major Asian actors, China, Japan, India, Pakistan, or Indonesia—each for a differing combination of reasons—has shown any particular enthusiasm over the idea. The People's Republic of China, which regards itself (probably correctly) as the original, main target of the Brezhnev plan, strongly opposes the notion. Other nations, large and small, seem to be asking, "What's in it for us?" In short, the idea seems to suffer increasingly with the Asian nations both from its vagueness and from the severe credibility gap that Moscow has inevitably created for itself by a series of past questionable actions in Eastern Europe, China, Korea, Cuba, and Japan and by recent policies and practices in Southeast Asia, the Middle East, the Indian Ocean, Africa, and elsewhere.

THE MILITARY IMBALANCE IN EAST ASIA

Although Japan ranks third after the United States and the Soviet Union as a major industrial power, militarily it is unranked, a relatively minor light. A number of factors and constraints combine to produce this situation: historical, constitutional, political, economic, and psychological.

The omnipresence and long shadows of the two superpowers, augmented by the growing presence of Communist China, have to date dominated and dictated the political and military balance in the area. The rapidly changing strategic imbalance on the Korean peninsula with North Korea emerging again as a substantial, regional military power and potential threat to the Republic of Korea is causing increasing and understandable concern in Seoul, Tokyo, and Washington. Here are some of the hard facts compiled by U.S. Intelligence sources:

- North Korea outguns South Korea in every measurement of ready military power. The disparity is most significant in artillery (2 to 1), armor (2½ to 1), combat aircraft (2 to 1) and naval combatants (2 to 1), even taking into consideration the fact that North Korea must maintain two separate navies.
- All evidence points to continuing North Korean efforts to increase its edge on land and sea and in the air.
- The combat forces north of the DMZ are so positioned that they can attack with little or no prior movement; and the counter-intelligence screen is so effective that a three-dimensional attack could be launched with no more than a few hours warning.
- The combination of interceptors, guns, missiles and hardening make North Korea the toughest air defense environment outside the Soviet Union. There is no prospect for interdiction of the type implemented by the U.S. Air Force during the 1950–1953 war.

- An augmenting inventory of submarines poses a dangerous threat to a South Korea totally dependent on sea lines of communication.
- An indigenous production base and stockpiling give North Korea the capability to sustain an offensive for several months without external support. Kim Il Sung has thus attained the capability to execute a wide variety of military options without the concurrence of or aid from his allies.[41]

These disturbing realities further serve to underline the vital importance of a continuing firm and credible U.S. defensive posture in Northeast Asia. A review of the overall strategic picture in the region during the past decade is not reassuring.

Figure 5 reflects trends in comparative, conventional force development, and deployment of the major strategic actors in the Northeast Asian region for the decade, 1965–1975. Military deployments in and around Japan are more graphically portrayed in Figure 6.

The key to Japan's strategic and economic viability between East and West in Asia must, then, necessarily continue to rest upon the U.S. nuclear umbrella as well as the relative strength of U.S. naval forces in the western Pacific. Early in 1978, Admirals Elmo Zumwalt and Worth H. Bagley warned of the strategic deterioration of the U.S. position in the Pacific and of its implications for Japan. "Today the [U.S.] Pacific Fleet," they wrote "is half the numerical size of 1964 and only 40 per cent of its maximum strength in 1968 during the Viet Nam War. . . . Total force (of the Soviet Fleet) of some 450 ships is twice the size of the U.S. Pacific Fleet, and its 139 surface combatant ships and submarines are about 20 per cent greater than the like American total."[42]

About the same time and on the same subject, the new American ambassador to Tokyo, the Honorable Mike Mansfield (who will be remembered as quite a dove when he was in the Senate) is reported to have lectured President Carter on the seriousness of the Soviet naval threat in the western Pacific when the ambassador paid a return visit to Washington in February of 1978. Shortly thereafter (March 1), he told correspondents that he "would anticipate that there would be no further reduction of (our) forces out there."[43]

Finally, Makoto Momoi, a staff member of Japan's Defense Research Institute and a specialist on Soviet naval affairs and security problems in Northeast Asia, sums up the strategic imbalance and, with it, Japanese concern for 1978 and beyond: "Japan," Momoi warned "is ten years behind recognizing the Soviet threat because we accepted the (old) American theory that the Soviet Navy wasn't to be taken seriously."[44]

Most authorities, U.S., Japanese, and others, seem to agree that the U.S.

FIGURE 5

OUTLINE OF CHANGES IN MILITARY DEPLOYMENTS
IN AND AROUND JAPAN

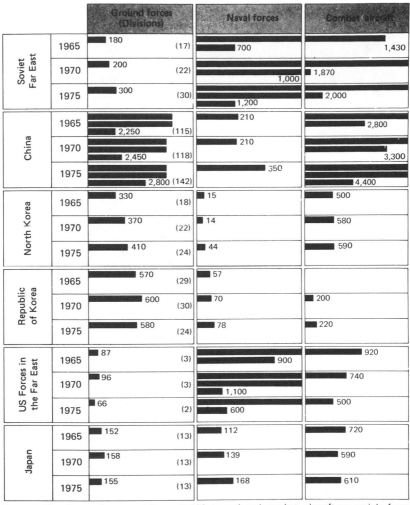

Note: 1. The figures for ground forces (1,000 troops) and combat aircraft are mainly from Military Balance of the corresponding year. Navy figures (1,000 tons) are mainly from Jane's Fighting Ships of the corresponding year.
2. Number of Chinese divisions excludes artillery and railway construction engineer divisions.
3. Ground force strengths of the ROK and U.S. Forces in the Far East include marines.
4. Naval strength of U.S. Forces in the Far East is that of the Seventh Fleet. Combat aircraft figures include carrier-borne elements of the Seventh Fleet.
5. U.S. Forces in the Far East refer to U.S. forces stationed in Japan, Taiwan, the ROK and the Philippines.
6. Figures for Japan indicate actual strengths.

SOURCE: Japan, Defense Agency, *Defense of Japan, 1976*, (1976 White Paper on Defense) Tokyo, 1977, p. 15.

FIGURE 6

MILITARY DEPLOYMENTS IN AND AROUND JAPAN
(Round numbers)

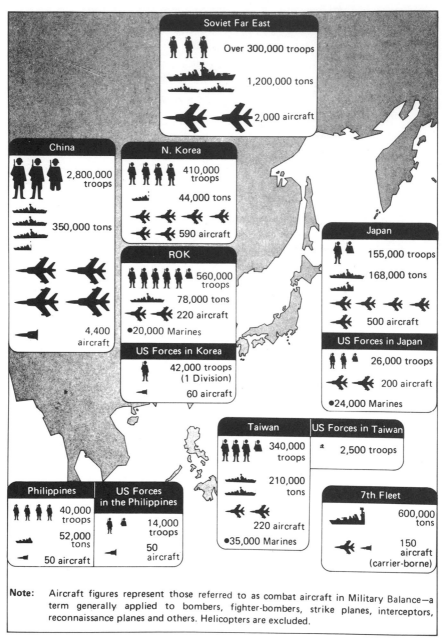

Soviet Far East
Over 300,000 troops
1,200,000 tons
2,000 aircraft

China
2,800,000 troops
350,000 tons
4,400 aircraft

N. Korea
410,000 troops
44,000 tons
590 aircraft

ROK
560,000 troops
78,000 tons
220 aircraft
●20,000 Marines

US Forces in Korea
42,000 troops (1 Division)
60 aircraft

Japan
155,000 troops
168,000 tons
500 aircraft

US Forces in Japan
26,000 troops
200 aircraft
●24,000 Marines

Taiwan
340,000 troops
210,000 tons
220 aircraft
●35,000 Marines

US Forces in Taiwan
2,500 troops

Philippines
40,000 troops
52,000 tons
50 aircraft

US Forces in the Philippines
14,000 troops
50 aircraft

7th Fleet
600,000 tons
150 aircraft (carrier-borne)

Note: Aircraft figures represent those referred to as combat aircraft in Military Balance—a term generally applied to bombers, fighter-bombers, strike planes, interceptors, reconnaissance planes and others. Helicopters are excluded.

SOURCE: Japan, Defense Agency, *Defense of Japan, 1976* (1976 Defense White Paper) Tokyo, 1977.

Pacific fleet still holds a strategic edge over its rapidly growing Soviet counterpart. This is due to the American monopoly of aircraft carrier presence in the Pacific (believed to be short-lived), the long tradition and superior training and combat experience of U.S. naval officers and men, plus the still somewhat more advanced design and technology of U.S. naval vessels and aircraft. The same authorities repeatedly stress, however, that the substantially larger Soviet budget allocation for naval research and development and Moscow's massive and ongoing submarine, ship, and aircraft production schedule when coupled with the improved training and experience of Soviet naval personnel are, in the aggregate, rapidly closing the gap. Moreover, these developments and trends if accompanied by a substantial and continuing U.S. force reduction, could soon produce a serious situation—a disturbing imbalance—where the Soviets would clearly be superior to the United States in the Pacific in virtually all categories. The implications for Japan are all too obvious.

When for purposes of worst-case scenario, the United States is left out of the East Asian military equation, the present Japan-centered military imbalance in East Asia becomes dramatically apparent. Even using rough data in broad categories, the picture emerges in stark and disturbing outline. To begin with, in the nuclear weapons area, the Soviet inventory is formidable; Communist China's nuclear weapons capability is growing; Japan's is nonexistent. Further, the contrast between the Soviet Union's 43 ground force divisions in East Asia; Communist China's 136 divisions, and Japan's inexperienced 13 Self-Defense divisions offers little by way of corollary reassurance. Nor are Japan's 15 vintage submarines presumed to be even a regional match for the Soviet expanding bluewater navy, with some 325 submarines (39 of them missile firing nuclear submarines), a substantial number of them in Pacific waters. When we turn to the air, the Soviets (in Northeast Asia) boast something like a four-to-one quantitative and an overwhelming qualitative superiority in the vital aircraft dimension.[45]

The Japanese authorities have shown increasing concern over this military imbalance as questions over the reliability of the United States as a defense partner have been repeatedly and understandably raised in the wake of Vietnam. Such questions were regularly asked of me during a visit to Japan in 1977. These questions were characteristically cast in the context of "concern over the new policies for Asia of the new administration in Washington," although the record, or at least result, of previous administrations' policies toward Southeast Asia and elsewhere could also hardly have been reassuring.

In December of 1977, the Japan Defense Council announced plans to buy 100 additional McDonnell Douglas F-15 fighter and 45 Lockheed P-3C antisubmarine patrol planes for a total price of $4.5 billion.[46] This will obviously improve Japan's regional defense posture but does little to redress the basic military imbalance in Northeast Asia. The Pentagon notified Congress in May of 1978 of the decision to sell the F-15s and P-3Cs to Japan for $2.2 billion. It will represent the largest U.S. arms sale to Japan in history. The purchases are to extend over eleven years with most of the aircraft to be built in Japan.[47]

Such comparisons leave aside—as, of course, realistically and practically one cannot—the formidable long- and medium-range Soviet nuclear missile launching capability (silo and mobile in addition to submarine). This dimension is understandably all the more disturbing and intimidating to the Japanese, crowded together as they are on four islands comprising three-fourths the area of the state of California, located 100 miles off the Communist mainland, and possessing essentially only four or five "targetable, *major* strategic urban-industrial centers."

The most dramatic and disturbing picture yet drawn of the escalation of security issues in Northeast Asia and of Tokyo's intensified concern emerged from Japan's fourth postwar White Paper on Defense approved by the Japanese Cabinet at the end of July 1978. An unusual Defense Agency briefing on the document, held for all foreign newsmen in Tokyo (including both Chinese and Soviets) as well as for representatives of the foreign embassies, underlined apprehension over the policies and practices of the Soviet Union and of the United States. The White Paper expresses serious reservations over President Carter's plan to withdraw ground combat forces from South Korea and points ominously to the limits of the U.S. 7th Fleet's diminishing capability to defend Japan's sea lanes. "The activities of the Soviet fleet around and beyond Japan [by contrast]," the report concludes, "are intensifying and these appear to be aimed at increasing political and psychological influence over this area, and not merely for training and intelligence purposes." Asked whether taken together this meant that Japan now considers the Soviet Union a direct threat, Ko Maruyama, Defense Agency vice minister, replied, "we make that interpretation."[48]

All of this suggests, rather ominously, that—Moscow's policy of detente notwithstanding—we may be witnessing only the first stage of the escalating Soviet challenge in Northeast Asia and of the increasingly vigorous Japanese response.

Appendixes

Following are the full texts of the important postwar treaties and agreements between the Soviet Union and Japan and summaries of the lesser agreements, 1956–1977.

Appendix A   Texts of the 1956 Joint Declaration and Protocol between the Soviet Union and Japan

Appendix B   Texts of two other 1956 bilateral agreements concerning high seas fisheries and rescue of persons in distress at sea between the Soviet Union and Japan

Appendix C   Text of Treaty of Commerce between the Soviet Union and Japan (with Annex and Exchange of Notes), 1957

Appendix D   Summaries of Soviet-Japanese bilateral treaties, 1956–1975 (translated from original Russian text unless otherwise indicated) chronological according to date signed; with effective date and date of publication by Ministry of Foreign Affairs (MFA)

Appendix E   Texts of Recent Fisheries and Whaling Agreements (1975–1977)

Appendix F   Text of Draft Treaty on Goodneighborhood [Neighborliness] and Cooperation between USSR and Japan, 1978

Appendix G   The Defense Budget in Brief, FY 1977

APPENDIX A-1

Joint Declaration by the Union of Soviet Socialist Republics and Japan[1]

Signed at Moscow, October 19, 1956.

From 13 to 19 October 1956 negotiations were held at Moscow between the Delegations of the Union of Soviet Socialist Republics and Japan.

The following representatives of the Union of Soviet Socialist Republics took part in the negotiations:

N. A. Bulganin, Chairman of the Council of Ministers of the USSR,
N. S. Khrushchev, Member of the Presidium of the Supreme Soviet of the USSR,
A. I. Mikoyan, First Vice-Chairman of the Council of Ministers of the USSR,
A. A. Gromyko, First Deputy Minister of Foreign Affairs of the USSR, and
N. T. Fedorenko, Deputy Minister of Foreign Affairs of the USSR.

The following representatives of Japan took part in the negotiations:

Prime Minister, Ichiro Hatoyama,
Ichiro Kono, Minister of Agriculture and Forestry, and
Shunichi Matsumoto, Member of the House of Representatives.

In the course of the negotiations, which were held in an atmosphere of mutual understanding and co-operation, a full and frank exchange of views concerning relations between the Union of Soviet Socialist Republics and Japan took place. The Union of Soviet Socialist Republics and Japan were fully agreed that the restoration of diplomatic relations between them would contribute to the devel-

---

SOURCE: *Japanese Annual of International Law*, no. 1 (1957): 129–131.
1. Came into force on December 13, 1956, as from the date of the exchange of the instruments of ratification at Tokyo, in accordance with paragraph 10.

opment of mutual understanding and co-operation between the two States in the interests of peace and security in the Far East.

As a result of these negotiations between the Delegations of the Union of Soviet Socialist Republics and Japan, agreement was reached on the following:

1. The state of war between the Union of Soviet Socialist Republics and Japan shall cease on the date on which this Declaration enters into force and peace, friendship and good-neighbourly relations between them shall be restored.

2. Diplomatic and consular relations shall be restored between the Union of Soviet Socialist Republics and Japan. For this purpose, it is intended that the two States shall proceed forthwith to exchange diplomatic representatives with the rank of Ambassador and that the question of the establishment of consulates in the territories of the USSR and Japan respectively shall be settled through diplomatic channels.

3. The Union of Soviet Socialist Republics and Japan affirm that in their relations with each other they will be guided by the principles of the United Nations Charter, in particular the following principles set forth in Article 2 of the said Charter:

a. To settle their international disputes by peaceful means in such a manner that international peace and security, and justice, are not endangered;

b. To refrain in their international relations from the threat or use of force against the territorial integrity or political independence of any State, or in any other manner inconsistent with the Purposes of the United Nations.

The USSR and Japan affirm that, in acordance with Article 51 of the United Nations Charter, each of the two States has the inherent right of individual or collective self-defence

The USSR and Japan reciprocally undertake not to intervene directly or indirectly in each other's domestic affairs for any economic, political or ideological reasons.

4. The Union of Soviet Socialist Republics will support Japan's application for membership in the United Nations.

5. On the entry into force of this Joint Declaration, all Japanese citizens convicted in the Union of Soviet Socialist Republics shall be released and repatriated to Japan.

With regard to those Japanese whose fate is unknown, the USSR, at the request of Japan, will continue its efforts to discover what has happened to them.

6. The Union of Soviet Socialist Republics renounces all reparations claims against Japan.

The USSR and Japan agree to renounce all claims by either State, its institutions or citizens, against the other State, its institutions or citizens, which have arisen as a result of the war since 9 August 1945.

7. The Union of Soviet Socialist Republics and Japan agree that they will enter into negotiations as soon as may be possible for the conclusion of treaties or agreements with a view to putting their trade, navigation and other commercial relations on a firm and friendly basis.

8. The Convention on deep-sea fishing in the northwestern sector of the Pacific Ocean between the Union of Soviet Socialist Republics and Japan and the Agreement between the Union of Soviet Socialist Republics and Japan on co-operation in the rescue of persons in distress at sea, both signed at Moscow on 14 May 1956, shall come into effect simultaneously with this Joint Declaration.

Having regard to the interest of both the USSR and Japan in the conservation and rational use of the natural fishery resources and other biological resources of the sea, the USSR and Japan shall, in a spirit of co-operation, take measures to conserve and develop fishery resources, and to regulate and restrict deep-sea fishing.

9. The Union of Soviet Socialist Republics and Japan agree to continue, after the restoration of normal diplomatic relations between the Union of Soviet Socialist Republics and Japan, negotiations for the conclusion of a Peace Treaty.

In this connexion, the Union of Soviet Socialist Republics, desiring to meet the wishes of Japan and taking into consideration the interests of the Japanese State, agrees to transfer to Japan the Habomai Islands and the island of Shikoton, the actual transfer of these islands to Japan to take place after the conclusion of a Peace Treaty between the Union of Soviet Socialist Republics and Japan.

10. This Joint Declaration is subject to ratification. It shall enter into force on the date of the exchange of instruments of ratification. The exchange of the instruments of ratification shall take place at Tokyo as soon as may be possible.

IN WITNESS WHEREOF the undersigned plenipotentiaries have signed this Joint Declaration.

DONE in two copies, each in the Russian and Japanese languages, both texts being equally authentic.

Moscow, 19 October 1956.

By authorization	By authorization
of the Presidium of the Supreme	of the Government
Soviet of the Union of Soviet	of Japan:
Socialist Republics:	I. HATOYAMA
N. BULGANIN	I. KONO
D. SHEPILOV	S. MATSUMOTO

APPENDIX A-2

Protocol Between the Union of Soviet Socialist Republics and Japan Concerning the Expansion of Trade and the Reciprocal Grant of Most-Favored Nation Treatment[1]

Signed at Moscow, October 19, 1956. [Translation.] No. 3769.

The Governments of the Union of Soviet Socialist Republics and Japan, with reference to the provisions of paragraph 7 of the Joint Declaration by the Union of Soviet Socialist Republics and Japan signed at Moscow on 19 October 1956, have agreed as follows:

1. Pending the conclusion of the treaties or agreements referred to in paragraph 7 of the aforesaid Joint Declaration, the Contracting Parties shall make every effort to expand trade between the two States, to which end each of the Contracting Parties shall accord the other Contracting Party the following treatment:

   a. Most-favoured-nation treatment with respect to customs duties and charges of all kinds, customs formalities and other rules applicable to the import of goods from and the export of goods to the other Contracting Party;

   b. Most-favoured-nation treatment with respect to the vessels of the other Contracting Party when in its ports, such treatment to cover the entering, clearing and stationing of vessels, all dues and charges, the loading and unloading of cargo and the supply of fuel, water and provisions.

2. The provisions of the foregoing paragraph 1 shall not restrict the right of either Contracting Party to enforce any prohibition or limitation designed to protect the vital interests of its security.

This Protocol is subject to ratification. It shall enter into force on the date of the exchange of instruments of ratification. The exchange of the instruments of ratification shall take place at Tokyo as soon as may be possible.

IN WITNESS WHEREOF the undersigned plenipotentiaries have signed the present Protocol.

SOURCE: *Japanese Annual of International Law*, no. 1 (1957): 131–132.

1. Came into force on October 12, 1956, as from the date of the exchange of the instruments of ratification at Tokyo, in accordance with paragraph 2.

Done in two copies, each in the Russian and Japanese languages, both texts being equally authentic.

Moscow, 19 October 1956.

By authorization
of the Presidium of the Supreme
Soviet of the Union of Soviet
Socialist Republics:
N. Bulganin
D. Shepilov

By authorization
of the Government
of Japan:
I. Hatoyama
I. Kono
S. Matsumoto

APPENDIX B-1

Convention Concerning the High Seas Fisheries of the Northwest Pacific Ocean

Signed at Moscow, May 14, 1956; in force, December 12, 1956.
[Unofficial Translation.]

The Governments of Japan and the Union of Soviet Socialist Republics,

Considering the common interest of the Contracting Parties with respect to the development, on a rational basis, of the fisheries in the Northwest Pacific Ocean, and their mutual responsibility with respect to the condition of the fish and other marine living resources, as well as to the effective utilization of those resources,

Recognizing that it will serve the common interest of mankind, as well as the interests of the Contracting Parties to maintain the maximum sustained productivity of fisheries in the Northwest Pacific Ocean,

Considering that each of the Contracting Parties should assume an obligation, on a free and equal footing, to conserve and increase the above mentioned resources,

Recognizing that it is highly desirable to promote and co-ordinate the scientific studies of the Contracting Parties, the purpose of which is to maintain the maximum sustained productivity of fisheries of interest to the two Contracting Parties,

Have, therefore, decided to conclude this Convention, and for this purpose have appointed their respective representatives who have agreed as follows:

ARTICLE I

1. The area to which this Convention applies, hereinafter referred to as "the Convention area," shall be all waters, other than territorial waters, of the Northwest Pacific Ocean, including the Japan Sea, the Okhotsk Sea and the Bering Sea.

SOURCE: *Japanese Annual of International Law*, no. 1 (1957): 119–124.

2. Nothing in this Convention shall be deemed to affect in any way the position of the Contracting Parties in regard to the limits of territorial sea or to the jurisdiction over fisheries.

ARTICLE II

1. The Contracting Parties in order to conserve and develop the fish and other marine living resources, hereinafter referred to as the "fishery resources," agree to carry out in the Convention area, the co-ordinated measures specified in the Annex to this Convention.

2. The Annex attached hereto shall form an integral part of this Convention. All references to the "Convention" shall be understood as including the said Annex either in its present terms or as revised in accordance with the provisions of paragraph (a) of Article IV.

ARTICLE III

1. In order to realize the objectives of this Convention, the Contracting Parties shall establish the Japan-Soviet Northwest Pacific Fishcrics Commission, hereinafter referred to as "the Commission."

2. The Commission shall be composed of two national sections, each consisting of three members appointed by the governments of the respective Contracting Parties.

3. All resolutions, recommendations and other decisions of the Commission shall be made only by agreement between the national sections.

4. The Commission may decide upon and revise, as occasion may require, the rules for the conduct of its meetings.

5. The Commission shall meet at least once each year and at such other times as may be requested by one of the national sections. The date and place of the first meeting shall be determined by agreement between the Contracting Parties.

6. At its first meeting the Commission shall select a Chairman and Vice-Chairman from different national sections. The Chairman and Vice-Chairman shall hold office for a period of one year. The selection of a Chairman and Vice-Chairman from the national sections shall be made in such a manner as will yearly provide each Contracting Party in turn with representation in those offices.

7. The official languages of the Commission shall be Japanese and Russian.

8. The expenses incurred by a member of the Commission in connection with participation in the meetings of the Commission shall be paid by the appointing government. Joint expenses incurred by the Commission shall be paid by the Commission through contributions made by the Contracting Parties in the form and proportion recommended by the Commission and approved by the Contracting Parties.

ARTICLE IV

The Commission shall perform the following functions:

a. At the regular annual meeting, consider the appropriateness of co-ordinated measures being enforced at the time, and if necessary revise the Annex to this Convention. Such revision shall be determined on the basis of scientific findings.

b. When it is required by the Annex to fix the total annual catch of a stock of fish, determine the total annual catch of such stock by the Contracting Parties and notify the said Parties.

c. Determine the kind and scope of statistics and other reports to be submitted to the Commission by each of the Contracting Parties for carrying out the provisions of this Convention.

d. For the purpose of studying the fishery resources, prepare and adjust co-ordinated scientific research programs and recommend them to the Contracting Parties.

e. Submit annually to the Contracting Parties a report on the operation of the Commission.

f. In addition to the functions stipulated above, make recommendations to the Contracting Parties with respect to the matter of conservation and increase of fishery resources in the Convention area.

ARTICLE V

The Contracting Parties agree, for the purpose of mutually exchanging experiences concerning the study and conservation of fishery resources and regulation of fisheries, to exchange men of learning and experience in fisheries. The exchange of such men shall be conducted by agreement from time to time between the two Parties.

ARTICLE VI

1. The Contracting Parties shall take appropriate and effective measures in order to carry out the provisions of this Convention.

2. When in receipt of the notification from the Commission concerning the total annual catch fixed for each of the Contracting Parties in accordance with paragraph (b) of Article IV, the Contracting Parties shall issue licenses or certificates to their fishing vessels and inform each other of all such licenses and certificates issued.

3. The licenses and certificates issued by the Contracting Parties shall be in both the Japanese and Russian languages, and the fishing vessels, when engaged in fishing operations, shall have on board their license or certificate without fail.

4. The Contracting Parties agree, for the purpose of rendering effective the provisions of this Convention, to enact and enforce necessary laws and regulations, with regard to their nationals, organizations and fishing vessels, with appropriate penalties against violations thereof and to submit to the Commission a report on any action taken by them with regard thereto.

ARTICLE VII

1. When authorized officials of either of the Contracting Parties have reasonable ground to believe that a fishing vessel of the other Party is actually violating the provisions of this Convention, such officials may board and search the vessel to ascertain whether the said provisions are being observed.

Such officials shall present credentials issued by their Government and written in both the Japanese and Russian languages, if requested by the master of the vessel.

2. If it becomes clear as a result of the search conducted by such officials that there is evidence that the fishing vessel or any person on board such vessel is violating the Convention, the said officials may seize such vessel or arrest such person.

In that case, the Contracting Party to which the officials belong shall notify as soon as possible the other Contracting Party to which such fishing vessel or person belongs of the arrest or seizure, and shall deliver such vessel or person as promptly as practicable to the authorized officials of the Contracting Party to which the vessel or person belongs at the place of arrest or seizure unless another place is agreed upon by the Contracting Parties. Provided, however, that when the Contracting Party which receives such notification cannot immediately accept delivery and requests of the other Contracting Party, the latter Party receiving the request may keep such vessel or person under surveillance within its own territory, under the conditions agreed upon by the Contracting Parties.

3. Only the authorities of the Party to which the above-mentioned fishing vessel or person belongs have jurisdiction to try cases arising in connection with this article and impose penalties therefor. Written evidence and proof establishing the offense shall be furnished as promptly as possible to the Contracting Party having jurisdiction to try the case.

ARTICLE VIII

1. This Convention shall become effective from the date of entry into force of the Peace Treaty between Japan and the Union of Soviet Socialist Republics or from the date of restoration of diplomatic relations between the said countries.

2. After this Convention has remained in force for a period of ten years, either Contracting Party may give notice to the other Contracting Party of an intention to abrogate the said Convention, and it shall terminate one year after the date of receipt of the said notification by the latter Party.

IN WITNESS WHEREOF, the undersigned representatives have signed this Treaty.

DONE in duplicate, in the Japanese and Russian languages, both equally authentic, at Moscow, this fourteenth day of May, one thousand nine hundred and fifty-six.

BY AUTHORITY OF THE GOVERNMENT OF JAPAN:
ad referendum
I. Kono
K. Matsudaira

BY AUTHORITY OF THE GOVERNMENT OF THE UNION OF SOVIET SOCIALIST REPUBLICS:
A. Ishkov

ANNEX

The Contracting Parties agree to regulate, within the Convention area, the fishing of the stocks of fish named below:

1. Salmon

Chum Salmon (Oncorhynchus keta)
Pink salmon (Oncorhynchus gorbuscha)
Silver Salmon (Oncorhynchus kisutch)
Sockeye Salmon (Oncorhynchus tschawytscha)

a. The area wherein the fishing will be regulated shall be the Northwest Pacific Ocean (including the Okhotsk Sea and Bering Sea) bounded on the east and south by a line running southeast from Cape Navarin to intersection of 55° North Latitude and 175° West Longitude; thence south to intersection of 45° North Latitude and 175° West Longitude; thence west to intersection of 45° North Latitude and 155° East Longitude; thence southwest to Akiyuri Island; and the Japan Sea north of 45° North Latitude.

b. With regard to fishing season for 1956, sea-fishery with movable fishing gear shall be prohibited in the Convention area within forty nautical miles from the coastline of the islands belonging to either of the Contracting Parties and from the continental coast within the area stipulated in (a).

Based upon scientific data, such prohibited areas shall be re-examined by the Commission as soon as practicable.

These regulations prohibiting sea-fishery with movable fishing gear shall not apply to small Japanese fishing vessels in the waters adjacent to Hokkaido within the prohibited area.

c. The total amount of catch shall be determined by the Commission. The total amount of catch for the first year the Convention is in effect shall be determined at the first meeting of the Commission.

d. With respect to mothership-type fishing operations, the catch per year (in raw fish weight) by each fishing vessel and investigation ship shall not exceed three hundred metric tons and one hundred and fifty metric tons respectively.

The total amount of catch by all the fishing vessels and investigation ships belonging to a mother ship shall not exceed the total catch fixed for such mother ship. Within the scope of such total catch the catch by each fishing vessel and investigation vessel may exceed to some degree the above amounts fixed for each fishing vessel and investigation vessel respectively.

e. The fishing season for each year shall end on 10 August.

f. The length of drifting nets set in the sea by a fishing vessel shall be as follows:

Not more than ten kilometres in the Okhotsk Sea; not more than twelve kilometres in the waters of the Pacific Ocean bounded on the east and south by the line connecting Cape Olyutorskiy, the intersection of 48° North Latitude and 170°25′ East Longitude, and Akiyuri Island; not more than fifteen kilometres in the other areas.

The distance between the drifting nets set by a fishing vessel shall be that confirmed immediately after the setting, and the distance between one net and the nearest net shall, in any direction, be as follows:

Not less than twelve kilometres in the Okhotsk Sea area; not less than ten kilometres in the waters of the Pacific Ocean bounded on the east and south by the line connecting Cape Olyutorskiy, the intersection of 48° North Latitude and 170°25′ East Longitude, and Akiyuri Island; not less than eight kilometres in the other areas.

These provisions, however, shall not apply to small fishing vessels operating in the waters south of 48° North Latitude and having their base of operations at a port in Japan.

With respect to meshes of a drifting net, the length from knot to knot shall be not less than fifty-five millimetres.

2. Herring (Clupea Pallasii)

Fishing of small immature herring of less than twenty centimetres in length (from tip of snout to the end of vertebral column at the caudal fin) shall be prohibited.

Incidental catch of such small herrings, if not in large quantity, shall be allowed. The allowable extent of such catch shall be determined by the Commission.

3. Crabs

King Crabs (Paralithodes camtschatica)
(Paralithodes platypus)

a. Fishing of female crab and immature crab whose carapace is less than thirteen centimetres in width shall be prohibited. The female crabs and the afore-mentioned immature crabs if caught in the nets shall be released back into the water immediately.

The incidental catch of female crabs and above-mentioned immature crabs, if not in large quantity shall be allowed. The allowable extent of such catch shall be determined by the Commission.

The Commission shall also determine the amount of incidental catch of female and above-mentioned immature crabs in a given area requiring suspension of fishing in that area.

b. In consideration of conservation of the resources, as well as efficiency of operations, restrictions shall be placed upon the length of the row of crab nets, the distance between the nets arranged in a row, and the distance separating the several rows. The Commission shall determine the restrictions.

APPENDIX B-2

Agreement for Cooperation for the Rescue of Persons in Distress at Sea

Signed at Moscow, May 14, 1956; in force, December 12, 1956.
[Unofficial Translation.]

The Governments of Japan and the Union of Soviet Socialist Republics,

Recognizing the need for making an arrangement to render possible co-operation for giving prompt and effective assistance, irrespective of nationality, to persons in distress in the Japan Sea, the Okhotsk Sea, the Bering Sea, and in the waters of the Northwest Pacific Ocean adjacent to the coasts of Japan and the Union of Soviet Socialist Republics,

Have for this purpose appointed their respective representatives who have agreed as follows:

ARTICLE I

1. In case any vessel (the term "vessel" as used in this Agreement is understood to include fishing vessels) is in distress in the Japan Sea, the Okhotsk Sea, the Bering Sea or in the waters of the Northwest Pacific Ocean adjacent to the coasts of Japan and the Union of Soviet Socialist Republics (hereinafter referred to as "the Soviet Union"), the sea disaster rescue agencies of the Contracting Parties shall give necessary assistance, to the furthest extent possible, in rescuing persons on board such vessel.

2. When a sea disaster rescue agency of either Contracting Party receives a report of a vessel in distress at sea, the agency concerned shall take the rescue measures deemed most appropriate with respect to persons on board such vessel.

3. In case the place of disaster is located near the coast of the other Contracting Party, or when it is deemed necessary, the sea disaster rescue agency receiving the information of the disaster shall make plans for rescue operations after consultation with the sea disaster rescue agency of the other Contracting Party.

SOURCE: *Japanese Annual of International Law*, no. 1(1957): 124–127.

Such consultation shall be held invariably when the sea disaster rescue agency of one Contracting Party receives a report that a vessel belonging to the other Contracting Party is in distress at sea.

ARTICLE II

The rescue operations within the territorial sea of Japan or of the Soviet Union shall be conducted in accordance with the laws and regulations of the country concerned.

ARTICLE III

1. The wireless stations of the sea disaster rescue agencies of Japan and the Soviet Union shall receive the distress signals sent in frequencies of 500 kilocycles (600 metres) and 2,182 kilocycles (137.5 metres) in compliance with the international regulations concerning transmission and receipt of distress signals.

2. Wireless contact between the sea disaster rescue agencies of Japan and the Soviet Union shall be made through Station JNL with respect to the rescue agency of Japan and Station URH with respect to the rescue agency of the Soviet Union.

In this event, call signals shall be made in the frequency of 500 kilocycles, and subsequent transmission in the case of Station JNL shall be in frequencies of 472 kilocycles, or 3,212.5 kilocycles at night and 6,386.5 kilocycles during the day, and in the case of Station URH in frequencies of 457 kilocycles, or 3,270 kilocycles at night and 6,365 kilocycles during the day. When call signals are made in frequency of 500 kilocycles and if reliable wireless contact cannot be made at a certain time of the day or night, sea disaster rescue agencies of the Contracting Parties may agree to make the call signals at such times in the other frequencies stipulated in this Convention.

3. The ships belonging to the sea disaster rescue agencies while conducting rescue operations shall maintain wireless contact with each other, as well as with the vessel in distress through Station JNL and Station URH respectively, and if necessary may make direct contact in frequencies of 500 kilocycles or 2,182 kilocycles.

4. The wireless communications mentioned in 1, 2, and 3 above shall be made in international code or when possible in the ordinary English language.

ARTICLE IV

1. The sea disaster rescue agency of either Contracting Party that commences rescue operations first for the purpose of rendering assistance, may when necessary for the completion of the operations request the co-operation of the rescue agency of the other Contracting Party, in accordance with the provisions of Article III.

2. The sea disaster rescue agency in receipt of the request mentioned above shall as far as practicable despatch means of rescue to the reported place of disaster for the purpose of rescue operations.

ARTICLE V

The Contracting Parties undertake to give detailed instructions concerning enforcement of the provisions of this Agreement to their respective sea disaster rescue agencies.

ARTICLE VI

The provisions of this Agreement shall not be deemed to be in conflict with the Convention for the Unification of Certain Rules respecting Assistance and Salvage at Sea signed at Brussels on 23 September 1910 and the International Convention for the Safety of Life at Sea, 1948, signed at London on 10 June 1948.

ARTICLE VII

1. This Agreement shall become effective from the date of entry into force of the Peace Treaty between Japan and the Union of Soviet Socialist Republics or from the date of restoration of diplomatic relations between the said countries, and remain in force for a period of three years.

2. If neither of the Contracting Parties announces the abrogation of this Agreement at least one year before the above-mentioned period expires, it shall continue in force for another three years, and it shall continue to remain in force for additional periods of three years each as long as neither of the Contracting Parties announces the abrogation of this Agreement at least one year before the expiration of each extended period of three years.

IN WITNESS WHEREOF, the undersigned representatives have signed this Convention.

DONE in duplicate, in the Japanese and Russian languages, both equally authentic, at Moscow, this fourteenth day of May, one thousand nine hundred fifty-six.

BY AUTHORITY OF THE GOVERNMENT OF JAPAN
ad referendum

I. Kono
K. Matsudaira

BY AUTHORITY OF THE GOVERNMENT OF THE UNION OF SOVIET SOCIALIST REPUBLICS:

A. Ishkov

EXCHANGE OF NOTES

Moscow, 14 May 1956

Excellency,

I have the honour to refer to Article II of the Agreement between Japan and the Union of Soviet Socialist Republics for Cooperation for the Rescue of Persons in Distress at Sea, signed today in Moscow, and to state that according to the views of the Japanese Government the provisions of the said Article shall not be deemed to affect in any way the position of the Contracting Parties with respect to the question of the limits of territorial sea.

Accept, Excellency, the assurances of my highest consideration.

Ichiro Kono

His Excellency
  Mr. A. A. Ishkov
    Minister for Fisheries
      The Union of Soviet Socialist Republics.

Moscow, 14 May 1956

Excellency,

I have the honour to acknowledge the receipt of your Excellency's note of this date stating as follows:

"I have the honour to refer to Article II of the Agreement between Japan and the Union of Soviet Socialist Republics for Cooperation for the Rescue of Persons in Distress at Sea, signed today in Moscow, and to state that according to the views of the Japanese Government the provisions of the said Article shall not be deemed to affect in any way the position of the Contracting Parties with respect to the question of the limits of territorial sea."

I have further the honour to state that the above are also the views of the Government of the Union of Soviet Socialist Republics.

Accept, Excellency, the assurances of my highest consideration.

A. Ishkov

His Excellency
  Mr. I. Kono
    Forestry Minister for Japan.

Moscow, 14 May 1956

Excellency,

I have the honour to refer to the Convention concerning the High Seas Fisheries of the Northwest Pacific Ocean, and the Agreement for Cooperation for the Rescue of Persons in Distress at Sea, between Japan and the Union of Soviet Socialist Republics, both signed today in Moscow, and to communicate to Your Excellency that the approval of the Diet is required to put the said Convention and Agreement into force with respect to Japan.

Accept, Excellency, the assurances of my highest consideration.

Ichiro Kono

His Excellency
  Mr. A. A. Ishkov
    Minister for Fisheries
      The Union of Soviet Socialist Republics.

APPENDIX C

*Treaty of Commerce between Japan and the
Union of Soviet Socialist Republics*[1]

Signed at Tokyo, December 6, 1957.

Japan and the Union of Soviet Socialist Republics, desiring to promote the development of trade relations between the two countries and acting in accordance with the provisions of the Joint Declaration by the Union of Soviet Socialist Republics and Japan, signed on 19 October 1956,[2] have resolved to conclude a Treaty of Commerce, provided for in paragraph 7 of the said Declaration, and have for this purpose appointed as their plenipotentiaries:

Japan:
   Sadao Hirose, Envoy Extraordinary and Minister Plenipotentiary;
The Union of Soviet Socialist Republics:
   Ivan Fedorovich Semichastnov, Deputy Minister of Foreign Trade of the Union of Soviet Socialist Republics,

who, having exchanged their full powers, found in good and due form, have agreed as follows:

ARTICLE 1

The two Contracting Parties shall, within the limits of their respective laws, make every effort to put their trade, navigation and other commercial relations on a firm and friendly basis.

ARTICLE 2

Each Contracting Party shall grant to the other Contracting Party most-

---

SOURCE: *Japanese Annual of International Law*, no. 2 (1958): 173–183.
   1. Came into force on May 9, 1958, the date of the exchange of the instruments of ratification at Moscow, in accordance with article 15.

favoured-nation treatment in respect of customs duties, charges and customs formalities of any kind and other regulations connected with the importation of goods of the other Contracting Party and with the exportation of its own goods to the other Contracting Party.

ARTICLE 3

The goods of one Contracting Party which have been conveyed in transit through the territory of one or more third States shall not be liable, on importation into the territory of the other Contracting Party, to duties or charges higher than those to which they would have been liable if they had been imported directly from the territory of the other Contracting Party.

These provisions shall likewise apply to goods which, while in transit through the territory of a third State, have been subjected to trans-shipment, re-packing, or warehousing.

ARTICLE 4

Each Contracting Party shall grant to the goods of the other Contracting Party unconditional most-favoured-nation treatment in all matters relating to all internal taxes or other internal charges of any kind and to all laws, regulations and requirements affecting internal sale, offering for sale, purchase, distribution or use of imported goods within the territory of such Contracting Party.

ARTICLE 5

Each Contracting Party shall, in accordance with the internal laws and regulations in force, grant most-favoured-nation treatment as regards exemption from duties and charges in respect of the temporary importation to its territory and exportation from its territory of the following articles of the other Contracting Party:

a. Samples of goods;

b. Articles intended for experiments or tests;

c. Articles intended for display at exhibitions, competitions and fairs;

d. Fitters' equipment, intended for fitting work and for the installation of equipment;

e. Articles intended for processing or repair, and articles which constitute processing or repair materials;

f. Containers for exported or imported goods.

ARTICLE 6

Any advantages, facilities, privileges or immunities with respect to the matters referred to in articles 2 to 5 of this Treaty, which are granted or may hereafter be granted by one of the Contracting Parties in respect of goods originating in any third country or intended for export to the territory of any third country, shall be granted in respect of similar goods originating in or intended for export to the territory of the other Contracting Party.

ARTICLE 7

No prohibitions or restrictions shall be applied by either Contracting Party on the importation or exportation of any goods from or to the Territory of the other Contracting Party which are not similarly applied to the importation or exportation of similar goods from or to the territories of all third countries in like circumstances for the purpose of safeguarding the external financial position and balance of payments.

ARTICLE 8

The merchant vessels of each Contracting Party shall have the right to enter, clear and stay in all the ports and territorial waters of the other Contracting Party to the same extent and on the same terms as the merchant vessels of any third State.

The merchant vessels of each Contracting Party, their crews, passengers and cargoes shall be accorded by the other Contracting Party in its ports and territorial waters treatment no less favourable than that which is accorded to the merchant vessels, crews, passengers and cargoes of any third State in respect of loading and discharging; charges and dues of every kind levied on behalf of or for the benefit of the State, municipalities or other organizations; the mooring of vessels and the assignment of places for loading and discharging in ports and roadsteads; supplies of fuel, lubricating oils, water and food; the use of pilotage services, signals and lights used to mark navigable waters; the use of cranes, anchorages, warehouses, shipyards, dry-docks and repair yards; the application of regulations and formalities, including health and quarantine formalities; and all other questions relating to commercial navigation.

Each Contracting Party shall also accord in customs and administrative matters and other formalities in its ports and territorial waters to the merchant vessels and cargoes of the other Contracting Party treatment no less favourable than that which is accorded to the merchant vessels and cargoes of any third country.

Any vessel flying the flag of either Contracting Party, supplied with the documents required by the laws and regulations of that Party for proof of nationality of the vessel, shall be recognized by the other Contracting Party as a vessel of the country whose flag it flies.

Tonnage certificates of the vessels of the Contracting Parties and other technical ship's papers, referring to the measurement of the capacity of vessels, issued or recognized by one of the Contracting Parties, shall be recognized by the other Party. In accordance with this provision, any vessel of either Contracting

Party carrying a valid tonnage certificate shall be exempt from re-measurement in the ports of the other Party, and the net capacity of the vessel entered in the certificate shall be taken as the basis for calculating harbour dues and charges.

ARTICLE 9

The provisions of the preceding article shall not extend to coastal shipping. Nevertheless, the merchant vessels of either Contracting Party proceeding from one port of the other Party to another, in observance of the laws and regulations of this Party, for the purpose of landing all or part of a cargo brought from abroad, or of taking on board all or part of a cargo for a foreign destination, shall not be regarded as engaged in coastal shipping.

ARTICLE 10

If a vessel of one Contracting Party is in distress or is wrecked on the coast of the other Contracting Party, such vessel and its cargo shall enjoy the same advantages and immunities as are granted by the other Contracting Party to its national vessel and cargo. In particular, the necessary aid and assistance shall be afforded at all times, and in the same measure as in the case of national vessels in the same situation, to the master, crew and passengers, and to the vessel and its cargo.

It is agreed that articles saved from a vessel in distress or wrecked shall not be liable to any customs duties, provided that these articles are not intended for use inside the country.

ARTICLE 11

In view of the fact that, under the laws of the Union of Soviet Socialist Republics, foreign trade is a State monopoly, Japan agrees that the Union of Soviet Socialist Republics shall establish in Japan a Trade Delegation, the legal status of which shall be governed by the provisions of the Annex to this Treaty, which shall constitute an integral part thereof.

ARTICLE 12

Japanese nationals and corporate bodies constituted in accordance with the laws in force in Japan shall, when engaged in business activity in the territory of the Union of Soviet Socialist Republics personally or through their appointed representatives under conditions prescribed by the laws in force in the USSR, enjoy in respect of the protection of their persons and their property the same treatment under the law as that accorded to the nationals and corporate bodies of any other State.

The nationals and corporate bodies of either Contracting Party, specified in this article, shall enjoy access to the courts of the other Contracting Party on the same basis as the nationals and corporate bodies of any other State.

Article 13

No provision of this Treaty shall be construed as precluding either of the Contracting Parties from taking any measures directed to the protection of its essential security interests.

Article 14

The two Contracting Parties undertake to enforce arbitral awards made with regard to disputes which may arise out of commercial contracts concluded by nationals and corporate bodies of Japan on the one hand, and by Soviet foreign trade organizations on the other hand, or relating to such contracts, if provisions for deciding the dispute by such arbitration has been embodied in the contract itself or in separate agreement drawn up in proper form.

The enforcement of the arbitral award may be refused in the following circumstances:

a. When the arbitral award has not become final and operative under the law of the country in which it was made;

b. When the arbitral award compels one party to the dispute to take some action which is contrary to the laws of the country in which enforcement of the award is sought;

c. When the arbitral award is contrary to public policy in the country in which enforcement of the award is sought.

An arrangement for submitting to arbitration disputes arising out of or relating to commercial contracts shall exclude the national courts of the Contracting Parties from jurisdiction.

Article 15

This Treaty shall be subject to ratification and the exchange of instruments of ratification shall take place at Moscow as soon as possible. The Treaty shall enter into force on the date of the exchange of the instruments of ratification and shall remain in force for a period of five years.

If neither of the Contracting Parties gives notice in writing six months before the expiration of the said period, of its desire to terminate the Treaty, the Treaty shall remain in force until the expiration of six months from the date on which either of the Contracting Parties notifies the other Contracting Party of its intention to terminate the Treaty.

In witness whereof the plenipotentiaries of the two Contracting Parties have signed this Treaty and have affixed thereto their seals.

Done at Tokyo, on 6 December 1957, in duplicate, in the Japanese and Russian languages, both texts being equally authentic.

Sadao Hirose   I. Semichastnov

ANNEX

THE LEGAL STATUS OF THE TRADE DELEGATION OF THE UNION OF SOVIET SOCIALIST REPUBLICS IN JAPAN

ARTICLE 1

The functions of the Trade Delegation of the Union of Soviet Socialist Republics in Japan shall be:

a. To facilitate and develop trade between Japan and the Union of Soviet Socialist Republics;

b. To represent the interests of the Union of Soviet Socialist Republics in Japan in regard to trade between Japan and the Union of Soviet Socialist Republics;

c. To take necessary action for the Government of the Union of Soviet Socialist Republics in connexion with commercial transactions between Japan and the Union of Soviet Socialist Republics;

d. To carry on trade on behalf of the Government of the Union of Soviet Socialist Republics between Japan and the Union of Soviet Socialist Republics.

ARTICLE 2

The Trade Delegation shall form an integral part of the Embassy of the Union of Soviet Socialist Republics in Japan.

The official premises of the Trade Delegation at No. 12 Shinruyudo-cho, Azabu, Minato-ku, Tokyo shall be invested with the privileges and immunities enjoyed by the official premises of diplomatic missions. The Trade Delegation may be transferred to other premises by agreement between the Government of Japan and the Government of the Union of Soviet Socialist Republics.

The Trade Delegation may establish branches in other Japanese cities with the prior agreement of the Government of Japan.

The Trade Delegation shall be entitled to use a cipher.

The Trade Delegation shall not be subject to any regulations governing commercial registration.

The Trade Delegate and his two deputies shall enjoy all the privileges and immunities accorded to members of diplomatic missions.

The number of employees of the Trade Delegation shall be limited by agreement between the two Governments.

The employees of the Trade Delegation who are citizens of the Union of Soviet Socialist Republics assigned to Japan shall be exempt from Japanese taxation on the emoluments they receive from the Government of the Union of Soviet Socialist Republics for the performance of the functions mentioned in the preceding article.

ARTICLE 3

The Trade Delegation shall act on behalf of the Government of the Union of Soviet Socialist Republics.

The Government of the Union of Soviet Socialist Republics shall be responsible for all commercial contracts concluded or guaranteed in Japan on behalf of the Trade Delegation and signed by two authorized persons.

The Trade Delegation shall communicate to the Government of Japan the names of the aforesaid authorized persons and the extent to which each such person is empowered to sign commercial contracts on its behalf. The Government of Japan shall publish the names and powers of these persons in the Government publication of Japan.

It is understood that any commercial contracts concluded without the guarantee of the Trade Delegation by any Soviet organizations whatsoever, which under the laws of the Union of Soviet Socialist Republics have the status of independent corporate bodies, shall be binding only on the organizations in question, and execution in respect of such contracts may be levied only on their property. No responsibility for such contracts shall be incurred by the Government of the Union of Soviet Socialist Republics by the Trade Delegation or by any other Soviet organization whatsoever except such as are parties to the contract.

ARTICLE 4

The Trade Delgation shall enjoy the privileges and immunities arising out of the provisions of article 2, with the following exceptions:

Disputes regarding commercial contracts concluded or guaranteed in the territory of Japan by the Trade Delegation under the provisions of article 3, second paragraph, shall, in the absence of an arbitration agreement or an agreement providing for any other jurisdiction, be subject to the jurisdiction of the Japanese courts and shall be settled in accordance with Japanese law, save as otherwise provided by the terms of individual contracts or by Japanese legislation. No interim orders may, however, be made against the Trade Delegation.

In respect of legal proceedings before the courts in connexion with actions which may be brought concerning the disputes mentioned in the preceding paragraph, the Government of the Union of Soviet Socialist Republics shall waive the privileges and immunities referred to in article 2 on behalf of the Trade Delegate and his two deputies and undertakes to authorize the Trade Delegate and, in the event of his absence, a deputy Trade Delegate to represent its country so that the Japanese courts may conduct legal proceedings in the actions which may be brought before them in accordance with the provisions of the preceding paragraph.

Execution of judgements relating to contracts to which the Trade Delegation is a party may be taken against all State property of the Union of Soviet Socialist Republics in Japan, in particular property, rights and interests arising out of contracts concluded or guaranteed by the Trade Delegation, with exception of property belonging to the organizations referred to in article 3, fourth paragraph, which are not a party to the contract guaranteed by the Trade Delegation.

Property and premises intended solely for the exercise in Japan of the diplomatic and consular rights of the Government of the Union of Soviet Socialist Republics, in accordance with international practice, and also the premises occupied by the Trade Delegation and the movable property situated therein. shall not be liable to execution.

ARTICLE 5

The establishment of the Trade Delegation shall in no way affect the rights of individuals and corporate bodies of Japan to maintain direct relations with the Soviet foreign trade organizations for the purpose of concluding and carrying out commercial contracts.

S. H.   I. S.

EXCHANGE OF NOTES

I

Tokyo, 6 December 1957

Sir,

I have the honour to confirm that in the course of negotiations on the conclusion of the Treaty of Commerce between Japan and the Union of Soviet Socialist Republics signed on this date, we have agreed as follows:

1. The Government of Japan and the Government of the Union of Soviet Socialist Republics, with a view to developing trade between their two countries, consider it desirable to establish regular steamship lines between Japan and the USSR, utilizing the merchant vessels of both countries.

2. For the successful execution of this agreement it is desirable that the maritime shipping firms and associations of the two countries should negotiate the conclusion of an agreement on the commercial arrangements necessary to the opening of such lines, in particular as regards tariffs, schedules and the appointment of agents. It is also desirable that the competent officials of the two Governments should confer if any questions arise requiring the consideration of the Governments.

3. Each Government shall inform the other which maritime shipping firms

and associations will take part in the aforementioned negotiations, which are to begin at Tokyo as soon as possible.

I have the honour to be, etc.

SADAO HIROSE

His Excellency Mr. I. F. Semichatnov
Plenipotentiary of the Union of Soviet Socialist Republics
Tokyo

II

Tokyo, 6 December 1957

Sir,

I have the honour to acknowledge receipt of your letter of this date . . .

I have the honour to be, etc.

I. SEMICHASTNOV

His Excellency Mr. Sadao Hirose
Plenipotentiary of Japan
Tokyo

APPENDIX D-1

*Exchange of Notes between the Government of Japan
and the Government of the USSR concerning the
Mutual Refusal of Consular Fees in the Granting of Visas*

Signed in Tokyo, February 26, 1965. Effective April 1, 1965 (MFA, April 1967).

A mutual exemption from all consular fees on visas required of Soviet and Japanese citizens traveling in Japan and the USSR. This agreement can be terminated in 30 days following notification by one of the parties.

APPENDIX D-2

*Exchange of Notes Pertaining to Procedures for the
Transfer of Fishing Vessels Seized and Persons Arrested
in Connection with their Violations of Fishing Laws
Established by the Convention on Open-Sea Fishing
in the Northwestern Region of the Pacific between
Japan and the USSR*

Signed in Moscow, April 15, 1965. Effective April 15, 1965 (MFA, January 1967).

SOURCE: Texts of bilateral treaties and agreements, 1956–1977 (Appendixes D and E) furnished in both Russian and Japanese by the Treaty Bureau of the Japanese Ministry of Foreign Affairs (*Gaimusho*). Unofficial translation/summaries, where not otherwise indicated, from Russian text.

The first exchange confirms that the procedures defined in the Soviet-Japanese Fishing Convention of 1956 are in effect in 1965.

Note N. 18: A Soviet proposal, accepted by Japan, establishing transfer procedures effective in 1962.

1. If an official of the violator's country is available, the transfer can be effected in the area where the vessel was seized. Such a transfer must be recorded in a Report in Russian and Japanese accompanied by a report of the violation itself (in both languages).

2. If a transfer in the area is not possible, the seized vessel is directed to a port in its own country of origin. The seizing vessel notifies by radio the other side's officials and submits similar reports which also include the vessel's destination and whether or not its nets were sealed. The seizing party must be notified within 12 hours of the vessel's arrival at its port of destination.

3. Whenever the vessel seized operates out of a "mother-ship" base, it is directed to this base and the official present on board the base must notify the seizing party within 12 hours of the seized vessel's arrival. The procedure is as per Pt. 2 of the present Note.

4. If an official meets a seized vessel on its way to a designated port or base, he may receive the vessel on the spot pending notification of the seizing party within 12 hours.

5. Whenever a vessel is detained or a person arrested, the detaining party must provide it with the water, food, fuel, and supplies needed. These supplies are to be paid for by the seized vessel's crew and an agreement to this effect is to be drawn up in both Japanese and Russian. Copies of this agreement are sent to the appropriate officials of the seized vessel's country, who must ensure that payments are made within four months of receipt of such documents.

6. All communication concerning the transfer of seized vessels is to be by radio through shipboard and coastal radio stations. A list of Japanese and Soviet radio stations, their locations, and call numbers follow. Frequencies are also given as well as the times when all radio stations maintain their channels open in order to be able to receive possible messages from the other party. Both Japanese and Russian can be used in these communications and in case of need, English. Telegrams in Japanese or Russian are to be written using the Latin alphabet and transmitted by Morse code. [Moscow, March 31, 1962.]

APPENDIX D-3

An Agreement on Trade and Payments between
Japan and the USSR for the Years 1966 through 1970

Signed in Moscow, January 21, 1966. Effective January 21, 1966 (MFA, December 1966).

The agreement is valid from January 1, 1966, through December 31, 1970. It includes two lists of trade merchandise: List I enumerates Soviet exports to Japan (mostly raw materials and mineral ores), and List II names Japanese exports to the USSR (fishing and cargo ships, factory and laboratory equipment, machinery and parts). Quantities are given in tons and pounds sterling.

There are also two additional lists of items to be traded between the Far Eastern region of the USSR (fish and whale products) and Japan (consumer goods).

The agreement also states that neither agreeing party shall in any way restrict the export and import of merchandise not included in these lists. Furthermore, quantities and sums stated in these lists are simply guidelines and not restrictions on future trade.

APPENDIX D-4

An Agreement between the Government of Japan and the Government of the USSR on Aviation Communication

Signed in Moscow, January 21, 1966. Effective March 3, 1967 (MFA, July 1967).

Paragraph I: Defines the terms *aviation authorities* (in Japan, the Minister of Transportation, and in the USSR, the Minister of Civil Aviation); *designated airline; air communication; international air communication; landing not connected with transportation;* and *Appendix I* and *Appendix II*. Both these Appendices can be modified as provided for in Article 2 of Paragraph XVIII and are integral parts of this agreement.

Paragraph II: Both designated airlines have the right to make landings not connected with transportation at points assigned by the other agreeing party within the boundaries of its own territory as well as transportation related landings at points specified in Appendix I. Schedules, payments, and technical servicing of aircraft is to be determined by a commercial agreement between the designated airlines. Each agreeing party will determine the itinerary of aircraft within its borders. If the other party is dissatisfied with an itinerary so determined, it can initiate a temporary halt in the exploitation of any line.

Paragraph V: All aspects of air transportation are subject to local rules and regulations.

Paragraph VIII: All profits from the agreed-upon flights are tax free. Passengers may choose any one of the two designated airlines; the same applies to cargo.

Paragraph X: All fuel, oil, and supplies brought by a designated airline onto the territory of the other agreeing party, and which are needed in the operation of these flights, are exempt from customs duties. However, they cannot be unloaded without the authorization of local customs authorities and must be returned to their country of origin whenever they remain unused.

Paragraph XII: The identification of aircraft, crew, passengers, and cargo: Standard.

Paragraph XIII: Each designated airline can maintain within the territory of the other agreeing party the technical, flight, and administrative personnel needed for the operation of these flights. The total number of personnel is to be determined by both agreeing parties. All personnel must be citizens of the agreeing parties.

Paragraph XIV: Both sides agree to exchange statistical information which might be helpful in determining the volume of passengers and cargo transportation.

Paragraph XV: Both sides agree to offer all forms of aid and assistance to all disabled aircraft on their territories.

Paragraph XVI: All accidents with aircraft must be reported immediately to the aviation authorities of the aircraft's country of origin. Procedures in case of serious injury or death of passengers and/or serious damage to the aircraft; standard regulations governing the investigation of such incidents.

Paragraph XVII: All disagreements must be settled through negotiations.

Paragraph XIX: This agreement remains in effect until a year following the notification of one of the agreeing parties of the intent to terminate said agreement by the other agreeing party.

Appendix I: The flights to be operated in both directions by "Nihon Koku Kabushiki Kaisha" and "Aeroflot" are: Tokyo-Moscow-points in third countries and Moscow-Tokyo-points in third countries.

Appendix II: Gives the technical details of flight operations including air traffic control zones, communication, and air traffic control procedures (current standards of the International Civil Aviation Organization; English will be the language used during communication).

Additional Minutes to the Agreement: In view of the fact that the USSR is not yet able to open Siberian air space to foreign air transports, it proposes that "Aeroflot" and "Nihon Koku Kabushiki Kaisha" jointly rent from the Soviet Ministry of Civil Aviation aircraft and flight crews. Each airline may provide a specialist as a member of the flight crew. The passenger service crew is to be composed of both Soviet and Japanese personnel. The distribution of profits is to be worked out by both airlines.

APPENDIX D-5

Consular Convention between Japan and the USSR

Signed in Tokyo, July 29, 1966. Effective August 23, 1967 (MFA, November 1967).

An agreement developed by Etsusaburo Shiina, Minister of Foreign Affairs of Japan and Andrey Gromyko, Minister of Foreign Affairs of the USSR.

Part I: Defines the terms *consulate, consular official, consulate head, consulate worker, consular area, citizen,* and *vessel.*

Part II: The establishment of consulates, the assignment of consular officials and workers. Standard procedures.

Part III: Privileges and immunities. Standard.

Part IV: Consular functions and activities; standard. Paragraphs 38–42 deal with consular functions pertaining to commercial sea and air shipping.

Part V: Concluding resolutions.

This convention is to be ratified by means of an exchange of ratification acts to take place in Moscow. It also comes into effect thirty days following this exchange and is valid five years. It remains in effect for twelve months following the notification by one of the agreeing parties of its intention to terminate said Convention.

Addendum to the Consular Convention agreed upon at the time of signing and pertaining to Paragraph 32 of said Convention.

Deals with the time period within which a consular official must be notified of the arrest of a citizen of the country represented by said official (1–3 days) and with his right to visit and communicate with an arrested person.

Letter from A. Gromyko, Foreign Minister of the USSR, to E. Shiina, Foreign Minister of Japan. Concerns the procedure in case of the arrest of Japanese citizens for violations of territorial waters regulations in the Northwestern area of the Pacific Ocean, including the seas of Japan, Okhotsk, and Bering.

The Japanese Consulate in the USSR is to be notified within 10 days of such arrests. Visits of arrested persons by consular officials are subject to current diplomatic agreements. Consular officials may communicate with these persons by means of letters or telegrams.

None of these procedural provisions are to be regarded as having any effect whatsoever on the policies of either country concerning the extent of territorial waters or their jurisdictions over commercial fishing activities.

APPENDIX D-6

*Exchange of Notes on the Implementation of the
Japanese-Soviet Agreement on Cooperation in the
Rescue of Victims of Sea Disasters*

Signed in Moscow, July 24, 1967. Effective July 24, 1967 (MFA, June 1968).

Formalizes the agreement on rescue cooperation and establishes additional channels for radio communication during such rescue operations, the various kilocycles being specified.

APPENDIX D-7

*Exchange of Notes Concerning the Implementation
of the Agreement between Japan and the USSR on
Cooperation in the Rescue of Victims of Sea Disasters*

Signed in Tokyo, July 24, 1967. Effective July 24, 1967 (MFA, June 1968).

Additional channels of radio communication during rescue operations are established, the frequencies are given in kilocycles.

APPENDIX D-8

*An Agreement between the Government of Japan and
the Government of the USSR on Scientific and Technical
Cooperation in the Area of Commercial Fishing*

Signed in Moscow, July 24, 1967. Effective July 24, 1967 (MFA, September 1967).

An agreement to share scientific and technical information in all areas of commercial fishing, fish farming, and research in related areas. The agreement is valid three years. Once two years have elapsed following the signing of said agreement, it can be terminated by either party by means of a notification of intent to terminate. In such case, the agreement expires a year following the date of notification.

APPENDIX D-9

Exchange of Letters Concerning Imports and Exports between Japan and the USSR Necessary in the Development of Forest Resources in the Soviet Far East.

Signed in Tokyo, August 14, 1968. Effective August 14, 1968 (MFA, September 1968).

The Soviet government expresses its support of the agreement reached by "Exportles" and "K-S Sangyo" pertaining to the joint development of forest resources in the Far Eastern region of the USSR. All export and import connected with this project is subject to the regulations stipulated by the Agreement on Trade and Payments for 1966–1970. New items may be added to the lists of import and export merchandise included in said Trade Agreement.

APPENDIX D-10

Exchange of Letters between the Government of Japan and the Government of the USSR Concerning the Beginning Date of Independent Flights by Japanese Airlines over Siberian Air Space.

Signed in Tokyo, March 7, 1969. Effective March 7, 1969 (MFA, April 1969).

Flights are to be conducted as stated in the agreement signed on January 21, 1966, and are to begin no later than March 31, 1970. In the meantime, beginning with April 1969 there will be two flights a week on IL-62 aircraft. A flight schedule and other details of the flights are to be worked out by "Aeroflot" and "Nihon Koku Kabushiki Kaisha" at a meeting to be held in Moscow in March 1969.

APPENDIX D-11

Minutes of a Meeting Devoted to the Development
of Lists of Trade Merchandise that Will Be Traded
between Japan and the USSR in 1969

Signed in Moscow, March 14, 1969. Effective March 14, 1969 (MFA, April 1969).

Includes two lists of import/export items: one is mostly mineral and raw minerals which will be exported by the USSR to Japan, and the other is technical and industrial equipment that Japan will export to the USSR. Quantities are given in either tons or pounds sterling of total value of each item.

APPENDIX D-12

Exchange of Letters concerning a Modification of
Appendix I to the Japanese-Soviet Agreement on
Aviation Communications

Signed in Moscow, December 27, 1969. Effective December 27, 1969 (MFA, December 1969).

A Japanese proposal, accepted by the USSR, that the Japanese airline "Nihon Koku Kabushiki Kaisha" be allowed to fly in both directions: the itinerary, Tokyo-Moscow-Paris and/or London and other points in third countries. "Aeroflot" is to fly in both directions, the line Moscow-Tokyo and points in other countries.
    Also includes a letter from A. Gromyko, Foreign Minister of the USSR,

addressed to Takeo Fukuda, Foreign Minister of Japan, concerning various aspects of cultural exchange between Japan and the USSR in the next two years. This exchange is to include among other things, official and informational publications, scientific data, films, etc.

APPENDIX D-13

Exchange of Letters concerning a Modification of Appendix I to the Agreement between the Government of Japan and the Government of the USSR on Aviation Communication

Signed in Moscow, April 30, 1971. Effective April 30, 1971 (MFA, March 1972).

A modification of Appendix I to the agreement signed in January 1966. A Japanese proposal accepted by the USSR:

1. The Japanese airline "Nihon Koku Kabushiki Kaisha" is to operate the following lines in both directions:
    a. Tokyo-Moscow-Copenhagen (or Amsterdam), Paris and/or London and other stops in third countries.
    b. Niigata-Khabarovsk.

2. The Soviet airline "Aeroflot" is to operate the following lines in both directions:
    a. Moscow-Tokyo and other points in third countries.
    b. Khabarovsk-Niigata.
These lines will be flown over the western coast of Japan and Siberia.

Stops in third countries are to be chosen by mutual agreement.

APPENDIX D-14

An Agreement on Trade and Payments between Japan and the USSR for 1971-1975

Signed in Tokyo, September 22, 1971. Effective September 22, 1971 (MFA, February 1972).

A trade agreement effective retroactively from January 1, 1971, through December 1, 1975. Contains lists of almost three hundred export/import items including two separate lists of items to be traded between Japan and the Far Eastern regions of the USSR.

An additional letter from the Soviet side proposes that the total value of exports in 1971 should not exceed £4,630,000 pounds sterling for either side and may reach £6,940,000 in 1975. Representatives of both governments are to meet yearly in Moscow and Tokyo to discuss the state of current trade operations.

A letter from N. Patolichev, Foreign Trade Minister of the USSR, expressing the Soviet government's satisfaction with the agreement reached by "YAV Kabushiki Kaisha" and "Mashinoimport" concerning the supply to the USSR of equipment, machinery, and materials necessary in the construction of a sea port at Wrangel Bay.

APPENDIX D-15

Exchange of Notes between the Government of Japan and the Government of the USSR concerning the General Agreement between "Nihon Chip Boeki Kabushiki Kaisha" and "Exportles"

Signed in Tokyo, February 23, 1972. Effective February 23, 1972 (MFA, March 1972).

The Soviet government pledges its support to the agreement developed by "Exportles" and Japan Chip Trading Co., Ltd. according to which "Exportles" will provide to Japan technological chip in exchange for machinery and equipment used in the production of chip.

APPENDIX D-16

Exchange of Letters concerning a Modification of Appendix I to the Agreement between the Government of Japan and the Government of the USSR on Aviation Communication

Signed in Moscow, June 12, 1973. Effective June 12, 1973 (MFA, July 1973).

A further modification of Appendix I to the agreement signed in January 1966.

A Japanese proposal accepted by the USSR:

1. The Japanese airline "Nihon Koku Kabushiki Kaisha" is to operate the following lines in both directions:

    a. Tokyo-Moscow-Copenhagen, Amsterdam, Paris, London, Frankfurt am/M, Rome, and/or other points in third countries.

    b. Niigata-Khabarovsk.

2. The Soviet airline "Aeroflot" is to operate the following lines in both directions:

    a. Moscow-Tokyo-and other points in third countries.

    b. Khabarovsk-Niigata.

These lines will be flown over the western coast of Japan and Siberia.

Stops in third countries are to be chosen by mutual agreement.

APPENDIX D-17

An Agreement between the Government of Japan and the Government of the USSR on Scientific and Technical Cooperation

Signed in Moscow, October 10, 1973. Effective October 10, 1973 (MFA, March 1974).

Paragraph I: Provides for the exchange of scientists and scholars, the convocation of joint conferences and symposia, and the exchange of scientific information.

Paragraph III: Creates a Japanese-Soviet Commission on Scientific Cooperation which is to serve as a consulting body to both governments. Yearly meetings are to be held in Tokyo and Moscow alternatively.

Paragraph V: This agreement is valid two years and remains in effect until six months following notification by one of the parties of its intent to terminate said agreement.

APPENDIX D-18

Exchange of Notes concerning the Exchange of
Scientists and Research Workers between State
Research Institutes in Japan and Research Institutes
of the Academy of Sciences of the USSR

Exchanged in Moscow, October 10, 1973. Effective October 10, 1973 (MFA, November 1973).

The exchange is to consist of no more than ten scientists and researchers whose stay in the host country is not to exceed ten months. In addition, ten scientists may be sent as lecturers or conference participants. Their stay is limited to two months. The host country is to provide funds for the visiting scholars' research expenses as well as housing and travel within the country whenever it is necessary for their work. All other expenses are to be covered by the scholars' own country.

APPENDIX D-19

Exchange of Letters between the Government of Japan
and the Government of the USSR concerning the
Exchange of Official Publications

Exchanged in Moscow, October 10, 1973. Effective October 10, 1973 (MFA, May 1975).

Concerns the exchange of official publications to be carried out by the Lenin State Library of the USSR and the National Diet Library of Japan. The list of exchange titles is to be worked out by both these institutions.

APPENDIX D-20

Exchange of Letters between the Government of Japan
and the Government of the USSR concerning the
Distribution of Informational Materials

Exchanged in Moscow, October 10, 1973. Effective October 10, 1973 (MFA, May 1976).

Japan may distribute 30,000 copies a year of the informational handbook *Japan Today* and 50,000 copies of the magazine *Photo-Japan*. The distribution of the latter is to be handled by "Soyuzpechat." The USSR may distribute in Japan the biweekly magazine *The Soviet Union Today* and one other informational publication.

APPENDIX D-21

Exchange of Letters between Japan and the USSR on the Extension of the Agreement on Cultural Exchange

Signed in Moscow, January 25, 1974. Effective January 25, 1974 (MFA, March 1974).

A letter from N. Firiubin, Deputy Foreign Minister of the USSR, addressed to T. Hasegawa, Interim Chargé d'Affaires of Japan in the USSR, confirming the extension of the Agreement on Cultural Exchange until January 26, 1976.

APPENDIX D-22

Notes Exchanged concerning the General Agreement between the Film "Minami Yakuto Kaihatsu-Kereku Kabushiki Kaisha" and "Soyuzpromexport" and the Credit Agreement between the Export-Import Bank of Japan and other Japanese Banks and the Bank for Foreign Trade of the USSR

Exchanged in Tokyo, July 26, 1974. Effective July 26, 1974 (MFA, February 1975).

A letter from I. F. Semichastnov, First Deputy Minister of Foreign Trade of the USSR, stating the Soviet government's intention to encourage and facilitate the development of the South Yakutian coal basin as it is foreseen in the general agreement between "Soyuzpromexport" and "Minami Yakuto Kaihatsu-Kereku Kabushiki Kaisha" ("South Yakutian Coal Development Corporation Co., Ltd.") and in the credit agreement between the Foreign Trade Bank of the USSR and the Export-Import Bank of Japan. These agreements are regarded as factors in the broadening of trade between the two countries.

APPENDIX D-23

Exchange of Notes concerning the General Agreement
between "K-S Sangyo Kabushiki Kaisha" and "Exportles"
and the Credit Agreement between the Export-Import
Bank of Japan and other Japanese Banks and the
Foreign Trade Bank of the USSR

Exchanged in Moscow, April 3, 1975. Effective April 3, 1975 (MFA, May 1975).

The Soviet government welcomes the agreement to exchange Japanese machinery, equipment, ships, and other materials for Soviet wood products as well as the projected joint development of forest resources in the Far East. It pledges its full cooperation in the future broadening of trade between the two countries.

APPENDIX D-24

Letters Exchanged between the Government of Japan
and the Government of the USSR concerning Crab Fishing
in the Northwestern Region of the Pacific

Exchanged in Moscow, May 15, 1975. Effective May 15, 1975 (MFA, July 1975).

Crab fishing areas open to Japanese vessels in 1975 are specified. These areas are off the western coast of the Kamchatka Peninsula, in the region near Cape Navarin, in the area of Oliutorsky Bay, and near the eastern coast of Sakhalin. The total catch allowed in some of these areas is also determined.

APPENDIX D-25

Letters Exchanged between the Government of Japan
and the Government of the USSR on the Fishing of
Tsubu (Prosobranchia) in the Northwestern Pacific

Exchanged in Moscow, May 15, 1975. Effective May 15, 1975 (MFA, July 1975).

Specifies the parameters of two fishing areas open to Japanese fishing vessels which deal in Tsubu. One area is located off the eastern Sakhalin, the other in the northern part of the Sea of Okhotsk. Valid in 1975.

APPENDIX D-26

Exchange of Letters concerning the Renewal of the
Agreement between Japan and the USSR Based on the
International Convention for the Regulation of Whaling
and Pertaining to Pelagic Baleen Whaling in the Pacific

Exchanged in Moscow, May 5, 1975. Effective May 5, 1975 (MFA, May 1975).

A letter from A. Ishkov, Minister of Fisheries of the USSR, confirming the establishment of an agreement effective May 5, 1975. Text of said agreement is given in English. Specifies open season for pelagic baleen and pelagic sperm whaling. Allocates to each country its share of the total catch of fin whales, Sei and Byrde's whales, and male and female sperm whales as authorized by the International Convention for the Regulation of Whaling. Signed in Tokyo, September 5, 1973.

For the Government of Japan: For the Government of the USSR:

HIROMICHI MIYAZAKI   O. A. TROYANOVSKY

APPENDIX D-27

*Exchange of Letters between the Government of Japan
and the Government of the USSR about Mutual Tax
Exemption of Incomes and Profits Received from
International Sea and Air Transports*

Exchanged in Moscow, July 31, 1975. Effective July 31, 1975 (MFA, October 1975).

An agreement on mutual tax exemption on all incomes stemming from sea and air transport, effective for all consecutive tax years beginning with January 1, 1969. The cessation of the agreement can be effected by one of the parties by means of a letter of notification six months in advance of cessation date. Additional statement on the mutual exemption of tax due for periods prior to January 1, 1969.

APPENDIX E-1

Agreement on Fishing Operations between the Government of Japan and the Government of the Union of Soviet Socialist Republics

Signed in Tokyo, June 7, 1975. Effective October 23, 1975 (MFA, November 1975).

In the hope of securing safety and order in fishing operations to be conducted by the two countries' fishing vessels and in consideration of the fact that it is desirable to take measures for preventing accidents on the sea in connection with the activities of the two countries' fishing vessels and the use of their fishing gear, and in case an accident happens, it is desirable to step up disposition thereof promptly and smoothly, the Government of Japan and the Government of the Union of Soviet Socialist Republics concluded the following Agreement:

ARTICLE 1

1. This Agreement shall be applied to the high-seas water areas off the coast of the country of Japan.

2. Provisions stipulated in this Agreement shall not be deemed to have any effect on the positions of the two countries' Governments concerning the scope of their territorial waters and the problem of their fishery jurisdiction.

ARTICLE 2

a. "Fishing vessels" as term in this Agreement means vessels which are mainly engaged in fishery, vessels which are engaged in fishery and which have fish storage and manufacturing facilities, or vessels which will mainly transport fish or products manufactured therefrom from fishing-grounds.

b. "Nationals," as termed in this Agreement, also includes "corporations."

c. "Damages," as termed in this Agreement, means damages which are caused in connection with accidents occurring between fishing vessels or fishing gear.

ARTICLE 3

1. Each country's Government shall take necessary measures in order for its own country's fishing vessels (with the exception of non-motorpower vessels of less than 1 ton of gross tonnage) to be registered in conformity with its own country's laws and ordinances in order to ensure their identification on the sea and observe the provisions stipulated in Attached Document I of this Agreement.

2. (1) The two countries' Governments shall notify each other the systems which have been already implemented in connection with the provisions stipulated in Attached Document I.

(2) The two countries' Governments shall notify each other as quickly as possible the changes which were made in the systems, as mentioned in (1).

ARTICLE 4

Each country's Government shall take necessary measures in order to ensure that its own country's fishing vessels will observe the provisions stipulated in Attached Document II of the Agreement as to the use of lamps and signals.

ARTICLE 5

Each country's Government shall take necessary measures to ensure that beacons shall be attached, in accordance with the provisions stipulated in Attached Document III of this Agreement, to its own country's fishing vessels' nets, long-lines, and other fishing gear, which have been placed into the sea by anchors, and to its own country's fishing vessels' nets and long-lines, which are floating in the sea, in order to show their locations and scopes.

ARTICLE 6

1. Each country's Government shall take necessary measures to ensure that in conducting sailing operations and fishing operations, its own country's fishing vessels shall observe the provisions stipulated in Attached Document IV of this Agreement.

2. In order to carry out stipulation I more accurately and exactly, the two countries' Governments shall take necessary measures so that communications designed to exchange emergency information on waters, where the two countries' fishing vessels and fishing gear are particularly crowded, can be carried out promptly and effectively, as occasion demands, between the two countries' authoritative Government officials in charge.

3. The two countries' Governments shall exchange information on the actual situation of fishing operations to be conducted by the two countries' fishing vessels (including information on fishing gear and fishing methods). In case of

need, the two countries' Governments shall hold consultations at their discretion on deciding appropriate measures to be taken, based on that information.

ARTICLE 7

1. In order to facilitate settlement of a claim for compensation for damages (hereinafter referred to as "claim for compensation"), which will be sought by one country's national against the counterpart country's national, the two countries' Governments shall set up a Fishery Damage Compensation Claim Disposition Committee (hereinafter referred to as "Committee") each in Tokyo and in Moscow.

2. Each Committee shall be composed of two Committee members who will be appointed by the Government of Japan, and two Committee members who will be appointed by the Government of the Union of Soviet Socialist Republics. Each Government shall notify the other side's Government of the names of the Committee members, whom it has appointed.

3. Each country's Government may appoint experts and advisers who will assist the Committee members.

4. A decision of the Commitee shall be made based on the principle of the unanimous concurrence of all the Committee members by vote of Committee members who have attended, on the condition that at least one Committee member, whom each country's Government has appointed, is present, respectively.

5. The Committee may hold its meetings at places other than its location, as occasion demands.

ARTICLE 8

The expenses required for experts and advisers to participate in the activities of the Committee shall be paid by the Government which appoints these persons. The expenses to be spent jointly by the Committees shall be paid by the two countries' Governments in the form and the ratio of the expenses which will be recommended by each country's Committee and approved by the two countries' Governments.

ARTICLE 9

1. (1) When one country's national desires settlement by the Committee as to a claim for compensation, which claim that person will make to the counterpart country's national, the one country's national shall apply to that effect to the Committee, which is located in that person's country.

(2) The application as mentioned in (1) shall not be made when a year has passed after the occurrence of the accident, which had become the cause of claiming compensation. In case the accident, which has become the cause of claiming compensation, occurs during a period of two years immediately before this Agreement becomes effective, he may make an application as mentioned in (1) in less than a year after the effectuation of this Agreement.

2. The above-mentioned application shall be made in writing and contain the following items in so far as the national, who will claim compensation, (hereinafter referred to as the "claimant") knows.

a. Description of the accident which has become the cause of claiming compensation.

b. Enumeration of persons, organizations, and vessels concerned with the said accident.

c. The amount of compensation claimed.

d. The list of the names of persons who are available as witnesses to the said accident.

All other data necessary for proving the justification of the claim for that compensation, shall be presented to the Committee, which is located in the country of the claimant, along with that application.

3. In case the Committee, which is located in the country of the claimant, accepts that application, the Committee shall send it to the Committee, which is located in the country of the national, from whom compensation has been claimed, (hereinafter referred to as the "claimee") as quickly as possible after having corrected that application and data, as occasion demands, in contact with the claimant or authoritative Government officials of the country of the claimant.

4. In case the Committee, which is located in the country of the claimee, receives the above-mentioned application from the Committee, which is located in the country of the claimant, the Committee shall immediately notify the claimee of the claim for the said compensation. The claimee may present to the Committee, which is located in the country of the claimee, a rebuttal in writing against that claim for the said compensation, and all data, which are deemed to be necessary to present in order to reject the claim for the said compensation. The rebuttal to be made by the claimee may include a counter-claim in so far as it is based on the same accident as the accident which has become the cause of claiming the said compensation. The counter-claim shall be screened by the Committee, which is located in the country of the claimee, simultaneously with the claim for compensation.

5. The Committee, which is located in the country of the claimee, may request, as occasion demands, the claimant, the claimee, and the two countries' authoritative Government officials to present additional information on the claim for compensation or a counter-claim.

6. In case the Committee, which is located in the country of the claimee, deems it necessary, or the request is made by the claimant or the claimee, the said Committee may listen to the situation as to the said accident. The claimant and the claimee or their proxies may attend the meeting(s) to listen to the situation, make statements, and receive assistance from any person whom they select. In case it deems it necessary, the said Committee may entrust hearing of the situation to the Committee, which is located in the country of the claimant.

7. In applying the provisions stipulated in this Article and the next Article, contact with the claimant and authoritative Government officials of the country of the claimant and the claimee shall be made through the Committee, which is located in the country of the claimant except in case where the Committee, which is located in the country of the claimee, shall listen to the situation in accordance with provision 6.

ARTICLE 10

1. (1) The Committee, which is located in the country of the claimee, shall screen the claim for compensation, which has been made by the claimant, based on evidence which has been presented either in written, oral or other forms. In screening a claim for compensation, which was caused by the accident which occurred after the effectuation of this Agreement, the said Committee shall pay due consideration to the provisions stipulated in Attached Documents of this Agreement.

(2) In case the Committee, which is located in the country of the claimee, deems it improper to continue its screening of the claim for the said compensation during its screening, the said Committee may suspend or discontinue its screening.

2. The Committee, which is located in the country of the claimee, shall make contact with the claimant and the claimee, based on the findings of its screening and act as an intermediary for re-conciliation. In case the said Committee reaches a conclusion that one of the parties concerned should pay compensation, the said Committee shall urge the said party concerned to that effect in acting as an intermediary for re-conciliation.

3. In case a compromise is not reached within a reasonable period of time, the Committee, which is located in the country of the claimant, shall prepare a written report, which lists the said Committee's authorization of the following items:

a. The facts which have been made the basis of claiming compensation.

b. The extent of damages.

c. The degree of the responsibility to be shouldered by the claimee or the claimant.

d. The amount of money to be paid by the claimant or the claimee as compensation for damages, which were caused as a result of the said accident.

In case the said Committee does not reach an agreed-upon conclusion on the above-mentioned items, the said Committee shall describe in detail various Committee members' views on these items and at the same time, to list that effect in the written report.

4. The Committee, which is located in the country of the claimee, shall send, without delay, a written report mentioned in 3 to the claimee and the two countries' Government authoritative officials in charge.

5. The claimant and the claimee may in writing request the Committee, which is located in the country of the claimee, to conduct a re-screening within 30 days from the day it has received the written report mentioned in 3. The request of the claimant for re-screening shall be made through the Committee which is located in the country of the claimant. In the letter, which will request re-screening, the reasons for that request shall be written together with data concerned. The Committee, which is located in the country of the claimee, shall decide on the suitability for conducting re-screening within 30 days from the day when the request for re-screening arrived. The said Committee shall notify the claimant, the claimee, and the two countries' Government authoritative officials in charge of that decision. In case the said Committee decides to conduct re-screening, the said Committee shall prepare the same kind of new report within 30 days from the day when the said Committee made that decision and send that report, without delay, to the claimant, the claimee, and the two countries' Government authoritative officials in charge.

6. Each country's Government authoritative officials in charge shall make efforts so that the demand for compensation can be settled between the claimant and the claimee in conformity with the Committee's authorization, as stated in the written report, except in the case where the Committee decides to conduct re-screening. In case re-screening is conducted by the Committee, each country's Government authoritative officials in charge shall make efforts so that the settlement will be made in accordance with a new authorization.

7. (1) The claimant and the claimee shall notify their own countries' Government authoritative officials in charge within 90 days from the day when they received the report, which listed the Committee's authorization, as to whether or not they will accept the Committee's authorization, except in the case where the Committee decides to conduct re-screening. In case the Committee decides to conduct re-screening, the claimant and the claimee shall make a similar notification within 30 days from the day when they received a new report.

(2) The two countries' Government authoritative officials in charge shall transmit to the Committee, which is located in the country of the claimee, as quickly as possible a notification from the claimant and the claimee as to the Committee's authorization.

8. When the Committee, which is located in the country of the claimee, admits that matters are in such a situation where the request for re-screening is no longer made, in the case where the Committee does not reach an agreed-upon conclusion on matters mentioned in 3, or in case the Committee receives a notice to the effect that the claimant or the claimee has rejected acceptance of the said Committee's authorization, the Committee shall urge the claimant and the claimee to settle the claim for the said compensation by means of arbitration.

9. Each Committee shall give a report every year to the two countries' Governments on the claims for compensation, which were screened by the Committee, and the findings of that screening.

ARTICLE 11

Any provisions stipulated under this Agreement shall not be deemed to produce any effects on the rights of the claimant or the claimee as to compensation for damages and on the two countries' laws and ordinances concerning the procedures designed to assert their rights.

ARTICLE 12

Each country's Government shall make it feasible for its own country's national to remit, without delay, compensation money for damages, to the counterpart country's national in convertible currency.

ARTICLE 13

Attached documents of this Agreement may be amended at any time or may be supplemented without revising this Agreement through mutual agreement of the two countries' Governments.

ARTICLE 14

In case a request is made by either of the two countries' Governments, the two countries' Governments shall hold consultations on the implementation of this Agreement.

ARTICLE 15

1. This Agreement shall be approved by each country's Government in compliance with the procedures stipulated under the respective country's domestic laws.

2. This Agreement shall come into force on the day when the official documents, which will notify the approval by each country's Government, are exchanged, and shall remain in force for a period of three years.

3. Unless one of the two countries' Governments notifies the counterpart country's Government of its intention to terminate this Agreement in six months before the expiration of the above-mentioned period of three years, even after the expiration of the above-mentioned period, this Agreement shall remain in force until the elapse of six months from the day when one of the two countries' Governments notifies the counterpart country's Government of its intention to terminate this Agreement.

Whereof the under-signed persons have signed this Agreement under due authorization of their own countries' Governments.

Two copies of this text were prepared in Tokyo on June 7, 1975, both in the Japanese and Russian languages which are equally the official text.

On behalf of the Government of Japan

KIICHI MIYAZAWA

On behalf of the Government of the Union
of Soviet Socialist Republics

A. ISHKOV

ATTACHED DOCUMENT I:
Signs on Fishing Vessels and Other Matters

1. A fishing vessel shall indicate clearly on both sides of the bridge, the bow and in other most visible places the letters and the registration number which show the area where it is registered.

2. A fishing vessel shall provide in its vessel the document, which was issued by its own country's Government authoritative officials in charge and which listed the name of the vessel, the general outline, the nationality, the number, the name or port where the vessel was registered, and the name of the owner, or a document which is treated the same as this. However, in case its own country's Government admits that the said fishing vessel is not able to equip itself with these documents due to unavoidable reasons, this rule will not apply.

ATTACHED DOCUMENT II:
Lamp-lights and Signals by Fishing Vessels

A. Lamp-lights and Signals to Be Used by All Fishing Vessels

A fishing vessel shall observe regulations concerning lamp-lights and signals as stipulated in the international regulations of 1960 designed to prevent collisions on the sea.

B. Additional Signals to Be Used in Case Fishing Vessels, Which Are Engaged in Drag-net Fishery or Purse-net Fishery, Conduct Fishing Operations in Conspicuously Near-by Places

1. Signals of Fishing Vessels Which are Engaged in Drag-net Fishery

   (1) Fishing vessels, which are engaged in drag-net fishery may raise, in the daytime, the following signal flags stipulated in the international signal book (hereinafter referred to as "international signal book"), which was adopted by the Government-to-Government Maritime Affairs Consultation Organization, depending on the cases as under:

   (i) In case a fishing vessel is casting nets, it shall raise a Z-flag (this fishing vessel is casting nets).

   (ii) In case a fishing vessel is hauling in a net, it shall raise a flag (this fishing vessel is hauling in a net).

   (iii) In case fishing-nets have coiled themselves round an obstacle, a fishing vessel shall raise a P-flag (fishing-nets of this vessel have coiled themselves round an obstacle).

(2) Fishing vessels, which are engaged in drag-net fishery, may put up, at nighttime, the following lamp-lights, depending on the cases stipulated as under:

(i) In case a fishing vessel is casting nets, it shall put up two white lamp-lights on a perpendicular line.

(ii) In case a fishing vessel is hauling in a net, it shall put up one white lamp-light in the upper part of a perpendicular line and one red lamp-light in the lower part of a perpendicular line.

(iii) In case fishing-nets coiled themselves round an obstacle, fishing vessels shall put up two red lamp-lights on a perpendicular line.

(3) Fishing vessels, which are engaged in drag-net fishery by the "kake-mawashi" fishing method, may put up, in the daytime, a red streamer, in addition to signal-flags as stipulated in (1), and one yellow lamp-light at nighttime, in addition to lamp-lights as stipulated in (2).

(4) Fishing vessels, which are engaged in drag-net fishery using two vessels, may raise, in the daytime, a T-flag (avoid this vessel. This vessel is now engaged in drag-net fishery using two vessels) as stipulated in the international signal book, in addition to signal-flags as stipulated in (1). At nighttime, they may turn on a searchlight so as to show the direction of the progress of the other side's fishing vessels, which are forming a pair, in addition to putting up lamp-lights as stipulated in (2).

2. Signals of Fishing Vessels Which Are Engaged in Purse-net Fishery

Fishing vessels, which are engaged in purse-net fishery, may put up two yellow lamp-lights on a perpendicular line. These lamp-lights shall be lamp-lights which emit a flashing light per each second, alternately, and that their respective on intervals and off intervals shall be equal. These lamp-lights shall not be put up in any case except where fishing vessels are restricted in their operation capacity by fishing gear.

3. The lamp-lights stipulated in 1 (2) shall be put up in the most visible place at a lower position than the lamp-lights stipulated in (c) (i) and (d) of Article 9 of the International Regulations of 1960 designed to prevent collisions on the sea at a distance of more than 0.9 meters mutually. These lamp-lights shall be lamp-lights which are visible from the surroundings at a distance of at least one nautical mile and their visible distance shall be shorter than the visible distance of the lamp-lights on fishing vessels, which are engaged in fishing operations, stipulated in the International Regulations of 1960 designed to prevent collisions on the sea.

4. Fishing vessels, which are engaged in fishing in the midst of fog, haze, and snowfall, or other situations where the visibility is restricted, shall flash the following signals stipulated in the international signal book, which show conditions for their activities, at intervals of longer than 4 seconds and shorter than 6 seconds after having flashed signals stipulated in (c) (viii) of Article 15 of the International Regulations of 1960 designed to prevent collisions on the sea:

(i) In case fishing vessels are casting a net, they shall signal a long tone twice and a short tone twice ("zuru" signal—phonetic).

(ii) In case fishing vessels are hauling in a net, they shall signal a long tone twice and a short tone once ("golf" signal).

(iii) In case fishing-nets have coiled themselves round an obstacle, fishing vessels shall signal a short tone once, a long tone twice, and a short tone once ("papa" signal).

ATTACHED DOCUMENT III:
Signs of Nets, Long-Lines, and Other Fishing Gear

1. Signs to be attached to fishing-nets, long-lines, and other fishing gear which were fixed in the sea by anchors.

(1) In the daytime, two red flags or one red flag and a radar reflector shall be attached to the upper and lower sides of a buoy at the western-most tip of fishing gear (west means a half circle on a compass from the south to the north point via the west), and one white flag or a radar reflector to a buoy at the eastern-most tip of fishing gear (east means a half circle on a compass from the north to the south point via the east).

(2) At night, one red lamp shall be attached to a buoy at the western-most top of the fishing gear, and one white lamp-light to a buoy at the eastern-most tip. These lamps shall be lamps which are visible from a place at a distance of at least two nautical miles, in case the visibility is good.

(3) In order to show the direction of fishing gear, a buoy with a flag or a radar reflector attached may be set up in the daytime, and a buoy with a white lamp attached may be set up at nighttime at a distance of more than 70 meters and less than 100 meters from the two tips of the buoy.

(4) To fishing gear, the length of which exceeds one nautical mile, additional buoys shall be fixed at a distance of not exceeding one nautical mile so that there is no fishing-gear part with a length of one nautical mile without signs. In the daytime, a white flag or a radar reflector and at night, a white lamp shall be attached to as many buoys as possible. In any case, the distance of the lamps, which were attached to the same fishing gear, shall not exceed two nautical miles.

2. To fishing-nets and long-lines, which are floating in the sea, buoys with a yellow flag or a radar reflector attached shall be set up in the daytime at a distance not exceeding two nautical miles, and a buoy with a white lamp, which is visible from a distance of at least 2 nautical miles in case the visibility is good, shall be set up.

3. With regard to fishing gear, which were fastened to a fishing vessel, it is not necessary to set up a buoy at the tip which is fastened to the fishing vessel.

4. A flag pole of each buoy shall be at least 2 meters in height from the surface of the buoy.

ATTACHED DOCUMENT IV:
Regulations Concerning Operation of Fishing Vessels
and Fishing Operations

A. A fishing vessel shall observe the International Regulations of 1960 designed to prevent collisions on the sea and conduct fishing operations lest it should obstruct fishing operations to be conducted by the counterpart country's fishing vessels' fishing gear.

B. 1. In case a fishing vessel has arrived at fishing-grounds where the counterpart country's fishing vessels already are conducting fishing operations or fishing-grounds where fishing gear was set up in order to conduct fishing operations, the fishing vessel shall confirm the site and the scope of fishing gear which was set up in the sea. Also, a fishing vessel shall not place itself or set up fishing gear in such a form as to provide an obstacle or a hindrance to the counterpart country's fishing operations which have been already conducted.

2. A fishing vessel, which is not. conducting fishing operations, shall not anchor or stop at such places as to provide an obstacle to the said fishing operations to be conducted in the fishing-grounds where the counterpart country's fishing vessels are already conducting fishing operations. This rule, however, does not apply to a case where an accident or an unavoidable reason exists.

3. A fishing vessel shall not use explosives in order to catch fish.

4. A fishing vessel shall watch the surrounding situation constantly and efficiently while conducting fishing operations or while anchoring or stopping at the fishing-grounds, and place an appropriate look-out, able to take necessary action, depending on circumstances at that time.

5. Fishing vessels, which are engaged in drag-net fishery, and other fishing vessels, which are using portable fishing gear, shall take every possible measure for not hooking fishing gear or sea-anchors of the counterpart country's vessels, in order to prevent causing damage to fishing gear.

6. Fishing vessels, which are engaged in drag-net fishery, and other fishing-vessels, which are using portable fishing gear, shall observe the following regulations in order to prevent causing damage to fishing gear:

(1) In selecting the places and the direction of casting drag-nets, purse-nets, or Denmark-style nets, the prevention of fishing operations by the counterpart country's fishing vessels, which are towing fishing gear, casting a fishing-net or hauling in a fishing-net, shall be prohibited.

(2) To cast a drag-net, haul in a fish-net, or cast a purse-net or Denmark-style fishing-net just in front of the bows of the counterpart country's fishing vessels, which are towing fishing gear, shall be prohibited.

(3) The distance between fishing vessels, which are engaged in drag-net fishery, and the counterpart country's fishing vessels, which are engaged in drag-net fishery, shall be as follows:

(a) Fishing vessels, which will come across counterpart country fishing vessels right ahead or almost right ahead, shall try to keep the distance between the two vessels at more than 400 meters at the point of time for passing each other (in case either one of the two countries' fishing vessels are engaged in drag-net fishery by means of the *kakemawashi* fishing method, the distance shall be more than 1,000 meters).

(b) In case the two countries' fishing vessels have proceeded in the direction of crossing course mutually, the fishing vessel, which will yield the course, shall try to keep a distance at the rear of the stern of the counterpart country's fishing vessel, which has had its course yielded, at more than 1,100 meters (in case the fishing vessel, which has had its course yielded, is engaged in drag-net fishery by means of the *kakemawashi* fishing method, it shall keep a distance to the rear of the stern or in the front of the bow of the said fishing vessel, of more than 1,500 meters).

(c) In case the two countries' fishing vessels have proceeded in the same direction, a fishing vessel, which will outsail the counterpart country's fishing vessel, shall try to keep the distance between the two fishing vessels at more than 400 meters at the point of time for passing each other (in case either one of the two countries' fishing vessels is engaged in drag-net fishery by means of the *kakemawashi* method, the distance shall be more than 1,100 meters).

(d) A fishing vessel, which is engaged in drag-net fishery, shall try to keep the distance between the counterpart country's fishing vessel, which is engaged in purse-net fishery, at more than 1,200 meters.

(4) A fishing vessel, which is engaged in purse-net fishery or Denmark-style-net fishery, shall try to keep the distance (distance between fishing vessels and between fishing-nets) from the counterpart country's fishing vessel, which is engaged in purse-net fishery or Denmark-style-net fishery, at more than 900 meters.

7. The setting of fishing gear by anchors into the sea and the throwing of floating fishing gear into the sea shall be conducted while keeping the distance from the counterpart country's fishing vessel or fishing gear, which will be thrown into the sea by this fishing vessel, at more than 900 meters.

8. Except in the cases stipulated from (3) to (4) of 6 and 7, a fishing vessel, which is conducting fishing operations, shall try to keep the distance from the counterpart country's fishing vessel or fishing gear, which were fixed in the sea by anchors of its fishing gear, which are floating in the sea, at more than 500 meters.

9. (1) In case fishing-nets of one of the two countries' fishing vessels have been entangled with fishing-nets of the counterpart country's fishing vessel, every possible measure shall be taken in order to disentangle them without causing damage to the fishing-nets. Except in the case where it is not possible to dis-

entangle them by any other method, fishing-nets shall not be cut without obtaining the consent of the parties concerned.

(2) In case long-lines of one of the two countries' fishing vessels have become entangled with long-lines of the counterpart country's fishing vessel, a fishing vessel shall not cut the long-lines except in the case where it is not possible to disentangle them by any other method. In case a fishing vessel has cut long-lines, the long-lines, which were cut, shall be connected as quickly as possible and be restored to the original state as much as possible.

(3) Except in the case of rescue and in the cases as stipulated in (1), a fishing vessel shall not cut fishing-nets, long-lines, and fishing gear of the counterpart country's fishing vessel, or catch them with hooks, or draw them up to the shore.

(4) In all cases where fishing gear have become entangled, the fishing vessel, which has brought about that entanglement, shall take every necessary measure in order to reduce any damage to be caused to the fishing gear of the counterpart country's fishing vessels to the maximum extent. At the same time, a fishing vessel, which has had its fishing gear entangled, shall not take such action as to increase the damage on fishing gear of both sides' fishing vessels.

10. (1) In case a fishing vessel has caused damage to the counterpart country's fishing vessel or its fishing gear, the said fishing vessel shall come to a stop immediately.

(2) In case a fishing vessel of one of the two countries has caused damage to the counterpart country's fishing vessel or its fishing gear, in case the fishing vessel, which has caused damage, does not come to a stop, the fishing vessel, which has suffered damage, may seek the stoppage of that fishing vessel by using the following signals as stipulated in the international signal book, which was adopted by the Government-to-Government Maritime Affairs Consultation Organization:

(i) To raise an L-flag.

(ii) To give an L-signal (short tone one time, a long tone one time, and a short tone two times) by means of a siren, steam whistle, or other sound signals.

(iii) To flash an L-signal (short light-signal one time, long light-signal one time, short light-signal two times) in succession by flood-light projectors.

(3) In case an accident has occurred between the counterpart countries' fishing vessels, the fishing vessel shall confirm the contents of the accident jointly with the other fishing vessel. Also, the fishing vessels shall notify as promptly as possible its own country's Government authoritative officials in charge of matters in connection with this accident.

11. A fishing vessel shall not throw into the sea any object, which is apt to provide an obstacle or an impediment to the counterpart country's fishing opera-

tions or which is apt to cause damage to fish, fishing gear or fishing vessels, except in the case where there is a justifiable reason.

Foreign Minister KIICHI MIYAZAWA
Agriculture-Forestry Minister SHINTARO ABE
Transportation Minister MUTSUO KIMURA
Prime Minister TAKEO MIKI

APPENDIX E-2

Agreement between Japan and the Union of Soviet Socialist Republics concerning an International Observer Scheme for Factory Ships Engaged in Pelagic Whaling in the Southern Hemisphere

Signed in Tokyo, October 9, 1975. Entered into force October 9, 1975 (MFA, December 1975).

The Governments of Japan and the Union of Soviet Socialist Republics, being Parties to the International Convention for the Regulation of Whaling, signed at Washington on December 2, 1946 (hereafter referred to as "the Convention"),

Proceeding from the mutual concern of the pelagic whaling countries in the Southern Hemisphere for the conservation of whale stocks, for the maintenance of the proper productivity of pelagic whaling and the ensuring of its being carried out rationally;

Have agreed on the following scheme for International Observers on board factory ships or catchers functioning as factory ships engaged in pelagic whaling in the Southern Hemisphere in accordance with the decisions taken by the twenty-third meeting of the International Whaling Commission on the necessity of establishing a scheme of international observation of whaling operations:

ARTICLE 1
Purpose of the Scheme

The purpose of this scheme is to maintain surveillance of pelagic whaling in the Southern Hemisphere whenever whales are being delivered to factory ships or are being processed at such ships or catchers functioning as factory ships.

ARTICLE 2
Appointment of Observers

Observers shall be responsible to the International Whaling Commission (hereafter referred to as "the Commission") and shall be appointed in accordance with the following provisions:

1. Each signatory Government shall have the right to nominate at least as many observers as it has expeditions under its jurisdiction.

2. From the observers so nominated, observers shall be appointed to the expeditions engaged in pelagic whaling in the Southern Hemisphere and not more than one observer shall be appointed to any expedition.

3. The Secretary of the Commission shall inform both signatory Governments of all appointments made under sub-paragraph (2) of this Article.

ARTICLE 3
Right and Function of Observers

1. The observers shall have the status of senior officers and shall be entitled to subsistence and accommodation accordingly. Each signatory Government receiving observers shall take appropriate measures to ensure security and welfare of the observers and interpreters in the performance of their duties, to provide them with medical care and assistance, and to safeguard their freedom and dignity. The observers and interpreters shall observe the customs and order existing on the expeditions on which they are serving.

2. The observers shall not be invested with any administrative power in regard to the activities of the expeditions to which they are appointed, and shall have no authority to interfere in any way with those activities. They shall neither seek nor receive instructions from any authority other than the Commission. They shall be given the necessary facilities for carrying out their duties, including cabling facilities.

3. An observer shall be enabled to observe freely the operations of the expedition to which he is appointed, so that he may verify the observance of the provisions of the Convention in regard to the taking of whales and their rational utilization. In particular, the observer shall be given facilities to ascertain the species, size, sex, and number of whales taken.

4. All reports required to be made, and all records and data required to be kept or supplied in accordance with the Schedule of the Convention, shall be made freely and immediately available to observers for examination, and they shall be given all necessary explanations as regards such reports, records and data.

5. The master, manager or senior officers of any of the vessels forming part of the expedition, or the national inspectors, shall supply any information that is necessary for the discharge of the observer's functions.

6. When there is reasonable ground to believe that any infraction of the provisions of the Convention has taken place, it shall be brought in writing to the immediate notice both of the master or manager of the expedition and of the senior national inspector by an observer, who shall, if he deems it sufficiently

serious, at once transmit it to the Secretariat of the Commission together with the explanation or comments of the master or manager of the expedition and the senior national inspector.

7. An observer shall draw up a report covering his observations, including possible infractions of the provisions of the Convention which have taken place, and shall submit it to the master or manager of the expedition and to the senior national inspector for information and such explanations and comments as they wish to make. Any such explanations and comments shall be attached to the observer's report, which shall be transmitted to the Secretariat of the Commission as soon as possible.

ARTICLE 4
Language

1. Any observer who knows neither the language of the country whose Government receives him nor the English language, must be accompanied by an interpreter who shall be of the same nationality.

2. Where an observer does not speak the language of the country whose Government receives him but speaks English or is accompanied by an English-speaking interpreter, then the expedition is required to provide at least one English-speaking person on the factory ship or the catcher functioning as factory ship.

ARTICLE 5
Finance

1. Each signatory Government which nominates one or more observers who are appointed to expeditions shall pay the salary and other emoluments, travel, cable costs, subsistence and accommodation and other necessary expenses of those observers.

2. Subsistence and accommodation on the factory ship or the catcher functioning as factory ship shall be provided to the observers at cost.

3. When it is necessary that an observer be accompanied by an interpreter, the salary and other necessary expenses of that interpreter shall be paid by the signatory Government nominating the observer.

ARTICLE 6
Entry into Force

The present Agreement shall enter into force on the day upon which it is signed by the signatory Governments referred to in the preamble.

ARTICLE 7
Duration

The present Agreement shall remain in force until August 31, 1976.

ARTICLE 8

The two signatory Governments shall meet in London before the twenty-eighth meeting of the Commission to review the operation of the present Agreement and to decide on future arrangements.

In witness whereof the undersigned, being duly authorized thereto by their respective Governments, have signed the present Agreement.

Done in duplicate in Tokyo, the ninth day of October, 1975, in the English language.

For the Government of Japan:
(Signed) BUNROKU YOSHINO

For the Government of the Union of Soviet Socialist Republics:
(Signed) O. A. TROYANOVSKY

APPENDIX E-3

Agreement between Japan and the Union of Soviet Socialist Republics on the Regulation of North Pacific Whaling

Signed at Tokyo, November 21, 1975. Entered into force November 21, 1975 (MFA December 1975).

The Governments of Japan and of the Union of Soviet Socialist Republics, being parties to the International Convention for the Regulation of Whaling, signed at Washington on Decebmer 2, 1946 (hereafter referred to as "the Convention"),
    Have agreed upon the following:

ARTICLE 1

a. For the purpose of this Agreement:
    i. The open season in 1976 for pelagic baleen whaling operations shall be the period from April 15 to October 15 both inclusive;

ii. The open season in 1976 for pelagic sperm whaling operations shall be the period from March 15 to November 15 both inclusive.

b. The Signatory Government having a land station or stations operating under its jurisdiction shall as soon as possible notify the other Signatory Government of the season or seasons for such station or stations.

ARTICLE 2

The total catch of baleen and sperm whales authorized under the Convention to be taken in the North Pacfiic Ocean and dependent waters in 1976 shall be allocated between the countries of the Signatory Governments in the following manner:

i. Bryde's Whales
   Japan 681
   Union of Soviet Socialist Republics................................ 681
ii. Sperm Whales
   a. Male Sperm Whales
   Japan 2,223
   Union of Soviet Socialist Republics................................ 2,977
   b. Female Sperm Whales
   Japan 1,325
   Union of Soviet Socialist Republics................................ 1,775

ARTICLE 3

The present Agreement shall enter into force on the day upon which it is signed by the Governments referred to in the preamble.

ARTICLE 4

The present Agreement shall be operative until December 31, 1976.

In witness whereof the undersigned, being duly authorized thereto by their respective Governments, have signed the present Agreement.

Done in duplicate at Tokyo, the twenty-first day of November, 1975, in the English language.

For the Government of Japan:

(Signed) HIROMICHI MIYAZAKI

For the Government of the Union of Soviet Socialist Republics:

(Signed) O. A. TROYANOVSKY

APPENDIX E-4

Arrangement between Japan and the USSR for the Regulation of Pelagic Whaling in the Southern Hemisphere

Signed at Tokyo, November 21, 1975. Entered into force November 21, 1975.

The Governments of Japan and of the Union of Soviet Socialist Republics, being Parties to the International Convention for the Regulation of Whaling, signed at Washington on December 2, 1946 (hereafter referred to as "the Convention"),

Have agreed upon the following arrangements:

ARTICLE 1

For the purpose of the Present Arrangement, the term "season" shall mean the season during which the taking of fin whales in the Antarctic and sei and Bryde's whales combined, minke whales and sperm whales in the Southern Hemisphere is permitted under sub-paragraphs (a), (b), (c) and (d) of paragraph 2 of the Schedule to the Convention.

ARTICLE 2

In the 1975/76 season, of the total quota of fin whales, authorized under the Convention to be taken in waters south of 40° South Latitude by pelagic expeditions, and of those of sei and Bryde's whales combined, minke whales and sperm whales, authorized under the Convention to be taken in the Southern Hemisphere by pelagic expeditions, the quotas alloted to Japan and the Union of Soviet Socialist Republics shall be allocated between the two countries in the following manner:

i. Fin whales:

Japan	132
Union of Soviet Socialist Republics	88

ii. Sei and Bryde's whales combined

Japan	1,331
Union of Soviet Socialist Republics	895

iii. Minke whales

Japan	3,017
Union of Soviet Socialist Republics	3,017

iv. Sperm whales
(a) Male

Japan	878
Union of Soviet Socialist Republics	3,658

(b) Female

Japan 665

Union of Soviet Socialist Republics.................................. 2,796

ARTICLE 3

1. The catches taken in any of the Areas or the Divisions as described below by pelagic expeditions under the jurisdiction of either Government shall not exceed the limits shown below:

   i. Fin whales, Sei and Bryde's whales combined and Minke whales

      (a) Area I   120°W—60°W

Japan .... 132 fin whales
                               118 sei and Bryde's whales combined
                               600 minke whales

Union of Soviet Socialist Republics...................... 88 fin whales
                             80 sei and Bryde's whales combined
                               600 minke whales

      (b) Area II   60°W—0°

Japan .... 337 sei and Bryde's whales combined
                               759 minke whales

Union of Soviet Socialist Republics
               226 sei and Bryde's whales combined
                               759 minke whales

      (c) Area III   0°—70°E

Japan .... 1,133 minke whales

Union of Soviet Socialist Republics............. 1,133 minke whales

      (d) Area IV   70°E—130°E

Japan .... 401 sei and Bryde's whales combined
                               445 minke whales

Union of Soviet Socialist Republics
               270 sei and Bryde's whales combined
                               446 minke whales

      (e) Area V   130°E—170°W

Japan ....414 sei and Bryde's whales combined
                               420 minke whales

Union of Soviet Socialist Republics
               279 sei and Bryde's whales combined
                             420 minke whales

      (f) Area VI   170°W—120°W

Japan .... 178 sei and Bryde's whales combined
                               300 minke whales

Union of Soviet Socialist Republics
               119 sei and Bryde's whales combined
                             300 minke whales

ii. Sperm whales

(a) Divisions 3 and 4   20°E–90°E

Japan ....   175 male sperm whales
    95 female sperm whales

Union of Soviet Socialist Republics......   729 male sperm whales
    400 female sperm whales

(b) Division 5   90°E–130°E

Japan ....   82 male sperm whales
    52 female sperm whales

Union of Soviet Socialist Republics......   340 male sperm whales
    217 female sperm whales

(c) Division 6   130°E–160°E

Japan ....   62 female sperm whales

Union of Soviet Socialist Republics....   262 female sperm whales

(d) Division 7   160°E–170°W

Japan ....   96 male sperm whales
    76 female sperm whales

Union of Soviet Socialist Republics......   399 male sperm whales
    320 female sperm whales

(e) Division 8   170°W–100°W

Japan ....   293 male sperm whales
    187 female sperm whales

Union of Soviet Socialist Republics....   1,219 male sperm whales
    785 female sperm whales

(f) Divisions 9, 1 and 2   100°W–20°E

Japan ....   387 male sperm whales
    373 female sperm whales

Union of Soviet Socialist Republics....   1,619 male sperm whales
    1,570 female sperm whales

2. Notwithstanding the above provisions, the sum of the Area or Division catches by pelagic expeditions under the jurisdiction of either Government shall not exceed the quotas for their respective countries as allocated in Article 2.

ARTICLE 4

If a factory ship under the jurisdiction of a Government which is not a Party to the present Arrangement should engage in pelagic whaling in the Southern Hemisphere and that Government is or becomes a Party to the Convention, the present Arrangement shall be terminated.

ARTICLE 5

The present Arrangement shall enter into force on the day upon which it is signed by the Governments referred to in the preamble.

ARTICLE 6

The present Arrangement shall be operative until the end of the 1975/76 season.

In witness whereof the undersigned, being duly authorized by their respective Governments, have signed the present Arrangement.

Done in duplicate at Tokyo, the twenty-first day of November, 1975, in the English language.

For the Government of Japan:

(Signed) HIROMICHI MIYAZAKI

For the Government of the Union of Soviet Socialist Republics:

(Signed) O. A. TROYANOVSKY

APPENDIX E-5

Agreement between the Government of Japan and the Government of the Union of Soviet Socialist Republics concerning the Fishing in 1977 in the Northwestern Pacific off the land of the Union of Soviet Socialist Republics

Signed in Moscow, May 27, 1977. Ratified by Japanese Diet, June 9, 1977. Effective June 10, 1977.

The Japan-Soviet fisheries negotiations which had begun on March 15, 1977, occasioned by the Russian establishment of the 200-mile fisheries zone, had met difficulties over the draft of the agreement, but the signing of the final draft of the agreement took place between Ministers Suzuki and Ishkov on May 27.

As a result, the fishing quota for the remainder of this year was set at 455,000 tons excluding salmon, trout, and herring. With the addition of the March catch of 245,000 tons, the total is 700,000 tons, a drastic decline as compared with the actual catch of 1,396,000 tons in the same area in 1975.

SOURCE: Text (in Japanese) provided by Japanese Fisheries Agency [unofficial English translation].

The present agreement was ratified by the Diet on June 9, and became effective upon the verbal note exchange between the two countries in Moscow on June 10.

The 21st meeting of the Northern Pacific Japan-Soviet Fisheries Committee, which is to discontinue after this year, agreed upon the quota of 62,000 tons for salmon and trout in Areas A and B, and Arakatsu and Nicholonov, representing the respective countries, signed the protocol on May 24.

The agreement between the Japanese and Soviet Governments and the content of the regulation of Japanese fishing in the 200-mile zone of the Soviet Union are as follows:

The Government of Japan and the Government of the Union of Soviet Socialist Republics,

considering the mutual concern regarding the preservation and optimum utilization of the fisheries resources in the Northwest Pacific,

considering the Third United Nations Law of the Sea Conference on various issues concerning the rights of coastal states with respect to fishing off the land of the coastal states,

recognizing the sovereign right of the Union of Soviet Socialist Republics over the living resources for the purpose of exploration, exploitation, and preservation as prescribed in the Edict of the Presidium of the Supreme Soviet of the USSR dated December 10, 1976,

considering the fact that the people and vessels of Japan have traditionally been engaged in fishing in the Northwest Pacific off the land of the Union of Soviet Socialist Republics,

desiring reciprocal cooperation between Japan and the Union of Soviet Socialist Republics in the area of fishing,

desiring to establish procedures and conditions for the use of living resources which are of mutual concern and over which the Union of Soviet Socialist Republics exercises sovereign rights,

agreed upon the following.

ARTICLE 1

This agreement aims at the establishment of procedures and conditions for the people and vessels of Japan to engage in fishing in the waters adjacent to the coasts of the Union of Soviet Socialist Republics in the Northwest Pacific to be established by Article 6 of the Edict of the Presidium of the Union of Soviet Socialist Republics dated December 10, 1976, concerning the tentative measures concerning the preservation of living resources and the regulation of fishing in the waters adjacent to the coasts of the Union of Soviet Socialist Republics.

ARTICLE 2

The right of the people and vessels of Japan to engage in fishing as in the preceding Article is afforded on the principle of mutual interest for the people and vessels of the Union of Soviet Socialist Republics to maintain the right to continue the traditional operations off the land of Japan.

ARTICLE 3

In this agreement:

1. "Living resources" are all species of fish resources in the waters prescribed in Article 1, all species of spawning fish that lay eggs in the fresh waters of the Union of Soviet Socialist Republics and migrate to the outer oceans, and all living things belonging to the non-migrating species on the continental shelves of the Union of Soviet Socialist Republics.

2. "Fishes" are fishes with fins, the Mollusca, the Crustacea, and all other marine animals and plants (with the exception of birds).

3. "Fishing" includes A through D below.

A. Catching of fishes.

B. Attempting to catch fishes.

C. Other activities which can rationally be foreseen to result in the catching of fishes.

D. Operations on the ocean which directly support or prepare for the activities listed from A. to C.

4. "Vessels" are ships and other boats which are used or equipped to be used for the purpose of A. or B. below.

A. Fishing.

B. Operations related to fishing (including preparation for fishing, replenishing vessels, storage, transportation, and processing of fishes, and loading and unloading).

This definition does not include Japanese fishing vessels which undertake scientific research related to fishing with a special license issued by the responsible authorities of the Union of Soviet Socialist Republics.

ARTICLE 4

1. With respect to the water boundaries referred to in Article 1, the catch quota and the composition of species for Japan in 1977 to be determined by the responsible authorities of the Union of Soviet Socialist Republics and specific zones and conditions for fishing by the people and vessels of Japan are set down in the note to be exchanged between Japan and the responsible authorities of the Union of Soviet Socialist Republics on the day of the signing of this agreement.

2. The catch quota for 1977 referred to in 1 includes the fishes which Japanese vessels caught during the month of March 1977 in the waters referred to in Article 1.

ARTICLE 5

1. The authorities of the Union of Soviet Socialist Republics shall issue a

license related to the conduct of fishing to the Japanese fishing vessels which desire to be engaged in fishing in the waters referred to in Article 1. When a Japanese vessel does not possess this license, it may not engage in fishing in the waters referred to in the same Article.

2. Procedures for application for and issuance of the licenses referred to in 1, procedures for submitting information concerning fishing by Japan, and procedures for keeping fishing diaries by Japanese vessels are prescribed in the attachment which constitutes an inseparable part of this agreement.

3. The responsible authorities of the Union of Soviet Socialist Republics may collect a proper fee for the issuance of the license referred to in 1.

ARTICLE 6

The Government of Japan guarantees that the people and vessels of Japan shall observe the prescriptions of this agreement and the regulations established in the Union of Soviet Socialist Republics for the preservation of living resources and the regulation of fishing in the waters referred to in Article 1. The people and vessels of Japan which do not observe these prescriptions and regulations shall bear responsibility according to the law of the Union of Soviet Socialist Republics.

ARTICLE 7

1. The Government of Japan guarantees that the official appointed by the responsible authorities of the Union of Soviet Socialist Republics shall be given an opportunity to embark without hindrance upon any vessel which possesses the license referred to in Article 5-1 and which engages in fishing according to this agreement and that while the said official is aboard the vessel the captain and the crew of the said vessel shall cooperate with the said official in the execution of inspection (including the taking of measures to eliminate the violation which has been discovered as a result of the inspection).

2. The Government of Japan guarantees that the cost related to the staying of the official of the Union of Soviet Socialist Republics referred to in 1 aboard the Japanese vessel shall be borne by the responsible authorities of the Union of Soviet Socialist Republics.

3. When a Japanese vessel is captured by the responsible authorities of the Union of Soviet Socialist Republics, the Japanese Government shall be so informed without delay through diplomatic channels. The captured vessel and its crew shall be freed without delay after proper securities or other guarantees are presented.

ARTICLE 8

No prescription in this agreement shall be taken to violate the position or opinion of either government with respect to the ocean law issues under discussion at the Third United Nations Law of the Sea Conference or issues in the [two nations'] mutual relations.

ARTICLE 9

1. This agreement shall be ratified according to the procedures of the domestic law of the respective states.

2. This agreement shall become effective on the day when diplomatic notes are exchanged informing its ratification and shall remain effective until December 31, 1977.

APPENDIX F

Draft Treaty and Goodneighbourhood and Cooperation between USSR and Japan
(TASS Headline)

[Text] Moscow, February 23 TASS—IZVESTIYA today publishes a draft treaty on good-neighbourhood and cooperation between the USSR and Japan.

"The Union of Soviet Socialist Republics and Japan, seeking to promote the consolidation of peace and security in the Far East, in the Pacific basin and throughout the world;

Convinced that peaceful cooperation between both states on the basis of the aims and principles of the United Nations Charter accord with the aspirations of the Soviet and Japanese peoples, the broad interests of international peace;

Guided by the desire fully to overcome the elements of estrangement and distrust in their mutual relations, engendered in the past;

Prompted by solicitude for creating an atmosphere of goodneighbourhood and goodwill between both countries;

Reaffirming their intention to continue talks on the conclusion of a peace treaty;

Desiring to express in contractual form their resolve to create a firm and long-term foundation for the development of all-around cooperation between them, above all, in the political sphere, and also in the sphere of the economy, science, technology and culture;

Have agreed as follows:

ARTICLE 1

The Union of Soviet Socialist Republics and Japan regard the maintenance of peace, extension and strengthening of relaxation of tension and strengthening of international security as one of the main aims of their policy.

They express a desire to exert efforts for the consolidation of universal peace on the Asian Continent, in the Pacific basin and throughout the world.

SOURCE: TASS Moscow in English 1232 GMT 23 Feb 78 LD.

ARTICLE 2

The Union of Soviet Socialist Republics and Japan shall settle their disputes exclusively by peaceful means and undertake in their mutual relations to refrain from the threat of force or its use.

The high contracting parties shall develop and strengthen relations of good-neighbourhood and mutually-advantageous cooperation on the basis of peaceful coexistence.

ARTICLE 3

The Union of Soviet Socialist Republics and Japan undertake not to allow the use of their territories for any actions, which could prejudice the security of the other party.

ARTICLE 4

The high contracting parties undertake to refrain from any actions encouraging any third party to take aggressive actions against either of them.

ARTICLE 5

The Union of Soviet Socialist Republics and Japan shall maintain and widen regular contacts and consultations on important international issues concerning the interests of both states through meetings and exchanges of views between their leading statesmen and through diplomatic channels.

Should a situation arise, which, in the opinion of both sides is dangerous for maintaining peace, or if peace is violated, the sides shall immediately contact each other with the aim of exchanging views on the question of what can be done for improving the situation.

ARTICLE 6

The Union of Soviet Socialist Republics and Japan declare their determination to continue efforts for ending the arms race, of both nuclear and conventional weapons, and attaining general and complete disarmament under effective international control.

ARTICLE 7

Considering trade relations to be an important and necessary element of strengthening bilateral relations and attaching great significance to economic cooperation between the Union of Soviet Socialist Republics and Japan, the parties shall actively promote the growth of such relations, contribute to cooperation between the appropriate organizations and enterprises of both countries and to concluding appropriate agreements and contracts, including long-term ones.

ARTICLE 8

Attaching great significance to scientific and technical cooperation between the Union of Soviet Socialist Republics and Japan, the parties will promote in every way possible an expansion of mutually beneficial and all-round cooperation in these fields on the basis of the treaties and agreements, which exist or will be concluded between them.

ARTICLE 9

Being interested in the preservation and rational use of biological resources of the world ocean, the Union of Soviet Socialist Republics and Japan shall continue broadening cooperation in this field on the basis of the appropriate agreements and with due regard for the legislation of the parties.

ARTICLE 10

The high-contracting parties shall encourage the development of relations between government institutions and public organizations in the field of science, arts, education, television, radio and sports, contributing to a mutual enrichment of achievements in these fields, to strengthening the feeling of respect and friendliness of the peoples of those countries for each other.

ARTICLE 11

The Union of Soviet Socialist Republics and Japan shall strive that the relations and cooperation between them in all the above listed fields and any other fields of mutual interest be built on a durable and long-term basis. With this aim in view, the parties shall establish, where it is deemed advisable, joint commissions, or other joint bodies.

ARTICLE 12

The Union of Soviet Socialist Republics and Japan do not claim and do not recognize anyone's claims to any special rights to advantages in world affairs, including claims to domination in Asia and in the area of the Far East.

ARTICLE 13

This treaty shall not affect the bilateral and multilateral treaties and agreements concluded earlier by the Union of Soviet Socialist Republics and Japan, and is not directed against any third country.

ARTICLE 14

This treaty shall be subject to ratification and enter into force on the day of the exchange of instruments of ratification to be done in the city of _____ done at _____ on _____ in two copies, each in the Russian and Japanese languages, both texts being equally authentic.

For the Union of Soviet Socialist Republics:

For Japan:

APPENDIX G

Defense Bulletin

1. Scope of Defense Budget (100 Million Yen)

	FY1973	FY1974	FY1975	FY1976	FY 1977
Defense Budget (Total) (A)	9,355	10,930	13,272	15,124	16,906
Percent of previous FY	116.9%	116.8%	121.4%	113.9%	111.8%
Defense Agency	8,549	9,854	11,974	13,707	15,349
Percent of previous FY	117.0%	115.3%	121.5%	114.5%	112.0%
Defense Facilities Administration Agency	804	1,076	1,298	1,415	1,549
Percent of previous FY	115.7%	133.8%	120.6%	109.0%	109.5%
National Defense Council	1	1	1	1	1
Finance Ministery	1	0	0	0	7
Gross National Product (B)	1,098,000	1,315,000	1,585,000	1,681,000	1,928,500
General Account (C)	142,841	170,994	212,888	242,960	285,143
Percent of previous FY	124.6%	119.7%	124.5%	114.1%	117.4%
(A)/(B)	0.85%	0.83%	0.84%	0.90%	0.88%
(A)/(C)	6.55%	6.39%	6.23%	6.22%	5.93%

SOURCE: Defense Bulletin 1, no. 1 (April 1977)
1. Defense Budget and General Account is Initial Budget.
2. Finance Ministry's figure shows Special Account for Consolidation of Special National Property.
3. GNP is initial foreseen.
4. Detail may not add to totals, because of rounding. (Following the same.)

2. Expenditures

(1) Breakdown by Organization

(Million Yen)

	FY1977(A)	FY1976(B)	(C)=(A)−(B)	(C)/(B)%
Ground Self-Defense Force (GSDF)	713,924	651,653	62,270	9.6
Maritime Self-Defense Force (MSDF)	357,156	314,051	43,105	13.7
Air Self-Defense Force (ASDF)	413,595	362,180	51,415	14.2
Sub-Total	1,484,674	1,327,884	156,790	11.8
Internal Bureau	5,540	5,023	517	10.3
Joint Staff Council	697	645	51	8.0
National Defense College	547	556	△8	△1.5
National Defense Academy	7,609	7,092	517	7.3
National Defense Medical College	11,520	8,418	3,102	36.8
Technical Research and Development Institute (TRDI)	21,176	18,282	2,894	15.8
Central Procurement Office	3,140	2,838	302	10.7
Sub-Total	50,229	42,853	7,375	17.2
Defense Agency (Total)	1,534,903	1,370,737	164,166	12.0
Defense Facilities Administrative Agency	154,914	141,515	13,399	9.5
Finance Ministry	686	0	686	−
DA + DFAA + FM (Total)	1,690,504	1,512,252	178,251	11.8
National Defense Council	110	98	11	11.5
Defense replated Budget (Total)	1,690,613	1,512,351	178,263	11.8

(2) Breakdown by Item

(Million Yen)

	FY1977(A)	FY1976(B)	(C)=(A)−(B)
General Administration Expenditure	1,036,659	940,389	96,270
1. Personnel (Military and Civil)	884,061	803,291	80,770
2. Travel	7,745	7,485	260
3. Office Administration	32,985	29,116	3,870
4. Clothing	6,296	6,237	60
5. Rations	31,250	30,479	771
6. Medical Care	12,186	9,374	2,811
7. Training and Education	21,949	16,226	5,723
8. Fuel	30,876	29,650	1,226
9. Others	9,311	8,531	780
Weapons and Vehicles, etc.	98,927	92,785	6,142
Aircrafts	140,819	110,730	30,089
Ships	54,109	44,992	9,116
Facilities	40,862	34,629	6,233
Equipment Maintenance	146,635	132,761	13,874
Facility Construction and Maintenance Incidential Administration	1,202	960	241
Research and Development	15,691	13,491	2,201
Defense Agency	1,534,903	1,370,737	164,166

	FY1977 (A)	FY1976 (B)	(A) − (B)
General Administration Expenditure	16,384	14,996	1,388
1. Personnel (Civil)	14,994	13,808	1,186
2. Others	1,390	1,188	202
Labor Administration Expenditure	4,129	5,265	△ 1,136
1. Solatia for the Dischanged USFJ Employees	1,110	2,116	△ 1,006
2. Labor Management for USFJ Employees granted to Local Gavernments	2,405	2,518	△ 113
3. Temporary GOJ Subsidy for USFJ HIS	480	373	107
4. GOJ Sabsidy for the organizations assisting re-employment of the discharged USFJ employees	49	49	0
5. GOJ Subsidy for Welfare Facilities for USFJ Employees	7	162	△ 155
6. Others	78	47	31
Expenditure in relation to Administration of Facilities and Areas	120,693	105,593	15,100
1. Rental	34,992	35,169	△ 177
2. Administration of Facilities and Areas	2,945	2,484	460
3. Subsidy for Projects to Improve Local Situation Adjacent to Facilities and Areas	61,839	51,870	9,969
4. Adjustment Grant-in-Aid for Improvement of Environs of the Special Defenses Facilities	6,500	5,000	1,500
5. Damage Compensation in relation to Administration of Facilities and Areas	6,812	4,772	2,040
6. Others	7,606	6,299	1,307
Relocation/Consolidation Expenditure of Facilities and Areas	13,626	15,582	△ 1,956
1. Relocation/Consolidation Expenses of Facilities and Areas	13,497	15,455	△ 1,958
2. Others	129	127	2
Contributions by GOJ under the Mutual Defenses Assistance Agreement between Japan and U.S.A.	83	79	4
DFAA (Total)	154,914	141,515	13,399
Personnel	87	78	8
etc.	23	20	3
National Defense Council (Total)	110	98	11
Finance Ministry	686	0	686
Defense Budget (Total)	1,690,613	1,512,351	178,263

3. Contract Authorization and Continued Expenditure

(1) Contract Authorization (New)

	FY1977(A)	FY1976 (B)	(A) – (B)
Ordnance	48,181	25,372	22,810
Ammunition	32,692	20,838	11,854
Aircrafts	127,986	140,131	△ 12,145
Ships	22,469	24,202	△ 1,733
Equipment Maintenance	93,680	72,096	21,584
Others	37,438	44,848	△ 7,410
DA (Sub-total)	362,446	327,486	34,961
DFAA (Sub-total)	10,858	6,665	4,193
Total	373,304	334,151	39,154

(2) Continued Expenditures (New)

	Total	Future Obligation				
		FY1977	FY1978	FY1979	FY1980	FY1981
DD	30,671	325	7,706	4,377	13,533	4,730
DE	12,702	74	3,323	6,078	3,228	–
SS	25,622	391	12,606	2,838	9,788	–
(FY1976) DDH	42,785					

(3) Future Obligation

	FY1977			FY1976		
	New	Scheduled	Total	New	Scheduled	Total
A. Contract Authorization						
Ordnance	45,023	135	45,158	25,337	496	25,833
Ammunition	32,670	0	32,670	20,838	6,246	27,084
Aircraft	123,830	121,320	245,149	134,482	122,169	256,651
Ships	20,476	17,261	37,737	22,855	5,504	28,359
Equipment Maintenance	92,254	3,791	96,045	70,735	4,270	75,005
Others	35,079	2,285	37,364	39,348	158	39,506
Sub-total	349,332	144,791	494,124	313,595	138,843	452,438
B. Continued Expenditure	68,206	74,086	142,292	41,803	72,438	114,242
DA Total	417,538	218,878	636,416	355,398	211,281	566,679
Contract Authorization	6,515	0	6,515	3,771	0	3,771
DFAA Total	424,053	218,878	642,931	359,169	211,281	570,451
Contract Authorization (total)	355,847	144,791	500,639	317,366	138,843	456,209
Continued Expenditure (total)	68,206	74,086	142,292	41,803	72,438	114,242

4. Personnel Ceiling

	FY1976			FY1977 Increase (Demanding)			At the end of FY1977 (Demanding)		
	Uniform	Civil	Total	Uniform	Civil	Total	Uniform	Civil	Total
GSDF	180,000	11,591	191,591	0	25(114)	25(114)	180,000	11,502	191,502
MSDF	42,199	4,467	46,666	79	4(43)	83(43)	42,278	4,428	46,706
ASDF	45,252	4,805	50,057	240	3(45)	243(45)	45,492	4,763	50,255
Sub-Total	267,451	20,863	288,314	319	32(202)	351(202)	267,770	20,693	288,463
Internal Bureau	0	511	511	0	4(3)	4(3)	0	512	512
Joint Staff Council	83	34	117	0	0	0	83	34	117
National Defense College	0	92	92	0	0	0	0	92	92
National Defense Academy	0	705	705	0	1(4)	1(4)	0	702	702
National Defense Medical College	0	311	311	0	249(3)	249(3)	0	557	557
TRDI	0	975	975	0	4(8)	4(8)	0	971	971
Central Procurement Office	0	600	600	0	3(5)	3(5)	0	598	598
Sub-Total	83	3,228	3,311	0	261(23)	261(23)	83	3,466	3,549
(DA TOTAL)	267,534	24,091	291,625	319	293(225)	612(225)	267,853	24,659	292,012
(DFAA)	0	3,499	3,499	0	31(27)	31(27)	0	3,503	3,503
TOTAL	267,534	27,590	295,124	319	324(252)	643(252)	267,853	27,662	295,515
Reserve Personnel		39,600			0			39,600	

Note: Figures in (   ) indicate personnel reduction (250 Men) and removed personnel (2 Men) to Ministry of Foreign Affairs.

5. Breakdown of Major Items

(Million)

		FY1977	FY1976
I	Promotion of Training and Education	(102,192) 201,027	(83,222) 178,637
	1 Training and Education	(9,938) 23,517	(12,486) 16,226
	2 Oil	30,876	29,650
	3 Maintenance of Equipment	(92,254) 146,635	(70,735) 132,761
	(1) Maintenance of Ordnance	(4,305) 11,018	(3,161) 10,200
	(2) Maintenance of Aircrafts	(59,371) 78,644	(47,758) 71,248
	(3) Maintenance of Ships	(7,509) 15,083	(3,906) 12,642
	(4) Others	(21,069) 41,889	(15,909) 38,671
II	Promotion of Personnel Inducement Measures	(76) 56,850	(4,271) 47,063
	1 Increase of Administration Expenditures, etc.	(76) 16,466	13,880
	2 Promotion of Living Environment	17,124	(83) 14,267
	(1) Barracks	6,075	5,006
	(2) Messhall and Bathroom etc.	1,711	(83) 1,334
	(3) Gyms and Swimming Pools	858	323
	(4) Housing for Government Employee	8,481	7,604

	FY1977	FY1976
3 Improvement of Health and Medical Measures	21,248	(4,188) 17,610
(1) National Defense Medical College	10,678	(4,188) 8,196
(2) Medical Facilities	162	41
(3) Expenditures for Medical Care	10,408	9,373
4 Increase of Payment for Reserve Personnel	1,258	797
5 Vocational Training for Personnel Returning to Civilian Life	754	510
III Improvement of Command and Control Function	(1,732) 1,862	0
1 Construction of Jointed Communication System	(1,732) 1,487	0
2 Build-up of Air Traffic Control System	376	0
IV Promotion of R & D	(8,089) 21,798	(7,192) 18,477
1 R & D	(6,583) 15,691	(6,879) 13,491
(1) Proto-type and Contracted R & D	(6,583) 10,524	(6,621) 8,752
(Major Items) (SAM)	375	(326) 1,682
(ASM)	(2,513) 3,679	(3,061) 2,496
Fan-Engine for Small Plane	(617) 336	72
High-speed Homing Torpedo (G-RX2)	1,541	(1,081) 279
New Type Mine	(361) 90	0
FADAC	(333) 82	0

	FY 1977	FY 1976
(2) Equipment and Apparatus for R & D	(258) 1,581	1,339
(3) Testing	3,587	3,400
2 Evaluation	(1,506) 623	(313) 195
3 Others	5,485	4,792
V Improvement of Civic Cooperation	(7,578) 4,943	(3,781) 4,798
1 Rescue Aircraft	(7,518) 3,250	(3,781) 2,915
2 Civic Engineering and Construction Equipment	1,344	1,571
3 Others	(60) 349	311
VI Improvement of Defense Facilities	(1,066) 41,367	(6,912) 34,629
1 Facilities for Base	(1,066) 9,960	(2,193) 9,583
2 Facilities for Livelihood	13,252	(83) 11,038
3 Facilities for Environment Protection	2,293	2,494
4 Facilities for Education, Communication etc.	15,863	(4,636) 11,515
VII Improvement of Environmental Protection and Prevention of Disasters	(3,996) 12,887	(4,352) 8,627
1 Air Safety Measures	(3,750) 7,833	(4,288) 4,073
(1) Improvement of Air Traffic Control Functions	(2,408) 4,778	(2,973) 1,436
(2) Aircraft Safety Measures	(1,342) 2,424	(1,315) 1,866
(3) Others	630	770

	FY1977	FY1976
2 Environmental Protection	(245) 4,074	(64) 3,872
(1) Anti-Air Pollution	1,110	711
(2) Anti-Water Contamination	1,168	1,689
(3) Anti-Noise	433	299
(4) Anti-Ocean Pollution	(245) 1,363	(64) 1,174
3 Prevention of Disasters	981	683
(1) Safety Measures for Oil Tank	482	108
(2) Safety Measures for Ammunition Dump	499	574

VIII Acquistition of Capital Equipments

    1. Summary

(Million Yen)

	FY1977			FY1976		
	New	Scheduled	Total	New	Scheduled	Total
Class A*	(24,633) 0	23,604	23,604	(23,604) 0	24,705	24,705
Class B**	(1,992) 10,688	1,011	11,699	(1,011) 10,746	392	11,138
SAM	(16,409) 945	969	1,914	(1,104) 15	2,209	2,224
Ammunition	(32,670) 5,851	27,084	32,935	(20,838) 7,405	21,480	28,885
Aircrafts	(123,830) 5,488	135,331	140,819	(134,482) 6,924	103,806	110,730
Ships	(88,682) 2,855	51,254	54,109	(64,658) 2,495	42,497	44,992
1 Total	(288,216) 25,827	239,253	265,080	(245,698) 27,585	195,088	222,673

(Note) 1. (   ) is Future Obligation.
         2. * is Combat Essential Items of GSDF.
         3. ** is Items except "Class A".

2. Breakdown of New Procurement

(Class A)

(Million Yen)

	Quantity	Total Amount	FY1977	Future Obligation
M64	5,500	721	0	721
M62 MG	94	145	0	145
M64 ATM Launcher	8	120	0	120
M60, 106MM SPRR	16	850	0	850
M73 APC	6	572	0	572
M74 Tank	48	15,032	0	15,032
M61 Weasel	5	97	0	97
35MM Twin AAMG	1	607	0	607
M73 Tractor	9	971	0	971
M74 105MM SP Howitzer	5	832	0	832
M75 155MM SP Howitzer	10	2,809	0	2,809
M75 130MM SP Multi Rocket Launcher	6	1,025	0	1,025
M75 SP Ground Wind Sound System	3	332	0	332
M64,81MM Mortor	64	129	0	129
M70 SP Dontoon Bridge	3	391	0	391
Total		24,633	0	24,633

(ASM)

(Million Yen)

	Total Amount	FY1977	Future Obligation
Nike	901	0	901
Hawk	16,454	945	15,508
Total	17,354	945	16,409

(Aircraft)

(Million Yen)

	Quantity	Total Amount	FY1977	Future Obligation
GSDF				
OH-6J	10	1,332	1,332	0
HU-1H	3	1,307	98	1,209
V-107A	1	890	71	819
LR-1	1	423	28	395
AH-1S	1	967	168	799
Sub-Total	16	4,919	1,697	3,223
MSDF				
PS-1	1	5,300	221	5,079
US-1	1	5,389	253	5,136
KM-2	5	671	45	626
TC-90	1	404	49	355
NSS-2A	4	7,502	270	7,232
S-61A	1	1,525	63	1,462
Sub-Total	13	20,791	902	19,889
ASDF				
F-4EJ	12	45,329	246	45,082
F-1	18	46,544	1,762	44,783
C-1	2	8,350	479	7,871
T-3	12	1,769	264	1,505
MU-2J	1	598	40	557
V-107A	1	1,018	98	920
Sub-Total	46	103,607	2,889	100,718
Total	75	129,317	5,488	123,830

(Ships)

(Million Yen)

	Quantity (ton)	Total Amount	FY1977	Future Obligation
DD	1 (2,900)	30,671	325	30,346
DE	1 (1,200)	12,702	74	12,629
SS	1 (2,200)	25,622	391	25,231
MSC	2 (880)	8,569	445	8,124
ARC	1 (4,500)	13,572	1,432	12,141
Sub-Total	6 (11,680)	91,137	2,667	88,470
(Miscellaneous Auxiliary)	3 (312)	400	188	212
Total	9 (11,992)	91,537	2,855	88,682

Notes

CHAPTER ONE

1. A detailed, well-documented account in English of Japan's earliest contacts with the Russians is John A. Harrison's *Japan's Northern Frontier: A Preliminary Study in Colonization and Expansion with Special Reference to the Relations of Japan and Russia* (Gainesville, Fla.: University of Florida Press, 1953).

2. Further details in Peter Berton, Paul Langer, and Rodger Swearingen, *Japanese Training and Research in the Russian Field* (Los Angeles, Calif.: University of Southern California Press, 1956); and in Harrison, *Japan's Northern Frontier.*

3. George Lensen, "Russo-Japanese Relations" (introduction). Unpublished manuscript kindly supplied to author. For a well-documented, detailed account (based heavily on Russian sources) see Lensen, *The Russians Push Towards Japan: Russo-Japanese Relations, 1697–1875* (Princeton, N.J.: Princeton University Press, 1959).

4. Details of exploration and discovery are recorded and documented in John J. Stephan, *The Kuril Islands: Russo-Japanese Frontiers in the Pacific* (Oxford: Clarendon Press, 1974).

5. *Memoirs of Captivity in Japan* by Captain Golovin of the Russian navy (London, 1824), pp. 32–35.

6. A useful collection of 37 articles by a variety of authors is George Lensen, ed. *Russia's Eastward Expansion* (Englewood Cliffs, N.J.: Prentice-Hall, 1964), which traces that process "Across the Continent," "Across the Pacific," "Into the Russo-Chinese Borderlands," and beyond.

7. Russian approaches to Japan within the broad framework of cultural, diplomatic, and treaty diplomacy are elegantly sketched in Sir George Sansom's *The Western World and Japan* (New York: Knopf, 1950).

8. A fairly detailed and valuable work on Russo-Japanese relations in the prewar era is the two-volume *Nichi-Ro Kosho-shi* [A History of Japanese-Russian negotiations] published by the Japanese Foreign Ministry in 1944.

9. Texts in Victor A. Yakhonotoff, *Russia and the Soviet Union in the Far East* (New York: Coward-McCann, 1931), pp. 379–380. An excellent account of

this situation, based on Japanese Foreign Ministry archives, as well as on Russian diplomatic correspondence is found in Peter Berton, "The Secret Russo-Japanese Alliance of 1916" (Ph.D. dissertation, Columbia University, 1959).

10. Text of recognition notes, background, and details in George Lensen, *Japanese Recognition of the USSR; Soviet-Japanese Relations, 1921–1930* (Tokyo: Sophia University Press in cooperation with the Diplomatic Press, Tallahassee, Fla., 1970).

11. Text of Anti-Comintern Pact in Royal Institute of International Affairs, *Documents of International Affairs* (London, 1936), pp. 297–299. Secret Protocol in: Germany, Foreign Office, *Documents on German Foreign Policy, 1918–1945*, series D, vol. 1 (London, 1949), p. 754.

12. An authoritative and detailed account (in Japanese) of prewar Soviet-Japanese relations is *Nis-so Kosho-shi* [A History of Japanese-Soviet negotiations] published by the Japanese Ministry of Foreign Affairs in Tokyo, 1942. The chapter entitled "Japan and the Soviet Union: The Policy of Ambivalence" in Leonid N. Kutakov's *Japanese Foreign Policy* (Tallahassee, Fla.: The Diplomatic Press, 1972) is an authoritative account, based upon Soviet archives. Its author is a senior Soviet official in the Ministry of Foreign Affairs and a well-known diplomatic historian. Chapters 1 and 2 in A. M. Dubinsky's *The Far East in the Second World War* (Moscow: "Nauka" Publishing House, Central Department of Oriental Literature, 1972) documents the Soviet position in a more dogmatic manner pointedly designed to refute the conclusions of Western (especially American) studies of the period after 1937.

CHAPTER TWO

1. World Peace Foundation, *Documents on American Foreign Relations, 1941–42* (Boston, Mass., 1952) 3: 609–610.

2. Message, General MacArthur to General Marshall, No. 198, 10 December 1941, U.S. Department of Defense, *The Entry of the Soviet Union into the War Against Japan, 1941–1945* (Washington, D.C., September, 1955). Subsequent citations in this chapter, unless otherwise identified, are from this document.

3. Cordell Hull, *Memoirs*, 2 vols. (New York: Macmillan, 1948), 2:732, 1627.

4. JCS 16, Note by Secys, Sub. *United States Action in Case of War Between Russia and Japan*, 6 March 1942.

5. Memo, Gen. Marshall and Adm. King to President, 30 March 1942.

6. Msg., President to Marshal Stalin, 17 January 1942.

7. Msg., President to Marshal Stalin, 23 June 1942.

8. Msgs., Amb. Standley to Sec. State, Nos. 227 and 231, 2 July 1942.

9. Draft Msg. with Memo, JCS to President, 30 December 1942.

10. Msg., Marshal Stalin to President, 5 January 1943.

11. Msg., Marshal Stalin to President, 13 January 1943.

12. CCS 168, Memo by JCS, Sub: "Conduct of the War in the Pacific Theater in 1943," 22 January 1943.

13. CCS 300, Memo by JCS, Sub: "Estimate of the Enemy Situation, 1943–1944, Pacific–Far East Area," 6 August 1943.

14. U.S. Department of Defense, *Entry of Soviet Union into War*, p. 21.

15. Msg., Major Gen. Dean to JCS, 31 October 1943. CM.IN 655.

16. Hull, *Memoirs*, 2: 1113, 1309–10.

17. JCS 606/2, Reported by JPS, Sub: "Collaboration with the U.S.S.R.," 25 November 1943.

18. John R. Deane, *The Strange Alliance: The Story of Our Efforts at Wartime Cooperation with the Soviet Union* (New York: Viking, 1947), pp. 229–235.

19. CCS 417, Reported by CPS, Sub: "Overall Plan for the Defeat of Japan," 2 December 1943.

20. U.S. Department of Defense, *Entry of Soviet Union into War*, p. 27.

21. Msg., Amb. Harriman to President, 2 February 1944. For a full discussion of these negotiations see Deane, *The Strange Alliance*, pp. 229–235.

22. Msg., Amb. Harriman to President, 23 September 1944.

23. Msg., President to Prime Minister, 30 September 1944.

24. Author's conversation with Prof. Philip Mosely, New York, October 1959.

25. Msg., JCS to Maj. Gen. Deane, 28 September 1944.

26. Msg., Amb. Harriman to President, 15 December 1944.

27. Msg., Maj. Gen. Deane to JCS, 16 December 1944. See also Deane, *The Strange Alliance*, pp. 259–260.

28. Ltr. Sec. Stimson to Acting Sec. Grew, 21 May 1945.

29. Msg., Hopkins to President, 30 May 1945.

30. CCS 645/3 Sub: Estimate of Enemy Situation, 8 July 1945.

31. The best account of this dimension of the war in the Pacific is Robert J. C. Butow, *Japan's Decision to Surrender* (Stanford Calif.: Stanford University Press, 1954).

32. *Ibid.*, pp. 121–122.

33. James Byrnes, *Speaking Frankly* (New York: Harper and Brothers, 1947).

CHAPTER THREE

1. *Naimusho Keihokyoku Hoanka Daiichi-Kakari* [Sect. One, Peace Preservation Bureau, Police Division, Japanese Home Ministry], *On Trends Among Communist Elements, With Special Reference to the Conclusion of the War* (Tokyo, handwritten, 1945).

2. Dispatch to Secretary of State, Washington, from George Atcheson, Political Advisor, Army (Secret), November 2, 1945. Box 2276, File 891. National Archives, Washington, D.C.

3. *Ibid.*

4. George Atcheson, "Japanese Democratic Political Situation," in U.S. Department of State, *Foreign Relations of the United States: The Far East* (Washington, D.C.: Government Printing Office, 1971), vol. 9, pp. 87–90.

5. Soviet indoctrination and repatriation of Japanese POWs, treated separately in chap. 4.

6. Russell Brines, *MacArthur's Japan* (New York, Lippincott, 1948), p. 72.

7. Past and present editions of Soviet encyclopedias were checked, and no reference to Derevyanko could be found.

8. V. K. Derevyanko, *Otets, Soldat, Diplomat* [Father, soldier, diplomat], (Moscow, 1971).

9. The Soviet leadership over the years, it may be noted, has been heavily sprinkled with Ukranians: Brezhnev, Podgorny, Grechko, and Kirilenko, to name but a few of the top-level figures.

10. Derevyanko. *Otets, Soldat, Diplomat*, pp. 5, 11.

11. His wife is still living in Moscow. One of the general's former aides, whom I encountered by chance at a lecture I gave in Moscow in the summer of 1976, offered to arrange a luncheon with Mrs. Derevyanko; but, unfortunately, time did not permit.

12. Derevyanko, *Otets, Soldat, Diplomat*, p. 36.

13. *Ibid.*, p. 59.

14. Allied Council for Japan (ACJ), *Verbatim Minutes (VM)*, 12 June 1946.

15. ACJ, 7th Meeting, *VM*, 7 August 1946.

16. ACJ, 15th Meeting, *VM*, 18 September 1946.

17. *Ibid.*

18. ACJ, 28th Meeting, *VM*, 19 March 1947.

19. ACJ, 30th Meeting, *VM*, 16 April 1947.

20. ACJ, 38th Meeting, *VM*, 7 August 1947.

21. ACJ, 41st Meeting, *VM*, 17 September 1947, p. 15.

22. *Ibid.*, p. 16.

23. *Ibid.*

24. *Ibid.*

25. *Ibid.*

26. *Ibid.*

27. *Ibid.*

28. *Ibid.*, p. 17.

29. *Ibid.*

30. *Ibid.*

31. *Ibid.*, p. 18.

32. *Ibid.*

33. "Planned Duty Roster—Personnel of the Soviet Section of the Allied Council for Japan," submitted by General K. Kerevyanko to the Chief of Staff, Armed Forces, Pacific, 11 April 1946 (Box 29, File 210.6, National Archives Record Group 331). Other SCAP documentation in this and subsequent chapters also from the National Archives.

34. *Ibid.*

35. SCAP, G-2 *Special Report.* S/a Br. CIS, Tabsa, 23 April 1947, subj: "Mitsubishi Bldg. No. 21" (June 1947).

36. See chap. 5, "The Metamorphosis of the Moscow-Linked 'Lovable' Japan Communist Party."

37. John Davies, "Comments on Study by SCAP entitled, 'Communist Party'," July 24, 1946. Embassy of the United States of America (Confidential), No. 388, Moscow, September 12, 1946.

38. Further details may be found in SCAP, G-2 "Front Organizations in Japan," *Summation*, No. 23 (Secret) (December 1947).

39. SCAP, G-2, "Soviet Broadcasts to Japan," *Summation*, No. 21 (November 1947).

40. SCAP, G-2, "Soviet Radio Warfare," *Special Article*, No. 34 (December 1948), pp. 24–28.

41. *Ibid.*, p. 29.

42. *Ibid.*, p. 30.

43. SCAP, G-2 (CIS Special Intelligence) "Soviet Radio Warfare," *Special Article* No. 35. (Based on "Soviet Radio Broadcasts to the Far East: October 1948," dated November 26, 1948; Compiled from Daily Reports on Foreign Radio Broadcasts, surveys of USSR Radio Broadcasts, and daily Foreign Broadcast Information Service monitoring service) (February 1949), p. 25.

44. *Ibid.*

45. See chapter 7, "Japanese Public Opinion and the Press."

46. Eidus died in 1974.

47. *Novoe Vremia*, No. 8, April 15, 1946.

48. *Novoe Vremia*, No. 9, May 1, 1946.

49. *Novoe Vremia*, No. 11, November, 1947.

50. *Novoe Vremia*, No. 33, August 16, 1950.

CHAPTER FOUR

1. General Kuzma Derevyanko, principal Soviet representative. Details on his background and role are given in chap. 3.

2. Discussion of this and other issues taken up by the Allied Council for Japan in chap. 3.

3. Rodger Swearingen and Paul Langer, *Red Flag in Japan: International Communism in Action, 1919–1951* (Cambridge, Mass.: Harvard University Press, 1952), pp. 231–234.

4. Summary of Information, CIC area 24, 6 January 1947; Subject: escaped PW from Russion PW camp in Manchuria, Summary No. 14, *Russian Indoctrination of Japanese Repatriates* (February 1947).

5. "The attitudes of Repatriates toward Russia," SCAP, Civil Information and Education Section, Analysis and Research Division, *Publications Analysis*, No. 196, 14 August 1948, p. 2.

6. *Ibid.*, p. 3.

7. *Ibid.*, p. 6. Recent Soviet overtures to Japan including proposals for further joint Soviet-Japanese Siberian development are discussed in chap. 9.

8. SCAP, G-2 Civil Censorship Division, No. 41. "Comment on Repatriation" (Secret) (July 1949), p. 5.

9. *Ibid.*

10. CIS G-2 FEC, 10 March 1947. Subject: "Conditions in Soviet Dominated Areas," *Summation* No. 14. Russian Indoctrination of Japanese Repatriates (Secret) (April 1947).

11. A study of postwar Japanese publications in the Russian field shows repatriation constituting roughly 20 percent of original (as opposed to translations from Russian) Japanese language output (books only) on Soviet and Communist affairs. One hundred and ten volumes on repatriation can be identified for the years 1946–1954. Peter Berton, Paul Langer, and Rodger Swearingen, *Japanese Training and Research.*

12. Perhaps the best account in English is chap. VIII, "Disinformation: Poisoning Public Opinion," (pp. 164–186) in John Barron, *KGB: The Secret Work of Soviet Agents* (New York: Readers Digest Press, 1974).

13. Civil Censorship, "PW Newspapers Continue to Present Dismal Picture of Postwar Japan " *Survey of PW Mail from the USSR*. No. 30. (December 1947).

14. SCAP, CIS/G-2. "Japanese Repatriates from Soviet Zones," Part I, "Communist Indoctrination in POW Camps," Special Article No. 37 (Secret) p. 14—a condensation of a Special Report, "Soviet Repatriates," 2 February 1949, based on reports of G-2 agencies in the Far East Command and compiled by Special Intelligence, CIS/G-2 (April 1949).

15. M. R. CIC Sasebo Repatriation Team No. 444, Hq. 8th Army. 1 February 1947, in "Russian Indoctrination of Japanese Repatriates," Summation No. 14. (Secret), March 1947, p. 93.

16. G-2, GHQ, FEC. *Intelligence Summary*, No. 1737, 27 February 1947.

17. M. R. CIC Sasebo Repatriation Team, 27 December 1946. Subject: "Japanese Repatriates from Russian Occupied Territories," *ibid.*, p. 4.

18. "Japanese Repatriates from Soviet Zones, Part I: Communist Indoctrination in POW Camps." Special Intelligence, CIS G-2 SCAP, *Special Article No .37* (Secret), 2 February 1949.

19. See chap. 5 for details and documentation. Also see Rodger Swearingen, "The Japanese Communist Party and the Comintern, 1919–1943. A Study of the Relationship Between the Japanese Party and Moscow and of the Success of the Japanese Higher Police (Thought Police) in Combating Communism in Japan." (Ph.D. dissertation, Harvard University, 1951), 164 pp.

20. U.S. Political Advisor for Japan, the Foreign Service of the United States. "Communist Influence among Japanese Repatriates from Soviet Russia," No. 551 (Confidential), Tokyo, August 24, 1948. p. 2.

21. 2 S/I, CIC Area 2. 20 December 1946. Subject: "Yenan School Japanese Communists enter Japan," *Summation* No. 14. Russian Indoctrination of Japanese Repatriates. Discussion of the role of the "Yenan Communists" can be found in chap. 5.

22. *Ibid.*, p. 3. Details of Nosaka's background, including information on his training and experience in Moscow, Yenan, the United States, and elsewhere may be found in Rodger Swearingen, ed., *Leaders of the Communist World* (New York: The Free Press, 1971).

23. "Japanese Repatriates from Soviet Zones—Part II." Special Article (Summary) No. 38, based on Special Intelligence, CIS/G-2, 2 February 1949, p. 36 (June 1949).

24. *Ibid.*

25. *Ibid.*, p. 37.

26. As cited (National Archives).

27. *Ibid.*

28. *Nippon wa do ugoku ka?* [How will Japan act?], quoted in CHQ SCAP, Civil Information and Education Section, Publications Analysis. No. 196. 14 August 1948.

29. SCAP, CIS/G-2. "Japanese Repatriates from the Soviet Zones—Part II," Special Article No. 38, Condensation of Special Report "Soviet Repatriates." 2 February 1949. Based on reports of G-2 agencies in the Far East Command, Special Intelligence CIG/G-2. April, 1949, p. 39.

30. Several hundred thousand repatriates from Soviet areas returned to Japan, but membership in the Japan Communist Party as of 1949 to 1950 reached a peak of only slightly over 100,000, relatively few of them repatriates from the Soviet Union. Registered party membership as reported by the JCP to the attorney general's office in March 1950 was 108,692. Informed sources suggest that an additional 10 percent for "secret party members" should realistically be added to this figure.

31. Interviews by the author in Japan over the years with Japanese government officials and former Japanese Communists.

CHAPTER FIVE

1. For an overall analysis of the period, strategy, tactics, and context see Rodger Swearingen, *Communist Strategy in Japan 1945–1960* (Santa Monica: The RAND Corporation, 1965). Further detail is also provided in Robert A. Scalapino, *The Japanese Communist Movement, 1920–1966* (Berkeley and Los Angeles: University of California Press, 1967), pp. 1–48; and my earlier book (with Paul Langer), *Red Flag in Japan.*

2. For detailed analyses of the JCP in prewar and wartime Japan see (in order of appearance), Swearingen and Langer, *Red Flag in Japan*; Scalapino, *The Japanese Communist Movement*; and George Beckman and Okubo Genji, *The Japanese Communist Party, 1922–1945* (Stanford, Calif.: Stanford University Press, 1969).

3. Lenin, speaking at the Second Congress of Communist Organization of the East, Moscow, November 22, 1919. Stalin was Chairman of the Congress. Lenin, *Sochinenii* [Works] (Moscow, 1932) 24:242–251. Reprinted from *Izvestiia*, December 20, 1919.

4. Details in Swearingen and Langer, *Red Flag in Japan.*

5. Lenin in conversation with Katsuji Fuse, Japanese Press correspondent, quoted in *Lenin i Vostok* (Moscow, 1925), p. 63.

6. Extensive Japanese government documentation on this point is available at the Hoover Institution and the Library of Congress. Relevant items are listed and annotated in my section on the Japanese Communist Party in Thomas T. Hammond, *Soviet Foreign Relations and World Communist Movements* (Princeton, N.J.: Princeton University Press, 1965) pp. 774–786. The book by former Japanese Communist Jokichi Kazama, *Mosuko Kyosandaigaku no omoide* [Memories of the Moscow Communist University] (Tokyo, 1949), details the story of Soviet training from 1925 to 1930 and is probably the most useful and reliable eyewitness account in Japanese.

7. I had occasion to talk at length with all three of them in Japan on numerous occasions while working on several studies of Communism and related subjects, earlier.

8. By far the best account in English of the origins, formulation, substances, nuances, and implications of these several theses is contained in Scalapino, *The Japanese Communist Movement*, pp. 27–42.

9. See chap. 2, "The Emergence of a Soviet Policy for Postwar Japan."

10. Discussed in chap. 3, pp. 29–32.

11. Discussed in chap. 3, pp. 32–34.

12. Details and documentation in Swearingen and Langer, *Red Flag in Japan.*

13. During these fifteen years in prison Tokuda managed to write his memoirs *Waga Omoide* (Tokyo Shoin, 1948) covering the period 1921 to 1927, in which he details his numerous trips to Russia and China on behalf of the party. He was arrested and imprisoned by the Japanese police in 1927. Further detail in Swearingen and Langer, *Red Flag in Japan*, chap. XII, "The Leaders."

14. Some of Nosaka's experiences in the Soviet Union and China are related in his autobiography, *Bomei Ju roku nen* [Sixteen years in exile] (Tokyo, 1948). A more complete record of his two trips to the United States may be found in my chapter, "Sanzo Nosaka—Japan's 'Lovable Communist,' " in Rodger Swearingen, ed., *Leaders of the Communist World.*

15. See chap. 7, "Japanese Public Opinion and the Press."

16. SCAP, G-2, "Tokuda Kyuichi: Orthodox JCP Leader" (based on spot report, CIS, October 1947, "Soviet Faction of JCP") Summation No. 28, March 1948, pp. 16–17.

17. SCAP G-2, "Communist Potential in Japan," Special Article No. 33. (Based on Special Report, "Estimate of Communist Capabilities in Japan," CIS, JPB, 1 September 1948, which brings up to date all previous surveys of Japanese Communism), November 1948, p. 15.

18. See also chap. 3, "Soviet Policy and Practice in Occupied Japan," pp. 35–36.

19. SCAP, G-2, "The Japan Communist Party," *Summation*, No. 21, (Information from Special Report, January 1947, CIS, G-2, FEC, "Soviet Cultural Front in Japan") October 1947, p. 13.

20. Kyuichi Tokuda, *Naigai josei to Nippon Kyosanto no Nimmu* [The foreign and domestic situation in the tasks of the JCP] (Tokyo, 1948).

21. Exclusive interview with representative of Kyodo News Service in *Nippon Times*, January 7, 1946.

22. Tokuda, *Naigai josei*, p. 236.

23. Stressed in numerous SCAP reports and in my interviews with former JCP leaders.

24. Sanzo Nosaka, *Senryaku, Senjutsu no Shomondai* [Strategy and tactics] (Tokyo, 1949), p. 99.

25. Sanzo Nosaka, "Do the Basic Work," *Zenei* [Vanguard], October 1949.

26. An excellent, concise treatment of the period, strategy, and tactics may be found in Toshio Tsukahira, *The Postwar Evolution of Communist Strategy in Japan* (Boston, Mass.: MIT, Center for International Strategy, 1954).

27. *Ibid.*

28. Discussed in detail in Swearingen, *Communist Strategy in Japan.*

29. Some of the documentation on the Cominform criticism and its aftermath is available in a useful compilation of some 800 pages by the non-Communist Nikkan Rodosha Tsushinsha [Daily Labor Press], *Nihon Kyosanto no Bunken Shu* [Japanese Communist Party documents] vol. 3 (Tokyo, 1952). Vols. 1 and 2 of the same series, equally substantial, contain the documents of the period of peaceful revolution. Vol. 4, published at the end of 1952, included many of the documents on underground and military activities.

30. Sanzo Nosaka, "My Self-Criticism," *Zenei*, March 1950.

31. An anti-Tokuda doctrinaire group headed by the then third- and fourth-ranking party leaders, Yoshio Shiga and Kenji Miyamoto.

32. Centering around Kuichi Tokuda, Sanzo Nosaka, and Etsuro Shiino. See Tsukahira, *Postwar Evolution of Communist Strategy in Japan*, for an excellent discussion of the issue.

33. A whole series of special reports on Japanese Communism put out by several private research groups in Japan treats the period in some detail. The organizations, which were reported to be in touch with Japanese police authorities, are identified and discussed in Peter Berton, Paul Langer, and Rodger Swearingen, *Japanese Training and Research in the Russian Field.*

34. Discussed in detail in Swearingen, *Communist Strategy in Japan.*

35. The suspension of the party newspaper *Akahata* [Red Flag] and its successors, June 26, 1950; dissolution of the Communist Union Zenroren (abbreviation for Zenkoku Rodo Kumiai Renraku Kyogikai or National Labor Union Liaison Conference), August 30, 1950; 1,171 persons dismissed from government service as Communists, November 18, 1950; propagandists arrested by the hundreds throughout Japan.

36. On June 6, 1950, General MacArthur ordered the Japanese government to remove and exclude from public service the 24 members of the Central Committee.

37. Cominform, "Immediate Demands of the Japanese Communist Party—New Program," *For a Lasting Peace; For a People's Democracy*, November 23, 1951; "Basis of the New Program of the Communist Party in Japan," *ibid.*, February 15, 1952; "Thirtieth Anniversary of the Communist Party of Japan," *ibid.*, July 4, 1952.

38. Day-to-day underground developments for the period are recorded in *Kyokuto Jijo Kenkyukai* [Institute of Far Eastern Intelligence], and *Kyokuto Tsushin* [Far Eastern Intelligence], a biweekly which regularly contained an analysis of JCP activities of the period.

CHAPTER SIX

1. Discussed in perceptive detail by Frederick S. Dunn, *Peace Making and the Settlement with Japan* (Princeton, N.J.: Princeton University Press, 1963).

2. *Political Reorientation of Japan*, vol. 2, p. 765.

3. SCAP, G-2, "Soviet Radio Broadcasts to Japan," *Summation*, no. 21, 15 October 1947 (Secret), p. 27.

4. "Three Years After the Rout of Japanese Imperialism," *New Times*, no. 37, September 8, 1948, p. 1.

5. SCAP G-2, Civil Censorship, "Reaction to the Occupation," no. 36 (Secret) December 1948, p. 27.

6. Detailed in Dunn, *Peace Making*, pp. 77–85.

7. M. Markov, "American-Japanese 'Peace Settlement' Without a Treaty," *New Times*, no. 26, June 22, 1949, pp. 5–7.

8. *Ibid.*, p. 8.

9. "Five Years After the Surrender of Imperialist Japan," *New Times*, no. 35, August 30, 1950, pp. 1–2.

10. Japan, Ministry of Foreign Affairs, Public Information Bureau, *Collection of Official Foreign Statements on Japanese Peace Treaty*, vol. 2, 14 September 1950 to 25 May 1951 (Tokyo, 1951), p. 1.

11. *Ibid.*, pp. 3–5; 117–120; Dunn, *Peace Making*, pp. 110–112.

12. A somewhat longer, formal, and precise response is documented in Japan, National Diet Library, *Nisso Kokka chosei mondai Kiso shiryo shu* [Basic documentation for the study of the normalization of Japan-Soviet relations] (Tokyo, 1955), pp. 33–34, quoted in part in Savitii Vishwanathan, *Normalization of Soviet-Japanese Relations 1945–1970: An Indian View* (Tallahassee, Fla.: The Diplomatic Press, 1973), p. 48.

13. The mixed reactions and various sundry suggestions of the Allies, especially the Communist nations, are detailed in Dunn, *Peace Making*, pp. 109–110.

14. Detailed account in Dunn, *Peace Making*, pp. 123–143.

15. "Statement by the Delegate of the Union of Soviet Socialist Republics," Second Plenary Session, Opera House, 3 P.M. September 5, 1951 (*Provisional Verbatim Minutes*), Doc. 12, *VM/3*, September 5, 1951, pp. 36–60.

16. *Ibid.*, pp. 58–60.

17. Quoted in Dunn, *Peace Making*, p. 184.

18. *Sovieto Nenpo*, 1955, p. 665, cited in Vishwanathan, *Normalization of Relations*, p. 66.

19. "Molotov's Statement on Relations with Japan," V. M. Molotov's answers to questions from Mr. Mitsuru Suzuki, editor of Japanese newspaper *Chubu Nippon Shimbun, Pravda* and *Izvestiia*, September 13, 1954.

20. Vishwanathan, *Normalization of Relations*, p. 67.

21. D. Petrov, "National Interests of Japan Demand Normalization of Relations with All Countries," *Pravda*, December 6, 1954.

22. Observer, "Japanese Neighbor," *New Times*, August 30, 1961.

23. "Good Prospects for Soviet-Japanese Trade," interview with Michael Nesterov, Chairman, USSR Chamber of Commerce, *New Times*, no. 19, May 15, 1963.

24. A. I. Mikoyan, Press Conference, Subject: "Soviet-Japanese Relations." Transcript in *New Times*, no. 23, June 10, 1964.

25. Donald C. Hellmann, *Japanese Domestic Politics and Foreign Policy* (Berkeley and Los Angeles: University of California Press, 1969), p. 206.

26. Details in chap. 13, "The Northern Territories."

27. *Union of Soviet Socialist Republics and Japan Joint Declaration*, signed in Moscow on 19 October 1956. Full text as Appendix A.

28. Observer "Japanese Neighbor," *New Times*, August 30, 1961.

29. "Good Prospects for Soviet-Japanese Trade" interview with Michael Nesterov, Chairman, Chamber of Commerce, *New Times*, no. 19, May 15, 1963, p. 23.

30. A. I. Mikoyan, Press Conference. Subject: "Soviet-Japanese Relations." *Ibid.*

31. "Japanese-Soviet Relations." Interview with Joru Nakagawa, Japanese Ambassador to the USSR, *New Times*, no. 46, November 15, 1965.

32. V. Mezentsev, ""Our Trading Partner Japan," *New Times*, no. 8, February 23, 1966, pp. 11–13.

33. The bilateral treaties in effect between Japan and the Soviet Union 1956–1975 are listed (with a brief descriptive note) as Appendices to this volume.

34. Details in chapters 12, "Fisheries," and 13, "Northern Territories."

35. *The Japan Times*, January 13, 1976.

36. Full list of treaties with brief descriptive note on substance and source as Appendices D and E-1.

37. V. N. Berezin, *Na Dobrososedstvo i sotrudnichestbo i ego proterniki* [Course on good neighborliness and cooperation—and its enemies—from the history of normalization of relations between the USSR and postwar Japan] (Moscow, International Relations Publishing House, 1977), p. 111.

CHAPTER SEVEN

1. An excellent, detailed and up-to-date analysis of this process is Akira Tsujimura's "Public Opinion and Political Dynamics in Japan: The Tripolar Relationship of Government, Press and Public Opinion," Text of Seminar on "Changing Values in Modern Japan," Tokyo: *Nihon Kenkynicai* (in association with Japan External Trade Organization [JETRO] and Japan Airlines). Essence of paper presented to meeting in Los Angeles, Calif., March 19, 1977, to which I was privileged to have been invited.

2. For a more detailed, comprehensive review of the nature, scope, and development of public opinion research in Japan during the Occupation years—its

origins, proliferation, problems, contributions, and limitations—see Allan B. Cole and Naomichi Nakanichi, *Japanese Opinion Polls with Socio-Political Significance, 1947–1957* (Medford, Mass.: Fletcher School of Law and Diplomacy and the Roper Public Opinion Research Center, 1963). Subsequent polls and data for Occupation period, when not otherwise identified, from Cole and Nakanishi.

3. *Ibid.*

4. SCAP, G-2, CIS, Civil Censorship, "Reaction to the Occupation," no. 36 (January 1949), p. 28. (National Archives.)

5. *Ibid.*, p. 30.

6. Breakdown and details of poll in Cole and Nakanichi, *Japanese Opinion Polls*, p. 648.

7. *Mainichi*, August 23–25, 1950. National stratified random sampling, 3,220 of 3,552 responding to interview sampling.

8. *Yomiuri*, March 10–12, 1951. National stratified random sampling, 3,070 of 3,501 responding; interviews.

9. "Party Comments on Soviet Memorandum," *Contemporary Japan* (April/ June 1951) 20: 238–241.

10. *Yomiuri*, September 29–October 21, 1951. Tokyo and Environs, 1,341 of 1,718 responding; interviewing.

11. *Mainichi*, September 13–14, 1951.

12. *Mainichi*, June 15–17, 1951.

13. *Mainichi*, September 13–14, 1951.

14. *Asahi*, September 13–15, 1951.

15. C. Martin Wilbur, "Some Findings of Japanese Public Opinion Polls," in Hugh Borton, ed., *Japan Between East and West* (New York: Harper and Brothers, 1957), pp. 299–312.

16. *Ibid.*, p. 302.

17. *Ibid.*, p. 308.

18. *Ibid.*

19. Nathan Newby White, *An Analysis of Japan's China Policy Under the Liberal Democratic Party* (Ph.D. Dissertation in Political Science, University of California, Berkeley, 1971), p. 196.

20. *Yomiuri*, May 31, 1970.

21. *Asahi*, January 20, 1975.

22. *Asahi*, June 22, 1975.

23. *Yomiuri*, July 6, 1975.

24. Mitsuru Yamamoto, "JSP's Understanding of the International Situation," *Sekai*, February 1976.

25. Masamichi Inoki, *Chuo Koron*, November 1976.

26. Yukio Nakajima (*Chuo Koron* resident editor in Paris), "Interview with Andrei Amalric, Soviet Historian in Exile," *Chuo Koron*, November 1976.

27. *Japan Report*, vol. 22, no. 9, May 1, 1976.

28. *Asahi*, January 1, 1977.

29. *Ibid.*

CHAPTER EIGHT

1. See Swearingen's *Leaders of the Communist World* for biographical studies of these and some 25 other leaders, each analyzed by an appropriate specialist.

2. Interviews by the author with Japanese Public Security authorities, Foreign Ministry officials, and former high-ranking JCP leaders in Tokyo during the years in question.

3. See *Akahata* and *Zenei* for the period. Discussed in some detail in author's previously cited RAND study.

4. Discussed in Kinya Niizeki, "The Postwar Activities of the Japan Communist Party," *Japan Problems* (Public Information and Cultural Affairs Bureau, Ministry of Foreign Affairs, Tokyo, March 1954). Mr. Niizeki remains one of Japan's top authorities on Soviet affairs. He is currently with Japan's Atomic Energy Commission. Over the postwar years it has been my pleasure and good fortune to consult with him and his colleagues on numerous occasions, both in Tokyo and in Moscow.

5. See, for example, my survey of *Akahata* for the critical 18-month period June 1952 through December 1953 showing 85 articles on the USSR (many of them devoted in part to China) as against 168 articles exclusively on Communist China. Included in my article "Japanese Communism and the Moscow-Peking Axis," in *The Annals of the American Academy of Political and Social Sciences* 108 (November 1956):68.

6. Space constraints coupled with a mandate to focus squarely on JCP relations with Moscow and Peking (within the context of Soviet-Japan relations) precluded the otherwise desirable inclusion of a full analysis of party strategic periodization, and the "mainstream" versus the "international" as well as other factions and splinter groups during these formation years of the "independent" party. Both important aspects are discussed in considerable detail in my 1965 RAND study (cited) and in Scalapino's excellent 1967 book on the JCP (also cited).

7. Interview by Robert Scalapino with Kasuga, November 26, 1963. Quoted in Scalapino, *The Japanese Communist Movement*, p. 96.

8. The first hints of trouble between Moscow and Peking were still few and veiled when I was in the Soviet Union looking into such matters during the summer of 1957. See my report, "Asian Studies in the Soviet Union" (Notes of the Profession), *The Journal of Asian Studies*, Fall 1958.

9. Apart from primary JCP sources, the most accurate and substantial overview of the early part of the period is found in the White Paper on the JCP issued by the Japanese authorities in November of 1957 and subsequently published (January 24, 1958) in Tokyo by the *Nikkan Rodo Tsushinsha* organization.

10. Hirotsu Kyosuki, "Strategic Triangle: Japan," in Leopold Labedz, ed., *International Communism After Khrushchev* (Cambridge, Mass., The MIT Press, 1966), p. 128. Also my discussions with Japanese government authorities and former high-ranking JCP leaders in Japan as noted.

11. On November 27, 1957, the Moscow Declaration was made public. Immediately, a number of JCP leaders insisted that the party take formal action on

this declaration. This move is thought to have initially been opposed by Miyamoto and Hakamada.

12. *Akahata*, April 29 and 30, 1958. Details of implementation of this policy during the 1958–1960 period may be found in my translation of the *Japanese Government White Paper on Communism in Japan*, RAND Study, Part II (cited).

13. I am indebted for the phrase "cautious neutrality" and for one or two other pieces of important documentation to Sei Young Rhee, whose dissertation, "The Impact of the Sino-Soviet Conflict on the Japanese Communist Party, 1961–1968" (University of Missouri, 1973), displays a commendable combination of research work and perception.

14. *Kommunist*, no. 1, 1961.

15. See *Pravda* and *Akahata* of the period.

16. Full text of Nosaka's speech at the 22nd Party Congress of the CPSU on October 23, 1961, appears in *Akahata*, October 26, 1961.

17. Full text in *Akahata*, November 22, 1961.

18. "For the Unity of the International Communist Movement and the Struggle Against Two Enemies," *Akahata*, December 29, 1961, p. 1.

19. Hans H. Baerwald, "The Japanese Communist Party: Yoyogi and its Rivals," in Robert A. Scalapino, ed., *The Communist Revolution in Asia* (Englewood Cliffs N.J.: Prentice-Hall, 1965), p. 198.

20. The details of interparty factionalism during this period are contained in Katsuichi Fukuda, "Trends Within the JCP Relative to the Sino-Soviet Dispute" (Report of the Public Safety Information Bureau, Tokyo, July 1964). Documentation on the Moscow-Peking confrontation within the Gensuikyo meetings in Scalapino, *The Japanese Communist Movement*, pp. 233–234, 247–249, and 278–280.

21. "Decisions on Problems Relating to the International Communist Movement," voted at the JCP's Seventh Central Committee Plenum, October 18, 1963. Reprinted in *Nihon Kyosanto Chuo Iinkai Sokai Ketsugishu* [Collection of the resolutions of the JCP's Central Committee Enlarged Plenum] (Tokyo, 1975), p. 333.

22. An interesting brief discussion of these expulsions is included with some documentation in Rhee, "The Impact of the Sino-Soviet Conflict on the Japanese Communist Party, 1961–1968," pp. 216–218.

23. Partial texts of some of the key letters quoted in Scalapino, *The Japanese Communist Movement*, pp. 171–195. See also *Pravda*, *Akahata*, and *Peking Review* of the same period.

24. *Nihon Kyosanto no Gojunen* [Fifty years of the JCP], *Nihon Kyosanto Chuo Iinkai Shuppan Kyoku* (Tokyo: Japan Communist Party Central Committee Publishing Bureau, 1972), p. 184.

25. *Shiso Undo Kenkyusho* [Research Center for the Study of Social Movements], p. 53–54. Quoted by Kiyoki Murata in Swearingen's *Leaders of the Communist World*, p. 539.

26. Kenjii Miyamoto, *Atarashii Nihon eno Michi: Nihon Kyusanto No Rosen* [The Road to a New Japan: The Course of the Japan Communist Party], vol. 1 (Tokyo, Shin-Nihon Shuppansha, 1975), p. 65.

27. *Akahata*, August 8, 1966.

28. *Akahata*, June 10, 1967.

29. *Akahata*, February 8, 1968.

30. *Akahata*, August 15, 1968.

31. *Akahata*, August 25, 1968.

32. *Akahata*, April 2, 1970.

33. John K. Emmerson, "Japan" in *1973 Yearbook on International Communist Affairs*, Richard F. Staar, ed. (Stanford, Calif.: Hoover Institution Press, 1973).

34. *Akahata*, May 13, 1975.

35. Emmerson, "Japan" in *1975 Yearbook on International Communist Affairs*.

36. *Akahata*, November 19, 1975.

37. Emmerson, in *1976 Yearbook on International Communist Affairs*.

38. For a brief biographical note on Fuwa, see Paul F. Langer, *Communism in Japan* (Stanford, Calif.: Hoover Institution Press, 1972).

39. Emmerson, *1977 Yearbook on International Communist Affairs*.

40. *Pravda* and *Izvestiia*, November 3, 1977.

41. John Emmerson provides a review of recent trends in the JCP in "The Japan Communist Party," a paper he presented at the Association of Asian Studies in Chicago, March 31, 1978. (Unpublished manuscript.)

CHAPTER NINE

1. During the spring of 1977, the author was invited by Boris Slavinsky of the New Far Eastern Center in Vladivostok to visit the Soviet Far East, traveling on the Soviet Motorship *Baikal* from Yokohama to Nakhodka and then by rail on the Trans-Siberia to Khabarovsk. Return was by Japan Airlines which operates flights on Thursdays and Fridays from Khabarovsk to Niigata, Japan. There were only two other passengers, both Japanese, on board the Boeing 727.

2. For an excellent Soviet overview of Siberian resources and much useful information and detail, see Boris Slavinsky, "Siberia and the Soviet Far East Within the Framework of International Trade and Economic Relations," *Asian Survey*, Spring 1977.

3. Alan B. Smith, "Soviet Dependence on Siberian Resource Development," *Soviet Economy in a New Perspective*, Joint Economic Committee, 94th Congress, 2nd Session, October 14, 1976.

4. *Pravda*, March 7, 1976.

5. *Pravda*, February 22, 1972.

6. Treated separately in chap. 11.

7. A list of all Soviet-Japanese bilateral treaties 1966–1975 with brief descriptive comment as well as full text of key treaties are included as appendices.

8. Keisukei Suzuki, *Shiberiya Hatten to Nis-so Keizei Kyoryoku* [Siberian development and Japanese-Soviet economic cooperation] (Toyko: Nikan Kogyo Shimbun-sha, 1977), p. 51.

9. *Ibid.*, pp. 52–53.

10. *Ibid.*, p. 53.

11. Kiichi Saeki, "The Second Trans-Siberian Railway," paper presented at Second Soviet-Japanese "Peace in Asia" Conference, Moscow, Spring 1974 (unpublished manuscript), pp. 3–4.

12. L. I. Brezhnev, *Along Lenin's Course. Speeches and Articles*, vol. 4, 1974, p. 457. Quoted in Slavinsky, "Siberia and Soviet Far East."

13. A. P. Derevyanko, ed., *BAM: Problems and Prospects* [in Russian] (Moscow, 1976), pp. 172–173.

14. Y. C. Kim, *Japanese-Soviet Relations: Interaction of Politics, Economics and National Security* (Beverly Hills, Calif.: Sage, 1974), p. 68.

15. Quoted in Suzuki, *Siberian Development*, p. 186.

16. *Ibid.*, pp. 187–188.

17. *Ibid.*, p. 189.

18. Discussed in some detail in chap. 11, Moscow versus Peking vis-à-vis Tokyo.

19. Jack F. Matlock, *Soviet-Japanese Economic Relations: Status and Prospects*, 30th Session, Senior Seminar on Foreign Policy, Department of State, Washington, D.C., 1970–1971 (Decontrolled following March 1973), p. 1.

20. *Ibid.*, p. 2.

21. *Ibid.*

22. Interview by author with Keisuke Suzuki, Tokyo, May 12, 1977.

23. N. I. Nikolaev and N. M. Singur, *Prospects of Economic Development in the Soviet Far East* (Khabarovsk: Publishing House), p. 11. Cited in Slavinsky, "Siberia and Soviet Far East."

24. Matlock, *Soviet-Japanese Economic Relations*, p. 6.

25. *Pravda*, April 22, 1974.

26. *Ibid.*

27. *Ekonomicheskaya Gazeta*, no. 5, January 1975, p. 13.

28. Suzuki, *Siberian Development*, p. 59.

29. Department of State, Matlock, *Soviet-Japanese Economic Relations*, p. 6.

30. Suzuki, *Siberian Development*, p. 6.

31. Summary description and further detail of Agreement as Appendix D-14.

32. *The Japan Times*, February 21, 1972.

33. Slavinsky, "Siberia and Soviet Far East."

34. Essence of Text of Agreement in Appendix D-15.

35. *Pravda*, July 23, 1972.

36. *The Japan Times*, March 24, 1974.

37. Brief of Agreement, signed April 3, 1975, in Appendix D-23.

38. *The Japan Times*, February 19, 1970.

39. Alan B. Smith, "Soviet Dependence on Siberian Resource Development," p. 439.

40. *The Japan Times*, February 2, 1974.

41. *Pravda*, April 23, 1974.

42. V. Syrokomsky, "Economic Cooperation Between the Soviet Union and Japan is Developing Successfully," *Literaturnaya Gazeta*, no. 15, April 9, 1975. Abstract in CDSP, April 30, 1975, p. 18.

43. Matlock, *Soviet-Japanese Economic Relations*, p. 8. See also N. V. Melnikov *Energeticheskiye Resursy. SSSR, Topivno-energeticheskiye Resursy* (Moscow, 1968). Cited by Smith in U.S. Congressional Study, *Soviet Economy in New Perspective*, p. 487.

44. V. Syrokomsky in *Literaturnaya Gazeta*, no. 15, April 9, 1975. CDSP, p. 17.

45. *Tyumen Native Ore.* Moscow, 1974, p. 42 (in Russian). Quoted in Slavinsky, "Siberia and Soviet Far East."

46. *Pravda*, March 7, 1976.

47. *The Japan Times*, February 21, 1972.

48. *Ibid.*

49. *The Japan Times*, March 24, 1974.

50. *Pravda*, June 1, 1974.

CHAPTER TEN

1. For Occupation policies, trade conditions, and Occupation restrictions, see SCAP, GHQ, Statistics and Reports Section, *History of the Non-Military Activities of the Occupation of Japan* (mimeographed). *Foreign Trade*, 1952, 265 pp.

2. V. Kudryavtsev, "The Fruits of MacArthur's Policy," *Izvestiia*, January 9, 1948.

3. I. Ivtsev, "The Colonization of Japan by American Monopolies," *Trud,* October 7, 1949, and Konstantim Popov, "The American Colonization of Japan," *Soviet Press Translations*, 5 (July 1, 1950): 403–409.

4. Details in Hugh Borton, *Japan's Modern Century* (New York: Ronald, 1955).

5. *Sovieto nenpo*, 1955, p. 681. Cited in Vishwanathan, *Normalization of Relations*, p. 93.

6. *The Strategic Trade Control System 1948–1956; Mutual Defense Assistance Control Act*, 1951; *Ninth Report to Congress*, 1957, pp. 1–22.

7. Vishwanathan, *Normalization of Relations*, p. 94.

8. *Sovieto nenpo*, pp. 374–376, cited in Vishwanathan, *Normalization of Relations*, p. 98.

9. See summaries of agreements in Appendix D.

10. Summary of agreement as Appendix D-3.

11. Summary of agreement as Appendix D-14.

12. Summary as Appendix D-23.

13. Full text (my translation) as Appendix E-5.

14. More detail on the Joint Committee may be found in William E. Bryant, *Japanese Private Economic Diplomacy* (New York: Praeger, 1975), and in Suzuki, *Siberian Development*.

15. For an excellent, overall evaluation and more detail, see Jan Stankovsky, "Japan's Economic Relations with the U.S.S.R. and Eastern Europe," in *Japan in der Weltwirtschaft*, A. Lamper, ed., *Probleme du Weltwirtschaft*, no. 17 (Munich, Weltform Verlag, 1974). See also Suzuki, *Siberian Development*.

16. Operating only on Thursdays and Fridays (as of May 1977).

17. Soren Too Boeki-kai, *Soren Too Boeki Chosa Geppo* [Developments in Soviet-Japanese trade during the first quarter of 1977] (Tokyo, April 1977), p. 127.

18. According to Soviet foreign trade statistics, the average FOB Soviet price for export to non-Communist countries in 1960 was $1.57 a barrel, and for Japan it was $1.34 a barrel; in 1964 the figures were $1.41 and $1.81, respectively; and in 1967, $1.50 and $1.42.

19. Further details in Lamper, *Japan in der Weltwirtschaft*.

20. Summary of treaty as Appendix D-14.

21. *New York Times*, March 23, 1973.

22. *Sankei*, October 22, 1976.

23. Japan External Trade Organization (JETRO) *White Paper on International Trade: Japan 1977*, (Tokyo), pp. 252–254.

CHAPTER ELEVEN

1. The following colleagues and specialists, with dates of their thought-provoking contributions, may be acknowledged: David E. Albright (January 1977;) A. Doak Barnett (1976); Paris H. Chang (April 1976); I-Kuei Chou (1970); Golam W. Choudhury (July 1977); Ralph N. Clough (September 1973); Edmund Clubb (September 1976); Shinkichi Eto (Fall 1972); Joachim Glaubitz (March 1976, Spring 1977); Harold C. Hinton (September 1976); Donald Hellmann (July 1973); Arnold L. Horelick (June 1977); Masataka Kosaka (Fall 1975); Shuo-chuan Leng (Fall 1975); Steven I. Levine (Winter 1975–1976); Richard Lowenthal (Autumn 1972); Malcolm Mackintosh (Fall 1975); Thomas W. Robinson (November 1973); Robert A. Scalapino (Fall 1975); Sheldon W. Simon (August 1976); Peter Van Ness (September 1976); Savitri Vishwanathan (April 1975).

2. It may be suggested that "detente" does not represent an essentially new Soviet strategy or policy, and that it may be characterized most accurately and strictly by the phrase "calculated cordiality" with, among others, three fairly obvious rationales or purposes.

Earlier periods of calculated cordiality may be recalled, each reflecting a distinct Soviet purpose: the New Economic Policy (1921–1927), the United Front (1934–1939), the Wartime Alliance (1941–1945), and the Coexistence Era (1954–1963). In every case, striking parallels, as well as some differences, may be observed.

As to the Soviet rationale for detente, three aspects stand out: first, the China angle—the felt Soviet need for allies against the new perceived immediate number one enemy (the United States is now assigned second, longer range place); second, the Soviet need for economic assistance—food, strategic raw materials, and technology where good public relations may be important; and, third, a kind of newly acquired Soviet respect for public opinion in the United States (after the lessons of Vietnam); thus the possibility of reducing U.S. defense spending if Congress and the American people can be convinced that the Soviet Union is a friend and not a potential enemy.

3. For a thought-provoking background piece see Richard Lowenthal, "The Soviet Union, China and Japan," *Survey*, Autumn 1972.

4. The author was in Vietnam at the height of the conflict on three separate occasions (in 1966, 1968, and 1969) for research and conferences relative to Soviet and Chinese Communist policies toward the area. Subsequent trips to Hong Kong, Taipei, Seoul, and Tokyo afforded direct opportunity to survey changing attitudes and to sense concern.

5. Discussed in detail in chapter 9, "Joint Economic Ventures in Siberia," and chapter 10, "Trade Between Japan and the Soviet Union."

6. See documentation on Soviet 25th Party Congress.

7. For two background overviews, see my "Moscow-Peking Relations in Perspective" in Swearingen, ed., *Soviet and Chinese Communist Power in the World Today* (New York: Basic Books, 1966), and Harold Hinton's *The Sino-Soviet Confrontation: Implications for the Future* (New York: National Strategy Information Center; published by Crane, Russak, 1976), the latter a more recent, excellent summary/analysis.

8. *Jen Min Jih Pao*, February 26, 1950.

9. Malcolm Mackintosh, "Soviet Interests and Policies in the Asian-Pacific Region," *Orbis*, Fall 1975.

10. O. Borisov, "Who is Preventing Normalization?" *Izvestiia*, May 16, 1974, p. 2. Cited in Stevin I. Levine, "China and the Superpowers: Policies toward the United States and the Soviet Union," *Political Science Quarterly*, Winter 1975–1976, p. 654.

11. Analyzed and elaborated upon, largely in terms of the changing military balance, in David E. Albright, "The Sino-Soviet Conflict and the Balance of Power in Asia," *Pacific Community*, January 1977.

12. On this point Shao-chuan Leng admonishes ". . . one should be extremely careful about interpreting Chinese foreign policy in terms of the traditional 'Middle Kingdom' concept presented in John K. Fairbank (1969) or in C. P. Fitzgerald (1967). It is one thing to say that the Middle Kingdom tradition is an important stimulus to modern Chinese nationalism and quite another to say that Peking wants to restore the Sino-centric world order and its tribute system." Shao-chuan Leng, "Chinese Strategy Toward the Asian-Pacific," *Orbis*, Fall 1975, footnote pp. 776–777.

13. Chou's Report of the Work of the Government to the Fourth National People's Congress, *Peking Review*, January 24, 1975, p. 24.

14. Kunming Military Region, Political Department, *Outline of Education on Situation for Companies* (Taipei: Institute of International Relations, 1974). During the summer of 1975, it was my honor and pleasure to have been invited to visit Taipei to discuss such questions with Chinese scholars from the Far

Eastern Institute, other research institutes, and appropriate government departments of the Republic of China.

15. Documented and elaborated in Leng's "Chinese Strategy toward the Asian-Pacific."

16. Periodization from Shinkichi Eto, "Postwar Japanese-Chinese Relations," *Survey* (Oxford) vol. 18, no. 4 (Autumn 1972), pp. 55–65.

17. *Peking Review*, April 17, 1964. Analysis of the *Peking Review* for the past two decades, 1958–1977, reveals the fluctuating attention given people-to-people diplomacy.

18. *Peking Review*, October 1972.

19. *Ibid.*, p. 17.

20. Donald C. Hellmann, "Japan and the Great Powers in Post-Vietnam Asia," *Pacific Community*, July 1975.

21. For an excellent analysis of postwar Sino-Japanese trade relations, see Chou I-Kuei, "Chinese (Mainland)-Japanese Trade Dynamics, 1950–1968, with Projections to 1975" (Ph.D. dissertation, Indiana University, 1970).

22. Further details, perspectives, and documentation in Ralph N. Clough (former Director of the Office of Chinese Affairs, Department of State), "Sino-Japanese Relations: A New Era?" *Current History*, September 1973.

23. Documentation and further detail in Saritri Vishwanathan, "The Japan-China-USSR Triangle: A View from Tokyo," *Indian Quarterly*, April–June, 1975.

24. *Japan Report* (Japanese Information Service, Consulate of Japan, New York, April 1, 1978).

25. Doak Barnett, "Peking and Asian Balance of Power" *Problems of Communism*, vol. 25 July–August, 1976.

26. Teng Hsiao-ping, speech to special session of the United Nations General Assembly, New York, in April 1974. *Peking Review*, April 19, 1974.

27. The document entitled "Reference Material Concerning Education on Situation" was edited and distributed by the political department of the Kunming Military Region to be used for "educating" cadres and soldiers of the People's Liberation Army. A copy of the document has found its way out of China. *Issues and Studies* (Taipei, June 1974). Cited in Paris A. Chang, "China's Foreign Policy Strategy: Washington or Moscow 'Connection,' " *Pacific Community*, April 1976, p. 98.

28. Leslie H. Gelb, *New York Times*, October 20, 1975. Quoted in an article by O. Edmund Clubb, "China and the West Pacific Powers" *Current History*, September 1976.

29. Robert Scalapino, "The Dragon, The Tiger and the World—Sino-Soviet Relations and Their Impact on Asia," *Orbis*, Fall 1975, p. 843.

30. *Peking Review*, September 1972, p. 5. For a detailed review of the issue and documentation, see Joachin Glaubitz, "Anti-Hegemony Formulas in Chinese Foreign Policy," *Asian Survey*, March 1976, pp. 205–215.

31. *Pravda*, June 1975. Cited in Glaubitz, p. 211.

32. Golan W. Choudhury, "Post-Mao Policy in Asia," *Problems of Communism*, July–August 1977, pp. 18–29.

CHAPTER TWELVE

1. William W. Lockwood, *The Economic Development of Japan* (Princeton, N.J.: Princeton University Press, 1954), p. 91.

2. Kutakov, *Japanese Foreign Policy*, p. 141.

3. SCAP, GHQ, Natural Resources Section, Report No. 152, "Fisheries Programs in Japan."

4. SCAP, GHQ, Natural Resources Section, "Mission and Accomplishment of the Occupation in the Natural Resources Field," January 1, 1950, p. 16.

5. More details in SCAP, GHQ, Natural Resources Section, Report No. 152, "Fisheries Programs in Japan, 1945–1951," Tokyo, 1951.

6. "Nisso Kosho to Suisankai no Ugokr" [Japanese negotiations and the fisheries (Marine Products) developments], *Chosa Geppo*, June 1957, p. 38. Cited in Vishwanathan, *Normalization of Relations*, p. 113. The chapter entitled "The Northern Fisheries" in Vishwanathan's book is probably the best overall brief account of the subject (to 1972) in English.

7. *Ibid.*

8. *Ibid.*, p. 39.

9. "Nisso Kosho to Suisan no Ugoki," pp. 43–44, 49. Quoted in Vishwanathan, *Normalization of Relations*, p. 116.

10. Report of the International Technical Conference on the Conservation of Living Resources of the Seas, 18 April to 16 May, 1955, at Rome, U.N. General Assembly A./Conf., 10/5 Rev. 2, A Conf. 10/6 of June 1955; also Norin Keizai Kenkyujo, *Hokuyo Gyogyo soran* [Overview of the northern fisheries], Tokyo, 1960. Cited in Vishwanathan, *Normalization of Relations*, pp. 78–82.

11. "Encompassing the entire Sea of Okhotsk and western parts of the Bering Sea, the Pacific Ocean adjacent to the territorial waters of the U.S.S.R., to the west and northwest of a line running from Cape Olyutorsky in the Bering Sea south along the meridian to a point 48° north 170° 21' east, then southwest until it reached the limits of the territorial waters of the U.S.S.R. at Anuchin island in the lesser Kuriles" (*Pravda*, March 21, 1956).

12. James H. Guill, "Soviet Maritime Expansion in the Pacific," *U.S. Naval Institute Proceedings*, November 1959, p. 59.

13. Full text of 1956 Fisheries Agreement given as Appendix B.

14. For a substantial summary of the situation to 1962, based in part on Soviet documentation, see George Ginsburg and Scott Shrewsbury, "The Postwar Soviet Fisheries Dispute," in *Orbis* 7, Fall 1963.

15. Details in Vishwanathan, *Normalization of Relations*, pp. 124–125.

16. Further details, technical data, and documentation in Ginsburg and Shrewsbury, "Postwar Dispute." See also *Asahi*, May 2, 1971, and *The Japan Times*, May 1, 1971.

17. *The Japan Times*, March 2, 1973.

18. *The Japan Times*, October 8, 1973.

19. *The Japan Times*, October 12, 1973.

20. *The Japan Times*, March 9, 1974.

21. *The Japan Times Weekly*, Saturday, June 14, 1975.

22. *Japan Times*, June 7, 1975. Further details in *Pravda*, June 8, 10, 14 and 27, 1975.

23. *Yomiuri Japan News*, May 16, 1975.

24. *Asahi Shimbun*, May 16, 1975.

25. *Yomiuri Shimbun*, May 16, 1975.

26. *Mainichi Shimbun*, May 16, 1975.

27. Documentation/Discussions Fisheries Agency, Tokyo, September, 1976.

28. Excellent discussion in Pamela Houghtaling, "The Contemporary Soviet-Japanese Fisheries Issue (Summary)" in *Soviet Oceans Development* (prepared for use of the Committee on Commerce and National Ocean Policy Study, 94th Congress, 2nd Session, October 1976).

29. *Ibid.*, p. 319.

30. A good discussion of the issues surrounding whaling may be found in Michael Douglas Bradley, "The International Whaling Commission: Allocating an International Pelagic Resource" (Ph.D. dissertation, University of Michigan, 1971).

31. Conference with representatives of the Fisheries Agency, Ministry of Agriculture and Fisheries, Tokyo, September 1976.

32. Japan Whaling Association, "Whaling Controversy: Japan's Position," (mimeographed) (Tokyo, April 1977), 24 pp.

33. *Gyogyo no Doko ni Kansuru Nenji Hokoku* [Annual Report—White Paper on Fisheries], 1976. Submitted to the 80th Diet (Regular) Session, May 1977.

34. *Agreement between the Government of Japan and the Union of Soviet Socialist Republics Concerning Fisheries in 1977 in the Northwest Pacific off the territories of the Soviet Socialist Republics.* [In Japanese] (Signed in Moscow May 27, 1977; ratified by the Japanese Diet on June 9 and effective upon the verbal note exchange between the two nations on June 10.)

CHAPTER THIRTEEN

1. These symposia have been held biannually, from 1972, alternately in Tokyo and Moscow.

2. Fuji Kamiya (Professor, Keio University), "The Northern Territories: 120 Years of Talks with Czarist Russia and the Soviet Union"; The Third "Peace in Asia Japan–USSR Symposium" (mimeographed) (Tokyo, April 1976).

3. For a succinct Japanese government statement of its position, see Japan, Ministry of Foreign Affairs, *The Northern Territory Issue: Japan's Position on Unsettled Questions Between Japan and the Soviet Union* (Tokyo: Public Information Bureau, 1968).

4. For an excellent brief, historical treatment of the Kuriles as an arena of Russo-Japanese interaction see John J. Stephan, "The Kuril Islands: Japan vs. Russia," *Pacific Community*, April 1976.

5. See John A. Harrison, *Japan's Northern Frontier: A Preliminary Study in Colonization and Expansion with Special Reference to the Relations of Japan and Russia.*

6. Discussions with United States and Japanese Foreign Ministry, Defense Agency, and Fishery Agency officials in Japan, September 1976 and May 1977.

7. Discussions with Japanese Fishery Agency officials in Tokyo, September 1976.

8. Discussions in Khakarovsk, May 1977, with Boris Slavinsky of the Soviet Scientific Institute at Vladivostok and with other Soviet economists of the region. See chapter 9.

9. John Stephan, "The Kuril Islands." Soviet views are typified by L. N. Kudashev, "Iz istorii Kurilshikh ostrovov," *Voprosy istorii* (August 1963): 42–58. For Japanese views: Takakura Shinichiro, *Chishima gaisha* (Tokyo, 1962); Ochiai Tadashi, *Hoppo ryodo* (Tokyo, 1971); Waki Tetsu, *Chishima to Nihonjin* (Sapporo, 1970). For a more comprehensive treatment see Stephan, *The Kuril Islands: Russo-Japanese Frontiers in the Pacific.*

10. John A. Harrison, *Japan's Northern Frontier.*

11. Japan, Ministry of Foreign Affairs, *The Northern Territories Issue* (Tokyo, 1970), p. 9.

12. Succinctly chronicled in Kim, *Japanese-Soviet Relations*, pp. 20–32.

13. See chapter 3 for details.

14. United States, Department of State, *Foreign Relations of the United States, The Conferences of Malta and Yalta*, 1945 (Washington, D.C.: U.S. Government Printing Office, 1955), p. 768.

15. Stephan, "The Kuril Islands," p. 321.

16. United States, Department of State, *Foreign Relations of the United States, The Far East VI*, 1947 (Washington, D.C.: U.S. Government Printing Office, 1972), pp. 537–538.

17. Hoppo Kyodo Fukki Kisei Domei, *Hoppo Ryodo no Shomondai* (Tokyo: Hoppo Ryodo Fukki Kisei Domei, 1967). Quoted in Kim, *Japanese-Soviet Relations*, pp. 27–28.

18. *U.S. Department of State Bulletin*, vol. 35, no. 900 (September 24, 1956), p. 484.

19. Details in Stephan, *The Kuril Islands*, pp. 211–212.

20. Japan, Ministry of Foreign Affairs, *The Territorial Issue* (Tokyo, 1970), p. 5.

21. Summaries from Shigeo Sugiyama, *Northern Territories of Japan.* Association in Northern Territories, monograph reproduced from *Japan in World Politics*, Institute for Asian Studies, January 1972, pp. 21–39.

22. *Pravda*, January 29, 1960.

23. *CDSP*, vol. 1, no. 3, pp. 26–27, cited in Vishwanathan, *Normalization of Relations*, p. 131.

24. Text in *International Affairs* (Moscow), November 1961, pp. 3–4.

25. *New York Times*, December 5, 1950.

26. *Asahi Shimbun*, July 14, 1964.

27. *Peking Review*, February 11, 1972.

28. *Peking Review*, September 21, 1973.
29. *Peking Review*, March 16, 1973.
30. *Peking Review*, June 21, 1974.
31. Quoted in Kim, *Japanese-Soviet Relations*, p. 41.
32. Text in *Pravda*, October 11, 1973.

CHAPTER FOURTEEN

1. An excellent overall analysis of the situation as Japan moved into the 1970s may be found in Donald Hellmann, *Japan in East Asia: The New International Order* (New York: Praeger, 1972).

2. Fuji Kamiya, "Security in Northeast Asia," The Second "Peace in Asia Japan–USSR Symposium" (mimeographed) (Moscow, 1974), pp. 2–3.

3. The first such symposium was held in Tokyo in 1972; the second in Moscow in 1974.

4. Shinkichi Eto, "New Trends in Asia," The Third "Peace in Asia Japan–USSR Symposium" (mimeographed) (Tokyo, April 1976), p. 13.

5. Masamichi Inoki, "How to Cope with the Soviet Threat," *Chuo Koron* November 1976.

6. I. A. Latishev, "New Foreign Policy Concepts of the Japanese Ruling Circles" (Moscow, 1971), pp. 10–11. Also text in *Asia Quarterly*, Bruxelles, 4, (1971): 359-371.

7. For details, see chapter 11.

8. *Pravda*, September 5, 1970, p. 5.

9. *Pravda*, November 26, 1970, p. 4.

10. *Pravda*, January 31, 1971, p. 1.

11. *Izvestiia*, May 13, 1971.

12. *Izvestiia*, January 14, 1972.

13. *Izvestiia*, May 13, 1973.

14. *Izvestiia*, April 9, 1975.

15. Details in "Soviet Pilot Lands Secret MIG-25 Jet on Hokkaido: Asks for Asylum in U.S." *Japan Times*, September 7, 1976; "MIG Causes Diplomatic Tangle," *Japan Times*, September 8, 1976, and (a major front-page story), "Soviet Defector Seen Being Turned Over to U.S. Today," *Japan Times*, September 8, 1976.

16. Martin E. Weinstein, *Japan's Postwar Defense Policy* (New York: Columbia University Press, 1971).

17. John Foster Dulles, "Security in the Pacific," *Foreign Affairs*, January 1952, p. 179.

18. For a comparative analysis of the main changes, see John Emmerson, *Arms, Yen and Power: The Japanese Dilemma* (New York: Dunellen, 1971).

19. Some of the legal aspects as well as political implications of Japanese rearmament are discussed in a brief article by Fukase Tadakazu (Professor of

Constitutional Law at Hokkaido University) in an article entitled, "The Self-Defense Forces Under the Peace Constitution," *Japan Quarterly*, July–September 1977.

20. The development of Japan's defense policies and self-defense forces are discussed and documented by Makoto Momoi in his chapter on "Basic Trends in Japanese Security Policies" in Robert Scalapino, *The Foreign Policy of Modern Japan* (Berkeley and Los Angeles: University of California Press, 1977), pp. 341–364.

21. First Plan, 1957–1961; Second, 1962–1966; Third, 1967–1971; Fourth, 1972–1976.

22. Japan, National Defense College, *Defense of Japan in Brief* (Tokyo, 1976).

23. For official Japanese Government summary of 1977 Defense Budget, see Appendix G.

24. *Pravda*, January 16, 1978.

25. *Sankei*, January 1, 1976.

26. Consideration in terms of budget, organization, personnel, public opinion, and legal restrictions are treated in John Emmerson, *Arms, Yen and Power*. The subject is updated and analyzed in greater detail in John E. Endicott, *Japan's Nuclear Option: Technical and Strategic Factors* (New York: Praeger, 1975).

27. Saburo Kato (a pseudonym), "Japan: Quest for Strategic Compatibility," in *Nuclear Proliferation, Phase II*, Robert M. Lawrence and Joel Larus, eds. Published for the National Security Education Program (Lawrence, Kansas: University of Kansas Press, 1974), p. 204.

28. *Nihon Kaizai*, June 26, 1970. Cited in Emmerson, *Arms, Yen and Power*.

29. Endicott, *Japan's Nuclear Option*, p. 235.

30. A substantial analysis of the problem may be found in Emmerson, *Arms, Yen and Power*, Chapter 7, "The Problem of Okinawa," and Chapter 8, "Back to Japan: Okinawa, 1970–1972."

31. For two up-to-date Asian perspectives on the issue see G. W. Choudhury, "China's Foreign Policy Goals," and Chang Pao-min, "Taiwan between Washington and Peking," in *Pacific Community*, January 1978.

32. James William Morley, "How Essential is the Republic of Korea to Japan," in *The Future of the Korean Peninsula*, ed. Young C. Kim and Abraham Halpern (New York: Praeger, 1977).

33. For a background, biographical sketch of Kim, which also traces North Korea's changing position between Moscow and Peking, see Young Hoon Kang's "Kim Il Sung, Mysterious North Korean Leader," in Swearingen, *Leaders of the Communist World*, pp. 397–413.

34. Donald S. Zagoria, "Moscow and Pyongyang: The Strained Alliance," in *The Future of the Korean Peninsula*, ed. Kim and Halpern.

35. *Ibid.*

36. Brezhnev's speech, "For Strengthening the Solidarity of Communists for a New Upswing in the Anti-Imperialist Struggle," *Pravda* and *Izvestiia*, June 8, 1969.

37. O. Borisov, "For Peace and Security in Asia," *New Times*, no. 39, September 1971, pp. 10–11.

38. See for example, Radio Moscow, August 18, 1973, in FBIS, August 24, 1973, pp. A9–10; D. Volsky, "Asian Security: Its Friends and Enemies," *New Times*, no. 34, August 1973, pp. 4–5; V. Pavlovskiy, "Collective Security in Asia," *Kommunist*, no. 16, 1973, pp. 55–66, cited in Howard M. Hansel's well-documented, and fairly comprehensive article, "Asian Collective Security: The Soviet View," *Orbis*, Winter 1976.

39. Justice M. van der Kroef, *Australian Security Policies and Problems* (New York: National Strategy Information Center, 1970), p. 27. For a useful review of the various Asian nations' reactions to the Soviet collective security suggestion see Alexander O. Ghebhart, "The Soviet System of Collective Security in Asia," *Asian Survey*, December 1973.

40. For a good, brief description of the Indian perception of the Soviet plan, see Ghebhart, *ibid.*

41. Richard G. Stilwell, "The Need for U.S. Ground Forces in Korea," *AEI Defense Review*, no. 2 (1977), pp. 19–20.

42. Quoted in Sam Jameson, "Growing Pacific Fleet Causing Alarm," *Los Angeles Times*, April 9, 1978.

43. *Ibid.*

44. *Ibid.*

45. Data from Institute for Strategical Studies, *The Military Balance* (London, 1977).

46. *Los Angeles Times*, December 29, 1977.

47. *Ibid.*, May 17, 1978.

48. *Los Angeles Times*, July 29, 1978.

Index